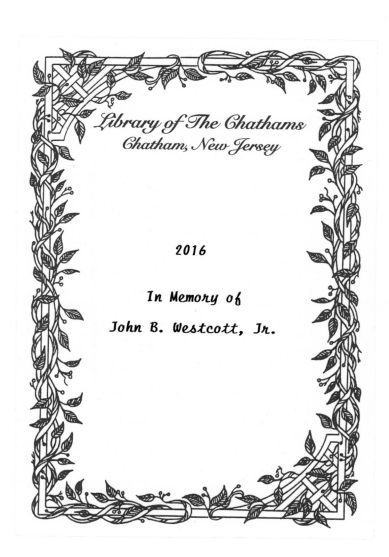

Advance Praise for *The Right Wrong Man*

"*The Right Wrong Man* is a fascinating exploration of what kind of justice the bit players in history's greatest crimes deserve. With the authority of an academic and the eye of a novelist, Lawrence Douglas sheds bright new light on the perplexing case of John Demjanjuk, a small cog in the Nazis' genocidal machine. Although Demjanjuk was not 'Ivan the Terrible,' as originally accused, Douglas argues that in the end he was Ivan-the-terrible-enough to have been properly convicted."

—Jane Mayer, staff writer with the *New Yorker*

"In this excellent book, Lawrence Douglas, a thoughtful student of legal attempts to punish atrocities committed in wartime, uncovers the strange case of the non-German who, impressed into serving as a Nazi concentration camp guard, was, many years later, repeatedly tried as a war criminal and ultimately convicted."

—Richard A. Posner, U.S. Court of Appeals for the Seventh Circuit

"Lawrence Douglas has once again provided us with a history-laden and provocative analysis of Holocaust trials. His riveting study of the Demjanjuk saga is of importance, not just to historians and jurists, but to all those who wonder how can justice ever prevail when the crime being adjudicated is genocide."

—Deborah E. Lipstadt, Emory University

"A wonderfully lucid book about the bizarre and fascinating case of John Demjanjuk, the only American to lose his citizenship twice, and about the much larger issues of law and morality that arise when individuals are held to account for crimes committed by the state."

—Scott Turow, author of *Identical*

"*The Right Wrong Man* is powerful, richly observed, and darkly entertaining. Anyone interested in postwar history will want to read it."

—Elizabeth Kolbert, staff writer with the *New Yorker*

"Douglas has produced an excellent account of the Demjanjuk case—or rather cases. His beautifully written book is the definitive work on the subject."

—William Schabas, author of *Unimaginable Atrocities: Justice, Politics, and Rights at the War Crimes Tribunals*

"In this insightful and gracefully written book, Douglas elevates the Demjanjuk case from a legal curiosity—one involving an initially mistaken prosecution followed by a later valid one—to a study in the uses and limits of the law when it confronts genocide."

—Michael B. Mukasey, former U.S. attorney general

"In this pathbreaking book, Lawrence Douglas reflects on how jurists in the Demjanjuk trial grappled with challenges of the passage of time, the infirmity of the accused, the hierarchy of perpetrators, inherited legal institutions, and different legal traditions. This is an essential work for understanding judicial reckoning with mass atrocity in our time."

—Michael R. Marrus, professor emeritus, University of Toronto

"Impeccably researched, imaginatively crafted, and beautifully written, *The Right Wrong Man* is a brilliant analysis of the longest, most complex and confusing, and most controversial series of legal measures ever initiated against any Holocaust perpetrator—John Demjanjuk. The story of the three decades of litigation required to convict him is told here as only Lawrence Douglas can tell it."

—Charles W. Sydnor Jr., Virginia Holocaust Museum

"A marvelous book and a gripping read, *The Right Wrong Man* dissects one of the most bizarre episodes in the adjudication of the Holocaust. It is reminiscent of, but superior to, Hannah Arendt's *Eichmann in Jerusalem*. Like Arendt, Douglas studied his subject from up close, from inside the courtroom. Combining eloquent reporting with trenchant analysis, he has produced a rare thing indeed—a learned page-turner."

—Jens Meierhenrich, London School of Economics

"This book cements Douglas's reputation as our leading guide to thinking about the difficult moral, political, and legal issues surrounding the postwar Nazi trials. *The Right Wrong Man* is brilliant, ambitious, and wide ranging."

—Devin O. Pendas, author of *The Frankfurt Auschwitz Trial, 1963–1965*

"A remarkable and important work that lays bare the limits of the justice system for the greatest crimes. Lawrence Douglas has woven out of the trials of John Demjanjuk a book that is utterly gripping and finely crafted, one that offers insights that are profound, troublesome, and enlightening."

—Philippe Sands, University College London

THE RIGHT WRONG MAN

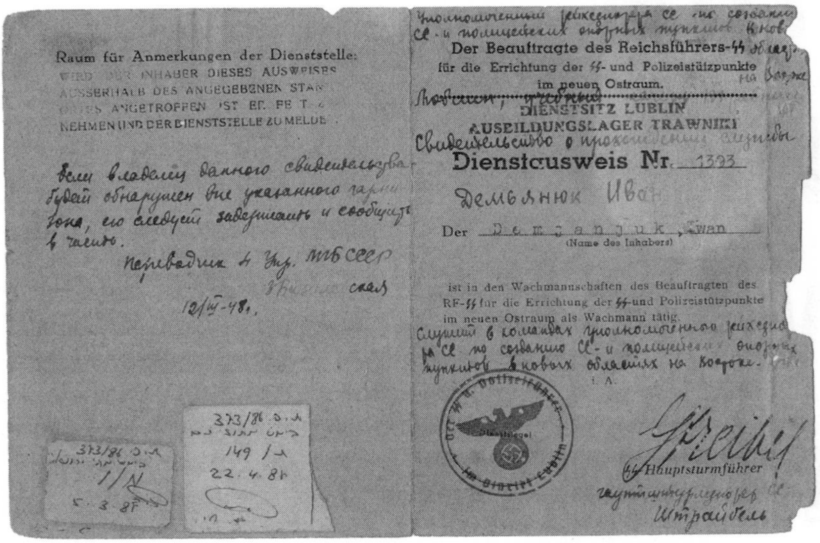

Perhaps the most exhaustively examined document in legal history: exterior face of Demjanjuk's Trawniki ID. Courtesy Office of Special Investigations, DoJ.

THE RIGHT WRONG MAN

John Demjanjuk and the Last Great Nazi War Crimes Trial

LAWRENCE DOUGLAS

PRINCETON UNIVERSITY PRESS
Princeton and Oxford

Published by Princeton University Press, 41 William Street,
Princeton, New Jersey 08540

In the United Kingdom: Princeton University Press, 6 Oxford
Street, Woodstock, Oxfordshire OX20 1TW

press.princeton.edu

Jacket image: John Demjanjuk's service card
© Marijan Murat / dpa / Corbis

Library of Congress Cataloging-in-Publication Data

Douglas, Lawrence, author.
The right wrong man : John Demjanjuk and the last great Nazi war-crimes trial / Lawrence Douglas.
pages cm
Includes bibliographical references and index.
ISBN 978-0-691-12570-1 (alk. paper)
1. Demjanjuk, John—Trials, litigation, etc. 2. War crime trials—United States. 3. War crime trials—Israel. 4. War crime trials—Germany. 5. World War, 1939–1945—Atrocities. 6. Holocaust, Jewish (1939–1945) I. Title.
KF228.D44D68 2015
341.6′90268–dc23 2015007801

British Library Cataloging-in-Publication Data is available

This book has been composed in Sabon Next LT Pro, Helvetica
Neue LT Std and Typewriter MT

Printed on acid-free paper. ∞

Printed in the United States of America

10 9 8 7 6 5 4 3 2 1

For Jacob and Milo, again

Oh what crazy ideas you get,
still thinking about justice . . .

—H. G. Adler, *The Journey*

CONTENTS

THE RIGHT WRONG MAN

Introduction

Die Zeit, the German weekly, called it the "last great Nazi war crimes trial," a designation that misled on almost every count.[1] The defendant stood accused of assisting the SS in the murder of 28,060 Jews at the Sobibor death camp—but not of being a Nazi. Nor did the trial involve war crimes, since the systematic extermination of unarmed men, women, and children was not an act of war. Then there was the question of "greatness." By all accounts, the defendant, John (Ivan) Demjanjuk, had been little more than a peon at the bottom of the Nazis' exterminatory hierarchy. Compared with Nuremberg, where twenty-one leaders of the Nazi state faced an international military tribunal, or with the Jerusalem trial of Adolf Eichmann, logistical mastermind of a continent-wide scheme of deporting Jews to their death—or even with the French trial of Klaus Barbie, the so-called Butcher of Lyon—the proceeding against Demjanjuk looked almost inconsequential. Add the fact that the defendant was at the trial's start a near nonagenarian, seemingly in frail health, and that sixty-seven years had elapsed since his alleged crimes, and the most remarkable aspect of the trial was the fact that it was staged at all. All the same, in putting Demjanjuk on trial, German prosecutors had assumed a radical risk. An acquittal would have been disastrous, a highly visible and final reminder of the failure of the German legal system to do justice to Nazi-era crimes. For *Die Zeit* was almost surely right on one count: whatever else one might say about the case, it was likely to be the *last*, or at least the last Holocaust trial to galvanize international attention.

Even the flood of attention had less to do with Demjanjuk's personal notoriety and more to do with the awkward fact that he had previously been mistaken for a truly notorious figure. Demjanjuk's legal odyssey traced back to 1975, when American officials first received sketchy word of the wartime activities of a Ford machinist living in a quiet suburb of Cleveland. Demjanjuk had been born in the Ukraine in 1920 and had entered the United States in 1952, settling in the Cleveland area and becoming a naturalized US citizen in 1958. By the late 1970s, American prosecutors had identified him as the former Treblinka guard whose wanton acts of sadism had earned him the fearful sobriquet Ivan Grozny, "Ivan the Terrible." In the most highly publicized denaturalization proceeding in American history, Demjanjuk was stripped of his citizenship and extradited to Israel, where he was tried as Treblinka's Ivan Grozny. Convicted in 1988 and sentenced to death, Demjanjuk idled in an Israeli prison for five years, while his appeals ran their course. Then, in the summer of 1993, the Israeli Supreme Court tossed out his conviction, after newly gathered evidence from the former Soviet Union showed the Israelis had the wrong Ivan. Demjanjuk returned to the United States a free man, ending one of the most famous cases of mistaken identity in legal history.

But it hardly spelled the end of Demjanjuk's legal travails. Resettled in suburban Cleveland with his American citizenship restored, Demjanjuk became the subject of a fresh denaturalization proceeding. While Demjanjuk might not have been Treblinka's Ivan the Terrible, evidence showed that he had nonetheless been a "terrible enough Ivan" who served at Sobibor, an equally lethal Nazi death camp. In 2001, Demjanjuk earned the distinction of being the only person in American history to lose his citizenship twice. Still protesting his innocence, he remained barricaded in his middle-class ranch house in Seven Hills, Ohio, while American officials searched fruitlessly for a country willing to accept him. After Poland and Ukraine declined, Germany, which had long resisted accepting alleged Nazi collaborators from the United States, somewhat surprisingly said yes. Demjanjuk was flown to Munich, arriving on German soil on May 12, 2009.

Two years later to the day, on May 12, 2011, a German court convicted the by-now ninety-one-year-old defendant of assisting the SS in the murder of 28,060 Jews at Sobibor. But punishment would never be meted out: ten months later, with his appeal still pending, John Demjanjuk died in a Bavarian nursing home. It was perhaps fitting that the most convoluted, lengthy, and bizarre criminal case to arise from the Holocaust never reached a definitive conclusion.

* * *

In the following pages, we will explore the elaborate and strange story of Demjanjuk's legal odyssey. But for all its extraordinary twists and turns, the Demjanjuk case also places deeper, more persistent claims on our attention. It asks us to think critically about the justice of trying old men for superannuated crimes. It invites us to reflect on the nature of individual responsibility in the orchestration of state-sponsored crimes. It demands that we think carefully about the nature, causes, and possible justifications of collaboration in the perpetration of atrocities. And it provides a crucible in which three distinct national legal systems—the American, the Israeli, and the German—sought to create legal alloys potent enough to master the legal challenges posed by the destruction of Europe's Jews.

Using criminal prosecutions to address that destruction severely tested traditional conceptions of law and jurisprudence. The law typically views criminal acts *microscopically*. The standard model, dutifully studied by law students around the globe, construes crimes as deviant acts committed by individuals against other individuals that harm community order. Different legal systems reach different conclusions about which specific acts constitute such a threat, but all legal codes condemn foundational wrongs such as murder, and instruct the modern nation-state to respond aggressively, mobilizing and deploying its investigatory and judicial resources to apprehend, prosecute, and ultimately punish perpetrators. In Thomas Hobbes' *Leviathan*, arguably the greatest work of Western political thought, the state is more than simply the bulwark of order; it is the force that protects us from the mortal violence of strangers. And in John Locke's *Two Treatises of Government*, the state both defends law and submits to its neutral dominion.

Nazi crimes exploded this model and its assumption that private violence represented the most basic threat to the fabric of social life. Nazism revealed the terrible capacity of the state itself to turn reprobate, a phenomenon the German philosopher Karl Jaspers designated with the term *Verbrecherstaat*, "the criminal state."[2] This idea—that the state, far from acting as the locus and defender of law and order, might itself commit the worst acts of criminality—simply lay beyond the ken of the conventional model of criminal law and was indeed unintelligible to it. Jaspers' term named the novel achievement of Nazism, how it turned the state into the principal perpetrator of crimes, the very agent of criminality.[3] In the peroration of his opening address at Nuremberg, chief American prosecutor Robert Jackson framed the legal challenge posed by the *Verbrecherstaat*: "Civilization asks whether law is so laggard as to be utterly helpless to deal with crimes of this magnitude by criminals of this order of importance."[4]

The Nuremberg trial and its progeny offered a distinctive answer to this question. Nuremberg insisted that law *was* adequate to the task, but that the effort would require extraordinary legal innovations. Mastering the crimes of the *Verbrecherstaat* would require special courts, new jurisdictional principles, unorthodox evidentiary conventions, and, most of all, novel categories of wrongdoing. These new categories would have to be sufficiently flexible and capacious to handle crimes that spanned a continent, enlisted the participation of tens of thousands of perpetrators, and were supported by a complex organizational and logistical apparatus.

The prosecution of the major Nazi war criminals before the International Military Tribunal (IMT) in Nuremberg marked a crucial first step. Nuremberg was not in the first instance a Holocaust trial; the twenty-one defendants in the dock were principally charged with "crimes against peace"—that is, of having planned and launched a war of aggression in violation of international law. Yet the trial conferred judicial recognition on "crimes against humanity," as it called acts of state-sponsored atrocity; and the prosecution used this novel legal channel to bring much of the evidence of the Holocaust before the IMT. American prosecutors subsequently built on this precedent in the twelve so-called successor trials staged by the US military, also at Nuremberg. In these trials of leading German state and economic functionaries, American prosecutors shifted away from the IMT's focus on aggressive war and now treated crimes against humanity as the Nazis' central offense.

Nazi atrocity prodded the legal imagination to recognize a second novel incrimination. In a book published in 1944, *Axis Rule in Occupied Europe*, Raphael Lemkin, a Polish-Jewish adviser to the US War Department, coined a new term to describe the Nazis' treatment of Jews in occupied countries. Wedding an ancient Greek word for group (*genos*) to a Latin word for killing (*cide*), Lemkin's neologism sought to describe something distinct from mass murder, and more grave: "a coordinated . . . destruction of the essential foundations of the life of . . . groups, with the aim of annihilating the groups themselves."[5] The newly coined word *genocide* made its way into the IMT indictment, then gained far greater currency in the Americans' successor trials at Nuremberg, where it served to characterize the Nazis' crimes against humanity. On December 9, 1948, the United Nations General Assembly voted to recognize genocide as denoting its own independent crime in international law. The Convention on the Punishment and Prevention of the Crime of Genocide officially entered into force early in 1951; 144 states have since ratified the Convention, and today genocide stands, in the words of William Schabas, as the "crime of crimes"—the most serious crime recognized by any legal code.[6]

The effort to punish Nazi atrocity also gave rise to novel jurisdictional principles capable of puncturing the shield of sovereignty that traditionally insulated state actions from outside legal scrutiny. Likewise it stimulated the development of specialized investigatory units that revolutionized the role that professional historians would play in preparing criminal cases. It led jurists to experiment with flexible rules of evidence equipped to facilitate rather than frustrate the prosecution of state-sponsored crimes. And it sparked the establishment of special courts, some international, some domestic, specially tasked with trying crimes of genocidal sweep. In large measure, the field that we now call "international criminal law" owes its existence to the law's attempt to grapple with Nazi mass atrocity.

Not all legal systems embraced what I shall call the "atrocity paradigm"—the use of special law and processes to respond to Nazi crimes. As we shall see, Germany, spurred by resentment of the Allies' war crimes trial program, rejected the new incriminations designed to facilitate the prosecution of Nazi exterminators. But even where these legal innovations gained acceptance, they encountered an even more fundamental problem raised by the atrocities of the *Verbrecherstaat*. In the classic model of retributive punishment that found its most enduring exposition in the works of Kant, punishment is seen as a *just dessert*. In this view, punishment is something the criminal has *earned*; its purpose is not to rehabilitate or correct the wrongdoer, but to restore the moral imbalance caused by his crime. Nazi atrocity introduced a radical disequilibrium into this Kantian equation. Writing about the Nuremberg trial, Hannah Arendt famously observed, "For these crimes, no punishment is severe enough. It may well be essential to hang Göring, but it is totally inadequate. That is, this guilt, in contrast to all criminal guilt, oversteps and shatters all legal systems. . . . We are simply not equipped to deal, on a human level, with a guilt that is beyond crime."[7] Years later, Israeli Attorney General Gideon Hausner would make much the same point during the Eichmann proceeding, openly acknowledging that "it is not always possible to apply a punishment which fits the enormity of the crime." The problem of the inadequacy of punishment was hardly a trivial matter; to the contrary, as Arendt suggested, it raised profound jurisprudential questions. Incriminations such as "crimes against humanity" and "genocide" may have enabled prosecutions of perpetrators of Nazi atrocity, but if such crimes exploded classic theories of retributive justice, then what purpose exactly did the trials serve? As Arendt understood it, the problem was not that the law would fail to do justice to the defendants; instead, it was that no juridically sanctioned punishment could serve as a coherent response to mass atrocity. Such crimes exposed the limits of law as a retributive scheme.

In an earlier book, I argued that jurists sought to solve this dilemma by reconfiguring the basic purpose of the atrocity trial.[8] In researching the records of Holocaust trials, I was struck by the fact that numerous prosecutors defended the proceedings as *didactic* or *pedagogic* exercises. Attorney General Hausner was explicit in this regard; in his account of the Eichmann trial, he insisted, "we needed more than a conviction; we needed a living record of a gigantic human and national disaster."[9] Hausner's words were hardly anomalous; American prosecutors at Nuremberg, German prosecutors at the famous Frankfurt-Auschwitz trial (1963–65), and French prosecutors at the Barbie trial (1987) sounded many of the same chords. In these cases, jurists explicitly sought to use the trial as a means of teaching history, creating narratives from which political lessons could be teased. In calling such cases *didactic trials*, I intended no criticism, and in fact sought to distinguish such legal exercises from the corrupt *show trials* staged in the Soviet Union under Stalin. My deeper argument was that far from being an incidental feature of Holocaust trials, the didactic aspect represented a juristic solution to a juristic problem. If Nazi atrocity revealed the limits of the conventional criminal trial as a retributive exercise, the didactic trial delivered an expanded justification for prosecuting. While the atrocity trial would continue to perform the conventional function of ascertaining guilt and assigning punishment, it would also serve to teach history and history lessons.

The atrocity trial as didactic exercise has not escaped criticism. Oddly and disappointingly, the most influential critic was Arendt herself, who, in her famous report on the Eichmann trial, first published in the *New Yorker* in 1962 and a year later in book form, vehemently attacked Hausner's prosecutorial tactics. "The purpose of a trial," Arendt insisted, "is to render justice, and nothing else; even the noblest of ulterior motives—'the making of record of the Hitler regime which would withstand the test of history' . . .—can only detract from the law's main business: to weigh the charges against the accused, to render judgment, and to mete out due punishment."[10] In making this argument, Arendt appeared to forget what she had written about Nuremberg—that Nazi atrocities had so distorted the fabric of justice that no amount of "due punishment" would suffice to "render justice." While Arendt was certainly correct that a criminal trial must first and foremost fairly weigh the evidence against the accused, her dismissal of all other purposes betrayed an odd shortsightedness. Far from serving merely "ulterior motives," the didactic trial represented a solution to the *very problem that Arendt herself first identified*.

The atrocity trial as didactic exercise reached its purest elaboration in the Eichmann trial. Everything about the case was unusual, beginning with Eichmann's spectacular capture and kidnapping by Mossad agents, who plucked the former SS *Obersturmbannführer* off a street in suburban Buenos Aires. At trial, Israel relied on unusual jurisdictional theories to buttress its authority to try a man whose crimes had been committed on a different continent before the birth of the Israeli state. It also used a special charging statute, the Nazis and Nazi Collaborators

(Punishment) Law, passed by the Knesset in 1950, that incorporated into domestic Israeli law both Nuremberg's definition of "crimes against humanity" and a modified version of the United Nations' definition of genocide. The three-judge tribunal that presided over the trial was a special court, specially constituted to try persons accused under the 1950 statute. And the trial itself presented a drama of legal didactics, undertaking to teach history through the lived memory of survivor witnesses. This effort represented a dramatic departure from Nuremberg, where prosecutors had relied on documentary evidence largely to the exclusion of victim and survivor testimony. Many observers had questioned Nuremberg's documentary approach, as a trial that aimed to serve as the "greatest history seminar" became dull, repetitive, and tediously long. The Eichmann prosecution sought to correct this misstep. By presenting history through the anguished memory of survivors, the trial turned a younger generation of Israelis into witnesses of the witnesses. It conferred honor and public recognition on the experience of survivors, and communicated to younger Israelis the existential perils that menaced the Jewish people. It delivered a comprehensive and gripping account of the Holocaust while casting Zionist self-sufficiency and military preparedness as the necessary bulwarks against the repetition of any such catastrophe. At the same time, it galvanized attention around the world, particularly in America and Germany, and so began the work of transforming collective understandings of the Holocaust—which in time would come to be seen not merely as a horror of World War II, but as the signature event of the twentieth century.

If the Eichmann trial represented the Holocaust trial in its purest form as a didactic exercise organized around survivor testimony, Demjanjuk's "Ivan the Terrible" trial in Jerusalem represented the collapse of the paradigm. While the causes of this disastrous case of misidentification were, as we shall see, far from straightforward, the calamitous trial made abundantly clear the perils of didactic legality, showing how the desire to honor the lived memory of survivors of atrocity can easily lead a criminal court badly astray. The collapse of the Israeli case against Demjanjuk also exposed the limits of the American approach to dealing with Nazi crimes, an approach that differed dramatically from the atrocity model I have sketched above.

American jurists had been the pioneering force at Nuremberg and in years immediately afterward gathered a store of experience in trying former Nazis—not just in Nuremberg, but also at the site of the former Dachau concentration camp, where the US Army tried hundreds of former camp guards and other Nazis for war crimes and crimes against humanity before specially constituted military commissions. By the 1970s, however, when American jurists began dealing with the problem that Eric Lichtblau has called "the Nazis next door," this institutional memory had faded. The bold legal creativity that American jurists showed at Nuremberg was either ignored or forgotten. Lawyers of the 1970s simply assumed that US courts lacked jurisdiction over Nazi crimes; with the very laws that Americans had pioneered at Nuremberg unavailable, jurists were left addressing our domestic Nazi problem with ordinary legal tools. Former Nazis and Nazi collaborators who had acquired American citizenship would only face civil charges, arising under immigration law. Those like Demjanjuk—persons alleged to have perpetrated or served as accessories to mass crimes—were simply handled as persons who had entered the country illegally or under false pretenses. These denaturalization trials had little in the way of a didactic component, and few attracted great attention, the one exception being the spectacular Demjanjuk/Ivan the Terrible case. Essentially, the cases served as a means of lustration—they symbolically sought to purge America of persons undeserving of membership in a nation based on tolerance and equality.

In theory, such civil cases should have posed fewer obstacles to prosecutorial success than criminal trials. In point of fact, several botched cases exposed the difficulty of using ordinary legal instruments to handle state-sponsored atrocities. Prosecutors learned that asking aging survivors of profound trauma to accurately identify their past tormentors could prove a perilous undertaking. A deeper problem was institutional, as a decentralized collection of immigration lawyers and local US attorneys struggled to assemble cases against persons alleged to have lied about crimes committed decades earlier in far-flung lands.

This scattered approach, and the mistakes it led to, demonstrated the need for a specialized organization to handle such cases; and the creation of the Office of Special Investigations (OSI) in the Justice Department in 1979 represented a critical step toward mastering the legal problems posed by the Nazi next door. Bringing together teams of lawyers and professional historians in unprecedented collaboration, the OSI developed a model for dealing with Nazis that would pay impressive prosecutorial dividends by the mid-1980s. Alas, this model had yet to be adequately developed by the time of Demjanjuk's first denaturalization trial, and the OSI would pay dearly for inheriting its signature case before it was sufficiently equipped to handle it. In denaturalizing Demjanjuk as Treblinka's Ivan the Terrible, the OSI committed a colossal blunder that its later successes—even in the second Demjanjuk denaturalization case—could never fully correct. Institutions managed with competence and integrity develop and learn over time, which is what the OSI did. Yet for the OSI, the course corrections came too late to avoid the early disaster that continued to taint its reputation.

As we shall see, the Cold War also contributed mightily to this early calamity; indeed, the Cold War—both its waging and its dissolution—profoundly affected the course of all Nazi atrocity trials in the United States, Israel, and Germany. The most basic and obvious challenge for jurists lay in gaining access to evidence secured in archives behind the Iron Curtain. But to call the Cold War a complicating backdrop to these cases is too anodyne a characterization; it was, in effect, a major player in them. It fostered doubts about the quality and authenticity of evidence; it shaped institutional responses; it infiltrated rhetoric, inculcated belief systems, and came ultimately to define the realm of action, the structure of political and legal choice. It supplied the very ether through which jurists moved. The end of the Cold War was no less profound in its influence. History by counterfactual is a tricky business, but we can say with some confidence that had the Cold War continued there would have been no second Demjanjuk denaturalization trial in the United States. And there certainly would have been no prosecution in Germany.

* * *

In May 2009, at the time of Demjanjuk's arrival by US government jet in Munich, I was living with my family in Berlin. Within a two-hundred-yard radius of our apartment were three separate monuments to Nazi atrocity. Embedded in the sidewalk in front of our building was a pair of *Stolpersteine* (literally, "stumbling blocks"), brass cobblestones memorializing two Berlin Jews deported to Auschwitz. Across the street in a small park stood a sculpture of what I first took to be a stack of waffles but that closer inspection revealed to be a pile of stylized corpses (the sculpture was called *Treblinka*). And around the corner, a plaque affixed to an elegant prewar building informed passersby that the building, now home to luxury condos, had formerly housed a military court that condemned thousands of innocent persons to death during the Third Reich.

Politically and culturally, Germany is the poster boy for national self-reckoning, the land willing to face down its monstrous past. Turkey and Japan have yet to accept responsibility for crimes of genocidal sweep. France still struggles with its complicity in Nazi crimes. Austria continues to indulge the myth of the "first victim" of Nazism. Spain, which fancies bringing foreign human rights violators to justice, suddenly becomes prickly when a local magistrate shifts his attention to Franco-era crimes. By contrast, Germany has approached the difficult collective task known as *Vergangenheitstbewältigung*—confronting the past—with Teutonic thoroughness, making its past atrocities the subject of countless memorials, symposia, films, and other public discussions. When all else fails, German law serves as the muscle of memory, stepping in to prosecute Holocaust deniers.

When it came to bringing Nazi perpetrators to the bar of justice, however, the postwar German legal system amassed a pitifully thin record. It is true that in the years directly following the war, German courts operating under the watchful eye of Allied zonal occupiers conducted over forty-six hundred trials of crimes committed during the Nazi period—yet the impressive-sounding number obscures the fact that the majority of these cases involved relatively trivial property crimes committed in the last months of the war, when Germany witnessed a collapse of public order.[11] In the early years of the Federal Republic, trials involving Nazi atrocities came to a virtual standstill; in 1955, for example, West German courts convicted a grand total of twenty-one persons for Nazi-era crimes. Early on, East Germany demonstrated greater resolve in pursuing Nazi criminals, but some of these proceedings amounted to little more than Stalinist shows; later, East Germany lost interest in trials, insisting that most unpunished Nazis remained in the West.[12]

Today, the field known as "transitional justice" asks what role a judicial reckoning with a previous criminal regime should play in the transition to a democratic one. The West German answer was: not much of one. In the Federal Republic, the obstacles to successfully prosecuting former Nazis were many and formidable. Where Nuremberg pioneered the notion that special law and institutions were necessary to do justice to Nazi crimes, Germany insisted on treating Nazi atrocities as ordinary crimes to be treated by ordinary courts applying ordinary German law. As a consequence, German law (here I will use "German" and "Germany" to refer to the Federal Republic; East Germany will be designated as such) often frustrated rather than facilitated prosecutions. Generous amnesty statutes insulated many former Nazis from prosecution, including virtually all the bureaucrats who had helped plan and implement the Holocaust. German prosecutors could not try former Nazis for genocide or crimes against humanity, as these special incriminations were dismissed as ex post facto law. Barred from using the very incriminations designed to facilitate the prosecution of Nazi atrocities, German prosecutors had to rely on conventional crimes as defined by German statute. And so the most a prosecutor could do was to charge a former Nazi with ordinary murder. After 1960, murder was the *only* charge that a prosecutor could file, as the statute of limitations had tolled for all other crimes committed during the Third Reich. Even murder was controlled by a prescriptive period, which was lifted only thanks to a series of stopgap measures by a German parliament ultimately unwilling to face the international opprobrium and internal rancor that would have resulted from letting the statute of limitations expire on all Nazi-era crimes.

As we shall see, the fact that German courts had to address acts of genocide through the category of conventional murder created immense problems for prosecutors. Investigations were abandoned midstream, charges were brought only to be dismissed, those trials that did go forward often resulted in bewildering acquittals or frustratingly lenient sentences, and the occasional stiff sentence rarely escaped reduction or commutation. Thanks to the peculiarities of German legal doctrine, judges treated the Holocaust as if it had been perpetrated by no more than a handful of men—Hitler, Himmler, Heydrich, and Göring, and a few others thrown in for good measure. Everyone else, including SS men who had directly participated in mass shootings or had supervised the exterminatory process, were treated as mere accessories.

We should not be entirely surprised by this record of disappointment. The simple fact is that postwar Germany was full of former Nazis. Many occupied leading positions in the Federal Republic's government and judiciary. Even among those who smoothly adjusted to the new realities of a democratic Germany, few welcomed the aggressive prosecution of their former confederates. There is no denying, then, that the continuing influence of former Nazis contributed to Germany's refusal to use the atrocity model to prosecute Nazi crimes. But this is not to say that all the political, institutional, legal, and doctrinal roadblocks to successful prosecution were exclusively the handiwork of former Nazis. The law is not infinitely pliable, at least not in a liberal democracy; doctrine may accommodate and reflect political interests and partisan agendas, but it also evolves by its own internal logic and rules.

Then there is the matter of institutions. Like the United States, Germany has a federated legal system, one that unavoidably frustrated the centralized, coordinated investigation and prosecution of Nazi atrocities. For some, of course, this was a blessing. But for others it was a national embarrassment—if not a direct scandal. And so a full two decades before the creation of the OSI in the United States, Germany established Die Zentrale Stelle der Landesjustizverwaltungen zur Aufklärung nationalsozialistischer Verbrechen (The Central Office of the Regional Administration of Justice for the Investigation of National Socialist Crimes, hereafter, the Central Office), a special unit empowered to launch investigations of Nazi-era crimes.[13] In contrast to the OSI's relatively unsexy civil law caseload, the Central Office dealt only with criminal matters; indeed, with the expiration of the statute of limitations for all other crimes, the Central Office investigated exclusively murder cases. And yet the Central Office has never enjoyed a basic authority granted to the OSI: to try its own cases. From its inception in 1958, the Central Office has served as an investigative agency only, able to prepare preliminary investigations but dependent on regional prosecutors to file charges and try cases. Partly as a result, of the 120,000 investigations launched by the Central Office since its creation, only 5,000 cases went to trial, resulting in fewer than 600 convictions.[14] But trials there were; and the efforts of German investigators, prosecutors, and judges to bring perpetrators of Nazi atrocities to justice were no less remarkable than the obstacles thrown in their way.

By the start of Demjanjuk's trial in November 2009, however, the last prosecution to attract substantial media attention lay decades ago, and most Germans assumed that Nazi trials were a thing of the past. Many who previously had defended such trials now favored closing the book on this chapter of German history. And so the decision to bring Demjanjuk to Germany to stand trial made for surprise, even alarm. What exactly did Germany hope to achieve? Those most familiar with German case law openly predicted that the prosecution—if the aged defendant survived it—would end in failure.

And yet the trial, I will try to demonstrate, resulted in an important and even a historic success. If Nuremberg was a trial by document and the Eichmann and Ivan the Terrible cases were trials by survivor testimony, Demjanjuk's Munich trial was a trial by historical expert. Here the testimony of professional historians did much more than provide background and context to the crimes under consideration; rather, it enabled the resolution of the basic legal questions facing the court. Demjanjuk's Holocaust-as-History trial reflected more than the inescapable actuarial reality that the defendant was an old man and no survivors were around to identify him. It showcased the unusual role that historians had come to play in every aspect of atrocity cases, from the drafting of the indictment to the core of the court's judgment. While the Jerusalem trial of Ivan the Terrible marked the end of the Holocaust trial as a didactic exercise organized around survivor testimony, Demjanjuk's Munich case represented the advent of a very different kind of Holocaust trial: the Holocaust as History.

* * *

In writing this book, I was drawn to many aspects of the Demjanjuk case. Primary among them were how the vectors of law and Cold War politics converged in Demjanjuk's trials, and how the case brought into stark relief the efforts of three different domestic legal systems to address the crimes of the Holocaust. I was also interested in how the trial threw into stark relief the difference between treating Nazi extermination as a special challenge—one demanding legal innovation—and treating it as an ordinary crime. The manner in which the trial brought the prerogatives of memory and the conclusions of history into collision raised the question of how law treats the passage of time and handles the vexed issue of collaboration. Furthermore, I wanted to explore how legal systems develop and self-correct, how doctrine responds to the pressures of politics, and how law accommodates, digests, and frames the conclusions of history.

My interest was not with Demjanjuk the person. No one familiar with the case can seriously doubt that Demjanjuk served as a camp guard—not just at Sobibor, but at Majdanek and Flossenbürg, too. All the same, no evidence has ever been adduced to suggest that Demjanjuk distinguished himself by his cruelty, and I am prepared to believe that he did not. I can also readily imagine how, by the end of his life, he had come to view himself as a victim—of the Germans, who took him as a prisoner of war, impressed him into guard service, and ultimately brought him to trial; of the Israelis, who demonized and nearly executed him in a badly handled case of mistaken identity; and of the Americans, whose dogged determination to see him brought to justice must have looked like prosecutorial vindictiveness to an old man with deep reserves of self-pity. It is true that Demjanjuk never chose to be taken prisoner of war or assigned guard duty at a death camp. But life, particularly in times of historic upheaval, often thrusts us in situations not of our making. In such situations we must ask ourselves whether a difficult, or even terrible choice is the same as having no choice at all. Alas, in his stubborn and dissembling claim of absolute innocence, Demjanjuk deprived the law of a frank and nuanced reckoning with the meaning of his collaboration.

At the end of the day, I cannot say with assurance that, had I been a prosecutor on the case, I would have supported the decision to try Demjanjuk in Munich. But in writing about the trial, I find myself strongly supporting the verdict—not because I believe it was vital to punish Demjanjuk, but because the German court delivered a remarkable and just decision, one which few observers would have predicted from Germany's long legal struggle with the legacy of Nazi genocide.

In the following pages, I hope to convince you that the German trial did more than bring the bizarre and meandering case against Demjanjuk to a fitting close. It demonstrated the power of courts to self-correct and to learn from past missteps, offering a powerful example of how criminal trials can deploy history in a responsible way to shift and recenter doctrine. As we shall see, while still nominally treating the Holocaust as an "ordinary" crime, the Munich court managed to shatter the old paradigm and comprehend the Holocaust as a crime of atrocity. It is perhaps ironic that a man whom prosecutors first mistakenly pursued because of his alleged singular viciousness ultimately was convicted in Munich as the ultimate replaceable cog in an exterminatory machine. Yet as the court rightly recognized, a machine cannot run without its small constituent parts. Demjanjuk was rightly convicted not because he committed wanton murders, but because he worked in a factory of death. He was convicted of having been an accessory to murder for a simple and irresistible reason—because that had been his job.

1

The Beginning of the End of Something

Munich, November 30, 2009, 7:00 AM. The city is quiet and the early morning sky still dark, but the plaza in the Nymphenburgerstrasse teems with TV and radio trucks, their generators humming. Hundreds of journalists and spectators stand waiting outside the courthouse, all of us bundled against the late November cold. Yesterday's *Süddeutsche Zeitung* reported that press accreditations have been issued far in excess of what the courtroom can accommodate, and as the crowd swells, the jostling begins.[1] A man in a tuxedo and kipah walks along the perimeter of the crowd, silently handing out candles; Noah Klieger, a retired Israeli journalist and Auschwitz survivor, turns to me and dryly observes, "These trials bring out the crazies."

A press release issued by the court announced that doors will open for accredited journalists at 8 AM, but a *Polizist* who is handed the statement stares at it blankly, as if seeing it for the first time. Another policeman shouts inaudible instructions. Although the police have had six months to prepare for this day, they appear utterly unprepared and bewildered, improvising on the spot. Soon the only topic of conversation among the journalists is not the trial about to get underway, but the staggering absence of organization. A letter of protest, hastily drafted, is passed through the crowd. "We, the undersigned, regret the absence of professionalism." But to no avail. Two hours pass. A correspondent for Bavarian radio calls out, "As of 9:45 we will return fire!"—an allusion to Hitler's words announcing the start of the Second World War.

Instead of creating cordons and an orderly queue, the police now inexplicably herd the crowd into a crude funnel, its mouth leading to a single courthouse doorway. A sign marks off the *Demjanjuk Sammelzone*—the Demjanjuk Collection Zone. Is this someone's idea of a joke? The Nazi era left the German language contaminated, infected with dreaded associations, and *Sammelzone* suggests the collection areas where Jews were sent to be packed off to the killing centers. "The only thing missing," comments one observer stuck in the throng, "are the train tracks."[2] For some, the fact that a crowd containing numerous Jewish journalists and several Holocaust survivors is being shoved toward a single narrow portal creates resonances that cannot be ignored. But others, and perhaps especially the Germans themselves, find reassurance in the disorganization. The SS, after all, was terrifyingly efficient. Not so the Munich police. *See, we have changed.*

After fours hours of delay—first the interminable wait in line, then screenings and pat-downs—I finally manage to enter *Gerichtssaal* 101. Considered the most secure in Munich, Courtroom 101 was built in the 1970s to accommodate the sensitive high-profile trials of the Baader-Meinhof terrorist group, though it was never much used for its intended purpose. A windowless octagon with seats for 147 observers, it is part shabby seminar room, part drab Lutheran chapel, part air-raid shelter. The vaulted ceiling bears a Brutalist touch: massive decorative blocks of poured concrete loom overhead, seemingly ready at any instant to jar loose and crush anyone sitting below. Curiously, at least to an American observer, one sees no flags anywhere, either national or municipal, and no scales-of-justice iconography to indicate a court of law. Nothing adorns the walls but a simple wooden cross.

Still, the atmosphere in the room is festive, perhaps because we who have made it in know we're the lucky ones; half of those seeking admission remain stuck outside. Plans for an overflow room with a video hookup have been scrapped amid constitutional concerns. German law holds that televising trials invades the privacy rights of defendants. These privacy laws also account for the quaint practice in German newspapers of referring to defendants by an anonymous initial—"John (Ivan) D. was arraigned today." The high profile of this trial renders that protocol moot, yet the matter of the video hookup raises thorny interpretive questions. Is connecting a live video feed to an adjacent room simply a matter of extending the physical space of the court, or is it akin to broadcasting the trial on primetime to the Bavarian hinterland?

Reluctant to deliver grounds for appeal before the trial has even begun, the Munich court errs on the side of caution. There will be no special accommodations, a decision that provokes the ire of Michel Friedman, TV pundit and former president of the European Jewish Congress. With his camel-hair coat, out-of-season tan and black suit, shirt, and tie, Friedman could pass as a Las Vegas singer or worse, and he angrily denounces the court's decision to a gaggle of eager journalists. The courtroom is abuzz with correspondents from around the globe hustling to interview Nazi-hunting luminaries and other leading members of the European Jewish community. Serge Klarsfeld, the Frenchman who helped capture and prosecute Klaus Barbie, chats with Efraim Zuroff, director of the Simon Wiesenthal Center's Jerusalem office, the world's leading organization for tracking Nazi fugitives, which had listed Demjanjuk at the top of its most-wanted list.[3] Journalists hover close by, scribbling down snippets of their conversation.

All at once the chatter in *Gerichtssaal* 101 dies down as a door at the side of the chamber swings open. Flanked by two medical orderlies and a court-appointed doctor, the defendant is maneuvered into the courtroom in a wheelchair. A sky blue blanket drawn all the way up to his chin covers his legs and body, and a blue baseball cap juts low over his brow. His eyes are closed, and it's unclear whether he is asleep or just fending off the explosion of camera flashes. Photographers, cameramen, and videographers clamor in front of the wheelchair, shooting away in a frenzy, as if Gisele Bundchen had just sashayed into the Munich courtroom. Demjanjuk's mouth hangs open; he appears to mutter words or moan in pain. Cameras flash. A helpless octogenarian, wheelchair-bound, grimacing before a relentless onslaught of publicity: it is not a sight to burnish the criminal justice system's reputation. The blanket briefly slips from Demjanjuk's feet, revealing a pair of incongruously jaunty Puma sneakers.

At 11:15 three robed judges, accompanied by two "jurors" and two alternatives, shuffle into the courtroom and find their places behind a raised semicircular table of dark walnut. We are instructed to take our seats, and the presiding judge, a bald sixty-year-old jurist named Ralph

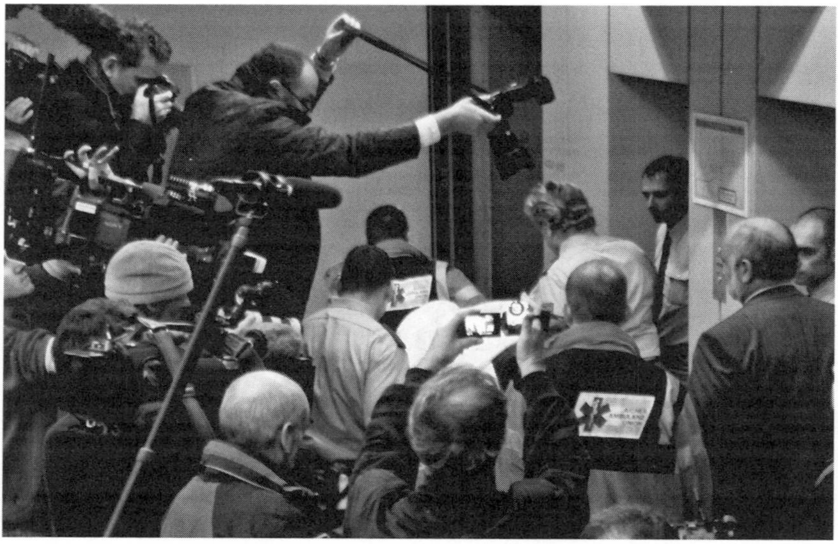

1.1. The media throng. Photo by Thomas Hauzenberger.

Alt, politely calls the court to order. "I apologize in advance for the delay," he begins. "We were unable to calculate the length of the entrance procedure." Derisive laughter ripples through the audience. (The head of the court later concedes that "there were organizational problems" and that the preparation was "not optimal.")[4] Bald, bearded, and bespectacled, Alt is soft-spoken and seemingly unaccustomed to speaking into a microphone, pressing the on button with needless vigor. A passionate chess player, he is known as a thorough, intelligent jurist with a strong understanding of white-collar crime.[5] But he has never before presided over a trial involving Nazi-era crimes, least of all one attracting international attention. Through the entirety of the Demjanjuk trial, he will remain intent on treating it like any other criminal case before an ordinary German court. Whatever the shortcomings of such an approach—shortcomings revealed in the court's very failure to plan for the first day's throngs—they can hardly be described as idiosyncratic. Since the Federal Republic's assumption of sovereignty, its legal system has tenaciously insisted that Nazi atrocities be treated as ordinary crimes, requiring no special courts, procedures, or laws to bring their perpetrators to justice.

It is an approach that will be tested, challenged, and attacked at every turn by Demjanjuk's defense. No sooner has Judge Alt apologized for the logistical snafu than Demjanjuk's chief counsel, a towering, bearded, and choleric criminal defense lawyer from Ratingen (on the outskirts of Düsseldorf) named Ulrich Busch, is on his feet. Busch seeks to dismiss the case on the grounds of *Befangenheit*—prejudice. While motions alleging prejudice typically are brought against a specific judge for harboring a personal bias against the defendant, Busch's opening salvo is directed against the *entire* German judicial system. It is an accusation he will repeat over and over: the German legal system is trying to make good on its pathetic record of dealing with Nazis by trying a man who is not a German and was never a Nazi. The charges against his client, Busch angrily declaims, represent a moral and legal double standard, a distortion of history, and a bald violation of the German constitution. What of all the SS higher-ups who were either acquitted or never even charged in the first place? Let us not forget, Busch cries, that his client was taken as a prisoner of war by the Wehrmacht. The killing of Red Army POWs was the first Holocaust! Ukrainian auxiliaries and death camp guards had no more freedom of action than the Jews themselves! A victim of forced deportation, his client was never on the radar of German prosecutors until Americans forced them to take the case. New standards are being used against his client. The rules of the game are being changed.

Busch's words tumble forth in seemingly tone-deaf fashion, and the parallel he draws between his client and the Jewish victims of genocide leaves spectators and journalists alike murmuring their disapproval. But his opening barrage clearly outlines the defense's strategy, which is to challenge the very legitimacy of the proceeding at the most fundamental level. In normal criminal trials, the law operates in a safe zone in which the motives and purposes of the prosecution and the rationale for the imposition of a sanction remain beyond the terms of dispute. Criminal law draws a line between violence permitted by the state in the form of a punishment and violence prohibited by the state as a delict; and in the overwhelming majority of criminal cases, this distinction is never called into question—nor is the state's authority to draw it. Not so with political trials. Political trials blur the distinction between state-authorized and state-prohibited force; they interrogate the purposes and procedures of prosecution.[6] Busch will seek to unmask the proceeding as a political trial, attacking at every turn the motives, purpose, justification, and fairness of the case.

It is 11:50 AM. Little more than half an hour old, the trial has already delivered exactly what a global news cycle craves from a legal spectacle: clamorous disorder—the dramatic entrance of a suffering, wheelchair-bound defendant; and an inflammatory opening challenge by the defense. Out on Nymphenburgerstrasse, film crews position themselves before the court building to tape their correspondents' first impressions, while wire service journalists, notes spread on the corridor floor outside the courtroom, bang out stories on laptops connected to portable satellite hookups.

Demjanjuk's reentry into the courtroom after the midday lunch break only adds to the carnivalesque atmosphere. Gone is the wheelchair, replaced by a monstrous orange ambulance gurney. Demjanjuk lies flat on his back, a white blanket drawn—so it appears from my vantage point—over his head. It seems that the defendant has died during lunch. A corpse has been wheeled in to stand trial.

Clearly the defense is seeking to deploy images of the defendant as a principal weapon in its attack on the legitimacy of the proceeding. Journalists viewing this apparition scribble furiously in their notebooks as Cornelius Nestler, a professor of criminal law representing relatives of persons murdered at Sobibor, jumps to his feet. Like Busch, Nestler is keenly aware that the prosecution of Demjanjuk is more than a colloquy over evidence and law; it is a competition over images that will be transmitted around the world. Indeed, this battle started well before Demjanjuk's arrival in Germany. In an attempt to challenge the American deportation order, Demjanjuk's family posted online a video purporting to document the medical exam of an enfeebled and dying Demjanjuk. Responding in kind, special agents in the office of Immigration and Customs Enforcement, a branch of the US Department of Homeland Security, covertly videotaped a seemingly able-bodied Demjanjuk walking unassisted and climbing into his daughter's car.[7]

"Excuse me," Nestler says, "I'd like to know why he's positioned like that."

A team of three doctors briefly confers and announces that the defendant has said he's uncomfortable sitting. Then would it be possible,

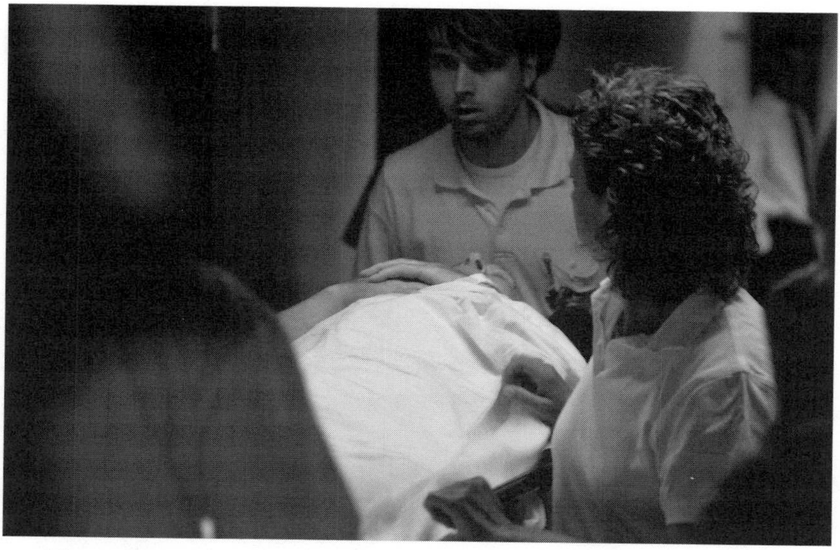

1.2. The corpse in the courtroom. Photo by Thomas Hauzenberger.

Nestler asks, at least to *raise* him? Through a Ukrainian interpreter, the lead doctor confers with Demjanjuk, who appears to reject the suggestion. Now a second lawyer representing victims' families rises and gestures at the gurney with a look of dismay.

"The picture this projects," he says, "is most disconcerting."

The court announces a recess to discuss the matter, and soon a compromise is reached: the defendant may remain on the gurney, but propped up at a 45-degree angle.

Appropriately enough, the rest of this first day of what will turn out to be a punishingly long trial is devoted to medical testimony concerning Demjanjuk's fitness to stand trial. Three physicians take their turns describing his various ailments, which include gout; gallstones; Myeledysplastic Syndrome, a preleukemia bone marrow disease; and spinal stenosis, a narrowing of the spinal cord. Of the trio of doctors, one—Dr. Albrecht Stein, an adjunct professor of medicine—will remain responsible for monitoring Demjanjuk's health in the months to come, emerging as one of the trial's most crucial actors. Decked out in his 1980s-style three-piece, double-breasted suit and jewel-studded, emerald green watch with matching green watchband, Dr. Stein could pass for a

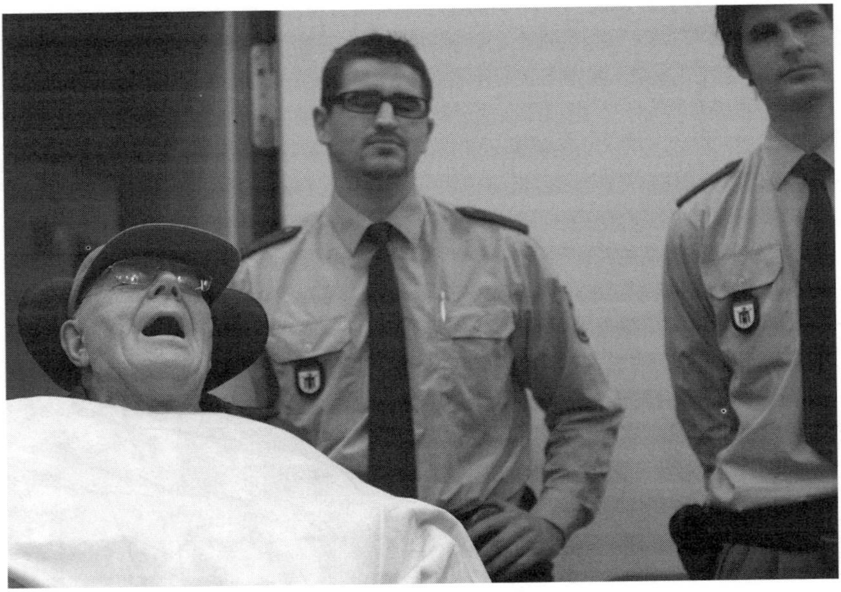

1.3. The performance of pain. Miguel Villagran / Getty Images.

dandified quack in a Fassbinder film. In a squeaky, exuberant voice, he delivers his opinion that despite the defendant's numerous chronic conditions, Demjanjuk is physically and psychologically able to stand trial. The three physicians are in agreement on this; nonetheless, they recommend that, in light of the defendant's advanced age and preexisting conditions, the court should operate on an abbreviated schedule: no more than three sessions per week, and no more than three hours per session.

The physicians' testimony concerning the defendant's medical state would seem completely unremarkable were it not for the grotesque pantomime playing itself out as a backdrop. While the doctors soberly attest to his essential fitness, Demjanjuk enacts a play of mute decrepitude and suffering. His face wrinkles in a silent grimace; he grips his forehead; he struggles to moisten parched lips; he stiffly moves his arms and then opens his mouth wide, like a dying elephant seal. The bizarre juxtaposition of the doctors' steady assurances and the patient's silent distress is the stuff of Monty Python, and journalists in the room exchange glances. The consensus is that the defendant is faking it; the defense is overplaying the martyr card. Demjanjuk's performance lends new meaning to the term show trial. One observer likens it to an Ionesco play.[8]

In the coming weeks Demjanjuk will remain inert, baseball cap pulled low over his brow, eyes hidden behind dark glasses. But the grimaces, the frowns of pain, the silent moans will cease. Someone, it seems, has passed him the message to tone it down.

2

John in America

The road backward from *Gerichtssaal* 101 toward some original point of complicity is long and serpentine, traversing the twentieth century's dreariest bloodlands. Ivan Demjanjuk was born in 1920 in Dubovi Makharyntsi, a tiny village nestled in central-west Ukraine, a place of quiet, rural poverty where farmers lived lives not unlike those of their ancestors in the Middle Ages. Yet the village also lay directly in the path of twentieth-century history, along a miserable corridor of Eastern Europe where ordinary people, caught between the horrific political engineering of two powerful nation-states—the forced famines of Stalin and the genocidal politics of Hitler—would be condemned to die by the millions. Demjanjuk was a simple man, whose greatest ambition was to live unobtrusively and undisturbed, but history would contrive to turn him into an icon of the lowly, shrewd figure charting a course of survival through collaboration.

Both his parents were invalids of sorts; during the First World War, his father lost several fingers on his left hand, and his mother, while pregnant with her son, lost her ability to bend her right leg and remained bedridden for a year.[1] The boy received little in the way of formal education, by his own account, attending school off and on for nine years but managing to complete only the fourth grade. He was twelve when the great famine of 1932–33 struck. Known in Ukrainian as the *Holodomor*, the famine is generally estimated to have killed perhaps three million people. Most historians view the catastrophe as the consequence of a stunning drop in agricultural productivity brought on by the Soviets' radical policies of forced collectivization.[2] But most

Ukrainians see it as an act of genocide. At his 1984 deportation hearing, Demjanjuk declared that "the entire world" understood "that the hunger was brought purposely to annihilate the Ukrainian nation."[3] At his trial in Jerusalem, he put the number of victims at seven million, a demonstrative trumping of the canonical tally of Jewish martyrs.[4] The very term *Holodomor,* which first gained currency in Ukrainian communities in the United States in the late 1970s, roughly translates as "extermination by hunger."

In his own telling, Demjanjuk's family survived the famine by selling the family farm for eight loaves of bread and moving to a *kolkhoz,* a Soviet collective farm, near Moscow, where his father's sister resided. Prohibited from staying, they returned to their village in the Ukraine, stopping first at the house of his father's brother, only to discover that "they [the brother and his family] were all dead by then."[5] Everywhere they "found death." As Demjanjuk recalled at his deportation hearing in 1984, people "were eating rats, they were eating birds. . . . People were lying around dead with flies attacking their bodies. It's impossible to tell it in words unless I use the word holocaust."[6] Later, at his Israeli trial, he characterized the famine as "beyond anything that humanity had known up until then"; his own family, he recalled, was forced to eat the house cat.[7]

When he was sixteen, Demjanjuk went to work in a coalhouse, and a year later, on a *kolkhoz.*[8] On the collective farm, he plowed fields by hand, but when the skilled tractor drivers were enlisted for the war against Finland, he became a replacement tractor driver, a job of distinction. He also joined the Komsomol, a communist youth organization. When asked in Jerusalem why a staunch anti-Soviet would join a communist organization, Demjanjuk offered an explanation that encapsulated his ethos of adaptation and survival: membership, he said, was "both mandatory and not mandatory."[9] Drafted into the Red Army in 1940, he at first did not report, because, by his own account, he lacked the two pairs of underpants that fresh recruits were required to bring to training camp.[10] After the German invasion in the summer of 1941, he was called up again; this time no one cared about his underwear.[11] Shortly after his first deployment, three months into the German invasion, he suffered a shrapnel wound to the back while his artillery unit was beating a retreat on the Dnieper River. After convalescing in a succession of military hospitals, he was redeployed, only to be taken as a prisoner of war in the Battle of the Kerch in the Crimean Peninsula in May 1942.

After the war, Demjanjuk bounced around several Displaced Persons (DP) camps in Germany, finding work for three years as a truck driver for the US Army, first in Landshut and later in Regensburg. There he married and celebrated the birth of his first child, a daughter, Lydia, in 1950. He originally hoped to emigrate to Argentina or Canada,[12] but here again larger political forces intervened, this time in the form of a law passed by the US Congress amid escalating Cold War tensions.

The Displaced Persons Act of 1948 was ostensibly designed to address a continuing humanitarian crisis—the fate of one million persons, mostly from Eastern Europe, who remained in DP camps a full three years after the war's end. President Truman believed it was America's moral responsibility to help relieve the postwar refugee problem, and on December 22, 1945, issued an executive order giving priority to the applications of displaced persons under existing immigration law.[13] Over the next two years, this executive decree worked foremost to benefit Holocaust survivors, thousands of whom entered the United States. Conservative members of Congress, notably unenthusiastic about this influx—and mindful that public opinion shared their prejudices—now stepped in, and fashioned a law designed, in the words of one senator, "to keep the Jews out."[14] Bemoaning it as "anti-Semitic," Truman nonetheless reluctantly signed the DP Act of 1948 into law.[15]

The new law effectively turned America's back to victims of Hitler while welcoming those of Stalin.[16] Of the two hundred thousand new refugees authorized to enter the country, fifty thousand spots were reserved for *Volksdeutsche*, ethnic Germans expelled from their homelands by the advance of the Red Army, while eighty thousand were set aside for DPs from countries now behind the Iron Curtain—Ukrainians, Byelorussians, Latvians, Lithuanians, and Estonians. Finally, an additional sixty thousand were reserved for farmers. Few Jews in Eastern Europe were farmers; indeed, official policy long prohibited them from owning or running farms.[17] So while the DP Act worked to restrict Jewish immigration, it opened the doors to the Demjanjuks of the world. According to his DP forms, Demjanjuk had spent most of the war working as an "independent farmer" in Poland; as a Ukrainian *and* a farmer, he was doubly qualified for a visa.

Alas for Demjanjuk, the 1950 extension of the law, which made possible the issuance of an additional 121,000 visas, eliminated the preference for farmers (as well as the restrictions on Jewish DPs). Applicants also needed a domestic sponsor, a requirement that originally had discouraged Demjanjuk from considering America. In December 1951, however, he and his wife received word that a farmer in Decatur, Indiana, would accept them.[18] A diagnosis of mild tuberculosis delayed Demjanjuk for several months, but once medically cleared and with visas secured, he set sail from Bremerhaven with his wife and child on the USS *General WG Haan*, arriving in New York Harbor on February 9, 1952. The family settled briefly in Decatur, where Demjanjuk was put to work on the farm castrating piglets, a job that did not agree with him.[19] They then moved to Cleveland, following a Ukrainian friend who had worked with Demjanjuk in Regensburg and now had a job at Ford.[20] Demjanjuk found employment at the Ford plant in Bookpart, Ohio, working as a motor balancer and later as a mechanic and machinist.[21] His wife got a job in the coiling department at General Electric.[22] A member of Local 250 of the UAW, Demjanjuk became a lifer at Ford, a beneficiary of the great postwar boom in well-paid, unionized, blue-collar manufacturing jobs.[23]

In 1958 Demjanjuk became an American citizen and officially changed his name from Ivan to John. Israeli prosecutors would later construe this as evidence of an attempt to hide his true identity, but in retrospect the name change seems to reflect no more than a desire to adapt and assimilate. "I was told by the official that all Ukrainians are changing their names to American versions," he would recall, "and that's when I did it."[24]

The family grew: a second daughter, Irene, was born in 1960, and a son, John Jr., in 1965. In 1970, the Demjanjuks moved into a brick ranch house in Seven Hills, a middle-class suburb of Cleveland. Demjanjuk became an avid gardener, spending his leisure time tending his vegetables.[25] The family regularly attended St. Vladimir's, the local Ukrainian Orthodox church, and the Demjanjuk children enrolled in the church school. At St. Vladimir's, Demjanjuk served as a member of the audit committee that reviewed the church's financial books and volunteered in the kitchen's pierogi fund.[26] He was considered an affable neighbor—"the kind of guy who would stop to help you fix a flat on the road."[27] And why not? After his years of famine and poverty in the Ukraine, and his harrowing experiences during the war, the life of a middle-class American émigré must have seemed like a miracle, a deliverance from the devastating intrusions of history.

* * *

In October 1975, Jacob Javits, a prominent senator from New York and a liberal Republican at a time when such a species still existed, received a letter from the editor of the *Ukrainian Daily News* purporting to list seventy Ukrainian war criminals residing in the United States. The editor and letter writer was Michael Hanusiak, an American of Ukrainian descent and a loyal communist, who, some years later, on the occasion of his seventy-fifth birthday, would receive the Order of Friendship of the Peoples from the chairman of the presidium of Ukraine's Supreme Soviet.[28] Javits was deeply engaged in the plight of Soviet Jewry, and had played a key role in drafting the Jackson-Vanik Amendment of 1974, which linked conferring most-favored-nation trade status for the Soviet Union to the easing of emigration for Soviet Jews. Hanusiak, who traveled often to Kiev, apparently received the list during one such trip directly from Moscow, which was vexed both by protests on behalf of Soviet Jewry and by the agitations of Ukrainian nationalists. Moscow hoped to deflect attention from the former and to discredit the latter by casting Ukrainian nationalism as a movement of former Nazi collaborators—thus driving a wedge between the two anti-Soviet movements.

Not that the two movements shared much in common, besides being anti-Soviet. Historically the Ukraine had unleashed horrific pogroms upon its large Jewish community. Many of these had occurred under the instigation or at least indulgence of some of the most prominent names in Ukrainian history. Bohdan Khmelnytsky, the seventeenth-century national hero whose visage adorns Ukrainian banknotes, is best remembered in Jewish history as the murderous Cossack who made the killing of Jews a rallying point of his political program.[29] Symon Petliura, the revered Ukrainian statesman who led the struggle for independence after the Russian revolution, figures in Jewish memory as having presided over a period of murderous pogroms, at best haplessly unable to stem the violence committed by his own military.[30] The Soviets clearly hoped to tap into the sentiment that saw Ukrainian nationalism as indistinguishable from anti-Semitism. Michael Hanusiak played a helpful role in this scheme. Two years before sending Javits the list, Hanusiak had published a short book called *Lest We Forget*, documenting the "psychopathic hatred" of the Jewish people among Ukrainian nationalists and the assistance that the latter provided in the "Hitlerites' program of ruthless extermination."[31]

The mid-1970s was also a time when the United States was finally beginning to address the disturbing legacy of the Displaced Persons Act of 1948. In theory, the act had barred the issuance of visas to persons who "assisted the enemy in persecuting civil[ians]." Yet Congress' Cold War priorities remained clear, as the law likewise barred persons belonging to a "Communist organization" or adhering to a "philosophy directed toward the destruction of free competitive enterprise and the revolutionary overthrow of representative government."[32] And while the DP Act had also put into place an elaborate screening process to filter out those who had been complicit in atrocities,[33] not everyone was convinced of the efficacy of these procedures. On January 12, 1949, six directors of prominent Jewish organizations published a letter in the *New York Times*, alerting the public that many "former Nazi collaborators and other persons . . . imbued with Nazi-like racist ideas" had swelled the ranks of the DP camps. The letter called for Congress to strengthen the screening provisions of the act to "prevent the settlement in this country of those whose infamous performance toward the hapless people of Europe makes them . . . unworthy of the high privilege of American citizenship."[34] This letter elicited a passionate response by a dozen leaders of Catholic relief services, who lamented the "widespread propaganda" suggesting "that a large proportion of the non-Jewish DP's are former Nazi collaborators." Challenging the need for additional screenings, the Catholic co-signatories insisted that every DP has passed through "at least seven or eight different screenings." Some had been screened "as many as thirty times."[35]

Where the latter number came from is anyone's guess; in reality, congressmen from districts with large Baltic or Slavic constituencies often pressured immigration officials to act with dispatch. Their efforts encountered little resistance, as many immigration officials shared strong anticommunist sentiments and showed little interest in making strenuous efforts to obtain evidence of collaboration, most of which had been destroyed in the war or carted off behind the Iron Curtain.[36] Thanks, then, to the law's skewed quotas and typically pro forma screening process, the DP Act of 1948 eased the passage of hundreds if not thousands of Nazi collaborators into the country. (The precise figure has been subject to some debate; *New York Times* journalist Eric Lichtblau estimates that the number of postwar immigrants with strong ties to the Nazis "likely surpassed ten thousand.")[37] Admittedly, actual Nazis had a much tougher time getting in; no one on Capitol Hill showed much enthusiasm for opening America's door to former members of the SS. That said, some sixteen hundred former Nazi scientists came to the United States under the auspices of Operation Paperclip, and perhaps another thousand ex-Nazis found gainful employment with the CIA, which in the early years of the Cold War recruited and protected even the most tainted war criminals if they promised to advance any national security or strategic interest, no matter how oblique or dubious. And in reserving thousands of visas for refugees from the Soviet Union, Congress had essentially extended an open invitation to Nazi collaborators, a fact that in time began to spark dismaying revelations.

The capture of Adolf Eichmann in Argentina in 1960 provided a stark reminder that prominent Nazis remained at large, in some cases living openly with impunity. Not all had fled to South America. In 1963, Charles Allen Jr., a freelance American journalist, published a three-part exposé in the journal *Jewish Currents* about fifteen presumed war criminals merrily residing in the United States.[38] A year later, Joseph Lelyveld of the *New York Times*, working on a tip from Simon Wiesenthal, broke the story of Hermine Braunsteiner-Ryan, an Austrian-born housewife living an unruffled life in New York City.[39] The Queens housewife and "good neighbor" had, it turned out, once been known as the "stomping mare" of Madjanek, a guard notorious for her brutal mistreatment of female prisoners at the Lublin camp. The high-profile case, which went on for years, reached a culmination of sorts in 1973, when Braunsteiner-Ryan, who had already relinquished her citizenship in an effort to avoid deportation, was extradited to Germany, where she was later convicted and sentenced to life imprisonment (she was released on medical grounds in 1996 and died three years later). It marked the first time that a naturalized American citizen was sent to another country to stand trial as a Nazi war criminal.

More generally, the late 1960s and early 1970s ushered in a period of growing sensitivity to what many saw as America's toleration of, if not outright complicity in, human rights abuses and war crimes. In 1968, historian Arthur Morse published *While Six Million Died*, a sharp indictment of the failure of the United States to bomb the rail lines to Auschwitz and of the general apathy of our wartime leaders to news of the extermination of European Jews. Morse's indictment resonated with protests against American war making in Indochina. Within liberal political circles, the war in Vietnam came increasingly to be seen as not merely misguided, but criminal. In the wake of the My Lai massacre, the bombing of Cambodia, and the Watergate scandal, Telford Taylor, the Nuremberg prosecutor, openly likened the Nixon administration to the Nazi leadership he had once tried.[40] After the indictment of Nixon's close advisers and the president's resignation, many saw lustration as the path toward the political renewal of a morally unhinged nation.

At the same time, Israel's brush with catastrophe in the opening days of the Yom Kippur War in 1973 introduced a new generation of American Jews to the existential vulnerabilities of the Jewish people. Politicians, such as Joshua Eilberg and Elizabeth Holtzman, began to take up the cause of ferreting out collaborators living domestically. Both Eilberg and Holtzman were members of the House, Democrats, and Jewish, with considerable Jewish constituencies. Eilberg, who had represented an urban Pennsylvanian district since 1966, chaired the House Subcommittee on Immigration, while Holtzman, a bright, tenacious Harvard-educated lawyer, entered the House in 1972, representing a Brooklyn district. Their efforts, reported on in the pages of the *Times* by Ralph Blumenthal, revealed the government's utter indifference to the Nazi collaborator problem. Eilberg and Holtzman brought attention to the ethos of apathy in the State Department, which had little interest in cultivating closer ties with the Soviets or in ruffling relations with West Germany. They also probed the resistance, faulty organization, and deficient procedures within the Immigration and Naturalization Service (INS), which handled all cases on the district level, with no central oversight or direction, and whose own chief trial lawyer in the Braunsteiner-

Ryan case openly complained of having "been hampered by superiors" in pursuing the matter.[41]

Eilberg's and Holtzman's agitprop finally prodded the INS to a largely symbolic concession: in 1973, it placed within its New York bureau a project control office responsible for investigating collaborators. The head of this office, or rather its sole dedicated employee, was a career INS investigator named Sam Zutty, and it was to Zutty that Senator Javits forwarded the list of seventy Ukrainians sent by Hanusiak, the American communist eager to foster "helpful exchanges." With virtually no staff, few resources, and little in the way of organizational support, Zutty focused on paring the list down. He quickly discovered that some of those named were dead and others no longer resided in America. Using such sophisticated investigative tools as phone books, Zutty trimmed the list of seventy down to a more manageable nine names. Included in this group were Feodor Fedorenko, then of Watertown, Connecticut, whom the list named as a former Treblinka guard, and Ivan Demjanjuk, a resident of suburban Cleveland, who allegedly had served at Sobibor.

In the case of Demjanjuk, a simple examination of visa and immigration records conducted by Harold Jacobs, an associate of Zutty's, led to an astonishing discovery. On his Application for Immigration Visa to the United States, filed in Stuttgart on December 27, 1951, Demjanjuk had listed his domicile from 1934 to 1943 as none other than Sobibor, Poland (see figures 2.1 and 2.2).[42] Over the years, in particular at his trial in Israel, this detail would cause headaches for Demjanjuk, forcing him to concoct increasingly involved stories to explain how he had come to list on this crucial form an utterly obscure Polish town, one that he later insisted he had never even *heard of*, let alone lived in.[43] To INS investigators, the visa application appeared to deliver powerful circumstantial corroboration of the information contained in the Hanusiak list. Yet neither Zutty nor Jacobs could find witnesses in the United States to aid the INS' investigations of Fedorenko and Demjanjuk—a fact that was hardly surprising, given that barely 120 Jews together had survived the Sobibor and Treblinka death camps. Most of those survivors had settled in Israel, and so American officials appealed to the Israeli police for help in preparing their cases.

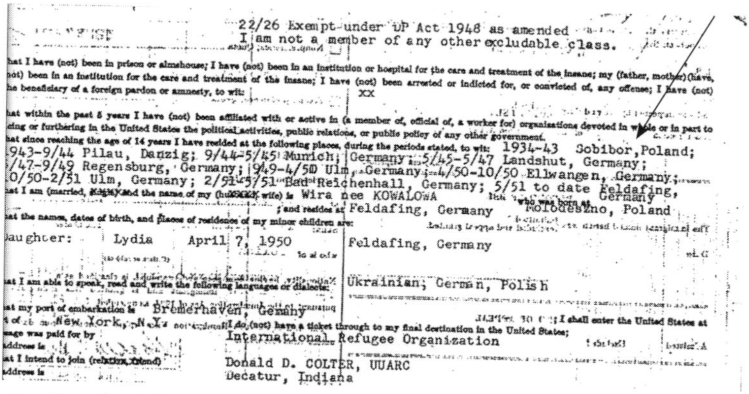

22/26 Exempt under DP Act 1948 as amended
I am not a member of any other excludable class.

hat I have (not) been in prison or almshouse; I have (not) been in an institution or hospital for the care and treatment of the insane; my (father, mother) (have, not) been in an institution for the care and treatment of the insane; I have (not) been arrested or indicted for, or convicted of, any offense; I have (not) he beneficiary of a foreign pardon or amnesty, to wit: XX

hat within the past 5 years I have (not) been affiliated with or active in (a member of, official of, a worker for) organizations devoted in whole or in part to ding or furthering in the United States the political activities, public relations, or public policy of any other government.

hat since reaching the age of 14 years I have resided at the following places, during the periods stated, to wit: 1934-43 Sobibor, Poland; 943-9/44 Pilau, Danzig; 9/44-5/45 Munich, Germany; 5/45-5/47 Landshut, Germany; /47-9/49 Regensburg, Germany; 9/49-4/50 Ulm, Germany; 4/50-10/50 Ellwangen, Germany; 0/50-2/51 Ulm, Germany; 2/51-5/51 Bad Reichenhall, Germany; 5/51 to date Feldafing, Germany

hat I am (married, single) and the name of my (husband, wife) is Wira nee KOWALOWA who was born at Molodeczno, Poland ; and resides at Feldafing, Germany

hat the names, dates of birth, and places of residence of my minor children are:
Daughter: Lydia April 7, 1950 Feldafing, Germany

hat I am able to speak, read and write the following languages or dialects: Ukrainian; German, Polish

hat my port of embarkation is Bremerhaven, Germany
hat I (do, not) have a ticket through to my final destination in the United States; I shall enter the United States at New York, N.Y.
age was paid for by International Refugee Organization
ddress is
hat I intend to join (relative, friend) Donald D. COLTER, UUARC
ddress is Decatur, Indiana

2.1. Demjanjuk's visa application listing Sobibor as residence (1934–43). Courtesy Office of Special Investigations, DoJ.

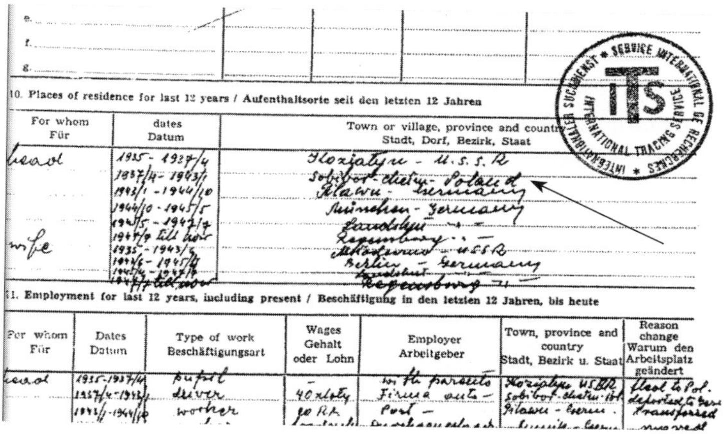

10. Places of residence for last 12 years / Aufenthaltsorte seit den letzten 12 Jahren

For whom Für	dates Datum	Town or village, province and country Stadt, Dorf, Bezirk, Staat
head	1935 - 1937/4	Slozjatyn - U.S.S.R.
	1937/4 - 1943/1	Sobibor-Cheln-Poland
	1943/1 - 1944/10	Pilawa - Germany
	1944/10 - 1945/5	München - Germany
	1945/5 - 1947/7	Landshut
	1947/7 till now	Regensburg
wife	1935 - 1943/6	[illegible] USSR
	1943/6 - 1945/	Berlin - Germany
	[illegible]	Landshut
	[illegible]	Regensburg

11. Employment for last 12 years, including present / Beschäftigung in den letzten 12 Jahren, bis heute

For whom Für	Dates Datum	Type of work Beschäftigungsart	Wages Gehalt oder Lohn	Employer Arbeitgeber	Town, province and country Stadt, Bezirk u. Staat	Reason change Warum den Arbeitsplatz geändert
head	1935-1937/4	pupil	–	with the parents	Slozjatyn USSR	fled to Pol.
	1937/4-1943/1	driver	40 zloty	Firma auto-	Sobibor-Cheln-Pol.	deported to Germ.
	1943/1-1944/10	worker	20 RM	Post –	Pilawa - Germ.	transferred

2.2. Demjanjuk's Application for Assistance listing Sobibor as residence (1937–43). Courtesy Office of Special Investigations, DoJ.

The plan was never to bring criminal charges against Fedorenko or Demjanjuk. As an author of an internal study of the OSI has noted:

No matter how egregious the prosecutory activity, the United States [could and] cannot file charges [against Nazi collaborators] because the alleged crimes—committed on foreign soil against non-US citi-

> zens—violated no US law at the time. Any legislation to criminalize such activity retroactively would be constitutionally barred by the Ex Post Facto clause.[44]

For decades, the American legal community has treated this notion—that without preexisting law, the constitutional bar against retroactivity disallowed the domestic prosecution of Nazi collaborators—as a legal fact. (As we will see, an even more obsessive concern with retroactivity would also dramatically restrict the prosecution of Nazi-era perpetrators in the German Federal Republic.) But legal facts differ from facts in the natural world. They represent less realities than assumptions, which, when prodded, may wobble. Consider, for example, the belief that a special law from Congress authorizing the trial of Nazis for extraterritorial crimes would have violated the ex post facto clause. At the time of Demjanjuk's extradition hearing, a federal judge held that "any violation of the law of nations encroaches upon and injures the interests of all sovereign states. . . . This is true irrespective of when or where the crime was committed, the . . . status of the punishing power, or the nationality of the victims."[45] In the same holding, the judge noted that the Allies in postwar Germany frequently "exercised extra-territorial jurisdiction" over persons "accused of war crimes and crimes against humanity." Reviewing the same matter, the Sixth Circuit Court of Appeals struck a similar note, observing that "some crimes are so universally condemned that . . . any nation which has custody of the perpetrators may punish them according to its law."[46]

To say, then, that Congress could never have given federal courts jurisdiction over Nazi-era crimes is misleading. It would be more accurate to say that for better or worse, the legal ingenuity that American jurists had shown in trying hundreds of Nazis at Nuremberg and under the auspices of the American military in occupied Germany never found resonance in the domestic legal imagination. Either backtracking from the spirit of Nuremberg—or perhaps unaware of its achievements—jurists in the United States never pushed for special legislation because they never seriously questioned the assumption that such special legislation would run afoul of the ex post facto prohibition.

This did not leave domestic prosecutors entirely powerless. Section 340(a) of the Immigration and Nationality Act of 1952 did authorize denaturalization proceedings in cases in which citizenship was "illegally procured or . . . procured by concealment of a material fact or by willful misrepresentation."[47] Denaturalization is a civil proceeding, but given what is at stake—the loss of citizenship—it typically takes on the character and feel of a criminal trial. With evidence supplied by Israeli investigators, INS officials hoped to denaturalize Fedorenko and Demjanjuk for having lied on their immigration forms, and then deport them to a country that *could* bring criminal charges.

The INS inquiry was assigned to Miriam Radiwker, a seventy-year-old lawyer in the Special Unit of the Israeli police devoted to the investigation of Nazi crimes. The Special Unit, previously known as Bureau 06, had helped prepare the case against Adolf Eichmann, the only former Nazi to have been tried in Israel. But it had also assisted the investigation of hundreds of Nazi cases in many other countries. Following a well-rehearsed protocol, Radiwker placed ads in an Israeli newspaper seeking Sobibor and Treblinka survivors to aid in an ongoing investigation, and also reached out to survivors directly. The Special Unit prepared a photo spread, a three-page album of seventeen photographs of Ukrainian suspects, which included Fedorenko's visa photo from 1949 and Demjanjuk's visa picture from 1951.

The results of these identification parades left Radiwker bewildered. On May 9, 1976, Eugen Turowski, a Treblinka survivor enlisted to aid in the identification of Fedorenko, instead identified Demjanjuk, the presumed Sobibor guard: "I can well remember this Ukrainian. I knew him personally because he sometimes came into the shop to repair something."[48] Fellow Treblinka survivor Abraham Goldfarb also failed to identify Fedorenko, and likewise paused over Demjanjuk's picture, insisting that the man "in picture number sixteen looks familiar."[49] Meanwhile, no Sobibor survivors recognized Demjanjuk.

Over the coming months, Radiwker sought out additional Treblinka survivors in an effort to make sense of these confusing results. On September 21, 1976, Josef Czarny, a government employee, pointed directly at Demjanjuk's photo: "This is Ivan Grozny, that is the Ivan, the infamous Ivan. Thirty-three years have gone by, but I recognize him at first sight with full certainty." When told that the man he had identified was "not at Treblinka but at Sobibor," Czarny was adamant: "This man, who was called 'Ivan Grozny' was in Treblinka when I came there. He was in

Treblinka until the last minute."[50] A week and a half later, on September 30, Gustav Boraks, a hairdresser who at Treblinka had cut the hair of naked women about to be gassed, pointed to the photo of Demjanjuk: "This is the photograph of Ivan Grozny. I recognize him with one-hundred percent certainty."[51]

"Ivan Grozny," a Russian sobriquet meaning "Ivan the Terrible," was not an unfamiliar name to students of the Holocaust. During the Eichmann trial, Treblinka survivor Eliahu Rosenberg had testified about a vicious Ukrainian guard named Ivan, who, along with a colleague, had run the gas chamber at Treblinka and had tormented Jews while forcing them toward their death. In his interview with Radiwker, Boraks recalled, "I saw him daily . . . as he brutally herded people in the gas chambers."[52] Czarny shared many of the same memories: "Ivan Grozny was a known sadist. . . . He maltreated the victims inhumanely. . . . He far surpassed the Germans in his cruelty. . . . He was one of the most gruesome characters in the Treblinka camp. That is why he stays in my memory forever."[53] As the number of Treblinka survivors to positively identify Demjanjuk climbed to ten, Radiwker became convinced that American investigators had stumbled upon one of the most notorious figures in the dismal history of the Holocaust. Her conclusion was forwarded to the INS, and on August 25, 1977, federal prosecutors in Cleveland filed a complaint seeking to strip Demjanjuk—aka Ivan the Terrible—of his citizenship.

* * *

By the time Demjanjuk's denaturalization case went to trial more than three years later, the legal landscape of domestic cases against alleged Nazis and collaborators had changed dramatically. The indefatigable Elizabeth Holtzman used House hearings to expose the continuing culture of inaction not only in the INS but also in the State and Justice departments. In response to a request filed in January 1977 by the House Subcommittee on Immigration, Citizenship, and International Law (formerly chaired by Eilberg and now by Holtzman), the comptroller general submitted a report, concluding that it had uncovered no proof of a "widespread conspiracy to obstruct investigations of alleged Nazi war criminals" in America. Nonetheless, the report noted that before 1973, investigations had been at best "deficient or perfunctory," and while it claimed that matters had "improved" since 1973, it conceded that there had been "no successful prosecutions."[54]

The INS took grudging note of the report's dry understatement—"improvements are still needed"—and announced the creation of a Special Litigation Unit (SLU) responsible for coordinating the investigation of all cases involving alleged Nazi war criminals. By July 1977, the INS had replaced the New York office where Sam Zutty had toiled alone with a Washington-based unit. Chosen to head the Office was Martin Mendelsohn, a young trial lawyer with a career in legal services and close connections to Holtzman. In May 1979, Mendelsohn's unit was moved out of the INS and into the Justice Department where it was renamed the Office of Special Investigations (OSI). In Justice, the OSI was lodged in the criminal division, a move largely orchestrated by Holtzman and designed to highlight the importance of the Office's civil caseload. Yet the reasons for the move from the INS to Justice—part bureaucratic, part strategic, part political—were not entirely happy. The SLU had hardly benefited from being housed in the Immigration Service. Many officials in the INS saw the fledgling unit as an indictment of the Service's handling of the collaborator problem, and rankled at the suggestion that the SLU had been created to correct a history of inaction and mistakes. Mendelsohn did little to dispel this impression; unsatisfied with the lawyering within the INS—"abysmal would have been an improvement" was how he described it—he assembled a staff almost entirely from outside the Service.[55]

A future director of the OSI, Allan Ryan, bluntly described the short-lived SLU as a "disaster,"[56] and it is true that in its two-year existence the SLU managed to file not a single new claim. In the denaturalization hearing of Vilis Hazners in 1977, a former member of the Latvian SS, Mendelsohn and his staff were exposed as ill-prepared, fumbling to produce documents.[57] It is far from clear, however, that Mendelsohn deserves the blame for the Unit's failures. Mendelsohn himself has argued that he was assigned an impossible task, one that he likened to "trying to build a skyscraper while also cleaning the Augean stables."[58] Certainly the fact that the unit lacked the statutory authority to prosecute its cases contributed to its woes. Having researched a case and prepared the evidence, its lawyers had to hand matters off to federal prosecutors, who formally filed the civil charges and led the litigation. This made for considerable resentment and friction between litigation teams, as US attorneys litigating denaturalization cases treated Mendelsohn like a meddling interloper. In the Demjanjuk matter, Mendelsohn found himself in something of a pitched battle with the US Attorneys' Office in Cleveland. Nearly two years had passed since federal prosecutors had filed the complaint, and Mendelsohn, concerned by the lack of progress on the case, sought to direct the litigation.[59] John Horrigan, the assistant US attorney in Cleveland in control of the case, tenaciously protected his turf, and Mendelsohn, who disliked Horrigan and had little confidence in his abilities, found himself struggling to get even basic information about the case from Cleveland. The turf battle continued through 1978, when an associate attorney general finally placed the case in Mendelsohn's hands.[60] But even this did not settle the matter. Soon after the SLU was reorganized as the OSI, Mendelsohn was eased out in an internal power struggle. Cooperation on the Demjanjuk case did not improve until Norman Moscowitz, a Harvard-educated lawyer hired by Mendelsohn, established a détente with Horrigan.

It would be wrong, however, to see the struggle between the two offices as merely the result of a battle over turf or a clash of personalities. At its heart, the dispute reflected a sea change in the understanding of the task facing the government. To Holtzman, Mendelsohn, and those within the fledgling SLU, it was clear that the historical and evidentiary complexities posed by Nazi collaborator cases required an entirely different organizational structure and litigation strategy. The basic problem nestled in the approach of the US Attorneys' Offices, which treated collaborator litigation as essentially no different from any other civil case. Holtzman and Mendelsohn recognized that while operating within the strictures of the civil law of denaturalization, the government essentially had to create a domestic war crimes unit—one capable of handling state-sponsored crimes perpetrated decades ago on a different continent. Standard strategies were doomed to fail in cases in which most evidence was held by America's principal political adversary, and in which lawyers and investigators lacked the requisite linguistic and research skills to make sense of what evidence they had.

Two botched litigations, the Walus and Fedorenko cases, dramatized the difficulty of handling atrocity proceedings with ordinary prosecutorial tools. Born in Poland, Frank Walus arrived in the United States in the late 1940s and settled in Chicago, where he became a naturalized US citizen and worked until his retirement in 1972. Five years later, in January 1977—that is, shortly before the creation of the SLU—federal prosecutors filed a complaint accusing Walus of having served with the Gestapo in Poland. The alleged "Beast of Kielce" was said to have committed numerous atrocities, including stomping a pregnant Jewish woman to death. The case was considered legally uncomplicated, as it turned exclusively on the testimony of eyewitnesses, all of whom claimed to identify Walus. With little supervision from the freshly whelped SLU, the case still was deemed of great importance, as it marked the very first denaturalization trial conducted in the United States against an alleged former Nazi collaborator.[61]

As a civil matter, a denaturalization trial does not provide the defendant with a Sixth Amendment right to a jury. Walus was tried, then, in the federal district court of Chicago before Judge Julius H. Hoffman, notorious for having presided over the "Chicago Seven" trial following the riots that rocked the Democratic National Convention in Chicago in the summer of 1968. In that trial, Judge Hoffman had let the antics and provocations of the defendants and their lead lawyer, William Kunstler, provoke him to the point that he ordered Bobby Seale, the Black Panther leader, bound to his chair and gagged. The defense taunted Hoffman, who was Jewish, for resorting to SS tactics; at one point, defendant Jerry Rubin marched to the judge's bench, screaming, "Heil Hitler!"[62]

The Walus trial began in March 1978,[63] as Hoffman was approaching his eighty-third birthday. As if to disprove the taunts of Rubin, the combative octogenarian displayed visible hostility to the defense, curtailing its cross-examination of government witnesses, including one who had previously described the 5′4″ defendant as standing well over six feet tall. Indeed, Hoffman was so brusque with the defense that the government feared he was delivering grounds for appeal.[64] On the face of it, the case seemed to favor Walus. While the prosecution was unable to supply any documentary evidence in support of the eyewitness identifications, the defense proffered documents in support of Walus' claim of factual innocence—that he had spent the war as a *Zwangsarbeiter*, a forced laborer, on a farm in Germany. These included a health insurance record of his employment in Germany—evidence that Hoffman dismissed as unreliable because it had been prepared by Nazis. After a seventeen-day trial, Hoffman ruled against Walus, ordering his denaturalization.

In the months following the ruling, Walus and his lawyers filed several increasingly desperate motions full of fresh exculpatory evidence, including statements of a French prisoner of war, a German priest, and a group of Polish forced laborers, all of whom claimed to have known Walus during his time in Germany. It also became clear that one of the key witnesses for the government had a deep personal animus toward Walus, apparently the legacy of having once been sued by him. Hoffman remained firm in his decision, but Walus found a more receptive audience in the Seventh Circuit Court of Appeals. Concerned both by Hoffman's "disturbing" behavior—particularly his curtailing of cross-examination by the defense—and by the weaknesses in the government's case, the circuit court ordered a new trial, observing that the recently unearthed evidence would "almost certainly compel a different result."[65] In light of this ruling, two government lawyers carefully reviewed its case "down to the floor nails."[66] One of them, Robin Boylan, who had made the move from the SLU to the OSI, became convinced of Walus' factual innocence. Yet dropping the case, he warned, "could cause hard feelings on the part of the Israeli police and Simon Wiesenthal."[67] Wiesenthal, the Viennese-based Nazi hunter, had supplied critical evidence against Walus while the Special Unit of the Israeli police had located and interviewed many of the survivor witnesses; the government did not want to alienate these crucial sources.

This was understandable. Cases against collaborators suffered from the difficulty of obtaining evidence, the bulk of which lay behind the Iron Curtain. Investigators were stymied by the refusal of officials in Moscow and Washington to cooperate with them or with one another. Neither side saw the point of cooperation; Moscow was reluctant to share evidence, and Washington essentially refused to ask for Soviet help. As the comptroller general's report noted, the State Department in particular refused to seek information from Soviet sources out of fear that "communist countries would use its actions for propaganda . . . to embarrass the West."[68] This problem did not simply complicate the process of preparing individual cases; it rose to the level of a structural issue that imperiled the very viability of the trial program.[69]

Investigators also received little in the way of assistance from America's own intelligence-gathering agencies. The CIA, perhaps fearing exposure of its own complicity in safeguarding former Nazis, was particularly stubborn in its refusal to share intelligence. During his brief tenure at the helm of the SLU, Mendelsohn did manage to receive modest assistance from the Agency, but this typically took the dispiriting form of the CIA quietly confirming that the subject of an immigration probe had previously been a former CIA operative.[70] But the CIA was hardly the only problem. In the years before the creation of the Special Litigation Unit, the INS, at the outset of any investigation, would routinely ask the CIA, FBI, Pentagon, and State Department to conduct record checks of persons of interest; often the INS would receive no response and just as often there would be no follow-up. The INS simply accepted the absence of an answer as indicating an absence of information.[71]

Given larger Cold War realities and this local culture of dysfunction, it was all the more imperative for those working on denaturalization cases to preserve and protect what sources they had. It was unsurprising, then, that Boylan should have fretted about imperiling relations with Simon Wiesenthal and the Special Unit of the Israeli police. But Boylan's concerns went further yet, issuing in a vague and disturbing alarm: "The [hard] feelings might spread throughout the Jewish community in the United States and lead to political repercussions."[72] The fear of "repercussions" notwithstanding, the Justice Department concluded that mounting a second trial against an arguably innocent man would be more calamitous than a quick, if inelegant, exit. The government dropped all charges, and quietly paid Walus $34,000 to help cover his legal costs.

The Fedorenko case represented the government's second go at denaturalizing an alleged collaborator. Feodor Fedorenko's early life bore striking resemblances to Demjanjuk's. Born to a poor family in a small Ukrainian village, meagerly educated, Fedorenko worked on the family farm until the Soviets launched their catastrophic campaign of forced collectivization. In 1933, Fedorenko moved to a *kolkhoz* in the Crimea, where he drove a truck. Only months after being drafted into the Red Army, he was taken as a POW by the advancing Wehrmacht, and interned in POW camps at Rovno and Chelm, the same camps as Demjanjuk.[73] After the war, Fedorenko found refuge in a displaced person camp outside of Hamburg. In 1949 he applied for admission to the United States under the DP Act of 1948, arriving later that year. After a brief stint as a farmhand in northern Connecticut, he settled in Waterbury, making a quiet life for himself as a foundry worker. After his retirement, he moved to Florida.

Fedorenko's denaturalization trial began in July 1978, in a federal district court in Ft. Lauderdale. Like Demjanjuk, he was accused of lying on his visa and immigration forms about his service as a guard at Treblinka. On these documents, Fedorenko claimed to have worked as a farmer in Poland from 1937 until 1942 in the small town of Sarny. He further claimed that in 1942 he had been deported to Poelitz in Germany, where he worked as a forced laborer until the war's end. But in sharp contrast to his fellow Ukrainian, who would remain unwavering in his insistence that he never served as a guard, Fedorenko admitted at trial that after short stints at Rovno and Chelm, he had been recruited, trained, and deployed to Treblinka. The heart of Fedorenko's defense was that his service had been involuntary. He testified that he had worked exclusively as a perimeter guard; it wasn't until months after his arrival that he even learned of the gassings that occurred inside the camp. He said that he never had mistreated any of the prisoners; indeed, he claimed to have had virtually no dealings with Jews at Treblinka whatsoever. In effect, Fedorenko admitted to having lied on his visa application and immigration forms, but argued that because his service had been involuntary and because he had behaved respectfully, he had not lied about any "material fact," which, if known at the time of his application, would have resulted in his exclusion.

Fedorenko's claims of involuntary service and good behavior were challenged by six survivors of Treblinka, who testified that Fedorenko had committed atrocities and had been an engaged participant in the killing process. These witnesses had flown in from Israel to tell their stories—only to find that the judge in the case, Norman Roettger Jr., refused to believe them. Roettger, a Nixon appointee, provided a reverse image of Judge Hoffman's behavior in the Walus trial, directing all his ire at the prosecution. Rejecting the government's case for denaturalization, he treated Fedorenko with open admiration, praising him as "a hard-working and responsible American citizen," who "did not speak unkindly of anyone" and whose "one failure as a resident and citizen in

29 years" was the receipt of a parking ticket.[74] In highlighting Fedorenko's record as a citizen, Roettger appeared to fashion a novel principle of equity, in which the defendant's irreproachable conduct since arriving in America more than excused whatever atrocities he might have once committed.

Judge Roettger went further still. In questioning the very fairness of seeking to denaturalize Fedorenko, he openly accused the government of wasting taxpayers' money—"never in six years on the bench has the court seen the Government indulge in such expenses"—and railed against demonstrators from the militant Jewish Defense League, who turned the trial into a "Hollywood spectacular [*sic*]."[75] Four of the six survivor witnesses—Eugen Turowski, Josef Czarny, Pinchas Epstein, and Gustav Boraks—had also identified Demjanjuk in the photo spreads used by Miriam Radiwker; Roettger doubted the credibility of them all. Czarny was "clearly the least credible of the survivor witnesses" because he claimed to recognize Fedorenko's "mean-looking face," when, in fact, the judge found the defendant to be "kind-looking." Ultimately none of the Treblinka survivors could be trusted, as "the court was convinced the witnesses were discussing the trial among themselves." It seemed likely, Roettger speculated, that "someone was coaching them."[76]

In ruling for Fedorenko, Judge Roettger concluded that the defendant's service had been involuntary. The misinformation recorded in his visa and immigration forms thus did not rise to the level of a lie about a "material fact," which would justify his denaturalization. If Fedorenko had fibbed, it was only as "a victim of Nazi aggression, fearful of repatriation. . . . and longing for a chance in America."[77] Hardly reasons to strip an otherwise upstanding naturalized American of his citizenship.

The constitutional bar against double jeopardy does not control civil cases, and so the government appealed. In a memo, Martin Mendelsohn presciently noted that Judge Roettger's concerns about the credibility of the eyewitness identifications were entirely irrelevant to the case. Fedorenko had admitted to serving at Treblinka, a pure death camp. "There were no neutrals at a death camp," Mendelsohn observed. "The choice was killer or victim."[78] The Fifth Circuit agreed, reversing unanimously. The court rejected Roettger's novel principle of equity, bluntly noting,

"The denaturalization statute, 8 U.S.C. §1451, does not accord the district courts any authority to excuse the fraudulent procurement of citizenship."[79] Even hard work and a record of good citizenship do not excuse lying about having served as a death camp guard.

Fedorenko appealed in turn, leading to a landmark ruling by the Supreme Court.[80] The 7–2 decision, handed down on January 21, 1981, reaffirmed that because citizenship is "precious" and its loss can have "severe and unsettling consequences," the government must supply evidence that is "clear, unequivocal, and convincing," a heavier burden of proof than in typical civil cases. That said, the Court nonetheless concluded that the government had shouldered its burden in this instance. Writing for the majority, Justice Marshall agreed with the Fifth Circuit that Roettger's considerations of equity went way beyond the judge's discretion under the terms of the Immigration and Nationality Act. Marshall further concluded that Roettger's argument that Fedorenko's service had been involuntary was irrelevant under the guiding statute, noting that Section 2(b) of the Displaced Person Act of 1948 barred visas to persons who "assisted the enemy in persecuting civil[ians]." He contrasted this with Section 2(a), which barred persons who "*voluntarily* assisted the enemy forces . . . in their operations." It seemed clear, Marshall reasoned, that while Congress introduced a "voluntariness" standard for determining the eligibility of those who had "assisted the enemy forces," it meant for courts to use a different standard in evaluating persons who had assisted the enemy in persecution. This distinction made the case "fairly straightforward."[81] Whether Fedorenko had served voluntarily or involuntarily at Treblinka was irrelevant. Because Fedorenko had failed "to comply with the statutory prerequisites for naturalization," his citizenship had been "illegally procured" and was now revocable.

After the Walus fiasco, the government presumably found the Court's ruling in *Fedorenko v. United States* a welcome vindication of its approach to denaturalizing Nazis and Nazi collaborators. In fact, both cases exposed serious problems. *Walus* underscored the perils of structuring cases on the testimony of survivor witnesses. While the lived memory of survivors could provide a poignancy absent in documentary evidence, survivors of atrocity were, alas, no less vulnerable to mistakes of identification than any other eyewitness in a trial—and perhaps more so, given the passage of time and the powerful desire to see past tormentors brought to justice. Fedorenko's trial made clear a related problem: the vulnerability of survivor witnesses to the indignities of the adversarial process. The open skepticism with which Roettger received the testimony of the Treblinka survivors, who had left their homes in Israel and had traveled thousands of miles to testify at the government's behest, left the witnesses feeling insulted and belittled, which, in turn, created a problem for the government. At the time of the Fedorenko trial, the government's larger litigation strategy in collaborator cases still focused on eyewitness identifications by survivors; indeed, many of the same survivors who had testified against Fedorenko would be needed in the future Demjanjuk trial. The possibility that these survivors would refuse to return to America if it meant being subjected to fresh indignities at the hands not merely of defense counsel but of the presiding judge himself threatened the viability of the Demjanjuk case.

The two cases also illuminated a corollary problem. If the government was to prevail in its case against collaborators, it would have to enlist support from professional historians. Whatever else we might say about his decision, Roettger's pointed observation that "no documentary evidence whatsoever was introduced by the Government . . . as to the duties . . . of the defendant at Treblinka" surely signaled a dramatic failure on the part of prosecutors.[82] Federal judges are not Holocaust historians; nor for that matter are INS investigators or assistant US attorneys. In the Fedorenko case, the government's failure to supply evidence on the operation of Treblinka invited misunderstandings and mistakes on both the trial and the appellate level. Both Roettger and Supreme Court Justice Marshall, for example, referred to the "Treblinka concentration camp,"[83] a designation no one familiar with the history of the Holocaust would use, as it erases the crucial distinction between a pure killing center and one that maintained a substantial prisoner or slave labor population. Roettger also accepted Fedorenko's assertion that he technically remained a POW during his tenure as a guard at Treblinka, a claim that a historian could have shown to be simply false.

Roettger's treatment of the voluntariness question also betrayed deep confusion about how Treblinka operated. Whether a person behaved voluntarily is, of course, a legal question to be answered by the judge (or, in a criminal case, by the jury), but a historian can clarify the constraints under which a person acted and the structure of rewards and punishments that shaped the performance of tasks. Perhaps the most disturbing aspect of Roettger's decision was his argument that, absent a voluntariness standard, the Displaced Persons Act would bar not only the Fedorenkos of the world from entry into America, but also "every Jewish prisoner who survived Treblinka."[84] According to Roettger, the government's reading of the DP Act meant that Jewish prisoners who performed tasks such as cutting the hair of women about to be gassed would also be guilty of assisting the enemy in persecuting civilians, and so would be ineligible for visas. The only way to safeguard against such a result was to emphasize the involuntariness of the Jews' service, an argument that effectively erased any moral distinction between guards such as Fedorenko and the Jews they guarded.

More unsettling still was the fact that Justice Stevens, in his *Fedorenko* dissent, accepted Roettger's position in its entirety. Convinced that the majority opinion committed the "profoundest sort of error," Stevens worried that actions such as "cutting the hair of female prisoners prior to their execution" would, under the Court's new construction, exclude "Jewish prisoners who assisted the SS in the operation" of Treblinka.[85] To use the term *execution*—which typically denotes a judicially authorized killing—to describe an act of extermination is bad enough; to compare the position of an armed guard with that of a prisoner slated for destruction seems almost perverse.[86] Marshall's majority opinion managed to avoid this pitfall, insisting that "an individual who did no more than cut the hair of female inmates . . . cannot be found to have assisted in the persecution of civilians. On the other hand, there can be no question that a guard who was issued a uniform and armed with a rifle and pistol . . . fits within the statutory language."[87]

Yet if Roettger's and Stevens' missteps were avoidable, they were hardly idiosyncratic. In the absence of guidance and correction from experts familiar with the functioning of a death camp, such mangling of truth was all but inevitable. As we've seen, even Marshall, who succeeded in drawing the relevant moral distinction between guards and their prisoners, failed to apprehend the difference between a death camp and a concentration camp. Ironically, this mangling of categories would prove exceptionally useful to prosecutors in the decades to come. Having swept Treblinka under the general rubric of "concentration camp," the Court in *Fedorenko* made the government's work in future cases much easier. Henceforth, it would have merely to prove service at *any* concentration camp—and not specifically a death camp—to prevail in denaturalization cases under the terms of the Immigration and Nationality Act.

It was the disastrous unraveling of the *Walus* case and the disappointing failure at the trial stage in *Fedorenko* that prodded the move of the Special Litigation Unit into the Justice Department and its reorganization into the Office of Special Investigations. The neat cause and effect was, of course, murkier in reality, with chronologies compressed and overlapping. In fact, the SLU had played a marginal role preparing the *Walus* and *Fedorenko* cases, but as Mendelsohn predicted, the unit "regardless of the degree of its involvement . . . will be blamed for any shortcomings." By the time the Seventh Circuit reversed in *Walus*, the OSI was already in place and took responsibility for reviewing the government's case. It likewise oversaw the appellate phase of *Fedorenko*, and Benjamin Civiletti, President Jimmy Carter's second attorney general, argued the case before the Supreme Court, his only oral argument as head of the Justice Department.

The SLU made the move over to Justice more or less in its entirety, but its perceived missteps predictably soon led to a shakeup in personnel. The directorship was first offered to Telford Taylor, who led the prosecution of the twelve American successor trials at Nuremberg; after Taylor declined, the job went to Walter Rockler, a senior partner at Arnold and Porter who had worked under Taylor at Nuremberg. Rockler forced out Mendelsohn: the two clashed; Rockler did not trust Mendelsohn and also came to resent his close, seemingly conspiratorial ties with Holtzman, who had lobbied for Mendelsohn's appointment as director.[88] By prior arrangement, Rockler stayed less than a year, and was replaced by Allan Ryan, an attorney in the solicitor general's office.[89]

The Justice Department welcomed the OSI no more warmly than the Immigration Service had welcomed the SLU. Still, the OSI now had an improved organizational plan, a clear institutional face, and a developing esprit de corps. With a dozen criminal investigators, a matching number of lawyers, and two professional historians on staff, the OSI could draw upon more substantial institutional resources, more sophisticated investigatory tools, and savvier litigation strategies than its predecessor in the INS. More importantly, the attorney general gave the OSI the power to "investigate and take legal action" in cases involving Nazi-era persecution. The OSI would continue to work with local US attorneys in filing complaints, but henceforth there would be no question about who had the power. The OSI would do all the heavy lifting.

All the same, the project of mounting a successful war crimes unit remained very much a work in progress. Certainly the addition of two historians to the Office was a critical step in the right direction. Adding academic historians to the government payroll represented a sharp departure for the Justice Department, which had done so only once before and long ago, while conducting land title research in cases involving claims to Native American reservation territory. Now historians would play an ever-more critical role in preparing the government's collaboration cases. Traditional investigators lacked the crucial linguistic and archival skills that constituted the core of the historian's training. In the words of Peter Black, who came to the OSI as its first full-time historian while still a graduate student at Columbia, historians would be called upon to "educate the attorneys so they could educate the judges."[90] This could make for tensions, as the historians often had a keener understanding of the issues than the lawyers running the cases. But such problems diminished as the OSI cultivated both a team of attorneys with detailed knowledge of the underlying history and a group of historians who came to appreciate the nuances of the legal process, such as the rules of discovery. As we shall see, the insertion of historians into the legal process would fundamentally alter the very nature of such proceedings, turning them into cases in which the resolution of basic historical questions became inseparable from the juridical determination of guilt.

Unfortunately, many of these changes came too late to save the government in the first Demjanjuk case. In the coming years, historians would eventually supplant conventional investigators altogether in the Office. But at the time that the government moved to denaturalize Demjanjuk, it had yet to dedicate a historian specifically to the case. This is not to suggest that a PhD alone could have prevented the calamity. Despite greater cooperation between the United States and the Soviet Union, information remained imperfect and evidence difficult to come by. But it is fair to say that *United States v. Demjanjuk* remained in the hands of a young and motivated but unsettled office yet to develop the practices necessary to master its complex caseload.

* * *

In the years since Miriam Radiwker watched stunned as one Treblinka survivor after another blanched at Demjanjuk's photo, the government's case had taken clear shape. Chastened by the collapse of the *Walus* litigation, the OSI was understandably wary about structuring a new denaturalization trial around survivor testimony. But in stark contrast to the *Walus* witnesses, the Treblinka survivors had seen and experienced Ivan Grozny on many occasions over a protracted period of time, a fact that lawyers reasonably believed lent greater reliability to the identifications. In addition, the OSI had secured the deposition of a former SS *Unterscharführer* (sergeant) named Otto Horn. Horn had served at Treblinka, but apparently with little enthusiasm and no displays of cruelty, and a Düsseldorf court had acquitted him of all charges at a major trial of Treblinka personnel in 1965.[91] Deposed by the OSI at his apartment in West Berlin, Horn identified Demjanjuk from two separate stacks of photos with a laconic declaration, "that is him."[92]

Investigators also had obtained valuable information from Demjanjuk himself. Walus had supplied a coherent and strongly corroborated alibi; Demjanjuk, by contrast, flirted with self-incrimination. In his statements and depositions, Demjanjuk claimed that he survived the war as a POW in Rovno and Chelm—although at his first deposition, he failed to mention Chelm, a bit of improbable forgetfulness that would come back to haunt him in Jerusalem.[93] By his own account, he was dispatched by the Germans toward the end of the war to Graz in Austria to serve with a unit of Ukrainians formed to fight the advancing Red Army. From there he was sent to Heuberg, a town in southern Germany, to join Vlasov's Russian Liberation Army, a fighting force of Russians organized with much the same mission. Demjanjuk insisted that he never actually saw any action in either unit, which probably is true. But he also acknowledged that while in Graz he received a blood-type tattoo, which he removed when assigned to the Vlasov force. The tattoo, and the scar near his left armpit created by its removal, would continue to prove troublesome to Demjanjuk. Two groups within the Nazi hierarchy had routinely received blood-type tattoos near their left armpit: members of the Waffen SS and members of the auxiliary forces that had assisted them. Demjanjuk claimed that "in Graz, everyone had a tattoo." But when he was transferred to Vlasov's force, he discovered that "in [the] Russian national army, tattoos weren't given and I took it off."[94] His desire to accommodate the cosmetics of the Vlasov force must have been very great indeed, as the casual phrase "*I took it off*" fails to do justice to the elaborate process of removal, which evidently consisted of rubbing the tattoo with a sharp rock until the skin bled, waiting for a scab to form, then repeating as needed.[95] Quite an involved process just to look like the rest of the Russian boys.

Finally, there was the pièce de résistance—a copy of an ID card issued at Trawniki, an SS facility designed to prepare specially recruited Soviet POWs for service as SS auxiliaries. In chapter 4, we'll have occasion to look at the structure and operation of the Trawniki camp in detail; for now, it suffices to note that approximately five thousand *Volksdeutsche* (ethnic Germans), Latvians, Lithuanians, Estonians, and, most of all, Ukrainians passed through the camp. Known alternatively as *Hiwis* (short for *Hilfswillige*, or "volunteer helper"), Blacks (for the color of the uniform that most received), or *Askaris* (after the local soldiers who fought on the side of the colonial forces of the German Empire in Africa in the late nineteenth century), the Trawniki men provided crucial assistance in the extermination of Poland's Jews, including serving as death camp guards.[96] Trawniki ID No. 1393 came to the attention of American investigators through an article in an issue of the Soviet-subsidized, English-language magazine *News from Ukraine* published in September 1977. Beneath a news story describing Demjanjuk's alleged "treachery" against his "Motherland" appeared a photo of a service ID that had been issued to DEMJANJUK, Ivan (see figure 2.3).[97] The ID included a photo of what was unmistakably a youthful Demjanjuk, a fact that over the years Demjanjuk neither denied nor acknowledged, but merely allowed, "Looks like me, but I am not 100 percent certain."[98] The photo ID accurately reported his birthplace, birthday, and father's name; under "special features," it noted, "scar on back," in the very place where he received the shrapnel wound in the early months of the war.

As a document discovered and reproduced by the Soviets, the card was treated by American investigators with due caution, especially in

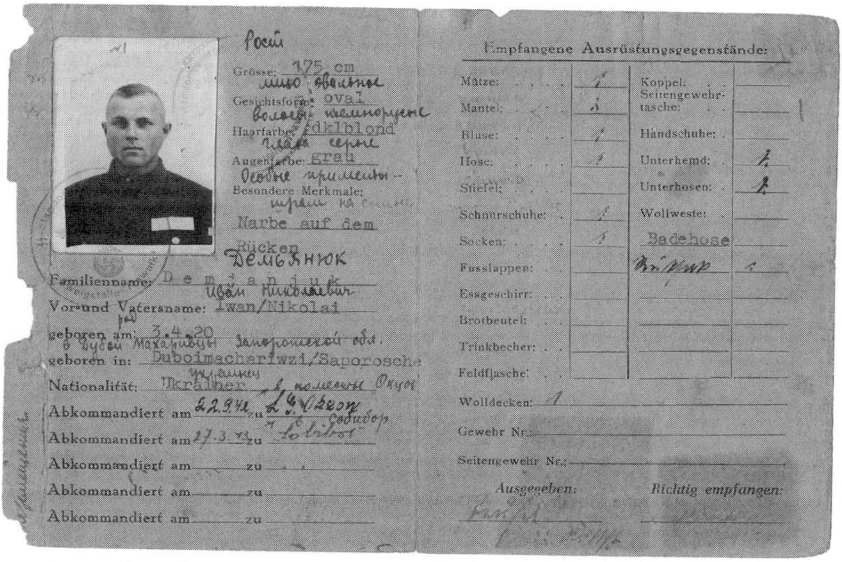

2.3. Trawniki service ID No. 1393, internal face. Courtesy Office of Special Investigations, DoJ.

light of its inaccuracies. Demjanjuk's defense was quick to note that the Trawniki ID listed Demjanjuk's eye color as gray and his hair as brown, whereas in reality his eyes were blue and his hair, at least when he still had it, blonde. Unfortunately for the defense, the government was able to show that Demjanjuk's immigration forms likewise listed his eyes as gray and his hair as brown.[99] Perhaps of greater significance was the fact that the ID listed the strapping 6′1″ Ukrainian as standing little over 5′8″. But even here, the mistake sounded less troubling in the metric original, as the listed height of 175 cm might have represented a simple typing mistake by a Trawniki clerk who meant to record 185 cm, Demjanjuk's actual height.[100]

At Demjanjuk's denaturalization trial, the defense was unable to proffer a shred of evidence impeaching the ID, except to stridently insist that nothing that came from Soviet sources could be trusted. The government meanwhile carefully established the card's authenticity. Although Wolfgang Scheffler, a prominent German historian called by the government as an expert witness, acknowledged that he had never before seen such a card, the OSI succeeded in locating a former paymaster at Trawniki who stated in a deposition that such cards had been standard issue. And although the Soviets had at first balked about sharing anything besides a reproduction, they later agreed to transport the original card to Chicago for examination. This provided the government's documents experts a chance to engage in close forensic analysis. Their conclusion: the German signatures on the card, which included that of the Trawniki commandant Karl Streibel, were authentic, as was the document as a whole.

Only one problem remained. Trawniki ID No. 1393 indicated that Ivan Demjanjuk had served at Sobibor, not Treblinka. This agreed with the information supplied in Hanusiak's original list of Ukrainian collaborators and with Demjanjuk's own account of his whereabouts (for, as we've seen, he inexplicably listed Sobibor as his Polish domicile in his DP documents). But the fact that Treblinka was nowhere mentioned on the Trawniki ID was hardly seen as fatal to the case against Ivan Grozny. Government lawyers advanced the theory that Ivan had served at both Sobibor and Treblinka, assigned first to one camp and then the other, and that his service ID simply failed to include the second entry. While such sloppiness would seem to contradict the Nazis' reputation for maintaining the most meticulous records, that reputation was often more myth than reality. For example, Demjanjuk's service ID lacked a date of issuance, suggesting that record keeping at Trawniki had been something less than fastidious. (Indeed, it now appears that the SS delegated most of the camp's day-to-day administrative work to *Volksdeutsche* (ethnic Germans), who, as one OSI historian drily noted, "were barely literate in any language, much less German bureaucratese";[101] even Commandant Streibel came to grumble about the camp's slovenly bookkeeping.) It was also possible, the government speculated, that Ivan might have on occasion shuttled between Sobibor and Treblinka; the two camps were separated by about 130 miles, and Demjanjuk was an experienced driver. If anything, the documentary evidence of service at Sobibor seemed to strengthen the testimonial evidence against Ivan the Terrible of Treblinka. The government case against Demjanjuk was thus built on a powerful trifecta of allegations—that he had trained at the SS facility at Trawniki, had served as a death camp guard at Sobibor, and had run the gas chamber at Treblinka.

Demjanjuk's efforts to refute these charges at his first denaturalization trial enjoyed little success. Like Fedorenko, he had no choice but to admit to having lied on his DP and visa forms. Having argued that he was taken as a POW in the spring of 1942, a fact accepted by all parties, he could not continue to insist that he had whiled away the six years between 1937 and 1943 as an independent farmer in the miniscule hamlet of Sobibor, of all places. But unlike Fedorenko, who claimed to have lied in order to conceal his involuntary service as a Treblinka guard, Demjanjuk remained adamant in his insistence that he had never trained at Trawniki or served as a guard anywhere at anytime. That he would deny having served at Treblinka was hardly surprising, as in fact that denial was truthful. But that he would deny everything was also unsurprising. The Supreme Court's ruling in *Fedorenko*, rejecting the involuntariness defense, had come down on January 21, 1981—scant days before the start of Demjanjuk's trial on February 10, 1981, before Judge Frank Battisti in a Cleveland federal district court. The *Fedorenko* decision effectively discouraged any acknowledgment of participation in Nazi crimes by any naturalized citizen intent on staying in the United States. Demjanjuk was doing—and saying—what he had to.

And so he insisted that he had lied on his immigration forms because he had feared repatriation to the Soviet Union. According to his testimony, in the years after the war, the Soviets would comb through DP camps, seizing refugees from the Soviet Union and forcibly repatriating them to their homeland, where a dire fate awaited. Repeating a familiar myth, he claimed that any Red Army soldier who had surrendered to the Germans would be summarily executed. Any Soviet citizen who had been impressed into an anti-Soviet fighting force likewise faced a firing squad. As a former German POW and as a member of not one but two anti-Soviet fighting forces, Demjanjuk had had to lie on his DP and visa forms. Had he reported truthfully, he would have signed his own death warrant.

The story of forced repatriation richly mixed fact and fantasy. It is true that the Yalta conference of February 1945 had included a repatriation agreement, and that in the early months after the end of the war in Europe, as Germany became engorged with seven million displaced persons, American forces briefly assisted the Soviets in searching through camps in the search of AWOL Soviet citizens. The practice, however, was short-lived, and by December 1945, American forces had already prohibited the forced repatriation of any person who had not actively collaborated with the enemy.[102] A year later, the United Nations Relief and Rehabilitation Administration issued Administrative Order No. 199, which permitted representatives from countries such as Yugoslavia and Poland to enter DP camps and try to pressure refugees to return home. But the State Department intervened within weeks to put an end to this practice.[103] By the time Demjanjuk filled out his assistance forms in 1948, whatever danger might have existed had long passed. And even if he continued to believe in the need to lie about his impression into the Vlasov army at the war's end, it wasn't clear why he had also lied about his whereabouts between early 1942 and late 1944.

Given the strength of the government's case, it came as no surprise that the five-week trial resulted in Demjanjuk's denaturalization. In stripping Demjanjuk of his citizenship, Judge Battisti cited "clear, unequivocal and convincing" evidence that Demjanjuk had trained at Trawniki and had served at Treblinka.[104] Battisti's ruling handed the government a resounding court victory and also displayed the dividends of the OSI's emerging litigation strategy. Although the OSI was yet to assign a dedicated in-house historian to the case, it had already begun relying heavily on the work of scholars of the Third Reich. Earl Ziemke, a professor at the University of Georgia, had opened the prosecution's case with testimony about the SS practice of recruiting select Soviet POWs for auxiliary service. And in turning to Wolfgang Scheffler, who supplied expert testimony about Aktion Reinhard, the planned extermination of Jews in German-occupied Polish territory, the government brought before the court Germany's leading Holocaust historian and expert on Nazi crimes.[105] Perhaps most notably, Scheffler is credited with having helped demonstrate that SS men who opted out of acts of extermination faced no draconian punishment, a study that punctured the myth that participation in genocide was compulsory.[106]

Compared, then, to Roettger's *Fedorenko* opinion, Battisti's holding in *United States v. Demjanjuk* is a far more informed, nuanced, and sophisticated document. Where Roettger failed to adequately grasp the role that guards like Fedorenko played in the operation of Treblinka, Battisti's opinion skillfully shows how Demjanjuk's personal wartime experience came to intersect with the larger trajectory of Holocaust history. In describing the Battle of Kerch where Demjanjuk was taken as a POW, Battisti refers to German war diaries that offered a daily chronicle of prisoners captured. In explaining the creation of the Trawniki camp, Battisti notes that the "SS lacked sufficient manpower in the Lublin district to carry out all the 'tasks' of Action Reinhard." He describes the "three extermination camps"—Belzec, Sobibor, and Treblinka—"constructed to implement the mass annihilation conceived by Action Reinhard."[107] This attention to history supplied a helpful anchor to the legal decision; more importantly, it clarified the function of Trawniki-trained guards, and so corrected the dangerous conflation of guard and prisoner that marred Roettger's *Fedorenko* holding.

Not that Battisti's opinion silenced the critics of the government. By now, the Demjanjuk affair had become something of a cause célèbre. The Ukrainian community rallied around one of its own, both morally and financially, ultimately raising more than two million dollars to cover Demjanjuk's legal costs. Much of this money came from Jerome Brentar, a wealthy Cleveland-based travel agent, who also had helped finance the defense of Frank Walus. Brentar had worked with the International Relief Organization (IRO), which was profoundly anti-Soviet in its bias, and over the years he had established ever-closer ties to Holocaust deniers. Later, he would serve as a character witness for and donate large sums to the defense of Ernst Zundel, a Holocaust denier twice tried and convicted in Toronto for publishing inflammatory lies.

While only a small number in the Ukrainian expatriate community openly flirted with Holocaust denial, the vast majority was deeply anticommunist and suspicious of Moscow, inclined to see their kinsman as the victim of a KGB framing. On the first day of Demjanjuk's denaturalization trial, 150 Ukrainian-Americans demonstrated in front of the Cleveland federal courthouse, protesting "a Soviet trial in American courts" and burning a Soviet flag for good measure.[108] Demjanjuk also received passionate support from his family, in particular from his son, John Jr., and from his son-in-law, Edward Nishnic, who likewise spoke of a KGB conspiracy. At trial, Demjanjuk floated a similar argument in an effort to challenge the authenticity of the Trawniki service ID, and the argument, as we will see, was not about to go away: the theory would feature prominently in his defense in Jerusalem and, long after the end of the Cold War and the passing of the Soviet Union, would find itself resurrected in the overheated rhetoric of Ulrich Busch, his lawyer in Munich.

The KGB conspiracy theory would also stray into the American political mainstream thanks principally to the noxious agitations of Pat Buchanan, the former Nixon speechwriter and future White House press secretary and presidential candidate.[109] Not long after the conclusion of Demjanjuk's denaturalization trial, Buchanan began to publish commentary accusing the OSI of engaging in a "fraternal collaboration" with the KGB. Buchanan was later joined by the likes of Ohio Congressman James Traficant, who rallied to Demjanjuk's side and trumpeted the conspiracy theory presumably to curry favor with his heavily conservative Eastern European constituency. (Decades later while in prison on federal corruption charges, Traficant displayed a wider affinity for conspiracy theories, claiming to be in the possession of privileged information about both the Waco attack and the Kennedy assassination.) Buchanan's commentaries came ever closer to espousing anti-Semitism and Holocaust denial, reaching a nadir of sorts in an article casting Demjanjuk as a victim of the "same satanic brew of hate and revenge that drove another innocent Man up Calvary that first Good Friday 2,000 years ago."[110] Yet Buchanan succeeded in exposing—and exploiting—a problem with our legal system's handling of the Nazi collaborators problem. We have already seen that because federal courts were never authorized to try former Nazis on criminal charges, denaturalization and deportation (D&D) represented a way around an otherwise intractable jurisdictional problem. But this solution to a legal conundrum came at a cost. The D&D approach inevitably trivialized crimes of atrocity by legally digesting them as mere acts of lying. The D&D approach magnified the significance of lying and drew attention away from the underlying criminal act, complicity in acts of genocide. This, alas, invited the willful distortions of Buchanan, who complained that "individuals are being taken into court, where horrific allegations are spread across the record, and then stripped of their citizenship—not because the allegations are proven, but simply because they 'lied' on their visa applications."[111]

The Supreme Court's *Fedorenko* decision also inadvertently compounded the problem. On one level, the decision provided a crucial precedent that enabled the government to successfully litigate future denaturalization cases. On another, it created powerful incentives for defendants to lie through their teeth in denaturalization proceedings. Admittedly, defendants in criminal proceedings often lie; but here the issue is not whether to lie or not, but how completely and what about. Had American jurists been able to bring criminal charges against Nazi collaborators, the structure of incentives would have been very different. In a prosecution of a person charged with crimes against humanity or genocide, the question of voluntariness would have played a central role. The involuntariness of participation could have supplied a full defense to the charges, and even if pled without success, it could certainly have been considered as a mitigating factor in sentencing. But because *Fedorenko* concluded that service alone, and not the voluntariness of service, was the question that controlled denaturalization proceedings, defendants henceforth had powerful incentives to concede nothing and to deny everything. Which is precisely what Demjanjuk did.

Finally, there was the sheer intricacy of the process, which, of course, was designed to protect the accused, but could in its excessive length look a good deal like a witch hunt. Federal law bars the deportation of American citizens, and so denaturalization was a necessary first step toward the government's ultimate goal of expelling Demjanjuk from the country. But it was only the first step. It is fair to say that under American law, sending someone to prison for the rest of his life without parole is easier than stripping a person of his citizenship and sending him abroad.

These difficulties notwithstanding, the Demjanjuk case supplied the fledgling OSI with a powerful and very public justification for the substantial commitment of public resources that had gone into its creation. If some saw Demjanjuk as the victim of a diabolical KGB conspiracy, many others, in particular American Jews, responded with outrage to the revelation that Ivan the Terrible had led a comfortable life, not in the lap of some South American dictator, but in the American heartland. To these groups, the Demjanjuk case underscored the vital importance of an organization dedicated to ridding America of such monsters. In prevailing at trial, the OSI demonstrated that it had learned from the missteps of its precursor, and that its able team could successfully litigate complex multilingual cases that required an unusual combination of legal savvy and archival expertise.

After the revocation of his citizenship, Demjanjuk lodged an appeal, arguing variously that Battisti had acted prejudicially, that the prosecution had committed fraud on the court, and that the OSI "collaborated with the Soviet government to conceal . . . the perjury of witnesses."[112] None of these arguments impressed the Sixth Circuit, and the Supreme Court summarily rejected his petition for review. Only after Demjanjuk had exhausted his appeals was the government statutorily permitted to begin the deportation process. Deportation cases are heard before a special immigration judge, and are controlled by their own procedural and evidentiary norms. In contrast to denaturalization cases, hearsay is permitted, and the government must make its case with "clear and convincing" evidence—a somewhat less exacting standard than the "clear, unequivocal and convincing" evidence required at denaturalization trials.[113] The ruling of the immigration judge can be appealed to the Board of Immigration Appeals (BIA), an administrative appellate body in the Justice Department. The decisions of the Board can, in turn, be appealed up the federal chain all the way to the Supreme Court. All told, the government must theoretically clear seven separate procedural hurdles in order to prevail in a D&D case: it must win at the denaturalization trial in federal district court and succeed in the appellate phase before the circuit court and Supreme Court; it must then succeed in the proceeding in immigration court, and prevail through the appeals to the BIA and then *back* through the circuit court and the Supreme Court. Not an easy course.[114]

Once this elaborate, expensive, and protracted legal process has run its course, federal law details yet another complicated calculus for determining the target country of deportation. The deportee may choose a country, on the condition that both our government and the designated country give their assent. In the absence of such an agreement, immigration officials work down a list of possible target countries. A preferred target might be one where the deportee was formerly a citizen, or from which he entered the United States, or in which he was born, and so on. All else failing, the deportee can be sent to *any* country willing to accept him. Assuming there is one.

The INS initiated deportation proceedings against Demjanjuk on December 6, 1982. The hearing itself began a little more than a year later, in early 1984, before immigration judge Adolph Angelilli, and moved along uneventfully, notable mostly for the less-than-stellar lawyering of OSI attorney Bruce Einhorn. Confronted with Demjanjuk's insistence that he had lied on the immigration forms to avoid forced repatriation to the Soviet Union and certain execution, Einhorn lamely challenged the defendant to "name . . . the law in the Soviet Union" that made being taken as a POW and serving in a foreign army punishable by death, to which Demjanjuk tartly answered, "How can you expect me to know a paragraph of the law? There is a general law that you cannot serve in another army." The government also found no occasion to press Demjanjuk on Sobibor. During the proceeding, Demjanjuk claimed to have randomly plucked the name of Sobibor off a map in the minutes before he was to fill out his DP forms: "I looked at the map and did find a location called Sobibor, but today when I'm checking the maps, I can't find a location called by this particular spelling. I do find a place called Sambor, but I don't know whether these two locations are the same place."[115] One might have hoped that Einhorn would push Demjanjuk on the remarkable coincidence of having randomly listed as his domicile a town that happened to be the site of the very death camp that his service ID showed he was first assigned to. The story begged for amplification, but because it had no direct bearing on Demjanjuk's attempt to be granted refugee status, Einhorn simply let the matter pass.

Weakest of all was Einhorn's effort to discredit Demjanjuk's claim that deportation, even to a country other than the Soviet Union, meant certain death because Demjanjuk would remain the quarry of the KGB. Dismissive of Demjanjuk's insistence that the Soviet Union targeted its enemies in foreign lands, Einhorn asked the defendant if he could name a single Ukrainian who had been assassinated abroad, to which Demjanjuk blithely responded, "Stepan Bandera was killed by Soviet agents." Einhorn had clearly never heard of the famous Ukrainian nationalist—he referred to him with misguided sarcasm as "this alleged Stepan Bandera"—who was in fact assassinated by the KGB in Germany in 1959.[116] (As we shall see in chapter 6, in a strange twist of legal history, the trial of Bandera's assassin, Bohdan Staschinsky, delivered a crucial precedent that powerfully affected how the German legal system prosecuted Holocaust perpetrators and accessories.)

Einhorn's ignorance did not prove fatal to the government, though it did expose a problem that might at first glance seem completely unrelated to the lawyer's missteps—namely, staff turnover in the OSI. Einhorn had joined the OSI toward the end of 1979 but had not participated in the case's discovery phase and had played at most a peripheral role in the denaturalization trial. Of the two OSI lawyers who worked closely on the denaturalization case, George Parker and Norman Moscowitz, Parker left the Office before the trial began and Moscowitz left shortly after Battisti's decision.[117] The Office also ran through its early directors: Rockler and Allan Ryan both left after short stints at the helm. Ryan was less than a hands-on leader; his deputy Neal Sher essentially ran the day-to-day operations of the Office. (Sher became director in 1983 and remained in the post for a decade; he was replaced in 1995 by Eli Rosenbaum, who has remained at the Justice Department to this day.)

Early turnover and a lack of strong executive stewardship created gaps in institutional memory, a problem that loomed large in a young institution burdened with cases that demanded a sophisticated command of history and context. Einhorn's shortcomings can, then, be seen less as the result of poor preparation and more as the consequence of upheavals in a fledgling unit struggling toward organizational stability. These problems diminished over time as the Office proved more successful in retaining its personnel, particularly its staff of historians, who became custodians of its institutional memory. Under Rosenbaum's directorship, the Office also ambitiously created the so-called OSI Bank, a veritable memory palace of exhaustively indexed documents, pleadings, reports, judgments, and memos. Henceforth institutional memory would no longer be lodged in the recall of any one person.

On May 23, Judge Angelilli found Demjanjuk deportable on all counts. He designated the Soviet Union as the country of deportation—but offered Demjanjuk the opportunity to leave voluntarily within thirty days to a country of his choice. Instead, Demjanjuk appealed the ruling, and on February 14, 1985, the Board of Immigration Appeals dismissed his appeal and reversed the grant of voluntary departure, paving the way to Demjanjuk's forced removal, more than seven years after US attorneys in Cleveland first filed their charges.

* * *

The deportation would never occur. Sixteen months earlier, on October 18, 1983, Israel had issued an arrest warrant for Demjanjuk and, two weeks later, had officially petitioned the United States for his extradition. Extradition is an entirely separate process from deportation. Drawing its authority from a treaty between the United States and a partner country, extradition permits a foreign government to petition the United States to arrest a suspect for an overseas crime and to send him to the requesting nation to stand trial. Extradition is an unusual process—many countries refuse to extradite their own citizens[118]—but in the United States, the hearing, conducted in a federal district court, is controlled by a substantially less onerous burden of proof than the "clear, unequivocal and convincing" standard in denaturalization trials. At an extradition proceeding, the United States appears as the representative of the foreign government. Here the government must show that the alleged crimes are "extraditable offenses" under the terms of the bilateral treaty between the United States and the petitioning nation, and must demonstrate to the court that there exists "probable cause" to believe the accused committed the alleged crime; under this standard the court need "not determine whether the evidence is sufficient to justify a conviction," but only whether there is sufficient evidence to "justify holding the accused to await trial."[119] Because deportation and extradition constitute separate and independent proceedings, the government is allowed, in cases such as Demjanjuk's, to proceed with both simultaneously.

As it happened, the normal process of assigning cases landed Demjanjuk's extradition matter back in Judge Battisti's court.[120] Demjanjuk's lawyers asked the judge to recuse himself; Battisti refused. (Recusal would typically only be required if the judge showed bias against the defendant.) Given his ruling in the denaturalization trial, it was hardly surprising that Battisti found ample evidence of probable cause—although in retrospect, one winces at his incredulous dismissal of the defense's argument that "there is 'absolutely no connection' between John Demjanjuk and Ivan Grozny."[121]

The only remaining matter of legal interest, then, was whether Demjanjuk's alleged crimes constituted an extraditable offense. This seemed utterly straightforward. Israel had charged Demjanjuk with the murder of "tens of thousands of Jews and non-Jews," and the Israeli-American extradition treaty clearly extended to acts of murder.[122] Still, the Israeli charging statute was not without its anomalous features. The Nazis and Nazi Collaborators (Punishment) Law had been passed by the Knesset in 1950, barely two years after the creation of the Jewish state. Reflecting the atrocity model pioneered at Nuremberg, the law incorporated "war crimes" into the Israeli domestic code along with the two novel incriminations born of the law's contact with the Holocaust. In proscribing "crimes against humanity," the Israeli law tracked the definition used at Nuremberg as later adumbrated by Allied occupation law and United Nations resolution. And in proscribing "crimes against the Jewish people," the law used the Genocide Convention's definition of genocide—with one critical substitution. In the convention of 1948, the contracting nations defined genocide as

> any of the following acts committed with intent to destroy, in whole or in part, a national, ethnical, racial or religious group, as such:
> (a) Killing members of the group;
> (b) Causing serious bodily or mental harm to members of the group;
> (c) Deliberately inflicting on the group conditions of life calculated to bring about its physical destruction in whole or in part;
> (d) Imposing measures intended to prevent births within the group;
> (e) Forcibly transferring children of the group to another group.[123]

By contrast, the Israeli law of 1950 defined "crimes against the Jewish people" as

> any of the following acts, committed with intent to destroy the Jewish people in whole or in part:

(1) killing Jews;
(2) causing serious bodily or mental harm to Jews;
(3) placing Jews in living conditions calculated to bring about their physical destruction;
(4) imposing measures intended to prevent births among Jews;
(5) forcibly transferring Jewish children to another national or religious group;
(6) destroying or desecrating Jewish religious or cultural assets or values;
(7) inciting to hatred of Jews;[124]

The Israeli law adapted the Genocide Convention, adding "incitement" and acts of "cultural genocide" to the list of offenses, while substituting "Jewish" for "groups" in general. The law was used to charge, prosecute, convict, and execute Eichmann; and it came in for a great deal of criticism during the trial in 1961. Hannah Arendt famously attacked it for failing to comprehend genocide as a crime "against human diversity as such."[125] An earlier and more stinging rebuke came courtesy of Telford Taylor, the former Nuremberg prosecutor, who argued that "to proscribe the murder of Jews as a 'crime against Jews' carries the implication that it is not a crime against non-Jews"—an astonishing charge that traded in ancient stereotypes of Jews as closed and clannish in their self-regard.[126] Thanks to his vociferous attacks on the legitimacy of the 1950 law, Taylor was asked by Demjanjuk's defense to testify at the extradition hearing, but declined for reasons that remain unclear.

In any case, both Arendt and Taylor had it wrong, for in truth the law could have been better faulted for its overreach than for its refusal to speak for all people. Indeed, the original draft of the law contained no mention of crimes specifically targeting the Jewish people, and simply specified "crimes against humanity" and "war crimes." Some Israeli lawmakers, however, objected. "After two thousand years without a state," wrote Knesset member Yaakov Gil, the young nation must recognize "[a crime] against Israel and humanity.[127] Yet the intent behind including the modified version of genocide was as much jurisdictional as symbolic. Once codified, "crimes against the Jewish people" would extend the juridical reach of the Jewish state to include Jewish people wherever they might reside and crimes of an earlier moment. It was a creative gesture, designed to address the reality that the state of Israel did not exist at the time of the Nazis' exterminatory acts. The law did not win the universal approval of Jews in far-flung locales, some of whom frankly resented Israel's attempt to sweep them within its jurisdictional protections.[128] But in attacking the law, Taylor clearly misunderstood its intent, which was to extend and not parochially restrict the reach of Israeli law.

As a second matter, Israeli lawmakers recognized that former Nazis would be far less likely to seek refuge in Tel Aviv, rather than, say, in Buenos Aires, Asunción, or Damascus. If the law were to have any practical use, it was meant to make possible the prosecution of European Jews who had collaborated with the Nazis and later settled in Israel. Indeed, until Demjanjuk and with the exception of Eichmann, the only persons prosecuted under the 1950 law were two dozen or so kapos—concentration camp prisoners assigned supervisory and disciplinary tasks by the SS—accused of particular abuses. These cases were of such sensitive nature that Israeli prosecutors only used the war crimes provision of the 1950 law, reasoning that a Jewish kapo could not engage in "crimes against the Jewish people," an offense that required a showing of a specific intent to "destroy the Jewish people in whole or part"—something that no Jew could have done.[129] Most of the trials ended in acquittals or relatively short sentences; in the case of Hezekiel Jungster, who in 1951 became the first and only Jew sentenced to death under the law, the Israeli Supreme Court stepped in to reduce the punishment to two years.[130] In 1964, the Israeli Supreme Court set aside the collaboration conviction of Hirsh Barenblat, the assistant conductor of the Israeli Opera House, holding that "it would be hypocritical and arrogant on our part—on the part of those who never stood in their place"—to condemn those who "did not rise to the heights of moral supremacy when mercilessly oppressed." This ruling effectively closed the book on trials of Jewish kapos in Israel.[131]

As Eichmann had been plucked off a dusty street outside of Buenos Aires by Mossad agents and bundled off to Israel in an audacious kidnapping, Demjanjuk would be the first person ever extradited under the 1950 law. In a last-ditch effort, his lawyers floated the novel argument that crimes against humanity and crimes against the Jewish people were not extraditable offenses, because they were not covered in the extradition treaty, which only mentioned murder, manslaughter, and grievous bodily harm. All parties agreed that Demjanjuk could not be charged with simple murder or manslaughter under Israeli law, as Israel's domestic murder statute lacked the extraterritorial reach of the Nazis and Nazi Collaborators law. But to extradite him for violations of the 1950 law, his defense argued, would be to change the terms of the extradition treaty by expanding the nature and number of extraditable offenses to now include crimes against humanity and crimes against the Jewish people. In later chapters, we will see how postwar German case law regrettably and even disastrously insisted that acts of extermination could be legally digested as simple murder; here, ironically, we find Demjanjuk's lawyers pleading for precisely the conceptual clarity lost on German jurists. "We would diminish the Holocaust," the defense argued, "were we to view the acts of the Nazis and their collaborators as 'ordinary' acts of murder."[132] The argument was at once provocative and perverse, and Judge Battisti dispatched it with characteristic pithy restraint. "There is no reason to presume," he wrote, "that the Treaty drafters intended to extradite for 'murder' and not for 'mass murder.' "[133]

On February 27, 1986, shortly after 6:00 PM, El Al flight 004 left JFK in New York bound for Ben Gurion airport. Few passengers on the regularly scheduled flight knew that behind a curtained-off section in tourist class sat John Demjanjuk. Less than a week earlier, the US Supreme Court had rejected Demjanjuk's habeas petition, clearing the way for Secretary of State George Schultz to sign the extradition order. More than eight years after federal prosecutors in Cleveland first filed their complaint, Demjanjuk had been forcibly removed from the United States and delivered to Israel to stand trial as Ivan the Terrible of Treblinka.

3

Ivan in Israel

Demjanjuk's arrival in Israel created a stir that reminded many of the capture of Adolf Eichmann a quarter century earlier. After flight 004 touched down, federal agents officially handed custody of the suspect over to Israeli police, who, with the help of a Ukrainian interpreter, read Demjanjuk his rights. For his part, Demjanjuk displayed a strange exuberance, as if he had arrived in the Holy Land as a religious pilgrim and not as a suspected perpetrator of mass atrocities. (Arguably, the Crusaders of centuries past had demonstrated the two identities weren't mutually exclusive.) His police escort, preventing him from falling to his knees and kissing the tarmac, bundled him into an armored van and whisked him off, accompanied by a heavily guarded convoy, to the maximum-security Ayalon prison in Ramla, fourteen miles southeast of Tel Aviv, where Eichmann had also been jailed. There Demjanjuk was placed in a cell monitored via closed-circuit television, and isolated—for his own protection—from the prison's other six hundred inmates. A contingent of seven guards was assigned to watch him round the clock, both to protect him from possible attack and to prevent any attempt at suicide—a concern which was clearly misplaced, given the fact that Demjanjuk's entire life was a study in shrewd survival and brute metabolic endurance.

As for the trial, Israeli authorities considered removing the iconic glass booth, which had protected Eichmann during his trial from assassination attempts, from its place on permanent display at the Ghetto Fighters' Holocaust Museum in northern Israel and retrofitting it for Demjanjuk, a much larger physical specimen. Like Eichmann, Dem-

3.1. The court as stage: Day 1 of the Israeli trial. Courtesy of the United States Holocaust Memorial Museum.

janjuk would be tried in a public theater converted to serve as a courtroom. An auditorium inside Jerusalem's convention center used for screening movies, Binyanei Haooma (Hall of the People), would now accommodate three hundred spectators for a very different kind of performance (see figure 3.1). Those who failed to secure a seat in the courtroom proper could follow the trial in an adjacent hall via closed-circuit television. And for everyone else, there was always television. Just as Israelis in 1961 had been able to listen to the Eichmann trial live on radio, now they could watch the Demjanjuk proceeding on television, the first televised broadcast of a trial in the nation's history.

But if Demjanjuk's Jerusalem trial was meant to channel the spirit of the Eichmann proceeding, not all Israelis were convinced of the wisdom of the effort. In April 1983, six months before Israel issued the arrest warrant for Demjanjuk, Neal Sher, who shortly before had become OSI's third director in nearly as many years, arrived in Jerusalem to discuss extradition matters. Nearly two years earlier, his predecessor, Allan Ryan, had met with officials from Israel's Ministry of Justice to press the Israelis to show a greater willingness to request the extradition of former Nazis. Ryan's efforts had met with little enthusiasm. Israeli officials were wary about becoming the dumping ground for the OSI, which at the time was pursuing some six hundred investigations. Why, these officials asked, should Israel assume the exclusive burden of bringing collaborators in Nazi genocide to justice? Countries such as Italy, Poland, and Germany should step forward to share the responsibility.[1] Sher now proposed that the Israelis request the extradition of Valerian Trifa, the Romanian cleric and former member of the Iron Guard suspected of instigating the massacres of Bucharest's Jewish population in 1941. A naturalized US citizen, Trifa had become the Archbishop of the Rumanian Orthodox Episcopate seated in Michigan and had offered the opening prayer to the US Senate in 1955 before falling afoul of American investigators in the mid-1970s.[2] Since 1982, following Trifa's voluntary surrender of his citizenship, US officials had been searching for a country willing to take him. The Israelis, who doubted that the evidence against Trifa could secure a conviction under the "incitement" provision of the 1950 law, rejected Sher's overture, fearing that in the case of an acquittal, Israel would be stuck in the odd position of having to supply permanent sanctuary to the stateless Trifa.

Israel's rejection of OSI's proposal predictably sparked controversy. Sher had found strong allies in Simon Wiesenthal, who evidently leaked news of the rejection to the press, and in Gideon Hausner, the former attorney general of Israel and the chief prosecutor in the Eichmann case who publicly criticized the decision, causing a rift with then Prime Minister Menachem Begin. But if Israeli officials resented the pressure from Washington, Washington was equally annoyed with the Israelis, who, from the OSI's perspective, were failing at this crucial moment to support its hard-won legal battles. To patch relations with the OSI and to ease domestic tensions, officials in the Justice Ministry agreed to petition for extradition but only in cases that satisfied three distinct criteria: the accused must have murdered with his own hands; he had to be relatively young and in good health; and Jewish witnesses had to be available to testify directly about the crime.

If any case satisfied these three criteria, it was Demjanjuk's. Nonetheless, when Deputy Assistant Attorney General Mark Richard traveled to Israel to discuss possible extradition, many Israelis continued to question the good to be gained by a domestic prosecution. Some officials continued to hope that Germany would step forward to take Demjanjuk. Others worried that the success of the Eichmann trial could never again be repeated. As I noted in the introduction, the Eichmann trial was a triumph of didactic legality: Attorney General Gideon Hausner openly acknowledged that winning a conviction and securing the death penalty had not been the "exclusive objects" of the trial. The trial had sought to create a "living record of a gigantic human and national disaster" by telling Holocaust history through the lived memory of survivor witnesses.[3] By presenting the prosecution's case through the testimony of the "brands plucked from the fire," Hausner aimed to correct the mistakes of Nuremberg.[4] Nuremberg, as we recall, was not in the first instance a Holocaust trial—the major Nazis tried before the International Military Tribunal were charged first and foremost with "crimes against peace," that is, with having launched an unprovoked war of aggression against Germany's European neighbors. While the trial did document the Nazis' crimes against the Jews in substantial detail, prosecutors chose to structure their case around captured documentary evidence, material considered more reliable than eyewitness testimony. In Rebecca West's memorable formulation, this trial by document turned Nuremberg into a "citadel of boredom." It also eroded support for the trial within victim communities, which criticized Nuremberg for leaving the victim absent, anonymous, and erased from memory.

Hausner's testimonial strategy in the Eichmann trial proved exceptionally successful. It provided a comprehensive, nuanced, and profoundly moving history of the Holocaust through the lived memory of survivor witnesses. It riveted an international audience, particularly in the United States and Germany, and created for posterity a powerful record of the destruction of European Jewry. Within Israel, it turned a generation of young Israelis into witnesses of the witnesses, sensitizing them to the perils that faced the Jewish people. The Eichmann trial became *the* great Holocaust trial. Enlisting memory in the service of justice and vice versa, the trial transformed global understandings of the destruction of Europe's Jews, making their near annihilation the grimly iconic event of a murderous century.

It was hard to imagine the Demjanjuk trial matching this success. Indeed, it wasn't clear what the trial was supposed to accomplish, other than convicting the accused—a sufficient justification in most cases, but arguably not in high-profile atrocity trials. In order to justify the undertaking, Israeli prosecutors rehearsed the same didactic themes sounded by Hausner a quarter century earlier. Even before the trial had started, Justice Minister Nissim asserted its "significance for the education of youth." Observers noted that 60 percent of Israeli citizens had been born after World War II, and a poll conducted by an Israeli newspaper purported to discover an astonishing level of ignorance about the Holocaust among Israeli teenagers. One fifteen-year-old thought the Holocaust dated from World War I, while another claimed never to have heard of Auschwitz.[5] In his summation at the end of the trial, state prosecutor Yonah Blatman gestured to the proceeding's pedagogic value. "The Holocaust," he declared, "seems to have been forgotten from the collective memory. . . . Here in Israel . . . people tend to push out of one's consciousness whatever is not to be found in the day-to-day reality."[6]

But even assuming that Israel's youth were in need of remedial Holocaust education, it was far from clear that Ivan's trial could provide it. In Eichmann, the prosecution found an ideal defendant for pursuing its didactic agenda. Eichmann had been an efficient, resourceful, and tireless facilitator of Nazi genocide, the logistical mastermind who organized the deportation of more than 1.5 million Jews to their deaths. At trial, though he fatuously insisted that he had never been an anti-Semite, Eichmann never denied his participation in the killing process. Instead, he insisted that he had acted out of a pure spirit of what he called "cadaver-like" obedience. This defense raised basic questions about how perfectly ordinary law-abiding persons, put to work in a system that authorizes the most extraordinary atrocities, utterly lose their moral compass—a phenomenon that Hannah Arendt called "the banality of evil." The Demjanjuk trial, by contrast, was far narrower in scope. Though clearly a brutal sociopath, Ivan Grozny remained a bit player in the Holocaust, a vicious outlier given free rein to act out his sadistic impulses. Moreover, Demjanjuk's defense was simple: the Israelis had the wrong man. The accused had never trained in Trawniki, had never served as a guard at Treblinka or anywhere else; he was the victim of a terrible mistake, a conspiracy orchestrated by the KGB. Such a defense offered little prospect of elucidating broader themes of Holocaust history.

Finally, many observers doubted that a new generation of Israelis really needed a refresher course in the traumatic history of their elders. Holocaust pedagogy, thanks in no small part to the Eichmann trial, had become firmly integrated into the curricula of Israeli schools, as had obligatory visits to Yad Vashem, the Israeli Holocaust museum and memorial. As the Demjanjuk trial was set to begin, Claude Lanzmann's mammoth and magisterial documentary *Shoah* was playing in Israeli theaters. Relying on a representational logic similar to that of the Eichmann trial, *Shoah* re-created Holocaust history through the voice of lived memory. Its screening became a national cinematic event, against which the Demjanjuk trial would have to compete. Yitzhak Raveh, one of the three judges who had presided over the Eichmann trial, publicly asserted that "after forty years, there is no educational, legal or historical value" in prosecuting Demjanjuk.[7] The *Jerusalem Post* shared these doubts. "Israel['s] post-Holocaust generation," it opined in an editorial, "needs no such boost."[8]

In a number of important ways, Israel was no longer the same country that it had been at the time of the Eichmann trial. In 1961, Israel had existed for barely a dozen years and faced existential threats from enemies sworn to its destruction. By linking the destruction of European Jewry to the continuing threats facing the fledgling Jewish state, the Eichmann trial used a legal stage to create a powerful historical and political narrative. This story cast Israel as the vehicle of renewal for the Jewish people, and depicted a commitment to Zionism and military preparedness as the keys to continued survival. A quarter century later, however, Israel boasted the region's most powerful military; it had secured peace with two neighbors, Egypt and Jordan, and had demonstrated its ability to do what it pleased in Lebanon. The belligerency of its neighbors no longer posed its most intractable problems; these now arguably came from within, from its uncomfortable role as an occupying power.

Perhaps unconvinced by his own argument, prosecutor Blatman offered a second rationale for the trial, justifying it as a rebuttal to "a phenomenon that is to be condemned outright, the denial of the Holocaust."[9] But here again we need to pause. Although Demjanjuk's defense was paid in no small part by an American with close ties to Holocaust deniers, Demjanjuk himself never denied the atrocities committed against the Jews of Europe. "My heart aches and I grieve deeply," he said, on the stand, "for what was done to your people by the Nazis . . . only because of the fact that you were Jews."[10] More to the point, it wasn't clear just how the trial could discredit the arguments of deniers. Anyone familiar with the copious literature of Holocaust denial—indeed, a Google search for "Demjanjuk" unearths a toxic landfill of such material—knows that its arguments resist empirical refutation. Voices of hate and malicious distortion do not answer to truth. Seen in this light, the trial of Demjanjuk was a lose-lose proposition: convicting him would do little to deter Holocaust deniers, while acquitting him would be proclaimed by those deniers as a validation of their lies. In this regard, Blatman's argument took on a desperate cast: the court had to convict, irrespective of the strength of the case, since an acquittal would provide succor to Holocaust deniers around the globe.

The trial began on February 16, 1987, and its first days appeared to confirm many of the concerns that had been circulating in the Israeli press. The expected crush of spectators failed to materialize. Seats remained empty, and broadcasters questioned the decision to interrupt normal programming to carry the trial on television. Observers viewed the defense team with dismay. Eichmann's team—led by Robert Servatius, a German lawyer with Nuremberg experience—had mounted an intelligent and dignified, if unsuccessful, defense, respectful of the survivor witnesses. Demjanjuk's team, by contrast, appeared disorganized, if not directly inept. Leading the team in the early phases of the trial was Mark O'Connor, an American lawyer who had represented Demjanjuk since the days of the deportation proceedings. O'Connor had come recommended by Jerome Brentar, the wealthy travel agent cum Holocaust denier who was footing the bill for the defense. Brentar knew O'Connor's father, Edward, from their joint involvement in postwar refugee issues.[11] The career of the elder O'Connor tied the politics of displaced persons, anti-Bolshevism, and neo-Nazism neatly together. Edward O'Connor had run the War Relief Services, a branch of the National Catholic Welfare Council, and in 1948 had been appointed by

President Truman to the Displaced Persons Committee, where he helped draft the controversial Displaced Persons Act of 1948. Later, he served as chairman of a private support group, Friends of the Anti-Bolshevik Bloc of Nations, an organization with ties to neo-Nazi groups. A strong supporter of Demjanjuk, Edward O'Connor had testified for Demjanjuk at his denaturalization trial and had served as the keynote speaker at a rally organized to protest his deportation.[12]

Mark O'Connor had inherited his father's political beliefs but not his rhetorical abilities, and his failings in the courtroom had earned him rebuke during the later phases of Demjanjuk's American proceedings. During the deportation hearing, he called Brentar to testify about IRO screening proceedings, despite the fact that Brentar had never served as a screening officer.[13] Commenting on the extradition challenge prepared by O'Connor, Judge Battisti testily observed that the "respondent has nowhere set out his views in a clear and logical progression."[14] And the Sixth Circuit, for its part, went out of its way to criticize the habeas action drafted by O'Connor as a "confusing mélange of arguments."[15]

The Israeli court did not have to wait long to take the measure of O'Connor's abilities. Scant minutes after Presiding Judge Dov Levin had gaveled the start of the trial, O'Connor rose to challenge the court's jurisdiction. We saw in the last chapter that the Nazis and Nazi Collaborator (Punishment) Law of 1950 granted Israel extraterritorial jurisdiction over crimes against humanity and crimes against the Jewish people. The 1950 law thus moved in the direction of accepting the universality principle, the idea that jurisdiction can be conferred not only by conventional measures, such as territory, but also by the sheer severity of the crime. According to the pure theory of universality, any domestic national court, no matter how tangentially related to the charged offenses, can try perpetrators of certain grave international crimes. By this standard, a court in New Zealand or Iceland or Costa Rica would have as strong a claim to try Demjanjuk for crimes against humanity as Israel.[16] Not surprisingly, universal jurisdiction in its pure form remains highly controversial, and the 1950 law can be understood as embracing the idea but limiting its application to cases in which the victims were principally Jewish. O'Connor appeared to misunderstand this, advancing an argument notable for its bizarre mode of expression:

> This is only the second time in history with regard to the State of Israel, the young State of Israel, that the sword of St. Michael has been taken out in the use of [the] long arm of jurisdiction to bring back into the House of Zion an international criminal, a criminal whose crimes offend all mankind.[17]

Stumbling onward, O'Connor tried to alert the court of the possible consequences of letting the genie of universal jurisdiction out of the bottle, warning that

> if a state not like Israel decides to take their sword on the basic lack of underpinning, the basic lack of rationale with mal-intent, your Honor, and the mal-intent is to bring a true enemy of all mankind, a true terrorist into the fold, before the forum and raped that individual with the veil of propriety in the law and then to acquit the individual. Your honor, that killer state will have followed the precedent of this Court, . . . acquitting the individual and letting him roam free forever, protected by the unnatural cloak of double jeopardy. Even more heinous, Justice Honor, even more heinous is the concept of a killer state determining that an individual, perhaps an Israeli citizen, is the enemy of all mankind, had committed crimes against persecuted people, thereby parroting in reverse in the concept of the children of darkness, not the children of light that sit before me now, the very principles that are being laid down, and in fact persecuting, not prosecuting, that individual with the improper application of universality.[18]

Daunting as it may seem, it *is* possible to paraphrase O'Connor's argument. Universal jurisdiction, he was trying to say, could in the future be abused in one of two ways: first, a criminal state could in principle lay claim to an ally in crime, try him, acquit him, and so insulate him from any future trials; alternatively, a state with a political axe to grind could, say, try an Israeli official for abuses against Palestinians. The first argument was mistaken, as the principle of double jeopardy does not typically apply across sovereignties;[19] the second argument, however, would prove prophetic, as Belgian prosecutors would one day try to use the concept of universality to indict Ariel Sharon (along with many other statesmen).[20] Still, it was an odd argument to bring before the court, for it was prudential, not legal in nature: O'Connor did not deny the court's jurisdiction, but simply tried to warn the judges of the consequences of exercising it. More notable than the substance of O'Connor's argument were its excesses and abuses of language—the bombast and tortured syntax, the odd rhetorical flourishes and incoherent phrasing. As the trial progressed, O'Connor's every utterance became an adventure in meaning, leaving the court and spectators bewildered—and the simultaneous interpreters, responsible for translating the proceedings into Hebrew and Ukrainian, in open despair.

Then there was the defendant. If ex-Gestapo officer Klaus Barbie, the so-called Butcher of Lyon, whose trial in a French courtroom was set to begin soon after Demjanjuk's, could be called (in the words of French writer Alain Finkielkraut) "a poor man's Eichmann,"[21] Demjanjuk was a poor man's Sergeant Schulz. Big, beefy, and boisterous, he looked as if he had just tumbled out of a beer hall. Philip Roth, who observed portions of the trial, described him as a "cheerful palooka."[22] As he plodded into the courtroom for the first time, Demjanjuk waved to the TV cameras and called out, "Hello, Cleveland!" During breaks in proceedings, he liked to joke with his guards, entertaining them with bits of mangled Hebrew he had picked up in prison. He showed a flair for interior decoration, adorning the cinder-block walls of his cell with images of religious icons and postcards from friends and well-wishers. In court, he followed the proceedings with an expression that mixed equal measures of indifference and bemusement; Michael Horowitz, an assistant prosecutor, commented that the defendant appeared "more tortured by his hemorrhoids than by his conscience."[23] Again, Philip Roth: "His arms were crossed casually over his chest, and ever so faintly his jaws moved up and down as though he were an animal at rest tasting the last of its cud."[24] Maybe we can best understand his demeanor by bearing in mind the fact that among all those involved in the proceeding—lawyers, judges, journalists, and spectators—Demjanjuk alone knew the giddy truth: that the Israelis had the wrong guy. A completely innocent man might have viewed his predicament with terror—Demjanjuk, after all, was charged with capital crimes. But Demjanjuk seemed to sense

3.2. The cheerful palooka. Courtesy of Israeli State Archives.

that the legal maelstrom gathering around him ironically offered the best chance to escape a reckoning with his past.

* * *

All the early concerns and misgivings about the trial vanished suddenly on day five, when Pinchas Epstein took the stand. The first of the five survivor witnesses to testify, Epstein called Ivan a "predatory animal" and said, "I dream of Ivan every night. . . . I see him, I see him, I see him. . . . I cannot free myself of this."[25]

Eleven years had elapsed since the identification parades conducted by Miriam Radiwker. Of the ten survivors who had positively identified Demjanjuk in her office, four had died, including the first two to recognize him, Eugen Turowski and Abraham Goldfarb. The encroachment of mortality was a defining feature of the case. We have seen how survivor testimony fueled the drama of the Eichmann trial, creating a courtroom oral history project that galvanized international attention. Watching footage from the Eichmann trial today, what most strikes an observer is the *youth* of the witnesses. Many were still in their thirties or early forties, recounting events fresh in memory. Eliahu Rosenberg, who testified before both courts, was a squat burly man of thirty-five when he first described the sadistic doings of the guard known as Ivan Grozny; now he was a retiree in his sixties. Of the remaining survivors to testify against Demjanjuk, one was now in his mid-seventies, and another, Gustav Boraks, a faltering eighty-six. Their experience of Treblinka lay more than four decades behind them.

If the passage of time should have raised concerns, it also made the testimony of the survivors all the more poignant—and urgent. In his opening statement, prosecutor Michael Shaked noted that "this may be one of the last trials where it is possible to bring to the stand witnesses who can say, 'We were there.' The subject sooner or later will have to step down from the witness stand and become a part of history."[26] The Israeli public appeared to grasp this; once the survivors took the stand, people seized the opportunity to hear these stories one last time before they became artifacts of history. Thomas Friedman, then the *New York Times*' Jerusalem bureau chief, described how, to "almost everyone's surprise," the trial quickly became a national "obsession":

> The proceedings are the background noise of Israeli society. Some people walk with transistor radios held to their ears.... Many bus drivers automatically keep their radio dials tuned to the proceedings.... One woman said her dentist now had the Demjanjuk trial on his office radio in the place of soothing classical music.[27]

As an Israeli government spokesman acknowledged, "We—the government, media and educators—were caught totally off guard by the public's reaction. No one anticipated it."[28]

Notwithstanding their initial ambivalence, Israelis now embraced the trial, which came to channel the Eichmann proceedings in ways no one could have scripted. At the Eichmann trial, Yehiel Dinur, a self-described "chronicler of the Planet of Auschwitz" who had penned several semi-hallucinatory novels about his camp experiences under the *nom de lager* Katzetnik (camp inmate), had famously collapsed during his testimony; ritualistically rebroadcast on Israeli TV every year on Yom Hashoah (Holocaust Remembrance Day), footage of the collapse came to symbolize the unspeakable horror, the unmasterable trauma of the Holocaust. At the Demjanjuk trial, Treblinka survivor Josef Czarny nearly reenacted Dinur's breakdown. Czarny, we recall, had testified at Fedorenko's denaturalization trial, but his characterization of the defendant's face as "mean-looking" had led Judge Roettger to doubt his credibility. Now, with photographs of a model of Treblinka framing the witness stand—just as they had at the Eichmann trial—Czarny also suffered a breakdown of sorts, stammering, "I am now in Treblinka" before succumbing to uncontrollable sobs.

Such moments made clear that the trauma of the Holocaust had remained undiminished in the years between the Eichmann and Demjanjuk trials. All the same, survivor testimony played a fundamentally different role at the two trials. While today we remember the Eichmann trial for its groundbreaking construction of Holocaust history out of survivor narratives, very few of the survivors who testified at Eichmann's trial had actually laid eyes on the defendant, let alone had any dealings with him. At the time this made for a fair share of controversy. Hannah Arendt sardonically quipped that the proceeding had conferred upon the survivors a novel legal entitlement—the "right of the witness to be irrelevant."[29] The court became increasingly troubled by the prosecution's habit of letting its witnesses present their testimony in the form of unstructured narrative. Indeed, the most testy and pointed exchanges during trial were not between the defense and the prosecution, or between the defense and the court, but between the prosecution and the court, which became increasingly impatient with the prosecution's determination to let survivors describe every aspect of the Holocaust, no matter how tangentially related to the activities of the accused.[30]

In principle, the survivor witnesses at Demjanjuk's trial played a far more conventional evidentiary function. The state's case stood on two pillars—the Trawniki card that purported to prove that Demjanjuk had trained as an SS auxiliary, and the identifications of the survivor witnesses, which purported to prove he was Ivan Grozny. The survivors' testimony could, then, have been limited to identifying Ivan and describing his sadistic acts. This alone would have provided the trial with more than its fair share of drama. Chil Rajchman, who had flown in from his home in Montevideo, Uruguay, testified that "I carry this demon within me. I see him everywhere," while Pinchas Epstein described Ivan as "a monster from another planet." The trial's emblematic moment came in a dramatic exchange between witness Eliahu Rosen-

3.3. Those murderous eyes. David Rubinger / The LIFE Images Collection / Getty Images.

berg and the defendant. Asked if he could positively identify the defendant, Rosenberg requested the court to "ask the accused to take off his glasses, I should like to see his eyes."[31] To inspect more closely, Rosenberg approached the defendant—who extended his hand in greeting and blurted out, "Shalom!" (see figure 3.3). The witness recoiled as if struck, his wife promptly fainted, and the spectators broke out in a chant of "Murderer! Murderer!" Once he recovered his composure, Rosenberg declared, "This is Ivan. I say unhesitatingly and without the slightest doubt. This is Ivan from the gas chambers. . . . I saw his eyes. I saw those murderous eyes"—words that the witness uttered in the Yiddish of the lost communities of Poland. Those *merderische oygen*.[32]

The court, however, refused to restrict the survivors' testimony to the task of identification. Instead, it granted witnesses the freedom to describe their encounters with Ivan as part of a larger narrative of surviving Treblinka and the Holocaust. The court's reasoning wasn't entirely unsound. The trial would turn on the accuracy of the survivors' identifications, and the court could best assess this accuracy by comparing it to the clarity and sharpness of the witnesses' more general memories of Treblinka. And yet the court also seemed influenced by the legacy of the

Eichmann trial; it acted as if the freedom to tell their story was *owed* to the survivors. Where the court in the Eichmann trial struggled with the prosecution to rein in the testimony of the survivor witnesses, the Demjanjuk court engaged in no similar effort. Indeed, during his testimony Rosenberg was asked: "You spent eleven months at Treblinka. How did you endure?"[33] The question—by all measures broadly irrelevant—came not from the prosecution, but straight from Presiding Judge Dov Levin.

In retrospect, we can clearly see that the impulse to honor survivor testimony—to treat it with dignity and to confer public recognition upon it—pushed the court badly in the wrong direction. On one notable occasion, when O'Connor's co-counsel, a Canadian lawyer named John Gill, prodded witness Rajchman to pinpoint where the female prisoners had hung the guards' shirts and socks to dry, Presiding Judge Dov Levin lost his composure: "Is it important to know where they hung up the laundry?" he burst out. "What is the difference where the laundry was hung when 850,000 human beings were killed at Treblinka?"[34] Certainly Levin was not the only person appalled by the defense's dreadful lawyering, which left the court and observers alike numb and dismayed. But we should pause over Levin's outburst. In asking about the location of the laundry, Gill was following O'Connor's strategy of seizing upon any act of mis-remembrance as evidence of the unreliability of a larger architecture of memory. One can question the underlying logic of such a position—after all, are we to measure a man's memory of the day his mother was murdered by whether he can recall the color of the socks he was wearing? Yet this logic was not fundamentally different from the court's. It was the court, after all, that insisted that the quality of the survivors' memories of the camp provided an index of the accuracy of their identifications, a notion that invited them to narrate broadly. O'Connor simply turned that logic on its head: the absence of textured memory might suggest that the identifications were also faulty. Yet in curtailing Gill's cross-examination, Levin was prompted less by the irrelevance of the question than by its impropriety. *What is the difference where the laundry was hung when 850,000 human beings were killed at Treblinka?* Here outrage and the desire to sacralize memory collided with the obligation to subject testimony to the rigors—and indignities—of the adversarial process. That collision proved fatal; the belief that traumatic memory deserved special dispensations and exemptions from adversarial scrutiny proved catastrophic for the court.

* * *

Five months into the trial, the Demjanjuk family lost patience with O'Connor and his disorganized defense, and formally removed him from the case. Taking his place was Yoram Sheftel, his Israeli co-counsel, a flamboyant lawyer who openly proclaimed his "fundamental distrust in governments as such."[35] Cut from the same mold as William Kunstler, the Chicago Seven defender who had driven Judge Hoffman to distraction, Sheftel would prove more of a gadfly to the court than O'Connor, in part because he was a more able lawyer, in part because as an Israeli and a Jew he felt free to engage in more outrageous provocations. Sheftel openly castigated the judges for conducting a show trial, a charge that left them visibly enraged.

Although a far more capable attorney than O'Connor, Sheftel managed to make his own share of dreadful miscues. His greatest blunder was to focus the defense's case on challenging the authenticity of the Trawniki photo ID. The prosecution called a small army of leading documents experts, including a German pioneer in the field of photo identification, an Israeli professor of dental morphology, and an FBI ink specialist, all of whom attested to the card's authenticity. Yet—parroting a theory rejected by every American court—Sheftel remained adamant that the Trawniki card was a KGB forgery, fashioned by the Soviets for obscure reasons that he never revealed. This strategy backfired terribly, and almost tragically, when one of Sheftel's own documents experts unraveled during cross-examination, revealing that she had lied about her credentials. Distraught, the witness retired to her hotel room at the conclusion of her testimony and tried to kill herself.

Absorbing such tactical setbacks, Sheftel never backed down from his larger insistence that the entire proceeding was a political show trial that would have made Stalin proud. Here again the argument didn't exactly parse; after all, what did Israel hope to gain politically by framing an innocent man? Sheftel's more sober version of this claim—"You don't hire a theater hall and invite television in order to show Demjanjuk will be acquitted"—would prove prescient in ways the lawyer could not have possibly anticipated.[36] But at the time, this argument got lost in his more outrageous provocations, which included calling the case the "Demjanjuk Affair" in obvious reference to the Dreyfus Affair, a notorious miscarriage of justice born of European anti-Semitism. Comparing Demjanjuk to Dreyfus accomplished little beyond infuriating the court and inflaming the spectators, who broke into chants of "Death to the defense!" At times, it seemed that the spectators would rather have seen Sheftel lynched than Demjanjuk executed—and, in fact, at a funeral of a prominent former judge, who, soon after joining the defense team, leapt to his death from a Jerusalem building, Sheftel had acid thrown in his face by a seventy-year-old man who had lost his family at Treblinka. One defended Demjanjuk at one's own peril.

Nor did the defendant's turn on the stand advance the defense's cause. Demjanjuk began his testimony five months into the trial, shortly after Sheftel took the helm, and his seven days facing his judges doomed him as much as any evidence submitted by the prosecution. A boisterous courtroom audience repeatedly greeted his testimony with jeers of derision. The transcript is filled with Presiding Judge Levin's interjections, "Silence in the hall! If anyone heckles, I will have to have him removed from the hall."[37] When a Hebrew interpreter misreported Demjanjuk's utterance that in 1941 he had been "eighty-two yards" tall, spectators assumed the defendant was mocking the court and exploded in shouts of outrage. There were moments of pathos, including Demjanjuk's plea, "Honorable judges . . . Please do not put the noose around my neck for the deeds of others," and his insistence that he was incapable of acts of cruelty: "I cannot even kill a chicken, my wife invariably did it."[38] (The latter claim oddly echoed Eichmann's frank acknowledgment to his Israeli judges that he could never have become a doctor because he could not stand the sight of blood.)

More generally, Demjanjuk's testimony offers a textbook illustration of a simple but elusive truth: if you intend to lie about your past, it's important to get the story straight from the outset. By the time that he took the stand in Jerusalem, Demjanjuk had made numerous statements to American officials over the years, creating a paper trail so rich in contradiction that Israeli prosecutors must have drooled in anticipation. Read in chronological order, his statements suggest that the speaker suffered from a disease new to the annals of neurology: reverse dementia. Facts, items, and events left maddeningly vague in earlier statements—or omitted altogether—gradually take form over time, grow sharp, and crystallize in later testimony. For instance, in his first deposition with lawyers from the Justice Department, on April 20, 1978, Demjanjuk reported that after his capture by the Wehrmacht he was taken to a POW camp in Rovno, where he slept in a railroad car and was put to work altering the gauge of rail tracks from the wide Soviet gauge to the narrower German. He also spoke of a second camp, though he could not account for its whereabouts: "I forget now."[39] Three years later, testifying at his denaturalization trial in March 1981, he recalled the site of this second POW camp as Chelm; his task in this camp, he said, was to build barracks. Now in Israel, he recalled that while it was true that he built barracks in Chelm, he had also and *mainly* dug peat, and did so with a group of sixty or so other POWs, whom he could "see before my eyes." And yet he could not recall a single surname of his fellow prisoners, nor could he recall how long he had stayed there.[40] (He first claimed that his internment lasted through the winter of 1944, but in light of testimony from historians showing that Chelm had been taken by the Soviets the previous summer, that changed to spring 1944.)

Some changes, expansions, and emendations in Demjanjuk's testimony could perhaps be overlooked, but not Chelm. *Chelm was his alibi.* By his own admission, Demjanjuk had spent only "a few weeks at Rovno"—probably no more than three. By contrast, he claimed to have been at Chelm for at least eighteen months—that is, during the entire period of his alleged training at Trawniki and his service as a death camp guard. Struggling to account for this disturbing bout of forgetfulness, Demjanjuk first blamed the very trauma of the POW experience, asserting that he "would like to forget all that I had been through" and asking rhetorically, "You think it's easy for me to recall what I did in those . . . two years in prison?"[41] The explanation flew in the face of the logic of the prosecution, which insisted that trauma leaves behind memories of eidetic intensity, clarity, and reliability, and also sat poorly with the rest of Demjanjuk's testimony. For when it came to describing other traumatic episodes in his life, of which, admittedly, there were many, Demjanjuk demonstrated a precise and excellent memory. He was able, for example, to recall the names and whereabouts of all four army hospitals where he was treated for the shrapnel wound suffered early in his wartime service with the Red Army. Describing his capture by the Germans, he said, "I remember this as if it happened yesterday." When asked by prosecutor Blatman whether it was possible to forget "the events of the famine," Demjanjuk responded that "it is impossible to forget. . . . Just as . . . anyone who survived the Holocaust cannot forget."[42] Yet when pressed by Blatman to account for having forgotten Chelm at his first deposition, Demjanjuk could provide no answer: "Mr. Prosecutor . . . What do you want from a person who only had four years of schooling? . . . I forgot. I can't say why I forgot. I forgot."[43]

This response was so lame that it prompted Presiding Judge Levin to intervene, explaining to the defendant the meaning and importance of an alibi in a criminal prosecution:

> HIGH JUDGE (HJ) LEVIN: A person who is . . . blamed for something can defend himself . . . by explaining that I was somewhere else at the time, at the very same time. This is called in legal jargon an alibi. Do you understand me thus far?
>
> MR. DEMJANJUK: Yes.
>
> HJ LEVIN: You say that . . . at the very same time, the end of 1942 and 1943, you were elsewhere, not at Treblinka, but somewhere else. And what is that other place?—Chelm.
>
> MR. DEMJANJUK: Yes.
>
> HJ LEVIN: That is your alibi . . . the prosecutor is saying to you, "that very same camp which serves as your alibi, that precise camp you failed to mention. How is that possible?"[44]

Then there was Demjanjuk's training as a driver, at first blush a matter of little consequence. In his PCIRO (Preparatory Commission for the International Refugee Organization) Application for Assistance form from 1948, Demjanjuk noted that during his seven years in Sobibor he had worked mainly as a farmer and, briefly, in 1943, as a truck driver.[45] He had no reason to lie about the matter. If he was trying to make himself a more attractive candidate for emigration, his record of employment as a driver with the US Army more than sufficed to establish that credential. Moreover, the claim seemed consistent with the established fact that he had been driving tractors since he was seventeen. Yet when confronted with the information stated in the form, Demjanjuk vehemently denied that he knew how to drive a truck back in

1943. He had not filled out the form himself, he said; the clerk who assisted him must have misunderstood him and entered the wrong information. True, he had learned to drive a tractor as a teenager, but trucks—never! He did not learn to drive a truck until after the war when the Americans taught him.

In part, one can understand these adamantine and implausible denials in light of the charges against him. The gas chamber at Treblinka, Ivan Grozny's bailiwick, was believed to have run on a diesel engine from a captured Soviet tank, and so Demjanjuk understandably sought to distance himself from any familiarity with diesels. (He bent over backward to emphasize that all the tractors on the collective farm had run on *petrol*, and that he likewise only worked on gasoline engines when he later went to work for Ford.[46] As it turns out, historians now believe that the gas chambers used gasoline engines, which produce larger volumes of carbon monoxide than diesels.) But Demjanjuk had even stronger reasons for insisting that he hadn't yet learned to drive a truck. In his testimony, he had already acknowledged that the SS had combed through POW camps searching for Ukrainians with truck-driving experience. His kinsman, Feodor Fedorenko, who had passed through Rovno and Chelm before being trained at Trawniki, was on record as stating that "we were lined up and the Germans picked out who could be useful . . . as drivers and technicians."[47] Indeed, Fedorenko claimed that he had been selected by the SS precisely because of his experience as a driver. And Demjanjuk had already conceded that, like Fedorenko, he might well have answered the SS's call had he only known how to drive a truck:

Mr. Shaked: If the Germans had come up to you and proposed to you that you collaborated with them, you might have agreed, would you not?

Demjanjuk: Perhaps, possibly.

. . .

HJ Levin: . . . You were [in] a very difficult situation in the POW camp . . .

Demjanjuk: I understand.

HJ Levin: . . . You worked like a slave and you were nothing but skin and bones.

DEMJANJUK: Yes.

. . .

LEVIN: If you were a mechanic or driver, when they asked you would [you] have gone to work for them? . . .

DEMJANJUK: Had I been a driver, then possibly, yes.[48]

By his own admission, the only thing that stood between him and serving for the SS was his lack of driving ability. When prosecutor Blatman noted that the famished POW and experienced tractor driver must have felt sorely tempted to claim that he could also drive trucks, Demjanjuk acted as if that had never entered his mind. "You are mixing up a tractor driver with a car driver," he said, further noting that "there is also a difference between Soviet tractors and German tractors."[49] How could a Soviet tractor driver possibly claim to know how to drive a German tractor, much less a German truck? The very thought was preposterous.

Finally, there was Sobibor. As we have seen, Demjanjuk insisted that he lied on his DP and immigration forms to avoid forced repatriation to the Soviet Union. Israeli prosecutors, following the lead of their counterparts in the OSI, treated this claim as fatuous, but even if one assumed its truth, Demjanjuk still had to explain how he had come to list Sobibor of all places. Indeed, given the defense's insistence that the Trawniki ID was a Soviet forgery, Demjanjuk's lawyers had to explain the remarkable coincidence that the Soviets, lacking any prior knowledge of Demjanjuk's DP forms, just happened to list him as having served in precisely the same spot where he claimed (falsely, by his account) to have lived.

We recall that at his 1984 deportation proceeding, Demjanjuk claimed to have randomly plucked "a location called Sobibor" from a map hanging in the office of the DP officer. The map must have been unusually detailed to include such a tiny cuff. It also was not clear how Demjanjuk could have read it, since, by his own admission, he only knew the Cyrillic alphabet at the time. Perhaps troubled by the improbability of this prior account, Demjanjuk changed his story in Jerusalem. Now he claimed that officials for the United Nations Relief Administration (UNRA) had advised Soviet citizens to "find yourself a place either in Poland, or Czechoslovakia, or anywhere else" to avoid forced repatriation. A total stranger ("a person like me who had to go through the commission") sitting with him in the waiting room "had a small map and in this atlas he found this place and said this is a good place, mention it." The place "randomly picked" was Sobibor.[50] The account required Demjanjuk to insist, implausibly, that he had arrived at the office without having given any prior consideration to where in Poland he was going to claim to have lived—even though naming a Polish residency was, by his own reckoning, essential to escape forced repatriation and likely execution.

Given the weaknesses of this story, perhaps Demjanjuk's strongest appeal was to simple logic. "Your Honors," he said, "if I had really been in that terrible place, would I have been stupid enough to say so?" For many observers the answer was an emphatic yes. Demjanjuk often presented himself as an affable oaf, an ignorant, uneducated peasant incapable of complex thinking: "My tragic mistake is that I can't think properly," he once lamented. "I can't answer properly."[51] But he was hardly a fool—a fact that the judges appreciated, his feints and dodges prompting Judge Levin to observe, "I see that you not only understand but you are clever."[52] Indeed, during Wolfgang Scheffler's testimony, Demjanjuk asked the court if he could directly cross-examine the professor, and while his questions may not have disclosed the workings of a sterling legal mind, they at least demonstrated that Demjanjuk had closely followed Scheffler's testimony and had done his homework on the camps.

So why, then, list Sobibor of all places? However bizarre or reckless the gesture may seem, we should bear in mind that when filling out the forms, Demjanjuk had absolutely no reason to believe that anyone would ever be able to link him to the death camp. Indeed, were it not for the Soviets' fortuitous discovery of his Trawniki service card (presumably this happened even before the war had ended), the connection would never have been made. It was also extremely unlikely that a screening official would have heard of the tiny death camp that had been razed by the Nazis in 1944 and made to look like a farm. On the other hand, it was more than possible that the official would test Demjanjuk's local knowledge of Poland, a test he could easily pass by accurately describing the environs he was most familiar with. In this regard, the fool's gambit made sense.

As damning as the Sobibor evidence might have seemed, it shed little light on the activities of Ivan the Terrible of Treblinka—and even could have been construed as exculpatory. Recognizing this, Israeli prosecutors offered what turned out to be a fatal construal of the lies on Demjanjuk's visa and immigration forms. By their lights, Demjanjuk had listed Sobibor to deflect attention away from the far more serious crimes he had committed at Treblinka. Sobibor served as a tactical misdirection, an implicit acknowledgment of a lesser offense designed to conceal the greater. Prosecutor Shaked noted that Fedorenko had done something similar, listing on his immigration forms that he had spent the crucial years at Pelitz, the site of another camp, in order to "hide Treblinka."[53] Only Pelitz, unlike Sobibor, was a work camp. How, in Demjanjuk's case, could listing service at one death camp cover service at another? It made little sense—unless his actions at the second camp had been far more notorious than at the first.

In any case, Demjanjuk's story was so implausible, the gaps in his memory so large and subject to belated correction, and his narrative so riddled with contradictions, that one can understand how experienced jurists became convinced of his guilt. Still, if his testimony strengthened the certainty that Demjanjuk was guilty of *something*, it added nothing to the case against Ivan Grozny. Nor for that matter did the Trawniki card, which had withstood all the defense's misguided efforts to unmask it as a KGB forgery. The case, then, ultimately rested on the identifications of the survivor witnesses. And these the court accepted in full. On April 18, 1988, the usually strong-willed Demjanjuk lost his composure in the minibus that brought him from prison to court. Sobbing, he had to be carried into the Binyanei Haooma. Refusing to attend this final session, he was placed in a holding cell behind the courtroom/stage where the proceedings were transmitted via closed-circuit television. Inside the courtroom, the judges addressed an empty seat. The absent defendant was found guilty and sentenced to death.

* * *

With hindsight, we can say with certainty that the survivors who identified Demjanjuk as Treblinka's gasman were wrong. Granted, there remain those who to this day believe that Demjanjuk was Ivan the Terrible. Gabriel Bach, who assisted in the prosecution of Adolf Eichmann and who was a member of the Israeli Supreme Court that overturned

Demjanjuk's conviction, continues to harbor suspicions.[54] But the historical record says otherwise, and does so convincingly.

Even during the trial, the prosecution's case began to show signs of fraying. On the stand, the eighty-six-year-old survivor Gustav Boraks appeared at times confused, telling the court that in order to testify at the 1978 Fedorenko trial, he had traveled from Europe to Florida—by train. More troubling was the statement of a former Sobibor guard named Ignat Danilchenko, submitted by the defense after closing summations. (The defense had received a copy of the statement through a Freedom of Information Act [FOIA] suit brought by Demjanjuk's son-in-law Ed Nishnic in October 1986 after an earlier FOIA request had been rejected. The suit, as we will see in the next chapter, proved calamitous for the OSI, which, a federal court determined, had failed to comply with the rules of discovery.) Deposed by Soviet authorities at the request of the OSI in 1979, Danilchenko had picked out three separate photos of Demjanjuk from a photo spread and had stated that he had known Demjanjuk as an "experienced and reliable" guard at Sobibor.[55] He also said that he and Demjanjuk were later transferred to Flossenbürg, a concentration camp in Bavaria, where they received, consistent with SS protocol, blood-type tattoos by their left armpit.[56] There was no mention of Treblinka.

Earlier, the defense had cast serious doubts on the testimony of the only non-survivor to place Demjanjuk at Treblinka. As we recall, in building its case against Demjanjuk, OSI officials had interviewed Otto Horn, a former SS sergeant at Treblinka, in his West Berlin flat, where Horn had identified Demjanjuk from a photo spread. Evidence acquired by the defense through bizarre means called that identification into question. For nearly two years, a pair of Demjanjuk supporters—both Baltic émigrés—had arranged to receive garbage from OSI dumpsters behind a McDonald's on K Street in Washington, DC. Evidently the OSI, for all its litigation savvy, never felt the need to use paper shredders when discarding confidential material. The pair passed the trash on to Demjanjuk's son, John Jr., and Nishnic. There, among "yogurt containers and apple cores," the two discovered notes taken by the OSI officials at the time of Horn's deposition.[57] These notes indicated that the SS man had in fact struggled to identify Demjanjuk, and had succeeded only after having been prompted.

Disconcerting as these flaws were, it wasn't until the appellate phase that the case began to completely unravel. Israel long ago abolished the death penalty for all crimes except treason in wartime, crimes against humanity, and crimes against the Jewish people; indeed, Eichmann remains the only person ever executed in Israeli history. Appeals in capital cases, heard by a special five-person panel of sitting members of the nation's Supreme Court, are mandatory, elaborate, and intended to occur soon after sentencing. After the acid-hurling incident, however, Sheftel needed two separate operations on his left eye, the first in Israel and the second in Boston; as a consequence, appellate hearings did not commence until mid-May 1990, over two years after Demjanjuk had been sentenced to death. All told, the special panel held twenty-five sessions that lasted until the end of June. There was little in the way of spectacular revelations. The defense once again squandered time and energy attacking the authenticity of the Trawniki ID. It continued to insist that Demjanjuk was absolutely innocent—that he had spent the years after his capture as a POW—despite the fact that the prosecution had long ago shredded his alibi.

But far more important than the substance of the hearings was their timing. World-historical events had again chosen to intervene in the life of John Demjanjuk. In the two years it took the special appellate panel to formally begin its sessions, the Iron Curtain had collapsed, and the USSR was beset by the political convulsions that would spell its dissolution. During the trial proper, Soviet officials had generally refused to cooperate with Israeli prosecutors. (The original Trawniki ID had been flown to Jerusalem, but only thanks to Shimon Peres' personal appeal to Armand Hammer, the American Jewish magnate of Occidental Petroleum, who, having spent much of his career working for closer ties with the Soviets, directly approached Brezhnev.) But the unraveling of the Soviet Union now meant that evidence long moldering in Soviet and KGB files might be available for inspection. Defense lawyers and prosecutors alike now traveled to the USSR to examine the so-called "Fedorenko protocols."

In 1984, in the wake of the Supreme Court's holding in the matter of his denaturalization, Fedorenko agreed to be deported to the Soviet Union, the country of his birth, perhaps unaware of the risk this entailed. He settled in the Crimea; a cable from the American embassy in

Moscow noted that he had applied for retirement benefits with the expectation of "enjoy[ing] his pension for the foreseeable future."[58] But to the surprise of the OSI, Soviet officials arrested Fedorenko and charged him with collaboration and participation in mass executions. Tried in 1986, he was convicted and executed the next year. Protocols from his case consisted of some twenty-two volumes of material associated with the Soviet investigation and trial. Included in these volumes were snippets of transcripts from other cases as well as passages lifted from earlier depositions and court statements. Perusing this material and in discussions with officials from the General Prosecutor's Office in Moscow, prosecutor Shaked and a colleague named Daphna Bainvol learned that the Soviets had begun investigating Trawniki-trained death camp guards as early as 1944, while the war was still ongoing, and had conducted numerous prosecutions through the end of the 1960s. Eager to examine the full files of these earlier cases, Shaked and Bainvol visited Moscow and Kiev several times over the next two years.

As material culled from Soviet trials, the statements contained in these files could not be taken at face value. Many confessions, for example, had a formulaic quality, repeating certain stock phrases ("while acting treasonously against the homeland, I . . ."). Others, however, were nuanced and textured, and when examined collectively, offered a rich body of information. Unsurprisingly in a totalitarian society, the archives were impressively organized; in an age before computers, Soviet archival science, relying on techniques pioneered in the 1920s, had developed elaborate methods of indexing information that one expert described as "the most sophisticated in the world."[59]

The new files contained a trove of material pertinent to the Demjanjuk case. It turned out that Ignat Danilchenko, the former Sobibor guard whose statement in 1979 had been submitted by Sheftel during summations, had been tried and convicted by the Soviets back in 1949. (Given a twenty-five-year sentence, Danilchenko was released after serving eight under the terms of the Soviets' general amnesty law of September 17, 1955.)[60] In an interrogation in 1949, Danilchenko named nine other guards with whom he had served, including Demjanjuk. This statement matched the one Danilchenko gave investigators thirty years later, including such details as Demjanjuk's later posting to Flossenbürg, where both he and Danilchenko received blood-type tattoos.[61]

Corroborating this statement were two transfer rosters of Trawniki guards that included Demjanjuk's name. The first, from March 26, 1943, listed those being transferred to Sobibor; the second, from October 1943, listed those transferred to Flossenbürg, including both Demjanjuk and Danilchenko. Yet another document from a separate archive indicated that before Sobibor, Demjanjuk had served as a guard at Majdanek, the camp in Lublin, where he was punished for ignoring a camp lockdown.[62] A rather complete picture of Demjanjuk's wartime service was now emerging.

Only nothing attached him to Treblinka. The Soviets had interrogated scores of former Trawnikis who served at Treblinka, yet the name Demjanjuk appeared nowhere in these statements. But an Ivan did figure prominently—a Ukrainian named Ivan Marchenko. To a man, the former guards identified Marchenko and yet another Ukrainian, Nikolai Shalaev, as the gasmen of Sobibor. Adding to that were Shalaev's own statements—twelve in all—which likewise named Marchenko as the second gasman.

Still, confusion remained. On his application for an immigration visa to the United States, Demjanjuk had listed "Martschenko" as his mother's maiden name, which evidently wasn't even true.[63] He later said that he had forgotten her maiden name and simply put down Marchenko, a claim that sounds no less bizarre than his Sobibor explanation, except that, in this case, Marchenko *is* a common Ukrainian name, the equivalent of Smith or Williams. In any case, the surmise of some and the desperate hope of his prosecutors—that Demjanjuk and Marchenko were one and the same—did not survive contact with the documentary record. This showed conclusively that Marchenko had been born in Dnepropetrovsk in 1911. Maria Dudek, a Polish woman who had consorted with Treblinka guards, positively identified Marchenko but did not recognize Demjanjuk. Furthermore, in the Soviet probes in the 1940s, a number of Treblinka guards had also positively identified Marchenko from an extant photo—and though the man in this photo had, like Demjanjuk, protruding ears and a receding hairline, his coarse brutal face was quite different (see figure 3.4). Shalaev reported that he had last seen Marchenko in the port village of Flume on the Adriatic where both had been brought, along with other former death camp

3.4. At left, Marchenko, Ivan the Terrible.

guards, to fight Yugoslavian partisans in the Balkans. Presumably Marchenko had been killed there in fighting.[64]

In its written judgment, the trial court had dismissed the possibility that there could have been "two *Wachmanns* [*sic*] (guards) from Trawniki, one in Treblinka and one in Sobibor, both Ukrainians named Ivan . . . and both with protruding ears, both the same age and becoming bald in the same way." This, the court noted, was simply too "far-fetched" to be believed.[65] Yet all the new information suggested precisely that: there *had* been two Ukrainian Ivans, one at Sobibor and one at Treblinka, who bore a slight but not entirely negligible resemblance to each other. And it was Marchenko, not Demjanjuk, who was Ivan Grozny. Of course, this information was less than entirely exculpatory. Not only did it strengthen the certainty that Demjanjuk had served at Sobibor, but it also indicated rather conclusively that he had also served at Majdanek and Flossenbürg. But not Treblinka. Israel was about to execute the wrong man as Ivan the Terrible.

After supplementary hearings in the summer of 1992, the Supreme Court retired to examine the by-now vast and complicated record. A year later, in July 1993, it issued its ruling. In a brave and necessary step, the Israeli Supreme Court threw out Demjanjuk's conviction as erroneous. Anyone inclined to question the courage involved in doing this should consider the fury the holding unleashed in Israel. Czarny's anguished cry "Am I not authentic?" captured the survivors' grief in the wake of the decision. To their mind, not only had the court set a barbaric criminal free; worse, it had denied their own lived reality. The minister of justice, David Liba'i, felt compelled to issue a statement tersely "condemn[ing] threats voiced against the Justices of the Supreme Court" and emphasizing that "respect for judges and acceptance of their judgments are vital to the rule of a law."[66]

The Supreme Court's opinion is long, over four hundred pages, of which just twelve address the grounds for reversal.[67] The judgment begins with an elaborate discussion of jurisdiction, which confirms Israel's authority to try Demjanjuk under the terms of the extradition treaty. A further two hundred pages are devoted to reviewing and validating the witness identification process. When it comes to weighing the fresh evidence, the court remains agnostic about whether Demjanjuk or Marchenko was Ivan Grozny; instead, it simply concludes that the new material introduced a reasonable doubt that mandated reversal.

At the same time that it acquitted Demjanjuk, the Supreme Court also sought to acquit the trial court. The opinion artfully avoids castigating the trial judges, insisting that their verdict was simply undermined by new evidence. Trial courts, after all, are not institutions of divine omniscience or Godlike perfection. Levin and his colleagues had not derogated their judicial function or strayed in their conduct of the trial. True, they had erred, but their verdict had been undermined by recently uncovered facts, the existence of which they could not possibly have known.

And in fact, the trial court was not alone in getting things wrong. Virtually all observers who followed the trial supported the conviction. Tom Teicholz, an American lawyer who attended the trial in its entirety and published a sturdily researched account called *The Trial of Ivan the Terrible* in 1990—that is, before the reversal—left no doubt that he agreed with the verdict. Philip Roth, who both praised Teicholz's account and went on to describe the trial (which he briefly attended) in his novel *Operation Shylock*, reached much the same result. Indeed, for observers such as Teicholz and Roth, the trial delivered its own unforgettable portrait of the perpetrator of atrocity. If the Eichmann trial, thanks in part to Arendt's treatment, had depicted the perpetrator as an efficient bureaucrat acting in blind obeyance to a warped notion of right, the Demjanjuk trial offered a far more intimate and, for Teicholz, more disturbing picture of the zealous, hands-on exterminator. In Teicholz's words, "Demjanjuk had given abstract evil a human face."[68]

Roth's *Operation Shylock* is, of course, a novel, and so we should be careful about approaching it with the same standards as a nonfictional account. As a work that plays with the boundary between fact and fiction and the stability of identity, the novel presents particular hazards for the reader who would read it as history—this despite Roth's deadpan insistence that it is "as accurate an account as I am able to give of actual occurrences." Still, in those sections devoted to the Demjanjuk trial, the book reads as reportage and we have no reason to doubt Roth's claim that the material was "drawn . . . from notebook journals."[69] The first-person narrator, who identifies himself as Roth, describes his first day at the trial where he finds himself "staring at John Demjanjuk, who claimed to be no less run-of-the-mill than he looked—my face, he argued, my neighbors, my job, my ignorance, my church affiliation, my long unblemished record as an ordinary family man in Ohio, all this innocuousness disproves a thousand times over these crazy accusations. How could I be both that and this?" But Roth does not leave the question unanswered. Like Arendt, who in the concluding pages of *Eichmann in Jerusalem* speaks to the defendant, supplanting the court's judgment with her own, Roth suddenly shifts to the second person, addressing Demjanjuk directly. To the question, "How could I be both this and that," Roth answers:

> Because you are. Because your appearance proves only that to be a loving grandfather and a mass murderer is not all that difficult. Your lawyers may like to think otherwise but this admirably unimportant American life of yours is your *worst* defense—that you've been so wonderful in Ohio at living your little, dull life is precisely what makes you so loathsome here. You've really only lived sequentially the two seemingly antipodal, mutually excluding lives. . . . The Germans have proved definitively to all the world that to maintain two radically different personalities, one very nice and one not so nice, is no longer the prerogative of psychopaths only.[70]

In Roth's account, Demjanjuk assumes iconic status as the perpetrator capable of living radically antipodal modes of existence. In contrast to the nineteenth-century exemplar of such a man—the fictional creation of Dr. Jekyll and Mr. Hyde—Demjanjuk suffers no inner struggle between his warring halves. To the contrary, the radically disconnected selves live as a harmonious whole. Identity, in this picture, is neither fixed nor stable, but is radically defined by and responsive to context.

Costa-Gavras' film *The Music Box*, released in 1989, presents a similar image of the perpetrator; indeed, screenwriter Joe Eszterhas based the screenplay in part on the Demjanjuk case. The film tells the story of a Hungarian émigré who settles in Chicago, becomes a US citizen, and later in life finds himself accused of wartime atrocities by the OSI. (In what Eszterhas describes as a bizarre coincidence, a year after the film's release, he learned that the OSI was investigating charges that his father had collaborated with the Hungarian fascist party, Arrow Cross.)[71] The old man vehemently denies any involvement in the atrocities and claims to be the victim of a Soviet conspiracy. In his struggle to avoid denaturalization, he is defended by his daughter, a lawyer, who gradually comes to harbor doubts about the kindly seeming father she loves. At the end, the daughter chances upon old photos hidden in a music box that shockingly reveal her father's participation in wartime atrocities. Although a conventional Hollywood production that lacks the subtlety of Costa-Gavras' masterpiece, *Z.*, *The Music Box* reveals how the image of the perpetrator as the man of sequential lives—the eastern European wartime beast, followed by the good American citizen and father—had crystalized around Demjanjuk. In journalism, fiction, and film, Demjanjuk had become an icon of atrocity.

Even those who had denounced Demjanjuk's conviction and protested his innocence did so largely for the wrong reasons. In a piece published in the *Washington Post* near the end of the trial, Pat Buchanan had described Demjanjuk as an "American Dreyfus" (echoing Sheftel's own hyperbolic and abrasive rhetoric). Then, in a *New York Times* op-ed that appeared two weeks before the trial court delivered its verdict, Buchanan demanded Demjanjuk's acquittal.[72] His argument, however, was largely based on attacking the Trawniki card—which he dismissed as a "laughable forgery"—and disputing the testimony of Eliahu Rosenberg, the survivor who claimed to recognize Demjanjuk's "murderous eyes." It turned out that in 1947, Rosenberg had told a Nazi hunter that Ivan Grozny had been killed in the uprising of Jewish prisoners in October 1943, and that he had included the same assertion in a short memoir that he penned in Yiddish two years earlier. Questioned about these prior statements at the trial, Rosenberg explained that he had not personally witnessed Ivan's killing, but merely heard about it from others.[73] For Buchanan, as for the defense, Rosenberg's prior statements revealed the witness to be a liar, a vengeful man prepared to finger Demjanjuk even though he knew that the real Ivan Grozny was long dead. But here again the argument fails, for evidence later unearthed showed that the real Ivan *did* survive the uprising. For Rosenberg to claim that he *believed* Ivan had been killed until presented with a photo showing him still to be alive was both internally consistent and in agreement with the factual record.

If some critics of the trial stumbled on the correct result through flawed reasoning, we still must ask whether the trial court's mistake arose, as the Supreme Court insisted, through no fault of its own. Supporting this position is the odd fact that Demjanjuk seemed perfectly prepared to let himself be executed rather than use Sobibor as an alibi, which the trial judges all but invited him to do. Might he not have saved himself and many others a great deal of grief by acknowledging his service at Sobibor? The German historian and journalist Gitta Sereny offered a psychological account to explain Demjanjuk's obstinate refusal to do so. Having so long concealed his past to his family, Demjanjuk could no longer back off from his story; in particular, he "could not bear to have his children know what he had done."[74] For Sereny, the point was not that Demjanjuk had somehow come to believe his own far-fetched story. Rather, his identity as a US citizen, as a husband, and most of all as a father was so firmly anchored in the narrative of complete denial that he could not now back away from it, even if it supplied him with his only lifeline.[75]

Yet the assumption that Sobibor could have served as an alibi remains highly questionable. Indeed, without making recourse to speculative psychology, we can identify excellent *legal* reasons why Demjanjuk refused to budge from his story. First, if Demjanjuk's ultimate goal was to return to his home in the United States, admitting his service at Sobibor would have been tantamount to confessing that he had lied on his immigration forms. Return would have been impossible. As a second matter, Section 216 of the Israeli Code of Criminal Procedure entitled the Supreme Court to

> convict the defendant of an offence of which he is shown to be guilty by the facts proven, even though it is different from that of which he was convicted by the lower court and even if those facts were not alleged in the lower court, as long as the defendant has been given a reasonable opportunity to defend himself.[76]

The Sobibor alibi required Demjanjuk to confess to having served as a death camp guard. Thus even if the Supreme Court dismissed the Treblinka charges, Demjanjuk had every reason to fear it would convict based on Sobibor. Granted, he might not have faced the death penalty under the substitution, but the prospect of a life sentence probably offered little succor. Yet even in the unlikely case that the court had accepted the alibi in full and had acquitted him, Demjanjuk still had reason to fear that a confession would cost him his life. On July 27, 1987, the day he took the stand for his first day of testimony, TASS, the official Soviet news agency, announced the execution by firing squad of Feodor Fedorenko.[77] The timing, clearly intentional, must have sent Demjanjuk a powerful signal. Fedorenko, as we recall, had acknowledged serving at

Treblinka. Not only had that acknowledgment cost him his American citizenship; now, Demjanjuk learned, it had cost him his life. Fearful that an acquittal would simply result in his deportation to the Soviet Union, Demjanjuk found himself in something of a double bind. Had he admitted Sobibor to extricate himself from Treblinka, he arguably would have simply exchanged one noose for another—or, to be more precise, a noose for a firing squad.

If we can make sense of Demjanjuk's behavior, we are still left with the perplexing and dismaying mistakes committed by the survivor witnesses. How could so many people, so convinced they were right, get things so very wrong? The answers are perhaps not so difficult to divine once we look more closely at the procedures used by the Israeli police—and, in particular, at the crucial first set of interviews, conducted in the summer and fall of 1976. At the outset, we should note that not all the survivors positively identified Demjanjuk. Schlomo Helman had spent more time in Treblinka than any of those who did; moreover, he had assisted in the construction of the Treblinka gas chamber, and so had been in close daily contact with Ivan. And though he had no trouble positively identifying Fedorenko, he did not recognize Demjanjuk. Alas, Helman died before the start of the trial.

As a second matter, the identification parades conducted by the Israeli police fell dramatically short of the protocols used by the OSI, and, if measured against the standard set by the US Supreme Court in *Manson v. Brathwaite*, arguably constituted an "impermissibly suggestive procedure."[78] In this country, guidelines for conducting photo arrays recommend that investigators "choose non-suspect fillers that fit the witness' description and that minimize any suggestiveness that might point toward a suspect."[79] If the suspect is bald, don't show a witness ten pictures of men with lush curly locks and one with no hair at all. Nor should any one photo stand out for its size or clarity. Miriam Radiwker's photo spreads failed on both scores. Of the seventeen photos included in the original spread, Demjanjuk's was larger and sharper than the others, and Demjanjuk was the baldest (see figure 3.5). Police procedure also recommends that investigators "specifically instruct eyewitnesses that the real perpetrator may or may not be present." Here again the Israelis goofed. The survivors examined the photo spread with the belief that their former guard was among those pictured.

3.5. The Israeli identification parade: No. 16 is Demjanjuk; No. 17, Fedorenko. Courtesy of Israeli State Archives.

In its ill-fated advertisement placed in local papers, the Israeli police invited Sobibor and Treblinka survivors to assist in "*an investigation against the Ukrainians Iwan Demjanjuk and Feodor Fedorenko*" (see figure 3.6).[80] It's hard to imagine a more colossal mistake. Treblinka survivors obviously had no way of knowing that they were being sought solely for the purposes of identifying Fedorenko and not Demjanjuk. As the Jewish prisoners typically would not have known the surnames of the Ukrainian *Wachmänner* (guards), the ad's naming of Ivan would naturally have triggered associations with the one Ivan whom all Treblinka survivors *would* had known, Ivan Grozny. It seems fair, then, to assume that the Treblinka survivors arrived at their interviews *anticipating* that the photo array might well present a picture of Ivan Grozny.

There were more problems, still. As we recall, Radiwker's first interviews were conducted in June 1976. Bewildered by the results, and clearly oblivious to the mistakes she had already committed, Radiwker arranged to interview additional survivors. The second round of interviews took place in September and October 1976, and the strength of the identifications they produced was what convinced the Israelis that

3.6. The Israeli ad, clearly naming DEMJANIUK [*sic*] Iwan, and FEDORENKO Teodor [*sic*]. Courtesy of Israeli State Archives.

Demjanjuk was Ivan. But the timing of the interviews proved fateful. Every year on August 2, the date of the Treblinka uprising, survivors gathered in Tel Aviv for a reunion. Either Radiwker did not know this or did not appreciate its significance. In any case, the reunion in the summer of 1976 presented an opportunity for those who had already identified Ivan to tell friends and associates the astonishing news that Ivan was alive, that the police were on his trail, and that they had seen his picture.[81] So when Radiwker conducted the second round of interviews, the investigation was already running away from her. The survivors arrived fully aware that Ivan had been positively identified—and eager to participate in the process that would bring their former tormentor to justice.

Perhaps, then, we should be less surprised by the fact that numerous Treblinka survivors got things wrong than by the assumption that they would get things right. This, of course, was the fatal assumption that led the trial court astray. Here there is no escaping the conclusion that the trial court committed egregious missteps. Under the terms of the Nazis and Nazi Collaborators (Punishment) Law, persons charged with its grave crimes receive a bench trial by a special three-judge tribunal; by law, the presiding judge must be a sitting member of the Israeli Supreme Court.[82] Elevated to the Supreme Court in 1982, Dov Levin presided over the Demjanjuk trial. Joining him were Zvi Tal, a future Supreme Court justice and an expert on rabbinic courts, and Dalia Dorner, who likewise would later take a position on the high court. Despite the experience and legal talent of the judges, the court let itself get caught up in the historic proceeding in a manner that the Eichmann tribunal had notably resisted. In its written judgment, the Eichmann court actually distanced itself from the prosecution's ambitious legal didactics, striking a note of modesty and sobriety:

> There are those who sought to regard this trial as a forum for the clarification of questions of great import . . . which arose out of the Holocaust. . . . In this maze of insistent questions, the path of the Court was and remains clear. It cannot allow itself to be enticed into provinces that are outside its sphere.[83]

The Demjanjuk court, by contrast, could not resist the enticement. The court called its written judgment a "Monument," to which the Israeli Bar Association subsequently paid tribute in an English-language version elegantly bound with an embossed cover. Striking a tone more fitting to the dedication of a public memorial than to the delivery of a legal verdict, the court introduced its holding with a blowy pronouncement:

> We shall erect in our judgment, according to the totality of the evidence before us, a monument to their [the victims'] souls, to the holy congregations that were lost and are no more, to those who were annihilated and did not receive the privilege of a Jewish burial because hardly a trace remained of them, to those who were burned on the pyre and whose skeletons became ashes and dust, used to fertilize the fields of Poland, which they made fertile when alive, and on which they found their horrible death.[84]

"We are charged with the duty to determine," the court continued, "through due process of law, historical truths in regard to the events that befell our world in one of the darkest periods in the history of all nations." As for the historical truths to be determined, the court swept

3.7. Justice Levin, center, reads the verdict. To his right sits Judge Zvi Tal; to his left, Judge Dalia Dorner. Courtesy of the United States Holocaust Memorial Museum.

past the narrow question of accurate identification and framed for itself matters metaphysical in their generality and biblical in their breadth:

> Is it possible that one of the nations of this world, which has produced people of the spirit, and of morality, giants of culture and science, should set before itself, as a target and supreme objective, "to destroy, to kill, and to cause to perish, all Jews, both young and old, little children and women" (like the plot of Haman the Agagite—Esther 3:13)?[85]

The court's worst missteps, however, came in its treatment of the identifications. All legal experts are familiar with both the power and the unreliability of eyewitness testimony. It may be tempting to believe that survivors of the Holocaust would prove themselves less vulnerable to mistakes than conventional eyewitnesses, but this is simply an article of faith, born of a desire to honor those who have experienced impossible loss and to spare them a cruel confrontation with their own frailties—particularly inasmuch as many were sustained by the prospect of one day bearing witness. Unfortunately, the court subscribed to this article of faith. In addressing "the possibility of treacherous memory"—the possibility that survivors might have sincerely misidentified Demjanjuk—it again struck a note less legal than poetical:

> We must ask: is it at all possible to forget? Can people who were in the vale of slaughter and experienced its horrors, who lived in an atmosphere of oppression, terror, fear, and persecution within the narrow confines of the extermination camp; people who saw, day after day, the killing, the humiliation, the brutality, the abuse by the German oppressors and their Ukrainian vassals in the Treblinka camp, forget all this?[86]

The question, of course, was the wrong one. At issue was not whether the survivors had forgotten their tormentor but whether they could identify him accurately. The court answered its own rhetorical question with bombast: "No, it is not possible to forget the scenes of horror, the atmosphere of terror, all that took place in the extermination camp. It is impossible to forget Ivan the Terrible and his atrocities."[87]

And so the judges adopted a posture more fitting for a victims' advocate than for a court. We have noted that the judges permitted the survivor witnesses to narrate broadly, reasoning that the accuracy of the survivors' larger narratives provided a valuable measure of the reliability of their identifications. But this approach boxed the court into an impossible position. It could no longer cast doubt on the accuracy of the identifications supplied by the Treblinka survivors without implicitly discrediting the deeper truth of the survivors' narratives about camp life.

This ill-fated posture led the court to ignore the testimony of defense witness Willem Wagenaar, an experimental psychologist from the University of Leiden and a leading expert on memory problems. Wagenaar testified that persons undergoing trauma often cannot reliably recount their experience.[88] But because these studies focused on isolated episodes of trauma, such as a rape or violent mugging, the court concluded that they had no bearing on the Demjanjuk case, which involved a repeated pattern of horror experienced daily for months on end:

> There is no room whatever for comparing the trauma experienced by the survivors of Treblinka with the traumatic experience undergone by a person who was a victim of harsh violence, rape, or similar crimes. . . . The traumatic shock suffered by the victims of Treblinka is a thousand times greater in its intensity and influence.[89]

A thousand times greater: the outrage packed into the phrase reveals how badly the court had strayed from its task. Even if we ignore the dubious logic of the claim, which simply assumes that the acuity of memory is directly proportional to the intensity of trauma, we cannot ignore the court's tone. For the court, the mere *suggestion* that the trauma of a Treblinka survivor could be compared to that of a rape victim was nothing short of impertinent, a grievous insult to survivors. The desire to sacralize and confer dignity upon the memories of survivors is understandable. But it is one thing to want to honor the stories of those who survived a death camp, and another to accord them legal probity in a criminal trial. It was this posture that nudged the court toward disaster.

Here again, a final comparison with the Eichmann trial is telling. As I've noted, the Eichmann trial remains famous for the way it succeeded in reconstructing the Holocaust through the lived memory of survivors. And yet the survivors at the Eichmann trial were basically *bearing witness to history*: they were not called upon as eyewitnesses in any conventional sense. If Hannah Arendt sounded callous in dismissing their testimony as utterly irrelevant, let us attend to the court's own characterization:

> Without a doubt, the testimony given at this trial by survivors of the Holocaust, who poured out their hearts as they stood in the witness box, will provide valuable material for research workers and historians, but as far as the Court is concerned, they are to be regarded as by-products of the case.[90]

The contrast to the Demjanjuk court could not be sharper. The Demjanjuk court's desire to vouchsafe the history of the Holocaust for a new generation and to honor the memory work of the aging survivors ushered it toward the precipice. Only a fortuitous opening of archives—and a brave gesture by the Supreme Court—spared Israel an inexpugnable legal catastrophe.

4

Demjanjuk Redux

Sixteen years had passed between the filing of the complaint in Cleveland and Demjanjuk's acquittal in Jerusalem. Another sixteen would pass before he would be removed from the United States for a second time and sent to Germany to stand trial. With the discredited Treblinka charges laid to rest, that trial would focus exclusively on Demjanjuk's service at Sobibor. All the same, it is unlikely that John Demjanjuk would ever have been brought to trial in Munich if not for the notoriety he gained as Ivan Grozny. Some might consider this Demjanjuk's misfortune; others, principally his German lawyer, would find it nothing less than scandalous that this quiet Ukrainian remained the quarry of overzealous Nazi hunters. Yet ironically the misidentification that nearly sent him to the gallows in Israel also possibly saved his life. Had he not been extradited to Israel, in all likelihood Demjanjuk would have been deported to the Soviet Union, like his compatriot Fedorenko. There he might well have met the same fate.

Like everything else in Demjanjuk's case, his acquittal by the Israeli Supreme Court aroused controversy. The court could hardly overlook the fact that the new evidence was less than entirely exculpatory. As we've noted, Section 216 of the Israeli Code of Criminal Procedure permitted the court to "convict the accused of an offence of which he is shown to be guilty . . . even though it is different from that of which he was convicted by the court below."[1] The high court had to consider, then, whether it could dismiss the Treblinka charges but still convict the appellant "as a result of his service as Wachmann in a Trawniki unit; or . . . as a Wachmann in Sobibor."[2] Complicating the question, Section

216 requires that in cases in which the court substitutes a conviction, the accused has to be given "a reasonable opportunity to defend himself."[3] Concerning the Trawniki and Sobibor charges, the court concluded that Demjanjuk had not been given such an opportunity. The "severe and outrageous facts" of his presumed service at Trawniki and Sobibor required that Demjanjuk be given a fresh chance to defend himself. This, the court explained, would require "starting the proceedings again"—language it placed in boldface, its only use of such highlighting in its four-hundred-plus-page opinion. After seven years of Demjanjuk, the court laconically concluded that reopening the proceedings "does not seem to us reasonable."

And so Israel prepared to set Demjanjuk free. Only now the stateless man needed a country willing to take him. Israelis were appalled at the prospect of a freed Demjanjuk stuck in Israel with nowhere to go. The United States appeared reluctant to let Demjanjuk back into the country. Germany showed no interest in taking him. A decade earlier, the United States had bundled Arthur Rudolf, a former Nazi rocket scientist who had become an American citizen before running afoul of the OSI, onto a plane and flown him to Germany. In an arrangement worked out with the OSI, Rudolf had agreed to return to Germany in order to avoid a denaturalization trial; once on German soil, he voluntarily surrendered his American citizenship, rendering him a stateless person and now Germany's headache.[4] Worried that the Israelis might pull a similar stunt—put Demjanjuk on a plane and dump him in Frankfurt—German officials went to the extraordinary precaution of putting Demjanjuk on a "no-entry" list, effectively barring him from the country.[5]

Ukraine was a very different story. A decade earlier, Demjanjuk's delivery to his homeland would have occasioned a Soviet war crimes trial and the defendant's possible execution. Now, in the post-Soviet world, the native Ukrainian was something of a national hero. Crowing that he was "not Nazi" but "pure Ukrainian," Demjanjuk received a personal invitation to return to his native country, and was vouchsafed a visa by the Ukrainian president, Leonid M. Kravchuk.[6] No sooner had the Ukraine extended an invitation to its native son, however, than the Sixth Circuit Court of Appeals in Cincinnati—the very court that had upheld Demjanjuk's denaturalization and extradition—suddenly cleared the path for his return to the States. Ruling on a motion brought by Demjanjuk's American legal team, the court ordered that he be granted reentry to the States.[7]

The prospect of Demjanjuk's release left many Israelis appalled. Expressing a sentiment shared by many of his countrymen, Efraim Zuroff, director of the Israeli branch of the Simon Wiesenthal Center and coordinator of its war crimes research, called the prospect of Demjanjuk's leaving Israel a free man "unthinkable," and "terrible."[8] A series of petitions urged the Israeli Ministry of Justice to file new charges—including one filed by Yisrael Yehezkeli, the distraught septuagenarian whose act of hurling acid in Sheftel's face had set in motion the delays that ultimately led to Demjanjuk's acquittal. In fact, the Supreme Court had not entirely foreclosed the possibility of filing new charges based on the Sobibor evidence, and now the court invited the Israeli attorney general to decide whether he would do so.[9]

In the middle of August, the attorney general offered his response, urging that the case be closed. The ministry had concluded that a Sobibor trial would require a new extradition order and would arguably violate bars against double jeopardy—at the very least it would invite appeals on such grounds. Voicing concern about the thinness of the evidence, the ministry concluded it would be better to drop the case altogether than risk a second acquittal. The conclusion disappointed officials in the OSI, who very much wanted to see Demjanjuk retried on the Sobibor charges. But the Israelis were in no mood to take legal advice from their colleagues in the States, who, they had come to believe, could have spared them the disaster in Jerusalem. The Supreme Court accepted the government's recommendation.[10]

Even that did not settle matters. Toward the end of August 1993, Esther Raab, a Sobibor survivor who had settled in suburban New Jersey, suddenly came forward, claiming to identify Demjanjuk, who, she said in an interview with the Associated Press, was "miserable like all of them." Raab stood by the reliability of her identification, citing her "good memory" and insisting that "every detail from Sobibor, every person, every face is so fresh in my mind. I might not remember what I ate yesterday, but I sure remember what happened there."[11] Raab represented the first Sobibor survivor ever to claim to be able to identify Demjanjuk, but it was unclear why she had waited all these years to come forward. The belated claim was clearly problematic; Israeli prosecutors, by now exhausted and dispirited, were hardly prepared to treat it as credible. Still, news of Raab's statement made headlines in both the United States and Israel, and complicated the efforts of Israeli officials to be done with Demjanjuk.

Finally, on September 22, two months after his acquittal by the Supreme Court, Demjanjuk's Israeli odyssey came to an end. Just as he had seven years before, Demjanjuk flew El Al—this time, however, seated comfortably in business class with his son John Jr., his son-in-law Ed Nishnic, Congressman Traficant, and two bodyguards. Jauntily attired in an outfit freshly purchased by his family in a shop in Tel Aviv, Demjanjuk wore a striped pullover, blue slacks, a green windbreaker, and a white beach hat—and a bulletproof vest, a precaution prompted by death threats. His presence on the 747 left many fellow fliers less than thrilled. The *Times* reported that Kochava Eden, an Israeli woman living in Los Angeles, moved her seat rather than sit directly behind Mr. Demjanjuk. "Instead of letting him fly with us," she commented acidly, "we should pull him behind the plane."[12] Still, the flight proceeded without incident. Nishnic praised El Al: "It's the safest airline in the world—their security is marvelous," a remark which seemed to overlook the fact that the airline typically sought to prevent attacks against, not by, Israelis. Awaiting Demjanjuk at JFK in New York was a small private plane that flew him to a secluded hideaway in Ohio where he remained until the first week of October, at which point he returned to his home in Seven Hills.

For some, Demjanjuk's return was an occasion for outrage, for others, celebration. Demonstrators dressed in the garb of concentration camp inmates gathered in front of his house, as did counterprotesters, including members of the local KKK. The City of Seven Hills rushed to pass a municipal ordinance that essentially barred all demonstrations from residential neighborhoods.[13] (The patently overbroad ordinance did not survive a constitutional challenge brought by the Aryan Nations, although it did permit the town to limit the scope of demonstrations that could be staged directly in front of Demjanjuk's house.)[14] On September 27, 1993, a day after Yom Kippur, a thousand protesters filled Public Square in Cleveland to demonstrate against Demjanjuk. In October, Demjanjuk's local church, St. Vladimir's, held a service in memory

4.1 Demjanjuk with Congressman James Traficant on a chartered flight from JFK airport to Medina, Ohio, September 22, 1993. AFP / Getty Images.

of those who had perished in the Holodomor and unveiled a small monument to the victims of the famine. "This," commented Reverend John Nakonachny, "is the era that Mr. Demjanjuk grew up in."[15]

* * *

Demjanjuk's acquittal and return were the beginning of an unhappy time for the OSI. In the fourteen years since its creation, the OSI had successfully denaturalized and deported three dozen Nazi collaborators—an impressive record, given the complexity of the cases and the procedural hurdles placed in the government's way. Now, the OSI had suffered a stunning reversal in its only case of true international stature. It was bad enough that the Israeli conviction had imploded and that Demjanjuk had been permitted, against OSI protests, back into the country—the only such instance of an OSI deportee ever being permitted to return to the United States. More damaging yet to the Office were the investigations into its handling of the case, triggered by the FOIA requests brought by Demjanjuk's tenacious American lawyers and political supporters.

As we've seen, the defense, thanks to some opportunistic dumpster-diving, had discovered OSI memos that contradicted the official report of Otto Horn's identification of Demjanjuk. The defense team had also tardily—and then only thanks to a suit following a rebuffed FOIA request—received from the OSI a copy of Danilchenko's interview with Soviet authorities in 1979. Challenges to the case had also come from independent media reports, including most notably a *60 Minutes* interview with Maria Dudek, the Polish woman who consorted with Marchenko and identified him as Ivan the Terrible of Treblinka. As the fissures in the case became visible, criticism of the OSI mounted. These attacks came not only from the usual suspects such as Buchanan and Traficant, but also from within the Department of Justice itself. The *Times* reported that Attorney General William P. Barr had lost faith in the Office and in its then director, Neal Sher. While Barr resisted the calls of critics like Buchanan to shut down the OSI altogether, the *Times* reported that he privately worked to undermine a unit he found "anachronistic" and whose work "sloppy."[16]

On June 5, 1992, the day after Israeli prosecutors first informed members of the Supreme Court at an oral hearing that they, too, shared doubts about Demjanjuk's conviction, a panel of the Sixth Circuit reopened Demjanjuk's habeas challenge to his extradition *sua sponte*. Weeks earlier, Gilbert Merritt, chief judge of the circuit, had read a *Vanity Fair* article exposing the weaknesses in the case.[17] Merritt had then written to Assistant Attorney General Robert Mueller requesting a copy of Soviet witness statements identifying Marchenko as Ivan Grozny.[18] Receiving no response, Merritt took matters into his own hands, convincing his fellow panel members to reopen the case. Not only was this a pointed act directed against the Justice Department, it also raised delicate diplomatic issues inasmuch as Demjanjuk remained in Israeli custody, convicted of capital crimes. But by now Merritt's principal concern was whether the OSI had engaged in misconduct by "concealing or withholding . . . evidence in their possession."[19] Merritt's court appointed Thomas A. Wiseman, a federal district court judge in Tennessee, as special master to report back on the matter.

For six months Wiseman conducted hearings and gathered evidence, and in June 1993, roughly a month before the Israeli Supreme

Court overturned Demjanjuk's conviction, the special master submitted a 210-page report to the Sixth Circuit examining charges that the OSI had engaged in prosecutorial misconduct. Wiseman's report, distinguished by its thoroughness and balance, left no doubt that the OSI had long been in possession of documents that cast serious doubts on its case against Demjanjuk. As early as October 1978, that is, before the OSI had even been created, lawyers working in what was still the Special Litigation Unit of the INS had received from Soviet sources copies of statements from two former Treblinka guards. Both had named Marchenko as one of the two operators of the Treblinka gas chamber. A year later, the Polish government's Main Commission for the Investigation of Hitlerite Crimes sent the OSI a list of guards known to have served at Treblinka. The list was hardly exhaustive; around 120 to 150 Trawniki-trained *Wachmänner* had guarded Treblinka at any given moment, and given transfers, desertions, and illness, the total number of Trawniki men to have cycled through Treblinka was probably more in the range of 200 to 250. The list from the Polish commission, by contrast, only included around seventy names. Nonetheless, missing from the list was Demjanjuk; appearing were both Fedorenko and "Marczenko, Iwan." The OSI had also received statements from several former Trawniki men who reported that all transfers were routed through Trawniki, a claim that at least arguably cast doubts on the prosecution's theory that Demjanjuk might have shuttled between Sobibor and Treblinka. Take the Marchenko material together with the Danilchenko statement (naming Demjanjuk as a guard at Sobibor and Flossenbürg) and the memos undermining Otto Horn's identification (Horn being the only camp official ever to have pinned Demjanjuk to Treblinka), and suddenly it seemed that the government's case had *never* been solid.

Worse still for the OSI was the discovery of the Parker Memorandum. George Parker was an OSI trial attorney who had worked closely with Norman Moscowitz on Demjanjuk's denaturalization trial. On February 28, 1980, that is, roughly a year before the start of the proceeding before Judge Battisti, Parker had penned a memo addressed to Walter Rockler, the OSI's first director, and Allan Ryan, his successor. Bearing the subject heading "Demjanjuk—a Reappraisal," Parker's memo soberly warned that "we may have the right man for the wrong act."[20] Canvassing the evidence, Parker offered a personal "assessment": "Demjanjuk could not have been Ivan the Terrible as well as the Demjanjuk known to Danilchenko at Sobibor. A reading of the Canons of Ethics persuades me that I cannot pursue this case simply as a Treblinka matter."[21]

One can almost smell the acrid pinch of gunpowder trailing from the proverbial smoking gun. The fact that Parker resigned shortly thereafter only strengthens the impression of a lonely voice of conscience struggling against government wrong. Not only did the memo make plain that an OSI lawyer with intimate knowledge of the case had harbored serious doubts from early on; it also raised troubling questions about the Office's failure to supply the defense with seemingly exculpatory material despite the numerous discovery requests. Indeed, according to Wiseman, the OSI also failed to share its doubts with Israeli prosecutors, who only learned of the exculpatory material from their own independent examination of KGB archives after the fall of the Iron Curtain.

If the special master's report offered a kernel of good news for the OSI, it was Wiseman's conclusion that the unit's missteps did not rise to the level of prosecutorial misconduct. Unfortunately this conclusion was largely overlooked in the contretemps that followed. Having received and reviewed the report, the three-judge panel of the Sixth Circuit accepted Wiseman's findings of fact but rejected his conclusion. In a surprising decision handed down on November 17, 1993—roughly two months after Demjanjuk's return to his home in suburban Cleveland—the panel held that in failing to "observe their obligation to produce exculpatory materials," the "OSI attorneys acted with reckless disregard for the truth." Such prosecutorial recklessness, the court concluded, prevented Demjanjuk's team from "presenting his [Demjanjuk's] defense fully and fairly" and so constituted "fraud on the court."[22]

The excoriation did not end there. The panel concluded that in denaturalization and extradition cases "based on proof of criminal activities of the party proceeded against," the government must follow the more exacting rules of discovery that govern criminal cases, rather than the more permissive rules that control civil litigations. These so-called

Brady disclosure rules—named after the landmark 1963 Supreme Court decision, *Brady v. Maryland*, that introduced the doctrine—hold that the failure to disclose exculpatory material in a criminal case constitutes a due process violation "irrespective of the good faith or bad faith of the prosecution."[23] The court's conclusion that *Brady* should also apply to the OSI's caseload was not entirely surprising; remarkable, however, was the fact that it admonished the OSI for failing to satisfy a standard that the court had only just imposed.

Finally, the panel lambasted the OSI for pursuing a "win at any cost" strategy. Quoting various documents that described the case as a "political 'hot potato,'" which, if lost, would "raise political problems for all of us, including the Attorney General," the court openly suggested that the OSI had gone forward with the prosecution to "please and maintain very close relationships with various interest groups because their [*sic*] continued existence depended on it."[24] This amounted to the bald charge that in order to satisfy a powerful political constituency (read: American Jews), the OSI recklessly conducted a witch hunt against a man it knew, or at least should have known, was innocent of the charges brought against him. Buchanan and Sheftel were no longer alone in calling Demjanjuk an American Dreyfus. The Sixth Circuit agreed. (As if to insulate itself from the charge of indulging in anti-Semitic conspiracy theories, the panel bent over backward to praise Israeli prosecutors for airing precisely the kind of ethical doubts that their American counterparts suppressed. Still, the damage had been done, and the Anti-Defamation League, World Jewish Congress, and Simon Wiesenthal Center used the fact of Judge Merritt's role in the intemperate decision—which, in fact, was written by his colleague on the panel, Judge Pierce Lively—to lobby against his consideration for a Supreme Court vacancy.)[25]

What explains the dramatic difference in the conclusions of the special master and the Sixth Circuit? Certainly timing played a role. While Wiseman's report came out before the Israeli acquittal, and thus called for diplomacy and even delicacy, by the time of the Sixth Circuit's ruling, Demjanjuk was back in Cleveland—and the panel was free to vent. The judges were clearly furious about the part they had played earlier in supporting what they now considered a clear miscarriage of justice. Regrettably, however, in rejecting Wiseman's more sober and balanced conclusions, the panel ended up treating history with the same kind of reckless inattention that it attributed to the OSI.

* * *

By the time of the Israeli acquittal, the Demjanjuk case had assembled its own lengthy history, which had come to rival and perhaps even surpass the complexity of the underlying subject of the litigation. The foibles of memory by now had assumed a meta-dimension, as the attempt to reconstruct lawyers' memories of interviews with camp functionaries and survivors became no less fraught than the first-order memories the lawyers sought to record. In finding the OSI guilty of fraud on the court, the Sixth Circuit panel did not exactly get things wrong. But it treated the OSI like a single, perfectly wired brain with complete knowledge of an expanding evidentiary base accumulated by all the various participants in the case. In fact, during the years leading up to Demjanjuk's extradition, no fewer than eight different federal prosecutors had worked closely on the case—some in a spirit of cooperation, others in open competition, and others still in foggy ignorance of the work of their colleagues. Largely dependent on Polish and Soviet sources for evidence, the lawyers struggled to make sense of a bewildering set of clues. In assessing how they handled the information, it is important to bear in mind that most of them (with the exception of Parker) were convinced by the survivors' identifications—which, if tallied together from around the globe, ultimately numbered eighteen. When it came to making sense of the contradictory evidence coming in infrequent bursts from behind the Iron Curtain, OSI lawyers cannot be said to have willfully or recklessly ignored transparently contradictory evidence; at worst, they struggled imperfectly to separate the germane from the irrelevant, while exploring pathways of plausible reconciliation.

Take, for example, the list of seventy known Treblinka guards forwarded to the OSI by Polish authorities. We have noted that the absence of Demjanjuk's name was disappointing, but could hardly have been considered worrisome, as the list was far from complete. The appearance of Marchenko's name might have raised concerns, but only if Marchenko was already on the OSI's radar. Otherwise, "Marchenko" was of no more interest than any other name on the list. We might insist that Marchenko *should* have been on the OSI's radar, thanks to the statements of the two Treblinka guards that the Office had received a year earlier from the Soviets. Apparently, however, Parker had never read those statements. Moscowitz had read them, but had not connected the dots—largely because they were few in number and all over the place. While the first guard, named Leleko, identified the operators of the gas chamber as "Marchenko and Nikolay," the second, Malagon, identified "Nikolai Marchenko" as the one "who drove the gas chamber van" and Demjanjuk as a "cook" who later worked as a "gas chamber van driver" at Buchenwald.

What is one to make of this mishmash? More to the point, do these statements represent exculpatory material? If Malagon was correct, then Leleko had it wrong—Marchenko in fact had been Nikolai's surname. Moreover, Malagon placed Demjanjuk at Treblinka, but as a cook. But what are we to make of Malagon's bizarre talk of gas van drivers? The SS had used mobile gas vans at Chelmno and Krasnodar, but not at Treblinka, which had fixed gas chambers, and obviously not at Buchenwald, which had no gas chambers at all. So maybe we should conclude that Leleko got things right and Malagon was mistaken—Marchenko and Nikolai were separate persons and the two had run Treblinka's gas chamber. This, we now know, turned out to be accurate: but, at the time, how should it have been interpreted? Moscowitz was aware that Demjanjuk, as we've noted, had once erroneously listed Marchenko as his mother's maiden name on an immigration form; could this be mere coincidence? Wasn't it possible that Demjanjuk and Marchenko were one and the same? Also, Leleko never said that Marchenko and Nikolai were the *only* guards to run the gas chambers.[26] So even if Marchenko was not an alias for Demjanjuk, Demjanjuk still could have been a third operator, the one known as Ivan Grozny. So while it is true that both Leleko and Malagon named Marchenko as one of the operators of the Treblinka gas chamber, a fact that, stated in this way, sounds exculpatory, our closer reading tells a very different story. What we are left with are two statements that contradict each other and sow confusion—but without challenging the case against Demjanjuk.

Given these confusions, we should at the very least expect Moscowitz to have asked the Soviets for additional statements from Treblinka guards who might have been able to clarify matters. Which is precisely what he did. Alas, the Soviets did not respond.[27] Although Moscow clearly possessed the Sobibor and Flossenbürg transfer rosters listing Demjanjuk, it never produced them. Why isn't entirely clear. It is possible that the Soviets were perfectly happy to see Demjanjuk hanged as Ivan the Terrible; indeed, executing the right man for the wrong crime hardly registered as an injustice in a legal system that had compiled an impressive record of executing persons for no crime at all. More likely is the possibility that the Soviets themselves had no idea what was in their files. Those files had been prepared decades earlier in investigations; as years passed, their importance waned, and the replacement of the original generation of archivists by neophytes brought a dramatic loss in institutional memory. After all, it is one thing to have a brilliant system of archiving material, and another to have archivists capable of navigating it and making sense of the material itself. The fact, for example, that many of these younger archivists knew little or no German makes clear the problems they would have had negotiating their own holdings.[28]

Even Parker's smoking gun memorandum looks less damaging on closer examination.[29] Malcolm Gladwell has nicely demonstrated that in the wake of a disaster it is not uncommon to find a warning that in retrospect appears to have foretold it all.[30] Such examples of prescience, Gladwell notes, cause us to overlook the innumerable instances in which alarms are sounded and yet the rocket takes off without incident or the stock market continues its steady rise. Certainly Parker was more concerned about the survivor identifications than was Moscowitz. But this is not to say that Moscowitz wasn't fully aware of the dangers. Both lawyers were intimately familiar with the Walus disaster, as was the OSI as a whole. The Office was determined to avoid the mistakes committed by the US attorneys in that case. Moreover, if some of Parker's worries proved prescient, others proved groundless. His concerns about the Trawniki card—his doubts about both its authenticity and its admissibility—were without merit, and the OSI was correct to ignore them. (It is worth noting that after Parker departed, the OSI amended the complaint against Demjanjuk to include service at Trawniki and Sobibor as alternative grounds for deportation, though the gravamen remained the Treblinka charges.)

This is not to absolve the OSI of all responsibility for the debacle. Wiseman's special master's report faults OSI prosecutors for committing certain acts of negligence and for indulging in "gamesmanship" with the defense on matters of discovery. But Wiseman was also correct to conclude that these missteps did not rise to the level of prosecutorial misconduct or fraud on the court. The problems he identifies as contributing to the calamity are familiar to us—the "intramural disputes" between the Cleveland US Attorneys' Office and the OSI; the "unstable and fractious character of the prosecution team"; the "hostile" relations between the two staffs; and the rapid turnover of lawyers that rendered "institutional memory" inconsistent and unreliable.[31]

Here again we must resist the impulse to personalize these hostile relations. Instead, we need to take a step back and consider the larger forces and structures that contributed to the debacle. These trace back to the very way in which our legal system chose to address the collaborator problem. Having failed to build on the Nuremberg model, American jurists were forced to treat acts of mass atrocity as violations of immigration law. Only with the creation of the short-lived SLU and the OSI did the system move away from what I have called an "ordinary crime model" toward the "atrocity model." In the OSI, the United States finally had an institutional mechanism capable of litigating crimes of state-sponsored atrocity. Even then, however, the absence of special legislation meant that such crimes still had to be litigated through ordinary law. Although dealing with underlying acts of the most extreme criminality, the OSI remained anchored in the world of civil litigation. In recognition of the severity of the civil sanction—denaturalization—OSI cases were controlled by a higher burden of proof, but still remained caught between civil and criminal rules of procedure. The hybrid character of OSI's cases and the absence of statutory guidance clearly contributed to the discovery problems identified by both the special master and the Sixth Circuit panel.

More crucially, the move from an ordinary crime model to an atrocity model inevitably created tensions between the US Attorneys' Offices, which had traditionally handled these cases, and the fledgling OSI. OSI officials understood that success in mastering crimes of Nazi atrocity required a centralization of prosecution and a sophisticated model of litigation based on cooperation with Cold War adversaries and unprecedented collaboration between lawyers and historians. To have such an understanding and to translate it into practice, however, are two entirely different matters. Here it is worth recalling that at the time of the denaturalization trial, the OSI had yet to assign a dedicated historian to the Demjanjuk case; that would not happen until Todd Huebner was brought on in November 1998. Norman Moscowitz was left, then, to puzzle out for himself the conflicting testimonies of Leleko and Maragon. Having studied Russian at Princeton and with a law degree from Harvard, Moscowitz was not unqualified to reason through the material. But it is possible that the presence of an expert, schooled in the relevant history and inclined to question assumptions that quickly hardened into certainties, might have led to a different result.

Ultimately, the OSI inherited the Demjanjuk case when it was less than fully prepared to handle its complexities. The fledgling office was right to wrestle control away from the local US attorneys, but this came at the cost of cooperation and good will between lawyers. The Office had to establish rapport with Soviet and Polish officials, even as it was busy assembling an able staff of lawyers and historians. On one level, Demjanjuk must have looked like a godsend: a case of international stature that promised to justify the existence of the young office (and make careers for its young staff). Alas, the Office had yet to put in place the apparatus, personnel, and practices that would, in the future, permit it to master such complexity. Had the case come to the OSI later in its institutional history, the Office would have handled it with greater sophistication and expertise. And indeed, when the Demjanjuk case did return to the OSI for a second go-around, the results proved very different.[32]

* * *

The finding by the Sixth Circuit panel that the OSI had committed fraud on the court occasioned yet more wearying litigation. The government appealed the ruling, asking that the matter be put before the Sixth Circuit *en banc*. A number of Jewish and Holocaust groups filed briefs in support of the government's petition, arguing, in part, that the panel's ruling would give succor to Holocaust deniers and neo-Nazis around the globe. The argument lacked legal merit, and served only to underscore the fact that the distinction between politics and law often vanishes in high-stakes atrocity trials. In the event, the Sixth Circuit declined to review the matter, and the US Supreme Court likewise turned the government down.

In the meantime, the OSI had asked Judge Battisti, who, as we recall, had presided over Demjanjuk's denaturalization trial and extradition hearing, to reinstate Demjanjuk's deportation order.[33] Battisti agreed to reopen the matter, but not until the government's petition to the Sixth Circuit ran its course. This was to be Battisti's last appearance in the Demjanjuk drama, as the hearty seventy-two-year-old, born eighteen months after Demjanjuk, suddenly succumbed to Rocky Mountain Spotted Fever, contracted from a tick bite that he got on a fishing trip to Montana. With Battisti's death, the Demjanjuk case was reassigned to Judge Paul Matia, a Harvard law graduate and a George H. W. Bush appointee. On February 20, 1998, in response to a motion brought by Demjanjuk's public defender, Matia agreed with the Sixth Circuit panel that lawyers in the OSI had acted with "reckless disregard for their duties to the court." As a result, he vacated Battisti's denaturalization order from 1981, in effect officially renaturalizing Demjanjuk. Seventeen years after being stripped of his citizenship, Demjanjuk was once again an American citizen. But in vacating the order from 1981, Matia did so "without prejudice," meaning that the OSI could again seek to re-denaturalize Demjanjuk—and strip him of his citizenship a second time.

It was not a foregone conclusion that the Office would do so. The implosion of its first case against Demjanjuk and the ruling by the Sixth Circuit had profoundly affected the psyche of the OSI, triggering a dramatic shift in how it handled its cases. In the wake of the "fraud on the court" finding, the American Bar Association and the Office of Professional Responsibility within the Justice Department each launched its own investigations of the Office. And while their separate reports rejected the Sixth Circuit's finding of prosecutorial misconduct, both identified substantial problems with the OSI's way of doing business.

Eli Rosenbaum, a Harvard-educated litigator who had served as the OSI's deputy director since 1988, had become head of the Office in 1995. Under Rosenbaum, a workaholic known for his meticulous preparation and fastidious dedication to doing things properly, the Office embarked on rehabilitating itself. Its database and method of filing evidence were

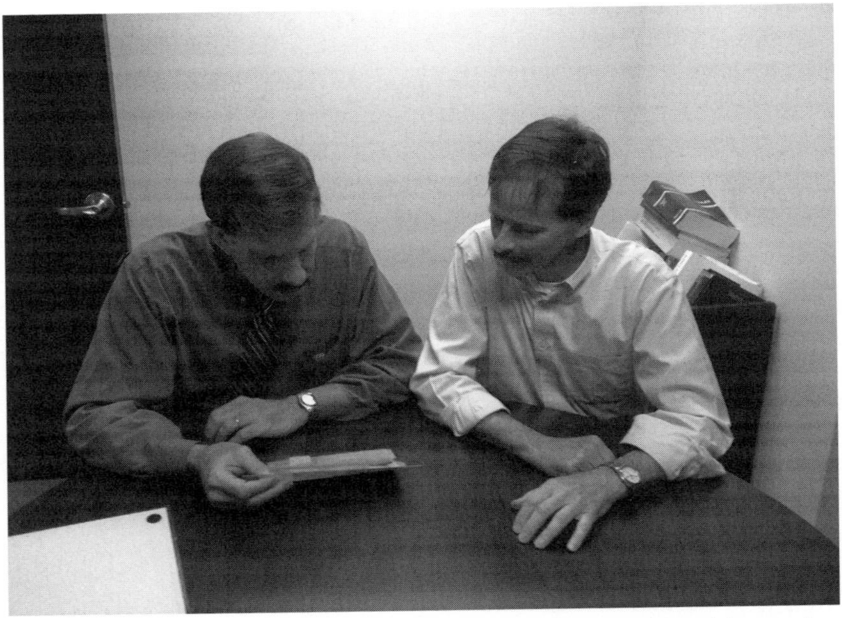

4.2. OSI Director Eli Rosenbaum (left) and OSI historian David Rich examine the Trawniki ID. Photo by author.

completely reorganized and digitized, steps taken to preclude the kind of mistakes that made documents disappear and sounded the alarm bells of conspiracy theorists. Under Rosenbaum, the standard for bringing charges would err on the side of excessive caution; the Office simply could not afford the perceptual costs of another high-profile acquittal. In light of the Sixth Circuit's application of *Brady*, the OSI put into place exceptionally liberal discovery practices that exceeded the *Brady* requirements; these came to resemble "open file" searches, granting the defense just about anything it wanted.

Such practices did not come without costs to the Office. One cannot simply hand—or rather, truck—vast amounts of material over to the defense and expect litigation to move forward expeditiously. The defense requires time to digest the material—months, sometimes years. With alleged collaborators, who are old and getting older, delay serves the interest of the defense. As we shall see, Demjanjuk's lawyer in the Munich trial would attempt to use discovery as a means of grinding the trial to a complete halt. In such time-sensitive cases, the adoption of liberal rules of discovery hands the defense a potent weapon to delay prosecutions and even disable them altogether. Yet the OSI was willing to absorb such difficulties as the acceptable costs of rehabilitating its reputation.

Perhaps the most dramatic shift in the Office's procedures was the move from witness-based proof to documentary evidence. This represented a bold but necessary repudiation of the basic paradigm of Holocaust prosecutions, which sought, as we've seen, to present Holocaust history through the lived memory of survivor witnesses. At first blush, the OSI's shift back to documentary evidence appeared to resurrect the Nuremberg approach, which privileged captured documentary evidence over eyewitness testimony. But this was in appearance only. Nuremberg eschewed survivor testimony chiefly for two reasons. First, since the IMT trial was structured around the Nazis' "crimes against peace"—their waging a war of aggression against their European neighbors—Allied prosecutors understood that few witnesses, except perhaps the defendants themselves, could testify meaningfully about Germany's war plans. As a second matter, given the unprecedented scope and horror of Nazi atrocities, prosecutors feared that survivor testimony would sound incredible. Here the concern was not about the reliability of memory—the events lay in the immediate past—but about the believability of the account. Documents, prosecutors hoped, would silence any skepticism.

Half a century later, proving the basic facts of Nazi atrocity was no longer the OSI's concern. Its cases turned largely on pinning suspects to places and actions. The Demjanjuk catastrophe established that no case could be safely structured around even the most unequivocal survivor identifications. Indeed, the OSI's dramatic shift away from witness-based cases was already well underway before the collapse of the Demjanjuk case: litigations prepared in the 1980s were already structured around documentary evidence, with witnesses brought in for the more modest purpose of educating the judge on the "impact" of persecution, not to identify the accused.[34] The Demjanjuk debacle only made patently clear what was already obvious to many in the Office—that the generation of survivors was disappearing, and the passage of decades had rendered the memory of those still alive vulnerable to distortion.

But if "memory evidence" had shown its unreliability, the same could not be said of the documentary evidence at the OSI's disposal. To the contrary, both the quantity and the quality of documentary evidence available to the Office had grown, and grown vastly, with the end of the Cold War. The disintegration of the Soviet Union made *millions* of pages of material available for scrutiny by the OSI—in principle, at any rate. For old habits die hard, and OSI officials continued to encounter KGB mentalities during research forays to the "New Russia." Still, with no statute of limitations hampering denaturalization cases, the sudden availability of troves of material gave the OSI a new lease on life.

On May 19, 1999, the OSI filed a fresh complaint against Demjanjuk. The decision to do so was Rosenbaum's, though it required the approval of Attorney General Janet Reno, who sought assurances that there would be no unwelcome surprises for the government. Everyone at the OSI recognized the hazards in seeking to denaturalize Demjanjuk a second time. The Demjanjuk disaster continued to cast a long shadow over the unit, marring its otherwise impressive record of success—a record that helped to quell the agitations of those who would have liked to shut down the Office completely. Before refiling charges, the Office had to be certain that such a move was fully supported by the evidence. Over the years, the OSI had assembled an impressive team of historians, a group that included Peter Black, Todd Huebner, David Rich, Steven Coe, and Elizabeth White. These historians did not merely help the Office win its cases; they redefined our historical understanding of the SS's process of recruiting and training the auxiliaries who crucially assisted in genocide. Allan Ryan, an early director, had failed to appreciate the need to fully integrate historians into the preparation of cases, but this changed under Neal Sher, and Rosenbaum further encouraged close collaboration between historians and attorneys. And so the OSI came to function as a kind of institute for advanced studies of Nazi genocide, with the work of its historians finding its way not only into briefs but also into leading scholarly journals.[35]

The new evidence against Demjanjuk found summary in a report prepared for the Office by an outside historian named Charles Sydnor, an expert on the SS death's head division. Sydnor, a charming Southern raconteur with a razor-sharp memory, had proved himself an invaluable expert for the government in fifteen prior cases involving service at concentration camps. His report, which would serve as the key submission at the second denaturalization trial, was, however, actually the work product of Todd Huebner, the first OSI historian to be specifically detailed to the Demjanjuk case. Shy, formal, and precise in his diction, Huebner recalls the actor Anthony Perkins in his twitchier performances. Like Peter Black, Huebner did his graduate training at Columbia under the supervision of István Deák, one of the leading historians of twentieth-century Europe.

The report, drawing extensively on documents made available by the Soviet Union's demise, offers an exceptionally textured history of Demjanjuk's wartime activities and of the operations of the camps to which he was assigned. By his own account, Demjanjuk had been captured by the Germans in the spring of 1942, in the Battle of Kerch, and confined at a POW camp in Rovno. According to Sydnor's report, on June 13 and then again on June 26, two contingents of recruits—men captured in May at Kerch, confined at Rovno, and plucked for special service—arrived at Trawniki, the SS training facility.[36] Each recruit received a *Dienstausweis* (service ID).[37] At the time of Demjanjuk's denaturalization trial in 1981, ID No. 1393 was a piece of exotica the likes of which even the renowned historian Wolfgang Scheffler confessed never to have encountered before. Huebner, by contrast, had examined some forty Trawniki IDs, including that of Danilchenko, the Sobibor guard whose statements helped unravel the Israeli case (see figure 4.3). In the case of Demjanjuk's card, the absence of a date of issuance and the incorrectly recorded height had fueled the allegations of forgery. Huebner's inventory made clear that such omissions and discrepancies were in fact characteristic of Trawniki's shoddy record keeping. Danilchenko's service card also misrecords the guard's height. Even officials at the time were aware of the problem. In 1942, a German policeman who reviewed the camp's records found them to be in a state of "total chaos."[38]

As Huebner demonstrated, Demjanjuk's service number 1393 suggests that he arrived on the June 13 transport.[39] At Trawniki, fresh recruits learned German marching songs and received a crash course in rudimentary Command German—*Achtung! Mach Schnell! Raus!* and the like. Instruction was in German, with a *Volksdeutsche* acting as interpreter, translating the simple lesson plan into, typically, Ukrainian. Basic ideological training also was part of the Trawniki curriculum.

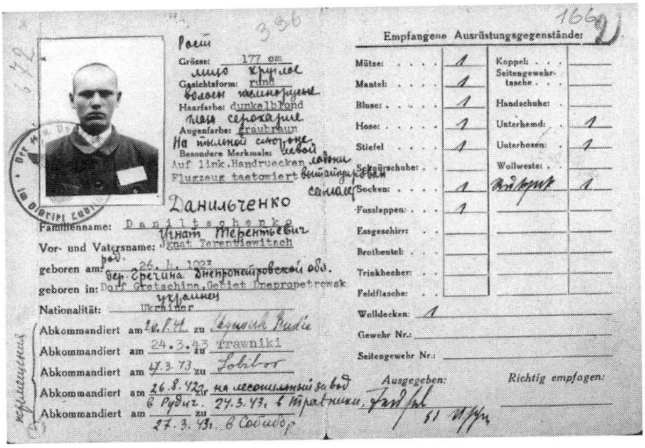

Grösse: 177 cm
Gesichtsform: rund
Haarfarbe: dunkelblond
Augenfarbe: graubraun
Besondere Merkmale: Auf link. Handruecken Flugzeug taetowiert
Familienname: Danilltschenko
Vor- und Vatersname: Ignat Terentiewitsch
geboren am: 26. 1. 1923
geboren in: Dorf Gretschinn, Gebiet Dnepropetrowsk
Nationalität: Ukrainer
Abkommandiert am 24.3.43 zu Trawniki
Abkommandiert am 27.3.43 zu Sobibor
Abkommandiert am ___ zu ___
Abkommandiert am ___ zu ___
Abkommandiert am ___ zu ___

Empfangene Ausrüstungsgegenstände:

Mütze	1	Koppel	
Mantel	1	Seitengewehrtasche	
Bluse	1	Handschuhe	
Hose	1	Unterhemd	1
Stiefel	1	Unterhosen	1
Schnürschuhe		Wollweste	
Socken	1		1
Fusslappen	1		
Essgeschirr			
Brotbeutel			
Trinkbecher			
Feldflasche			

Wolldecken: 1
Gewehr Nr.:
Seitengewehr Nr.:
Ausgegeben:
Richtig empfangen:

4.3. Ignat Danilchenko's Trawniki service ID. Danilchenko recalled serving with Demjanjuk at Sobibor and Flossenbürg. Courtesy Office of Special Investigations, DoJ.

Civilization was in a pitched battle with the *jüdisch-bolschewistisches Hauptfeind* (the Jewish-Bolshevik archenemy); as one alum recalled, recruits were taught "to despise the Soviet system and the Jews," a lesson that presumably many of the Ukrainian and Baltic recruits had already mastered.[40] Recruits were typically issued their own rifles after a week of weapons training. Trawniki also maintained a slave labor camp of Jews, which provided the guards an opportunity to practice their training techniques of herding, guarding, and shooting on live subjects. Training typically lasted two to three months, after which the Trawniki men were assigned to various tasks assisting in the extermination of Jews.

Demjanjuk's service ID indicates that he was assigned to the Manorial Estate Okzow on September 22, 1943.[41] The Okzow estate was part of a system of SS and police bases housed in seized Polish manorial estates. Here Demjanjuk would have guarded the base from partisan attacks, engaged in sweeps against partisans, and possibly also guarded Jewish prisoners.[42] His brief service at Okzow ended on October 14, when he was returned to Trawniki, which served as a hub for further assignments. From there he was transferred to Lublin, where he briefly served as a guard at Majdanek, the vast concentration camp located just outside that city. Part POW camp, part slave labor camp, Majdanek was

4.4. *Falsch Richtig. Wrong Right: A Primer for the SS*. Such illustrated manuals were used to train prospective guards. (Text: "Guarding a group of inmates in the open—above: wrong; below: right. Unloading a transport of inmates—above: wrong; below: right.") Bildarchiv Foto Marburg / Art Resource.

not a death camp per se, but did maintain its own gas chambers for the elimination of weak or enfeebled workers. A camp disciplinary record dated January 18, 1943, firmly places Demjanjuk at the camp. Evidently four *Wachmänner*, including "Deminjuk [*sic*], identification number 1393" had violated a camp quarantine put in place to control a typhus epidemic, traveling to a nearby village to "buy salt and onions."[43] The four were not simply indulging a taste for ethnic cuisine; "salt and onions" was apparently a code for a brothel,[44] and the infraction cost them "25 blows with a stick," a punishment administered three days later.

This was hardly the only instance in which the Trawniki-trained guards showed a lack of discipline; indeed, the entire Trawniki detachment acquitted itself so dismally that it was withdrawn from Majdanek by April 27, 1943. Well before that date, Demjanjuk had already been rotated back to Trawniki, and on March 26, 1943, he was dispatched to Sobibor.[45] We will have occasion to look at Sobibor more closely in chapter 7, but for now it suffices to recall that Sobibor, Treblinka, and Belzec comprised the three pure extermination facilities constructed by the SS in early 1942 as part of Aktion Reinhard, the planned elimination of the Jews of the Generalgouvernement (the large chunk of Poland occupied by Germany but not formally annexed to the Reich). Erected three kilometers from Sobibor, a village of less than five hundred, the camp stood on the edge of a swampy pine forest an hour's walk from the Ukrainian border. With a staff of 15 to 20 SS men and 100 to 120 Trawniki men, the death camp also had a small inmate population of Jews. This group, whose numbers fluctuated but on average included 600 to 700 persons, was forced to assist in the operation of the camp, including the exterminatory process. Demjanjuk remained as a guard at Sobibor for five and a half months, during which time passenger lists show that at least thirty thousand Jews were gassed. Documents do not make clear precisely when he left the death camp, but we know that he returned to Trawniki before October 1, 1943, for on that date he was transferred to Flossenbürg along with 140 other Trawniki men, including his fellow guard Ignat Danilchenko, to serve as part of the Reich's concentration camp system.[46]

Located amid granite quarries in Bavaria's Upper Palatinate, near the Czechoslovakian border, the Flossenbürg concentration camp saw its inmate population grow exponentially in the later stages of the war, from four thousand in June 1943 to over fifteen thousand by March 1945. This growth led to a dramatic deterioration in conditions. Counting its numerous subcamps, Flossenbürg had more than fifty thousand prisoners, including common criminals, political prisoners, and a number of Allied POWs.[47] Its guard force numbered over three thousand. The Sydnor/Huebner report described four separate documents placing Demjanjuk at Flossenbürg, including a weapons log from April 1, 1944, which states not only the make of the rifle and bayonet assigned to "W[achmann] Demianiuk," but also its serial number. While at Flossenbürg, Demjanjuk received a blood-type tattoo under his left armpit; this tattoo was meant to facilitate blood transfusions in case of injury.[48] Demjanjuk remained at Flossenbürg from October 1943 until at least December 10, 1944; from then until the end of the war, his whereabouts could not be clearly established.

The Sydnor/Huebner report conclusively demonstrated the former *Wachmann*'s service at not one camp but *four*. While none of the painstakingly assembled documents casts any light on Demjanjuk's conduct and actions as a guard—a fact that would loom large at his Munich trial—for the purposes of the OSI, the study more than satisfied the standard established by the Supreme Court in *Fedorenko*. The mere fact that Demjanjuk had served as a guard at Okzow, Majdanek, Sobibor, and Flossenbürg established that he had "directly assisted the Nazi government of Germany in implementing its racial and political policies toward the peoples under its control."[49] Demjanjuk had participated in precisely the kind of persecution that should have barred him from acquiring American citizenship.

Evidence alone, however, was not enough; there was also the question of equity. In deciding whether to pursue a second denaturalization trial, the OSI had to consider the fact that Demjanjuk had already spent nearly seven years in an Israeli prison—five of those under a sentence of death. In addition, he had suffered the stigma of being condemned as Ivan the Terrible, in large measure thanks to the mistakes, if not direct misconduct, of the OSI. Then there was the matter of age. Demjanjuk had been sixty-seven at the start of his trial in Jerusalem. Despite a formidable gut, he was a man vigorous enough to humble his young Israeli guards with his punishing regimen of push-ups. Now Demjanjuk was nearing eighty. Would justice be served by bringing charges against an octogenarian who already had experienced a lengthier deprivation of liberty than the overwhelming majority of Holocaust perpetrators? Finally, the Office had to consider the optics of refiling charges. Even if officials believed in the justice of pursuing Demjanjuk, many others would view it as a vendetta, an attempt to punish Demjanjuk for the Office's own previous mistakes. One former government prosecutor expressed this view crudely, recalling later that "the OSI had a hard-on for this guy."

Yet equity also pushed in the other direction. Demjanjuk had succeeded in having his conviction overturned and his citizenship reinstated despite continuing vehemently—and falsely—to deny his wartime service as a *Wachmann*.[50] Concerning the charges brought against him in Israel, his larger lies just happened to tell a local truth: in denying that he had served anywhere, he happened to truthfully claim that he had not served at Treblinka. But after the Sydnor/Huebner report, no fair-minded person could continue to accept Demjanjuk's insistence that he had never trained as an SS auxiliary or served as a guard. To let him live out his years in suburban quiet would reward him for persistent lying. The argument that his advanced age supplied a reason to drop the case was also less than persuasive. Why should age alone, in the absence of infirmity or incapacity, counsel against prosecuting? On April 13, 2014, a gunman opened fire at two Jewish community centers in Kansas City, killing three persons. The alleged gunman, a white supremacist and former leading member of the local Ku Klux Klan, was seventy-three at the time of the attack; no one questioned whether it was fair to arrest the septuagenarian on murder charges.

Age, then, seems less the concern than the passage of time since the alleged crimes. Yet as we have seen, a central and legitimate concern with superannuated prosecutions—that evidence deteriorates with time—most emphatically did not apply in this case. If anything, the passage of decades had made possible the assemblage of a far sturdier scaffold of incriminating documents. Congress, moreover, had already decided that no statute of limitations should apply to such cases; had the OSI placed a de facto prescriptive period on acts of collaboration in Nazi atrocities, it could arguably have been charged with effectively altering federal law, supplanting the intent of legislators.

Still, the passage of time remained relevant as it informed the matter of Demjanjuk's relative complicity. Ivan Grozny was a monster who committed unspeakable atrocities. Demjanjuk, it turned out, had "simply" served as a guard. The evidence does not tell us whether he behaved cruelly; it does not say whether he killed, maimed, or tortured. The material unearthed by Huebner showed that Demjanjuk had presumably visited a brothel and that Danilchenko called him an experienced guard. That is basically all. But while Ivan Grozny engaged in far worse crimes than Demjanjuk, we need also to recall that the question facing the OSI was not whether Demjanjuk had murdered. The question was whether he had assisted in persecuting civilians. The fact of his service at four different camps answered this question clearly. When all factors were considered—and however fraught the matter of equity—OSI's decision to reprosecute was solidly grounded.

Demjanjuk's second denaturalization trial began on May 29, 2001, roughly eight years after his acquittal in Jerusalem. It lasted for two weeks. Trying the case for the OSI was Jonathan Drimmer, a prosecutor known for his hard work and trial smarts. Working closely with him was Huebner, who observed the trial as a spectator and helped draft questions to pose to witnesses.[51] Compared to the carnivalesque atmosphere surrounding Demjanjuk's first denaturalization trial and the Israeli proceeding, the second trial was something of a nonevent. Only a handful of spectators attended the two-week trial presided over by Judge Matia in Cleveland's federal district court, and few media outlets covered it. Demjanjuk was no longer a figure of notoriety, but now just a lowly Ivan, a run-of-the-mill auxiliary in the Nazi system of atrocity. This, of course, made him a far more representative figure of those who facilitated the Holocaust, few of whom were bona fide sadists. But the media weren't necessarily interested in representative figures. A story about a vicious psychopath will trump one about a lowly foot soldier every time.

Significantly, the trial brought neither the accused nor survivors to the stand. Demjanjuk's Jerusalem trial had made it clear to his defense team—which now featured Michael Tigar, an experienced attorney and law professor—that little good could come from letting the accused testify. Indeed, Demjanjuk did not even attend the proceeding (in civil trials the defendant need not be present). The OSI, for its part, was determined to try its case without the testimony of survivors, none of whom could identify Demjanjuk as a guard in any case. Absent allegations of spectacular crimes, absent the drama of survivors describing atrocities, absent the testimony of the defendant (or even his attendance), the trial predictably was largely absent of observers. It resembled an intimate academic conference, with Professor Sydnor offering the sparsely attended keynote address. No longer vouchsafed in the lived memory of survivors, the crimes of the Holocaust had become the stuff of forensic history, to be digested and reconstructed in the sober reports of professionals.

* * *

On February 21, 2002, Judge Matia stripped Demjanjuk of his citizenship for a second time. His short ruling came with a separate Findings of Fact, which essentially offered a digest of the OSI's case. The ruling could hardly be considered a surprise, since Demjanjuk had basically failed to offer a defense. Perhaps hopeful that what had worked once might work again, his team had floated the argument that he was the victim of yet another case of mistaken identity. Now the claim was that the Trawniki ID actually belonged to Ivan *Andreevich* Demjanjuk, Ivan's cousin, about whom no court had ever previously heard a single word.[52] The defense had very little else to offer, beyond insisting that the eighty-year-old was presently in a state of cognitive deterioration and could no longer participate in his defense—a claim supported by no evidence, except perhaps by the bizarre assertion that his cousin had been the guard.

To think, however, that Matia's ruling signaled the end of the American phase of the litigation would be foolishly optimistic. The defense appealed Matia's holding to the Sixth Circuit, which dismissed the appeal and affirmed the denaturalization ruling. The deportation proceeding, assigned to Chief Immigration Judge Michael Creppy, began in December 2004 and ended a year later on December 28, 2005, with the judge's order that Demjanjuk be removed to the Ukraine, Poland, or Germany.[53] In December 2006 the Board of Immigration Appeals upheld the deportation order, as did the Sixth Circuit in January 2008. Almost fifteen years after his return to the States, Demjanjuk again was stateless, financially strapped, and at the end of his legal tether. But the saga was still far from over. John Broadley, a Demjanjuk lawyer of long standing, was convinced that although the OSI had won the most recent skirmish, the larger war would end in stalemate. "You'll never deport my client," he told Rosenbaum.[54]

Broadley's confidence was not unfounded. For all the effort and expense devoted to getting rid of Demjanjuk, American officials could find no country willing to take him. At his deportation hearing, Demjanjuk had argued that his forced removal to Ukraine would violate the Convention against Torture, as he would face brutal mistreatment if returned to his homeland, a claim that Judge Creppy found groundless. Yet Demjanjuk's concern reflected his fluctuating status in his native country. In 1983, his deportation to Ukraine would have meant his trial and possible execution; in 1993, he could have returned home as a national hero. Now, however, Ukraine wanted nothing to do with him. The Ukrainian attorney general's office noted that Demjanjuk had never technically been an Ukrainian citizen, had never applied for Ukrainian citizenship, and moreover was ineligible for extradition as no extradition treaty existed between Ukraine and the United States. In truth, Ukrainian officials worried that a trial would arouse anti-Semitic and nationalist sentiment, while simply accepting Demjanjuk without trying him would complicate Ukraine's efforts to integrate with the West. Facing a lose-lose proposition, Ukraine said no.[55]

As did Poland. In 2002, Poland's Institute for National Remembrance (IPN), a government office responsible for investigating and prosecuting both Nazi and Communist-era crimes, began an investigation of Demjanjuk and other SS auxiliaries who had served on Polish soil. Oddly, the Poles continued to weigh the possibility that Demjanjuk was Ivan the Terrible, and a historian at the Collegium Varsoviensis claimed to have irrefutable proof of this. But at the end of 2007, the IPN suspended its investigation, concluding that there was insufficient proof that Demjanjuk had personally participated in killings.[56] Without the evidence to successfully try Demjanjuk, Poland certainly was not going to provide him sanctuary.

Most vexing of all was Germany's position. Germany over the years had stubbornly refused to accept collaborators whom the United States had denaturalized; indeed, in the years since Hermine Braunsteiner-Ryan's extradition in 1973, Germany had filed only a single additional extradition petition. Typical were the cases of Bronislaw Hajda and Anton Tittjung. Like Demjanjuk, Hajda was a former Trawniki guard who allegedly had participated in massacring Jews, while the Yugoslavian-born Tittjung, a former member of the Waffen SS, had served as a guard at Mauthausen. In 2004, Germany's foreign minister, the former leftist firebrand Joschka Fischer, acting on behalf of the Gerhard Schröder administration and invoking dubious jurisdictional arguments, categorically refused to accept the two.

The reasons for German intransigence, however frustrating to the OSI, were clear. As we will see, German court rulings had made the trial of non-German collaborators in Nazi genocide all but impossible. But if their courts could not try former collaborators, German officials were not about to offer them safe haven. In 2004, the German Foreign

Office (*Auswärtiges Amt*) summarized its view that the country must "avoid the impression that Germany offers refuge for persons with an NS [National Socialist] past."[57] Unable to try such persons, and unwilling to admit them into the country, Germany arrived at the simplest solution. It refused to accept deportees from the United States.

Germany appeared particularly disinclined to have anything to do with Demjanjuk. In October 1993, shortly after Demjanjuk's return to the US, German investigators made the following entry in their file on him: "Was not in Treblinka—was, however, in Sobibor. No proof of individual criminal acts."[58] This conclusion agreed with the later findings of the Sydnor/Huebner report, which likewise offered no account of Demjanjuk's actions as a guard. But whereas service alone—without proof of individual bad acts—sufficed to support a denaturalization action under American law, it did *not* constitute a crime under German law, as interpreted at the time. And if the Germans could not try Demjanjuk, on no account were they going to let him enter the country. Periodically German investigators would review Demjanjuk's file and add a fresh notation of *nein*. In 2003, the director of Germany's Central Office for the Investigation of Nazi Crimes (Zentrale Stelle) noted that Demjanjuk was a "*Wachmann*" in "Trawniki, Okzow, Majdanek, Subobir [*sic*], and Flossenbürg," but added, "The proffered documents do not support an allegation of individual criminal wrong-doing."[59]

So matters stood until early 2008, when an investigator in the German Central Office named Thomas Walther chanced upon the Sixth Circuit's deportation order against Demjanjuk from January of the same year. Walther had been looking for evidence against an eighty-five-year-old who had run the SS kennel at the Ravensbrück concentration camp when a Google search called up the Demjanjuk ruling. Walther was familiar with the general outlines of the Demjanjuk story, but had had no idea that American officials had resuscitated their case and that Germany had been listed as a potential destination. Intrigued, Walther began reading through the Demjanjuk file, setting in motion a process that would culminate in Demjanjuk's arrival on German soil on May 12, 2009, to stand trial as an accessory to mass murder.

5

Demjanjuk in Munich

A German criminal trial lacks the *Law & Order-*, *Perry Mason*-style theatrics that inform American court lore. There are no passionate opening statements or folksy summations designed to sway a jury, for the simple reason that there is no jury. The *Grosse Strafkammer* ("criminal chamber"), the adjudicative instrument in felony trials, is a hybrid body, consisting of three professional judges and two *Schöffen*, or "lay deliberators." In American adversarial justice, the contesting parties—the defense and prosecution—control the flow of information, with the judge playing the role of neutral referee. In Germany, things are very different. The judges manage the case; they decide who will testify and are largely responsible for examining the witnesses.

In the first chapter, we briefly met the presiding judge in the Demjanjuk trial, the tall, bald, and tidily bearded sixty-year-old Ralph Alt (see figure 5.1). Some judges relish attention, but not the soft-spoken, scholarly, chess-playing Alt, who often needed to be reminded to speak audibly, and continued to treat his microphone as a source of puzzlement and discomfort. We saw how the determination to treat the Demjanjuk proceeding like any other criminal case before an ordinary German court resulted in an embarrassingly chaotic first day, with the Munich court wholly unprepared for the crush of media and spectators. Yet as an institutional matter, Demjanjuk's Munich trial *was* an ordinary criminal case. As opposed to Demjanjuk's Jerusalem trial, which convened a specially selected panel that applied international law as incorporated into the Israeli legal code, the Munich court was a stan-

5.1. Presiding Judge Ralph Alt. Photo by Thomas Hauzenberger.

dard German criminal court and Demjanjuk was charged with crimes under the ordinary German penal code.

Joining Judge Alt were the two associate judges, Thomas Lenz and Helga Pflüger. Pflüger remained a quiet but attentive presence at trial, often casting expressions of concern, if not sympathy, toward the defendant propped up on his gurney. Lenz cut a different figure altogether. Black hair combed severely back and glistening with gel, Lenz perfected an expression of chilly superciliousness, dispensing arrogance in liberal doses to all participants in the case, reserving special contempt for Demjanjuk's lead lawyer, Ulrich Busch. Lenz also served as the court's *Berichterstatter*, which means that he prepared the ongoing court holdings in advance of the final written verdict.[1] (That German courts deliberate during the course of the trial is another unusual feature of the system from an American perspective. A friend, who now sits on the Bundesgerichthof [hereafter BGH], Germany's highest appellate court, once invited me to attend a criminal trial he was presiding over; in advance of the final arguments, he blithely told me how he would rule and what sentence he would impose.)

The two lay members of the court, the *Schöffen*, are the closest things to jurors in the German system. Their function, however, is largely symbolic. They are not permitted to see the extensive dossier that has been prepared for the court in advance of the trial, and while they are allowed to question the witnesses, in the course of the eighteen-month trial the two *Schöffen* uttered not a word. Nor did they take any notes. Rather, they sat with fingers crossed, their faces expressing dutiful attention without absorption. A guilty verdict requires a two-thirds majority of the five—an odd mathematical formulation to say the least—so in theory, the laypersons have the power to acquit. But no lawyer I spoke to can recall a single instance of renegade *Schöffen* upsetting the verdict of the professional judges. Even if this were to happen, the *Schöffen* still lack the power to nullify that American juries enjoy, as German prosecutors have an authority that their American counterparts would covet—they can appeal *acquittals*. In these cases, an appellate court can either order a new trial or, in rare cases, directly replace the acquittal with a conviction (typically, though, with a suspended sentence).[2]

Compared to its American counterpart, a German trial is also a remarkably informal affair. Anglo-American rules of evidence are tailored to the jury system. Put less generously, the American system doubts the capacity of laypersons to assess the quality of evidence, and so has developed elaborate rules that carefully police the kind and scope of testimony and proof that can be presented to a jury. Because the German system has no jury, it has few such rules. Hearsay is admissible, as is a history of past convictions. There are no objections per se, as judges are considered experts in weighing the relevance and probity of proof. There are no statements to be stricken from the record, as there is no record. There is a court reporter, but his role is strangely limited to keeping a record of the witnesses, not a transcript of their testimony. (Imagine a transcript that ran *9:04 AM, Mr. Simpson took the stand; 12:20 PM, Mr. Simpson left the stand.*) In certain cases, the general rule against transcripts can be relaxed,[3] and, after Demjanjuk's arrival in Germany, an experienced stenographer named Josef Hrycyk, once honored as the fastest stenographer in all of Germany, wrote to the court suggesting that he be hired "in view of the historical importance" of the case. Alt's two-sentence response—the presiding judge saw "no cause to depart from the prescribed regulations"—underscored his determination to treat the trial as an ordinary proceeding."[4] And so while Hrycyk attended the first week of trial and posted transcripts of these early days on his website, without support from the court his project foundered, and by the third week, he had vanished from the trial.

The informality of the German system generally makes for shorter, more expeditious proceedings. Without the elaborate process of voir dire, without lengthy sidebars, conferences, and debates over the admissibility of evidence, most German trials hum along at a clip. But not all. The Demjanjuk trial, originally expected to last four months, dragged on for eighteen. As we saw in chapter 1, the court, deferring to the doctors who had examined the eighty-nine-year-old defendant, adopted a highly abbreviated schedule of no more than three hours of court per day, and no more than three days per week. The crush of motions brought by the defense slowed the trial even more. But the German court system also enjoys an unusual capacity to absorb and tolerate such delays. Once a jury is impaneled in the Anglo-American system, it is essential for the trial to run continuously. Not only does jury service represent a substantial disruption to ordinary life, but some jurisdictions bar jurors from taking notes, making it all the more critical that the trial proceed in a manner that permits the case to be followed and evidence and arguments to be remembered. The German system operates under no such constraint, and so a trial can be conducted something like a play at a repertory theater—scheduled intermittently over nonconsecutive weeks. German criminal procedure places a limit on the number of weeks that can pass between sessions—a limit that will be tested in the Demjanjuk case—but a court is perfectly capable of presiding over a discontinuous trial.

To an observer, such discontinuities can make for an exceptionally uneven proceeding. Even a typical German trial, one free of delays, does not necessarily provide a more coherent or satisfactory account of the crime than its Anglo-American counterpart. In the adversarial system, the parties construct a version of the events for the jury. The trial becomes a forum for narrative construction and contestation: each side attempts to tell a story that is coherent, followable, and persuasive, while trying to convince the jury that the other side's story is weak, implausible, and riddled with contradictions. Whatever one might say about such a system, it puts a premium on effective storytelling. Not the German system. Indeed, narrative coherence is largely irrelevant in a German trial. Because the court is essentially telling a story to itself, calling witnesses who can present and clarify material contained in the extensive dossier prepared in advance of trial, it is free to move about willy-nilly, jumping from one matter to the next. To an observer, this can make for a most disconcerting experience, as the logic of the case remains utterly opaque until the end.

Here the two systems offer another striking contrast. The American jury remains something of a black box. Occasionally jurors will consent to post-trial interviews, and now and then one will write a memoir of the case. But typically all we hear from a jury is the terse pronouncement, *guilty* or *not guilty*. The German court, however, offers a written verdict. If the trial itself lacks a logical presentation of evidence, coherence is now achieved retrospectively, in the form of the court's written opinion. Not only, then, is the power over judgment concentrated in the hands of the judges; so too is the power over narrative and story. Left blurry during the trial proper, narrative clarity in the German system emerges through the judges' retrospective act of turning opaque proceedings into a coherent judgment.

Because the judges control the flow of information in the German trial, the prosecution's main responsibility—the drafting of the indictment—is completed by the time the trial starts. The two prosecutors in the Demjanjuk case, Hans-Joachim Lutz and Thomas Steinkraus-Koch, were both in their late thirties. In contrast to Judge Alt, Lutz, the chief prosecutor, had previous experience with Nazi cases, having recently successfully prosecuted the former Wehrmacht lieutenant Josef Scheungraber for leading a massacre of Italian civilians (Scheungraber was convicted in 2009 and given a life sentence, though medical experts then declared him *haftunfähig*—incapable of being incarcerated). Lutz's experience notwithstanding, the youth of the prosecutors underscored the noteworthy fact that in Germany the task of bringing the crimes of the

Holocaust to justice has fallen not to the children of the perpetrators but to their grandchildren. To Lutz and other prosecutors of his age, the Holocaust is largely an artifact of history—a subject to be neither quietly avoided nor obsessively debated, but rather soberly treated as a vast and coordinated crime whose remaining perpetrators must be duly prosecuted, however belatedly.

The prosecution's work in a German case is basically completed by the time the trial begins. Once Lutz finished reading the indictment, a task he performed while seated and in a near monotone, his job was largely over.[5] He continued to attend court (his colleague Steinkraus-Koch did so less regularly), at times piping up to reject allegations by the defense that the prosecution had suppressed exculpatory documents. But he rarely questioned a witness.

As for the indictment, it was in certain respects an unremarkable document.[6] Running some eighty-six pages, it was far longer than a standard American indictment, but this is because German indictments typically provide a rather detailed summary of the government's case. Most of the historical and evidentiary material summarized in the indictment restated the OSI's case, and whole passages were lifted from a final investigatory report prepared by the Central Office in Ludwigsburg. The indictment described the creation and recruitment practices of the Trawniki camp, the development of Aktion Reinhard, and the creation of Treblinka, Belzec, and Sobibor. From the general it moved to the specific charges and evidence against Demjanjuk—again relying heavily on the OSI's work product.

Nonetheless, the German indictment did offer some surprises. As the Sydnor/Huebner report had made clear, the evidence of Demjanjuk's service at Majdanek and Flossenbürg was actually more detailed than the material about his time at Sobibor. This is not to suggest that Demjanjuk's time at Sobibor can be subject to reasonable doubt; Demjanjuk's service as a Sobibor *Wachmann* remains irrefutable, particularly when triangulated with the evidence of his service at Majdanek and Flossenbürg. The point is that the Majdanek and Flossenbürg deployments are better documented, as they include details such as Demjanjuk's punishment for indulging his appetite for "salt and onions" during a typhus lockdown at Majdanek, and the serial numbers of his rifle and bayonet at Flossenbürg. It's also worth noting that Demjanjuk's service at Sobibor was far shorter than his service at Flossenbürg—some five and a half months, compared to at least fourteen months at the latter camp. And in a significant coup, Thomas Walther, the German investigator, managed to locate a surviving Flossenbürg *Wachmann* named Alex Nagorny, also a Trawniki man, who served with Demjanjuk and agreed to testify at trial. Yet the German indictment conspicuously avoided charging Demjanjuk with any crimes associated with his service at Majdanek and Flossenbürg; indeed, these two camps hardly receive mention in the detailed indictment, which restricts itself to his service at Sobibor.

The peculiar omission revealed a great deal about the German legal system's handling of the Nazi past. In Demjanjuk's denaturalization trial in the United States, evidence of his service at Majdanek and Flossenbürg importantly supported the OSI's claim that he had assisted in the "persecution of civilian populations," a civil wrong that should have barred him from becoming a US citizen. For German purposes, however, service as a concentration camp guard did not constitute a crime—at least not one that could be prosecuted in a German court. (Courts in the Soviet occupation zone and in East Germany had convicted guards for mere service, but these convictions were set aside after German unification; several guards convicted by these courts were actually *indemnified* by the unified German state.)[7] In fact, even if prosecutors had possessed incontrovertible evidence that Demjanjuk had mercilessly and gratuitously beaten dozens of inmates at Majdanek and Flossenbürg, the indictment would still have focused solely on Sobibor, for the simple reason that such beatings also did not constitute triable offenses. By the time the Demjanjuk trial started, a full half century had passed since Germany had been able to charge Nazi-era criminals with any crime other than perpetrating murder, or with aiding and abetting its commission, the charge leveled against Demjanjuk. The number of victims attributed to Demjanjuk—27,900 (later amended to 28,060)—was extraordinary, but the basic charge, of being an accessory to murder, was strictly conventional.

The Israeli trials of Eichmann and Demjanjuk, as we've observed, used a statute that incorporated crimes against humanity and crimes against the Jewish people, a form of genocide, into Israeli domestic criminal law. Many other Western European nations, including France,

Austria, and the Netherlands, likewise enacted legislation to bring international crimes within the purview of domestic courts. So too did all the countries in the Eastern Bloc, including East Germany. Germany, however, remained an outlier. (Here again I am using "Germany" to refer to the Federal Republic, or West Germany.) German courts rejected the concept of crimes against humanity; and while Germany incorporated genocide into its domestic criminal code in 1954—some thirty-four years before the United States got around to it—its jurists concluded that the crime could not be applied to atrocities committed during the Nazi era, including the extermination of Europe's Jews. The irony in this cannot be overlooked, inasmuch as Raphael Lemkin, the Polish-Jewish adviser to the US War Department whose parents perished at Treblinka, had coined the term *genocide* specifically to name and condemn the extermination of Europe's Jews.[8] In the next chapter, we will examine in detail the complex, politically fraught, and even tragically misguided reasons that prompted German courts to reject the very incriminations designed to facilitate prosecuting Holocaust perpetrators. For now, it suffices to note that without genocide and crimes against humanity in their quiver, German prosecutors were drastically limited in how they could charge participants in Nazi atrocities. By 1960, the statute of limitations had tolled for every crime committed during the Nazi era except for murder. Even murder had long been controlled by a twenty-year statute of limitations. Had this bar remained in place, no German court would have had jurisdiction over *any* crime committed during the Nazi era, no matter how horrific, after May 8, 1965.

The approach of that deadline had triggered a passionate debate in Germany, one followed with consternation around the globe. In 1964, the German minister of justice, Ewald Bucher of the Free Democrats, a small right-centrist party that enjoyed great power as the minority party in the ruling parliamentary coalition, announced his intention not to seek an extension of the statute of limitations for murder. Supported by polls showing that Germans had grown weary of trials of Nazi-era crimes (not that there had been so many to grow weary of), Bucher dismissed concerns that permitting the prescriptive period to toll would insulate perpetrators of atrocity from prosecution. "I can hardly believe," he observed, "that anyone can take seriously the claim, that comes from certain quarters, that tens of thousands of Nazi murderers remain free and unpunished."[9] By "certain quarters," Bucher presumably meant either the international Jewish community or communist East Germany, which took great pleasure in publishing a veritable "Who's Who" of alleged former Nazi perpetrators living freely in the Federal Republic. Beginning in 1957 with a brochure titled *Gestern Hitlers Blutrichter—Heute Bonner Justiz-Elite* (Yesterday, Hitler's Blood Judges—Today, Bonn's Judicial Elite), the East Germans had periodically published the names of legal officials implicated in issuing death sentences to "political and racial" prisoners during the Third Reich.[10] Among those named was Ernst Kanter, president of the criminal chamber of the BGH (Germany's highest appellate court), who had issued draconian sentences as chief judge of the Reich's special war court in Denmark. Nearly three dozen high court judges appeared on the DDR's lists, as did fifteen officials in the Ministry of Justice.

Predictably these lists were dismissed as communist propaganda, and Bucher's opposition to extending the statute of limitations received strong support from Thomas Dehler, himself a former minister of justice, who questioned the justice of trying persons for "actions that happened twenty-five years ago under exceptional circumstances."[11] Dehler further questioned the constitutionality of any attempt to extend or lift the statute of limitations, arguing that "the state cannot expand its powers to punish after the fact."[12] The argument was formalistic in the extreme—after all, granting prosecutors more time to press charges is hardly as problematic as increasing the severity of a punishment after the fact, a favorite practice of Nazi jurists.

The Ministry's opposition to extending the prescriptive period for murder suffered a blow with the arrest in the summer of 1964 of a member of Chancellor Ludwig Erhard's personal security detachment, for having participated in wartime mass executions on the Eastern front. The arrest spurred support for a proposal, drafted by the opposition Social Democrats (SPD), to extend the existing statute of limitations, or drop it altogether. Adolf Arndt, a leading SPD jurist, described his proposal as a "tiny drop of justice owed to honor all those who lie in unknown mass graves."[13]

Matters came to a head with the Bundestag debate of March 10, 1965. Perhaps never before has a technical legal matter occasioned such a moment of national self-reckoning and elevated political discourse. The speeches were of such a quality that they were later collected and published (and excerpts can still be accessed online at the Bundestag's official homepage). Most famous was the speech given by Ernst Benda of the Christian Democrats, the majority party in the ruling coalition. Breaking ranks with many of his fellow conservatives, Benda insisted that the "honor of the nation" was at stake. Certainly Bonn was under pressure from abroad—Jewish groups had weighed in vocally against letting the statute of limitations expire, the *New York Times* had called it a "monstrous distortion of justice to permit men and women who helped to perpetrate the greatest crime of genocide in all history" to go unpunished,[14] and even the Roman Catholic Primate of Poland joined the protests. Speaking from his "own convictions," Benda, who later became president of the Verfassungsgericht (Constitutional Court), passionately argued that it was crucial for Germans to be able to say that "one did what was possible to do." He concluded with words inscribed at Yad Vashem: "The desire to forget lengthens exile, and the mystery of salvation is called remembrance."[15]

For all the impressive rhetoric, the Bundestag in the end only managed to pass a stopgap measure—and that only via a bit of clever legal reasoning. Arguing that Nazi criminals should not benefit from the years of Allied occupation, during which German courts were limited in their ability to try atrocity cases, the government simply recalculated the start date for the statute of limitations for murder, bringing it forward from Germany's capitulation to January 1, 1950. Thus, without actually altering the statute, the Bundestag effectively gave prosecutors another five years—until New Year's Day 1970—to bring charges against those who had committed or aided and abetted Nazi-sponsored murder. Five years later, the approach of this date predictably occasioned a fresh parliamentary debate and the hasty decision to simply extend the prescriptive period for murder from twenty to thirty years. This second stopgap measure gave German prosecutors and legislators a ten-year reprieve, but failed to solve the deeper problem, which once again resurfaced in 1979. The government's third go at addressing the vexing problem happened to coincide with the screening on German TV of the NBC miniseries *Holocaust*. Decried by both German and Jewish pundits as, in Elie Wiesel's words, "a trivialization of the Holocaust," the four-part miniseries unexpectedly struck a tremendous chord within the German public, which watched in record numbers.[16] Whether *Holocaust* influenced the parliamentary debate has itself been debated; in any case, with little discussion the Bundestag finally agreed to lift the statute of limitations for murder altogether.

Welcome as this was, the Bundestag could have done better. In parliamentary deliberations, the jurist and future Interior Minister Werner Maihofer, of the ruling coalition's Free Democratic Party (FDP), had argued in favor of a "more differentiated" and "nuanced" extension. Hoping to introduce a conceptual difference between ordinary murder and genocide into German law, Maihofer argued in favor of letting the prescriptive period toll for the former, but not for the latter—in other words, exempting only exterminatory killings committed during the Nazi period from the statute of limitations on murder. While Maihofer recognized that doing so would make some ordinary killers happy, he insisted that the measure would "write into national memory, even more powerfully than a Holocaust memorial could do," Germany's recognition of the distinctiveness of acts of mass atrocity.[17] Here, as with Israel's passage of the Nazis and Nazi Collaborators (Punishment) Law in 1950, we find a lawmaker proposing a criminal statute as a memorializing gesture—an act of remembrance etched into the penal code. Except in Maihofer's case, the effort failed, as the Bundestag simply lifted the statutes of limitations for all murders.

This meant that German prosecutors could continue to file charges against former Nazis for decades to come, as long as those charges involved committing or aiding and abetting murder. Another problem remained, however. German law, at least in the wake of a Frankfurt trial court's holding in the famous Auschwitz trial (1963–65), appeared to require evidence of an *Einzeltat*—a specific criminal act. In its verdict in the case against twenty-one Auschwitz functionaries, affirmed by the BGH in 1969, the trial court rejected the proposition that "everyone who was integrated [*eingegliedert*] into the camp's exterminatory program, or was somehow active in it, objectively participated in murder." If accepted, the court insisted, such a proposition would compel the conclusion that "a doctor, who was assigned to treat the guardforce, and who narrowly kept to this task, could nonetheless be held guilty as an accessory to murder."[18] The Sydnor/Huebner report, we recall, had adduced no evidence of Demjanjuk's specific behavior or conduct as a guard. This posed no problem in the civil proceeding; as Judge Matia noted, as long as the government could prove that the defendant assisted in persecution, "the degree of participation or involvement in the hostile movement is irrelevant."[19] In the wake of the Frankfurt-Auschwitz proceeding, however, German prosecutors worked from the assumption that the degree of participation or involvement was *directly* relevant—indeed, essential. "Mere" service as a concentration camp guard could not be considered a crime; German courts, it was assumed, could convict only on specific evidence that the accused had participated in an act of murder. Absent such evidence, charges could not even be brought in the first place.

* * *

To understand how Demjanjuk's prosecutors got around this problem, we need to return to Thomas Walther, the German investigator whose diggings into Demjanjuk's case set the Munich trial in motion. Balding but still wild-haired at seventy, with a gaze that holds a touch of Dennis Hopper-like monomania, Walther was, until 2006, a municipal court judge facing a cushy retirement. But while his fellow retirees set about purchasing sailboats for Lake Constance or vacation cottages on Mallorca, Walther had different plans. After stepping down as a judge, he stunned his colleagues by taking a job as an investigator with Germany's Central Office for the Investigation of Nazi Crimes. His motivations were of the deeply personal nature one often finds among Germany's immediate postwar generation. In 1939, Walther's father, who ran a construction firm, had hidden two Jewish families in an overgrown garden and eventually helped them escape Germany. "I hoped," Walther said, "to leave a similar example for my children."[20]

The Central Office in Ludwigsburg bears certain similarities to the OSI. It was created in 1958 to prepare cases against Nazi perpetrators, many of whom were living in Germany with impunity. As I have noted, during the Allied occupation, German courts conducted over forty-six hundred trials of Nazi-era crimes—a number that sounds more impressive than it really is, as few of these cases involved major offenses. After the creation of the Federal Republic, trials of Nazi perpetrators came to a virtual standstill. In 1948, German courts, operating under the watch-

5.2. Central Office investigator Thomas Walther. Walther's fortuitous Google search set in motion the German investigation. Photo by Thomas Hauzenberger.

ful eye of Allied occupiers, condemned 1,819 persons for Nazi-era crimes; by 1955, that number had fallen to twenty-one.[21] The reasons for this dramatic falloff were many. With thousands of former Nazis occupying positions in the administration of justice, from street cops to high court judges, there was precious little political will to confront the problem. Moreover, as in the United States in the years before the creation of the OSI, German efforts to prosecute were stymied by a lack of institutional support and centralized organization. Crime tends to be local, and Germany's federated system, like its American counterpart, was well equipped to deal with ordinary criminal acts, but not with a continent-wide campaign of extermination. Lacking not only the will but the resources, expertise, and even the statutory authority to prepare complicated cases against alleged Nazis, German prosecutors in the 1950s simply did not pursue them.[22]

The situation came to a scandalous head in 1958, when Bernhard Fischer-Schweder, a former member of an *Einsatzgruppe*, a mobile extermination unit responsible for the murder of thousands of Jews in western Lithuania, sued for the reinstatement of his state job. After the war,

Fischer-Schweder, using the imaginative pseudonym Bernd Fischer, had worked his way up to the directorship of a refugee shelter near Ulm. Fired—but not prosecuted—when his wartime activities came to light and frustrated in his efforts to secure another public-sector job, Fischer-Schweder brought suit in a labor court. A survivor of the Lithuanian campaign chanced upon a newspaper article about the lawsuit and wrote a letter to the local paper about the plaintiff's role in mass shootings; the letter, in turn, was forwarded to authorities. This led to the Ulm-*Einsatzgruppen* trial, a watershed in Germany's juridical reckoning with its Nazi past. Ten men from the SS commando Tilsit—including the litigious and foolhardy Fischer-Schweder—were tried in Ulm for the murder of more than five thousand Jewish men, women, and children.

The trial, which lasted from July 28 to August 29, 1958, received extensive press coverage and delivered a shock to the German national psyche. Although the court imposed lamentably light sentences, which varied from three to fifteen years (Fischer-Schweder received ten years and died in prison in 1960), the convictions brought home the fact that the great majority of the Nazis' most extreme atrocities had taken place in the East, in regions now obscured by the Iron Curtain. The Ulm case also gave the lie to the happy myth that most perpetrators had already been punished in the years directly following the war. Finally, it brought to light manifold problems with the existing prosecutorial model, as the Ulm prosecutors themselves complained about the investigative and organizational difficulties they had encountered in mounting their case.[23] Committed jurists tactically used the problems revealed by the Ulm trial to build the case for a special prosecutorial unit. Among politicians, support came less from a moral commitment to the idea—it would be an exaggeration to say that German public opinion was pushing for it—than from a sober calculation of the points that could be scored internationally (and against East Germany) by demonstrating a renewed resolve to take the Nazi problem seriously.[24] And so with the establishment of the Central Office in 1958, Germany finally had a unit specifically dedicated to leading the investigation of Nazi-era atrocities.

From its inception, the Central Office was limited to certain kinds of cases: any crime or constellation of crimes that could not be shoehorned into the statutory law of murder could not be pursued. There were other limitations. The Central Office was denied jurisdiction to investigate crimes of the judiciary. (It was oddly feared that such investigations would encroach on judicial independence.) More fatefully, it was not granted the power to prosecute its cases.[25] And so like the short-lived SLU—and in contrast to the OSI—the Central Office prepared investigations to be forwarded to regional prosecutors. The Central Office developed its own in-house team of investigators, often former prosecutors, in part because it did not trust normal police channels,[26] but, in contrast to the OSI, never hired a staff of dedicated historians. Over the years, it produced thousands of preliminary investigations, but often these went to naught. All too often charges were never pressed, and cases that did go to trial often resulted in acquittals. In the case of convictions, sentences tended to be shockingly lenient. Since the abolishment of the death penalty in 1949, German courts have imposed a life sentence on 170 perpetrators of Nazi-era crimes. The overwhelming majority of those convicted received less than two-years' imprisonment.[27] For Fritz Bauer, the German-Jewish attorney general of Hessen, such paltry sentences came "close to making a mockery of the victims' suffering."[28] Or as one official in the Office characterized it, "ten minutes prison for each dead."[29]

A final difference between the OSI and the German Central Office is worth noting. In 2010, the OSI was officially renamed Human Rights and Special Prosecutions (HRSP) and given expanded authority. No longer limited to prosecuting Nazi-sponsored acts of persecution under US civil law, HRSP could now bring criminal charges against any US resident suspected of serious human rights violations, such as torture, war crimes, and genocide, wherever those atrocities were perpetrated. The change in 2010 did not change the Office's handling of Nazi collaborator cases, but in the case of, say, a naturalized American citizen from Africa accused of human right abuses in the Darfur region, prosecutors could now file criminal charges. This change empowered the Office to function as it might have from the outset—as one charged with prosecuting crimes of atrocity. Yet the change has been something of a mixed blessing to OSI historians, experts in the Nazi era who suddenly found themselves reassigned to cases involving Bangladesh or Somalia, areas about which they knew next to nothing, and resulted in a small exodus of historians from the Office, including Todd Huebner.

Nonetheless, it meant that the OSI, reconfigured as HRSP, would continue to have a future—unlike Germany's Central Office, which even now remains statutorily bound to the investigation and prosecution of Nazi-era crimes alone. When the last perpetrators die off, the Central Office will simply close shop.

Indeed, when Walther joined in 2006, the Central Office was already winding down its operation. In the preceding decade, German courts had convicted exactly four Nazi-era criminals.[30] The Office, housed in an old building on the outskirts of Ludwigsburg that once served as a prison for women, had a neglected feel. Of a staff once totaling over 120, a group of just six lawyers, judges, and investigators remained, assisted by a dozen other staffers. Presiding over the Office's gradual dissolution was Kurt Schrimm. A career prosecutor, Schrimm had successfully tried Josef Schwammberger, a former SS commandant of Jewish slave labor camps, who was convicted in 1992 and sentenced to life imprisonment for atrocities committed in Przemysl, in southeastern Poland.[31] As opposed to Walther, who saw his work in Ludwigsburg as a calling, Schrimm described his elevation to the directorship as a "pure career move."[32] His prosecution of Schwammberger notwithstanding, he professed no particular interest in Nazi cases and no great expertise—in fact, when he assumed directorship of the Central Office in 2000, he had never heard of the OSI. This was the beginning of an inauspicious relationship with his American counterparts, who considered Schrimm an intelligent though colorless bureaucrat, unwilling to rethink received positions or to explore fresh prosecutorial angles. This assessment was largely shared by his own investigators, who viewed their boss as a man moved by two passions: gardening and collecting model Märklin trains, one of which he kept proudly displayed on his office desk.

About Demjanjuk, Schrimm showed little interest: it was Schrimm who in 2003 had penned the comment: "Wachmann: Trawniki, Okzow, Majdanek, Subobir [*sic*], and Flossenbürg; proffered documents do not support an allegation of individual criminal wrong-doing." Still, Schrimm indulged Walther's desire to take a fresh look at the case. Walther promptly enlisted the help of another investigator at the Central Office named Kirsten Goetze. Appointed to a Berlin judgeship in 1993 at the age of twenty-seven, Goetze had also felt a calling to work at the

5.3. Central Office investigator Kirsten Goetze. Goetze framed the legal theory used by the Munich prosecution. Photo by Todd Huebner.

Office, which she joined in 2006, shortly before her fortieth birthday. Walther and Goetze began putting in twelve-hour days and took fact-finding trips, to Israel in April 2008, and then to D.C. the next month. On May 28, 2008, they gave Schrimm an eight-page document sketching out the outlines of the case.

2008 happened to mark the fiftieth anniversary of the founding of the Central Office, and some have speculated that Schrimm saw a high-profile case as a fitting valedictory for the Office. Others have speculated that a man as constitutionally cautious as Schrimm would never have made the decision to order a full investigation on his own—the OK must have come from above. *Die Zeit* reported that, far from simply assenting, then Bundespräsident Horst Köhler actually pressured the Office to move against Demjanjuk, a claim that Schrimm dismissed as "utter nonsense."[33] In any case, Schrimm provisionally gave a green light, and Walther and Goetze began preparing their full report, with Walther handling the evidentiary questions and Goetze dealing with the legal ones. A tireless investigator, Walther was obsessed by what he called Demjanjuk's "microcosmos"—the circle of friends, social acquaintances, and associates around whom he had orbited. Walther took trips to Landshut, one hour northeast of Munich, where Demjanjuk had spent nearly three years as a displaced person. He plunged into the vast holdings of the International Tracing Service at Bad Arolsen. While searching for a list of witnesses at Demjanjuk's wedding in Regensburg, he discovered that Jakob Reimer, another Trawniki man, had lived less than a kilometer from the newlyweds. (Reimer also later emigrated to the United States where he too became the subject of a protracted deportation case.) Using an old address registry and Google Earth, Walther also discovered that a group of former Trawniki guards had all lived in Landshut in close proximity to one another, like former frat brothers reestablishing old bonds. This led Walther to Alex Nagorny, the former Trawniki and Flossenbürg guard, who later testified at trial. Address in hand, Walther drove to Landshut, where Nagorny still lived, and knocked on his door. Asked if he had known an Ivan Demjanjuk, the small wiry Nagorny simply answered, "Yeah, Ivan lived here in my apartment."[34]

Walther still hoped to find evidence of an *Einzeltat*—a specific act of killing that could be attributed to Demjanjuk. In an email to OSI director Eli Rosenbaum, Walther wrote, "I pray (yes indeed) that we will find the single concrete murder which we can tie together with the person of D."[35] But no amount of research could find it. Rosenbaum, for his part, had long considered the *Einzeltat* requirement a dreadful mistake in German case law that erected all-but-insuperable obstacles to prosecution. In conversation with Walther, he insisted that the American *Fedorenko* doctrine, which held that mere service as a concentration camp guard sufficed to establish complicity in persecutory acts, provided a template that the Germans could follow. He provided Walther with a list of American cases that had adumbrated this understanding, starting with the US Army trial of SS personnel in Mauthausen in 1946, in which an army military court had held that ". . . a member of the Waffen SS, Allgemeine SS, or any guard or civil employee, in any way in control of or stationed at or engaged in the operation of the Concentration Camp Mauthausen, . . . is guilty of a crime against the recognized laws, customs, and practices of civilized nations."[36] He also cited the Seventh Circuit's decision in *Kairys v. INS* in 1993, in which Judge Richard Posner had upheld the deportation of a Treblinka guard. "If the operation of such a camp were treated as an ordinary criminal conspiracy," Posner had ruled, "the armed guards, like the lookouts for a gang of robbers, would be deemed coconspirators, or if not, certainly aiders and abettors of the conspiracy; and no more should be required to satisfy the . . . provision . . . that makes assisting in persecution a ground for deportation."[37]

Actually, Rosenbaum might have quoted holdings much closer to home for Walther. In a number of earlier trials of death-camp functionaries, German courts had appeared to accept precisely the argument rejected in the Frankfurt-Auschwitz trial—namely, that service alone *was* tantamount to aiding and abetting murder. In upholding the conviction of SS functionaries at Chelmno, the small death camp that made use of mobile gas vans, the BGH reasoned that "the nature of the specific task that persons assigned to the specific killing actions performed is . . . without importance."[38] In cases brought against Sobibor functionaries, such pronouncements assumed even sharper form. As early as 1950, in the trial of two SS officers at the camp, Hubert Gomerski and Johann Klier, a court in Frankfurt held that "all those active in Sobibor . . . were linked to a single process [*Geschehensablauf*] whose sole purpose was the killing of Jews."[39] The court's comments on Klier, who had overseen the camp's bakery and later the *Schuhkommando*—the group responsible for collecting, sorting, and storing the shoes of the murdered Jews—were particularly remarkable. "Every activity," the court insisted, "was necessary for the operation of the camp. In this regard, the activities of the accused Klier in the bakery, as well as in the *Schuhkommando* were causally related to the success [of the killing operation]."[40] Sixteen years later, in a trial of a group of SS functionaries at Sobibor, a court in Hagen held that "in the case of these nine defendants, it has not been proved that any of them killed Jews with their own hand or that they caused Jews to be killed out of their own individual initiative. Nevertheless, in their organizational deployment within the camp, they facilitated the mass murder of Jews through their functional participation [*funktionelle Mitwirkung*]."[41]

Still, Rosenbaum's arguments left Walther and Goetze less than convinced. What sufficed for establishing assistance in persecutory acts would not suffice for establishing complicity in murder. German criminal law, moreover, was far less receptive than American law to prosecutions based on conspiracy. As for the earlier German decisions, it appears the investigators were not even aware of them. But even if the investigators had known of these holdings, it's not clear what difference it would have made. First, as I noted previously, after the BGH's appellate ruling in the Frankfurt-Auschwitz proceeding in 1969, the Central Office simply worked from the assumption that success at trial required proof of an *Einzeltat*. As a consequence, many investigations were dropped or never pursued in the first place. Certainly the Frankfurt-Auschwitz ruling came in for its share of criticism—including a short but probing critique by Hannah Arendt, which accused the court of failing "to take into account . . . nothing less than the everyday reality of Nazi Germany in general and of Auschwitz in particular."[42] And yet we find no evidence of jurists arguing that the Central Office had drawn the wrong inference from the BGH's ruling.[43] Secondly, the earlier Sobibor holdings were hardly as decisive as the language quoted above might suggest. The theory of "functional participation," for instance, was often iterated in the context of *acquittals*. The Frankfurt court that concluded in 1950 that supervising Sobibor's bakery constituted support of the killing process nonetheless acquitted Klier on all charges; similarly, the Hagen court that embraced the idea of "functional participation" in the killing process acquitted five former Sobibor SS men. (These acquittals, as we shall see in chapter 8, were typically based on putative necessity—the idea that death camp guards reasonably believed that the refusal to participate would have put them in jeopardy of life and limb.)[44] The fact that the judicial embrace of a theory of functional participation appeared in acquittals certainly obscured its importance. Finally, we should note that even when courts in these earlier cases could not attach the accused to specific acts of killing, they had been certain of the specific tasks and responsibilities of each of the individual SS men. In Demjanjuk's case, investigators only knew that he had served as a guard—nothing more or less.

It was Kirsten Goetze who saw a way to adapt the American approach to the drastically more restrictive doctrinal realities of German law. Her breakthrough argument, which perhaps can be better understood as a resuscitation of a doctrine that never properly took hold, did not challenge the high court's decision from 1969 in the Auschwitz case, but instead crucially sought to distinguish Sobibor from Auschwitz. Like Majdanek, Auschwitz-Birkenau had been a hybrid facility, part death camp, part prison and forced labor camp. Of the 1.2 million persons sent to Auschwitz, about 100,000 survived. This is a death rate in excess of 90 percent; considered as a disease, Auschwitz was astonishingly lethal. But compare this figure to the three pure extermination facilities built as part of Aktion Reinhard. About 1.5 million Jews were "resettled" to the killing centers of Treblinka, Belzec, and Sobibor. No more than 120 lived, a death rate of 99.99 percent.[45]

In their final report submitted on November 11, 2008, Walther and Goetze argued that Sobibor had been a pure extermination facility, whose sole purpose was to murder Jews. Even in the case of hybrid facilities such as Auschwitz and Majdanek, it would be hard to say what exactly a guard's specific responsibilities had been absent actual proof; prosecutors would indeed need evidence of an *Einzeltat* in order to prove the accused had aided and abetted murder. Not so with Sobibor. Sobibor had been a pure killing center, whose small staff of SS men and Trawniki guards were there to operate a killing machine; this exclusive function, she argued, made the absence of evidence about Demjanjuk's specific behavior at Sobibor irrelevant as a matter of law. The fact alone that he served as a *Wachmann* at a death camp should suffice to prove guilt. Sobibor guards were accessories to murder because facilitating murder was their job.

And so the report focused exclusively on Demjanjuk's five and a half months of service at Sobibor, hardly mentioning Flossenbürg and Majdanek. Only at Sobibor had Demjanjuk *necessarily* been an accessory to murder. About this five-plus-month period, the report offered gruesome detail. As I have noted, the killing centers of Aktion Reinhard were designed to exterminate Jews in the Generalgouvernement, the large tract of occupied Poland under Nazi colonial administration. But as the Final Solution turned into a continent-wide killing program, these camps were also used to murder Jews from other countries. During the months of Demjanjuk's service—from late March until mid-September 1943—most of the Jews killed at Sobibor came from the Netherlands. The Dutch numbers during this period are known quite exactly: 29,579 delivered on fifteen trains.[46] Of these 29,579, some presumably would have died in transit, though this number would have been quite small, as the

Dutch Jews at times arrived on regular passenger trains, and even the conditions in the freight transports were far more tolerable—and survivable—than was the case with the transports of Polish Jews, who were mercilessly crammed into cattle cars without food, water, or adequate ventilation. (A sixty-kilometer trip within occupied Poland could result in the death of 10 percent of the passengers; transports from Warsaw to Treblinka, barely a one-hundred-kilometer trip, could take as long as three days, as trains idled on sidings.) A tiny fraction would also have been chosen by the SS on arrival as *Arbeitsjuden*, "work Jews." By deducting these two groups, the indictment settled on the number 27,900, a figure that later was bumped up to 28,060 in light of evidence that two truckloads of Polish Jews were also dispatched to Sobibor during the months in question.

Walther and Goetze's examination of the deportation lists from the Netherlands also helped solve a second potential obstacle to prosecution—the matter of jurisdiction. The question of which German court should handle the case proved easier to answer than the question of whether *any* German court could. Because Demjanjuk had lived in DP camps close to Munich, Munich would hear the case—assuming a German court had jurisdiction. Demjanjuk, after all, was not a German citizen, and his alleged crimes did not occur on German soil (the Nazis had never claimed the Generalgouvernement as formally part of the Reich). In the past, German courts had concluded they lacked jurisdiction over non-Germans accused of extraterritorial crimes. Walther and Goetze offered two arguments in response. First, they argued that as a Trawniki-trained *Wachmann*, Demjanjuk had functioned as a German *Amtsträger*—essentially, a person holding an official position—and so fell under the jurisdiction of German law. Second, having scoured the lists of Jews deported from the Netherlands to Sobibor during the spring and summer of 1943, Walther and Goetze discovered 1,939 Jews who formerly had been German subjects.[47] Like the family of Anne Frank, these were Jews who had fled Germany for the presumed safety of the Netherlands. This discovery permitted Walther and Goetze to argue jurisdiction based on the principle of "passive personality"—the notion that a domestic national court can hear cases involving extraterritorial crimes committed by a foreigner against the court's own nationals.

This latter argument, which would have limited the trial to Demjanjuk's role in assisting the murder exclusively of the 1,939 German Jews, potentially raised interesting legal questions, inasmuch as an amendment from November 25, 1941, to the *Reichsbürgergesetz* (the Reich's citizenship law) had technically rendered any German Jew who took up residence abroad stateless.[48] (The Nuremberg laws of 1935 had stripped German Jews of full Reich citizenship but had continued to treat them as *Staatsangehörige*, "legal subjects.") By virtue of this amendment, any Jew deported, say, from Berlin to Auschwitz immediately ceased to be a German legal subject as soon as the train crossed the frontier. In 1968, the Bundesverfassungsgericht (the Constitutional Court) declared the odious law as legally nugatory, effectively reconferring legal subjecthood on exiled and deported German Jews.[49] However laudable the decision, it was hard to square with the more general juristic practice of the Federal Republic, which, as we shall see in the next chapter, tended to give legal effect to promulgated Nazi law. In any case, the potentially interesting colloquy over jurisdiction based on the nationality of the victims was preempted by the court's decision that Demjanjuk, as a *Wachmann*, had indeed served as a German official. This meant not only that Germany had jurisdiction, but also that it could try Demjanjuk for his role in the murder of all known deportees to Sobibor during the period of his service, and not merely the Germans among them.

On November 4, 2008, Walther and Goetze sent a draft of their report to Munich, traveling three days later to discuss their investigation with state prosecutors. (The ever-cautious Schrimm chose not to accompany his investigators to this crucial meeting.) In early January 2009, Eli Rosenbaum flew to Germany to urge prosecutors to answer the victims' last mute cry for justice, a histrionic appeal that infuriated though also may have helped convince Rosenbaum's recalcitrant German colleagues. On January 30, 2009, the Bayerisches Landeskrimininalamt, the Bavarian State Office of Criminal Investigations, having completed its review of Walther and Goetze's report, recommended prosecution; and on March 10, 2009, an investigative magistrate of Munich's district court issued the arrest warrant. Goetze briefly looked into the feasibility of renting a private jet to bring Demjanjuk from the States to Germany. (Not realizing that the jet was intended for a different kind of client, the rental agent politely inquired whether Goetze also wanted a case of champagne.) As it turned out, the OSI arranged the flight. At the last moment, officials in the German Ministry of the Interior had to be reminded to remove Demjanjuk's name from the no-entry list he had been placed on in the aftermath of the Israeli acquittal. Eli Rosenbaum, terrified that a last-second snafu would abort the whole effort, found himself too nervous to follow the course of the flight. Only after he received the thinly coded pronouncement "the albatross has landed" did he allow himself to feel a measure of relief.[50]

The case against Demjanjuk looked strong. German jurists had accepted jurisdiction over the accused, and by focusing exclusively on Demjanjuk's activities as a *Wachmann* at Sobibor, Goetze had seemingly found a way around the presumed need to show evidence of an *Einzeltat*. It was, by all measures, a simple and an elegant theory. The only problem was that in the recent history of the Federal Republic, no court had come close to adopting it. Christiaan Rüter, a Dutch professor of criminal law and lead editor of the comprehensive series *Justiz und NS-Verbrechen* (Justice and Nazi Crimes), has dedicated his career to the study of German court decisions involving Nazi-era crimes. On the eve of the historic trial, Rüter found little reason for optimism. "It is entirely bewildering," he ruefully noted, "how anyone familiar with the German legal system could expect a conviction of Demjanjuk with this evidence."[51]

6

Was damals Recht war . . .

To understand Rüter's pessimism we need to step back and take a closer look at the vexed history of how German courts dealt with Nazi-era crimes. Germany, as we've observed, rejected the "atrocity paradigm," the approach to Nazi criminality pioneered at Nuremberg, which called for special courts and special law to address the juridical challenges posed by state-sponsored mass crimes. Instead, the German legal system insisted on using ordinary criminal courts and its ordinary criminal code. The reluctance to use *Sondergerichte*—"special courts"—was understandable, as the very term conjures images of Nazi jurists handing out death sentences left and right. But the refusal to use special law is another matter. As we saw in the last chapter, Germany could have avoided the entire debate over the statute of limitations for murder had it chosen to charge Nazi-era perpetrators with crimes against humanity or genocide, both imprescriptible crimes. But this Germany refused to do.

The perversity of this refusal can be better appreciated when we consider the fact that Germany incorporated genocide into its legal code early on, in 1954—and that it has in fact successfully mounted genocide prosecutions. Genocide prosecutions remain a rarity and have typically been staged before specially constituted international criminal courts, such as the two UN ad hoc tribunals created to address crimes committed during the Yugoslavian civil war and the Rwandan genocide, respectively. Only a few countries in the world have tried and convicted perpetrators of genocide before their own domestic national courts, and Germany is one of them. But these trials are all of recent vintage, involving perpetrators from the Yugoslavian war who fled to Germany.[1] No German court has ever tried a perpetrator of Nazi-era atrocities on charges of genocide.

German courts are also among the few domestic national courts to have prosecuted persons for crimes against humanity. But these trials are all old, having been conducted by German courts in Allied occupation zones between 1946 and 1950. Indeed, in the very first German trial involving atrocities at Sobibor, a court in Berlin convicted the camp's *Gasmeister* (gas master) Erich Bauer of crimes against humanity.[2] (Bauer's death sentence was later commuted to life imprisonment.) The assumption of sovereignty by the Federal Republic, however, brought trials involving crimes against humanity to a screeching halt (although they continued in East Germany).[3] The last German trial involving crimes against humanity concluded over six decades ago.

What makes this all the more remarkable is the fact that the legal concepts of crimes against humanity and genocide were, as we have seen, fashioned to facilitate the prosecution of Nazi perpetrators. Crimes against humanity were first recognized as international crimes at Nuremberg, and genocide, coined by Lemkin in 1944, became a crime in international law by UN convention in 1948.[4] Why, then, have German courts consistently refused to use the very incriminations designed to name and condemn Nazi atrocities?

At first glance, the answer seems straightforward: German jurists concluded that the bar against retroactivity (*Rückwirkungsverbot*) prohibited such prosecutions. The idea that "an act can only be punished if its criminal wrongfulness [*Strafbarkeit*] was legally determined before the act was committed" is a principle both anchored in the German Basic Law (GG Artikel 103, Abs. 2) and repeated verbatim in the criminal code, where it appears as the first and most fundamental norm of the system of criminal justice (§1 StGB).[5] Bars against retroactivity are, of course, familiar to virtually all theories of jurisprudence and legal systems. The bar is essential to the rule of law; Montesquieu and Beccaria described it as foundational to the concept of justice, and the German legal theorist Feuerbach is credited with formulating the principle into the Latin maxims dutifully committed to memory by all students of international law: *nullum crimen sine lege, nulla poena sine lege*—no crime without (preexisting) law; no punishment without (preexisting) law.[6]

Today, virtually all German jurists reflexively accept that the bar against retroactivity erects a legally compelled, unavoidable obstacle to trying former Nazis for genocide or crimes against humanity. Kurt Schrimm of the Central Office put it this way:

> This [Article 103 of the Basic Law] has meant that German investigative and judicial officials, in contrast to the Allies, who . . . introduced and largely defined the elements of war crimes and crimes against humanity, have had to rely on the incriminations that already existed at the time of the so-called Third Reich.[7]

Schrimm acknowledges that by forcing prosecutors to rely on the ordinary crime of murder, the *Rückwirkungsverbot* hampered efforts to bring perpetrators of Nazi atrocities to justice: "It was . . . the task of the German judicial system to deal with these atrocities with legal instruments that weren't . . . equal to the task."[8] And yet he has never questioned the received wisdom that prosecuting former Nazis for genocide or crimes against humanity would violate the retroactivity bar. Because the crimes in the former Yugoslavia occurred well after genocide became part of the German criminal code, prosecuting Serbs who surfaced in Germany posed no retroactivity problems. Only when it came to trying former Nazis did the bar come crashing down.

Indeed, a belief in the *justice* of applying the bar to Nazi crimes enjoys near universal acceptance among jurists in Germany today. At Demjanjuk's Munich trial, I asked Stefan Schünemann, a lawyer representing a Sobibor survivor, if he regretted that the defendant could not be tried for aiding and abetting genocide. His response was automatic: "It would be wrong to use retroactive law to try even the worst criminals."[9] To be sure, German jurists are not alone in this belief. Article I, Section 9, of the US Constitution erected the world's first constitutional bar to ex post facto law, and we have seen that concerns about retroactivity discouraged American jurists and lawmakers from exploring the creation of new law to enable criminal prosecutions of ex-Nazis living within our borders. And yet not all domestic legal systems shared these concerns. As we have observed, the German response to Nazi crimes very much described the minority position among European legal systems. While it is true that the American response bears some resemblance to the German, we must remember that the problem of "quiet neighbors" only began to register as a political and legal issue in the United States in the 1970s, long after America had wrapped up its postwar trial program. The statutes that today authorize the reconstituted OSI to file criminal charges are all of recent ilk; the Senate did not get around to ratifying the Genocide Convention until 1988, a full four decades after the Convention, and the international crimes of torture and war crimes were incorporated into federal law in 1994 and 1996, respectively. For better or worse, American lawmakers never seriously had to debate whether applying these laws to "quiet neighbors" would have violated the Constitution, as the laws all came too late.

In Germany, by contrast, the argument over retroactivity represented *the* most important jurisprudential debate of the immediate postwar period. The problem surfaced early and often, starting at the trial before the International Military Tribunal at Nuremberg (IMT). Of the three substantive crimes charged to the defendants—crimes against peace, war crimes, and crimes against humanity—the first charge, crimes against peace, raised the greatest concerns. André Gros, French delegate to the London Conference that drafted the IMT Charter, made the point most bluntly, initially insisting that the crime of aggressive war was "a creation of four people who are just four people."[10] The tribunal sought to address the retroactivity problem with two arguments. On the one hand, it allowed that as a technical matter the Charter may have framed retroactive law, but held that such retroactivity was justified in a case involving such extreme acts. On the other, it insisted that settled law "had been clearly pronounced when these acts took place"—that is, there was *no* violation of *nulla poena*.[11]

This argument—conceding, on the one hand, that justice required a relaxation of the bar against retroactivity while insisting, on the other, that Nuremberg's law was not retroactive—largely failed to answer the continuing criticisms of crimes against peace. But it did appear to silence doubts about crimes against humanity, perhaps because such doubts had never really surfaced in the first place. As one commentator has observed, "Although the expression [crimes against humanity] was codified for the first time in the IMT statute, no violation of the *nullum crimen* principle was linked to this charge."[12]

But shortly after the conclusion of the trial of the major war criminals, the retroactivity problem did come to engulf crimes against humanity. *United States v. Josef Altstoetter, et al.* was one of the twelve so-called subsequent trials staged by the Americans in their zonal military tribunal in Nuremberg (the Nuremberg Military Tribunal, or NMT).[13] Known to posterity as the "Justice" case, *United States v. Josef Altstoetter* placed sixteen legal figures from the Nazi state on trial—nine former officials in the Reich Ministry of Justice and seven members of the People's or Special Courts. Missing were the Nazis' most notorious jurists, as they had been killed in the war or had died of their own hand. (Roland Freisler, chief judge of the *Volksgericht* and perhaps the Reich's most infamous legal figure, died, appropriately enough, in his own courtroom during an Allied bombing.) But if the case lacked notorious defendants, it nevertheless captured attention for effectively putting Nazi law itself on trial. As Telford Taylor aptly put it in his opening statement, "This case is unusual in that the defendants are charged with crimes committed in the name of law."[14] (This unusual confrontation, in which jurists stood trial for perverting the very fabric of ordered legality, delivered the material for the screen classic *Judgment at Nuremberg*, certainly one of the great legal dramas to come out of Hollywood.)[15]

The prosecution's case focused on the defendants' participation in crimes against humanity as defined by the trial program's authorizing statute, Control Council Law No. 10 (CCL 10). This Allied document, signed on December 20, 1945, less than five months after the promulgation of the Nuremberg (IMT) Charter, authorized the Allies to conduct independent trials in their respective occupation zones for the same three substantive crimes charged to the IMT defendants: crimes against peace, war crimes, and crimes against humanity.[16] And yet rather remarkably, CCL 10 altered Nuremberg's definition of crimes against humanity.[17] According to the IMT, only those crimes against humanity that had a clear connection or "nexus" to the Axis' aggressive war were deemed justiciable before the international tribunal. This meant that any crime against humanity committed before the start of the war—such as the Nazi-orchestrated pogrom in November 1938 known as *Kristallnacht*—fell outside of the IMT's jurisdiction. This holding was consistent with the tribunal's understanding that aggressive war was the crime that gave rise to all other Axis atrocities—and with its belief that the Nazis' treatment of fellow Germans before the outbreak of hostilities was none of its business.

CCL 10 severed this so-called nexus requirement.[18] This meant that Allied zonal trials could in principle condemn *all* Nazi crimes against humanity, even those unconnected to Nazi war making.[19] Just as remarkable as the change itself, however, was the fact that many judges of the successor trials refused to accept it or utterly failed to grasp it, and continued to hew to Nuremberg's nexus requirement. But not the judges in the Justice case. According to one observer, the judges in this case "deliberately went out of their way" to recognize and endorse CCL 10's new construction of crimes against humanity.[20] In doing so, they claimed an authority specifically repudiated by their colleagues on the IMT, namely, the right to condemn Nazi officials for peacetime crimes against their own citizens—in other words, for acts that were lawful under then operative domestic law.[21] This bold assertion made the retroactivity problem for crimes against humanity inescapable, and it is no surprise that the defense in the Justice case attacked CCL 10 as a violation of *nulla poena*.

What principle of legality authorized the judges in the Justice case to condemn acts permitted under German domestic national law? In an attempt to sidestep the entire problem, the court insisted that the defendants' actions had violated both international law *and* German law in effect at the time: "Many acts constituting war crimes and crimes against humanity as defined in CCL 10 were committed in direct violation . . . of the provisions of the German criminal code."[22] This argument was crucial for the court, enabling it to insist that "the rule against retrospective legislation . . . should be no defense if the act which he committed in violation of CCL 10 was also known . . . to be a punishable crime under his own domestic law."[23] Because Nazi jurists had violated *both* German law operative at the time *and* international law, the Justice case could not be accused of violating *nulla poena*.

This argument, however—that Nazi jurists had committed crimes under German law in effect during the Third Reich—was hard to square with the defendants' insistence that Hitler's orders *constituted* law. At trial, Hermann Jahrreiß, professor of law at the University of Köln and associate defense counsel at Nuremberg, was called as a witness for the defense to "explain to the Tribunal the constitutional status of the so-called Hitler decrees [*Führerbefehl*]."[24] In a long-winded expostulation, Jahrreiß insisted that an order from Hitler was not simply an order but a decree with the status of law, even if delivered in secret and in violation of then-operative German domestic statutes. It was incoherent, therefore, to argue that Hitler had issued illegal or criminal orders, as his orders constituted the final and ultimate word on what was lawful in the Third Reich. This claim brought about an important exchange between the professor and Presiding Judge James Brand:

> BRAND: I understand your view to be that judges were obliged to obey the law of their State of Germany even though in doing so they violated a principle of international law. . . .
>
> JAHRREIß: The general validity of the principles of the charter as international law could, in regard to judges of those states which require that their officials apply the law of the state as the final will, bring about tragic conflicts of conscience, for which, in my opinion, there is no indubitable legal solution at all.[25]

However dry and opaque, the professor's answer actually made a crucial concession to the court. For while insisting on the binding legal status of the *Führerbefehl*, Jahrreiß appeared to concede that a body of international law had existed *at the same time and in competition with* Hitler's power of decree. In conjuring a tragic conflict, in which a jurist had to choose between conflicting norms, Jahrreiß inadvertently surrendered the *nullum crimen* argument. The clash between the *Führerbefehl* and the law concerning crimes against humanity was not a *post hoc* creation of the IMT and CCL 10, but rather one that confronted German jurists *at the time*—even though the specific term crimes against humanity had to wait until Nuremberg for formal recognition. Thus against the defense's attempt to argue that the court was using retroactive law to condemn actions that were fully lawful when committed, the court was able to successfully argue that the defendants had in fact faced *competing* legalities: on the one hand, a perverted and usurped domestic law; and on the other, an existing body of international law expressive of basic norms of superior obligation.

This handling of the retroactivity problem looked decisive. Indeed, even Carl Schmitt, the "crown jurist" of the Third Reich, recognized after the war that Nazi atrocities deserved to be regarded as *mala in se*: "Their inhumanity is so great and so evident," he wrote, that criminal liability can be grounded "without any regard for hitherto existing positive law."[26] Given such statements, one might have predicted a gradual acceptance of trials involving crimes against humanity among German jurists in the postwar years. But it was not to be. To the contrary, trials involving crimes against humanity became ever more controversial in occupation Germany, at least in the western zones, where they were relentlessly attacked on grounds of retroactivity. Indeed, at the precise moment when the Justice case was being decided, German jurists were turning aggressively against their own domestic prosecutions for crimes against humanity.[27]

* * *

To make sense of this regrettable development, we need to return to Control Council Law No. 10. We have noted that CCL 10 authorized zonal trials by occupation courts. It also empowered—or rather tasked—German courts to conduct their own trials. Germany's unconditional surrender had brought its domestic legal system to a "complete standstill."[28] In October 1945, the Control Council, the Allied governing body for all of Germany, issued Law No. 4, essentially reorganizing the German judiciary according to the German Judicature Act of 1877. At first, the reconstituted German courts were permitted to deal only with ordinary domestic crimes committed during the occupation, but CCL 10 extended this jurisdiction of German courts to a limited number of acts that occurred during the Nazi period—namely, to those involving "crimes committed by persons of German citizenship or nationality against other persons of German citizenship or nationality, or stateless persons."[29] Even this grant was conditional, to be exercised only "if authorized by the occupying authorities." (In actuality, German courts occasionally strayed from these regulations and conducted trials technically beyond their mandate; the prosecution of Sobibor's *Gasmeister* Erich Bauer, in which a Berlin court convicted the Sobibor functionary for crimes against humanity, even though few of the victims were either German or stateless, provides an excellent case in point.)[30] The principle was clear: the Allies wanted to reserve to themselves the authority to try Germans suspected of perpetrating atrocities of an international character—that is, those whose victims were Allied nationals or the nationals of other countries attacked by Germany.[31]

Yet more noteworthy than the restrictions placed on German courts was the Allies' willingness to permit those courts to deal with *any* cases involving Nazi atrocities. This willingness had less to do with confidence in German courts than with the challenge of reestablishing the rule of law in a conquered country with a badly tainted judiciary. As many as 90 percent of judges and judicial officers had been Nazi party members,[32] and finding suitable postwar replacements was no small order for the Allies. The so-called vintage rule, which assumed that judges who had joined the party early on were more ardent Nazis than those who joined later, was more a work-saving contrivance of the Allies than an empirically supported proposition.[33] And reinstalling Weimar-era judges, many of whom had been purged by the Nazis, supplied no magic solution, since, as one American official observed, these jurists tended to be fierce nationalists "by no means necessarily democratically inclined."[34] The Allies also recognized that their own jurisdiction, even if technically authorized by CCL 10, was at its most tenuous with regard to certain crimes committed by Nazis against their fellow Germans. Such cases would, then, provide the safest and least controversial crucible for the reconstruction of the German judicial system.

Each Allied zonal authority was left to decide which cases to hand over to German courts. The Americans adopted the most restrictive approach, basically refusing to let German courts conduct any trials under CCL 10; the French and the British proved less chary.[35] On August 30, 1946, as the IMT trial was drawing to a close, the British zonal authority officially handed German courts jurisdiction over cases involving Nazi-era German-on-German crimes—with the proviso that German courts were to be bound by the precedents of the British military courts.[36] German courts in the Soviet occupation zone were granted the widest scope to try cases, but with the least independence.[37] Jurists with a Nazi past were absolutely barred from judicial positions in the Soviet zone; to fill the gaps, the Soviets appointed lay judges, persons who were "legally unqualified but politically reliable."[38]

Depending on their zonal location, German courts thus enjoyed varying degrees of authority to use international law, as codified in CCL 10, as the basis for trying certain Nazi-era crimes. Technically speaking, CCL 10 extended to four crimes: crimes against peace, war crimes, crimes against humanity, and membership in criminal organizations. Three of these four were of little or no concern to German courts, given the nature of the Allies' jurisdictional grant. By definition, crimes against peace and war crimes had to have an international character, and so remained beyond the jurisdiction of German courts. As for membership in criminal organizations, this crime largely fell from prosecutorial favor as it smacked of collective punishment. Thus of the four substantive crimes named in CCL 10, only crimes against humanity would play an important role in the trials conducted against Nazis in German courts. This, in effect, guaranteed that German domestic courts would have to revisit debates concerning retroactivity similar to those encountered in the Justice case.

Only now, with German judges presiding, the results were very different—except in the Soviet Occupation Zone (SBZ), where Marxist critiques of law dismissed the bar against retroactivity as an ideological construct of bourgeois legality, a device used to rationalize the status quo. In March 1947, Ernst Melsheimer, a German representative of the Soviet military administration in Sachsen, offered a distinctly Marxist gloss on the bar, arguing that "from a dialectical perspective there are no eternal principles of justice," and that "everything, including the principle of *nulla poena sine lege*, is subject to . . . changing economic relations."[39] It is no surprise, then, that Soviet occupiers showed little patience for the retroactivity argument, and German courts in the SBZ "after initial ambivalence . . . barely concerned itself with the retroactivity problematic."[40] Characteristic was the pronouncement of the provincial high court (*Oberlandesgericht*, OLG) of Gera, which declared that CCL 10 "is by its nature equipped with retroactive force [*rückwirkender*

Kraft] as it applies to criminal acts that were committed during the Hitler regime"[41]—an argument that appeared to defend the law *precisely for* its retroactivity.

The cavalier treatment of the retroactivity issue in the Soviet zone only exacerbated the concerns about it elsewhere, while also raising questions about the quality of justice dispensed under CCL 10. These concerns came to a head at the Constance Jurists' Day (Konstanzer Juristentag), convened June 2 to June 5, 1947, while the Justice trial was in recess. Organized by the French zonal military government, and following on the heels of similar conferences organized by the English and American military governments in the prior year, the convention brought German jurists together with representatives of the Allied occupation zones for four days of lectures and discussions on topics such as "the Constitution of the United States and individual rights" and "guarantees against a dictatorial judiciary."[42] These meetings, which included lectures, seminars, and social gatherings, were designed "to provide German jurists with an overview of democratic principles and institutions"[43]—what we would today call workshops in transitional justice.

During a session devoted to the "question of the punishment of crimes against humanity under CCL 10," Franz Arthur Müllereisert, president of the Lindau district court, rose to make the following point:

> A grave concern must be expressed that habits, which resemble Nazi abuses, repeat themselves in veiled fashion. In the case of Control Council Law [10], we are applying a law designed with a narrow purpose [*ein zweckbedingtes Gesetz*] and given retroactive power, even though we all have denounced legal retroactivity as a form of Nazi injustice.[44]

Müllereisert essentially urged German judges to resist applying CCL 10, lest they compromise their judicial independence in a manner akin to the worst of Hitler's judges. To try former Nazis for crimes against humanity, he argued, would be to apply retroactive law, thus tainting judges with precisely the evil they were attempting to rectify. In other words, the resurrection of the rule of law required the rejection of the very law—CCL 10—designed to effectuate its reintroduction.

Müllereisert was admittedly something of a crackpot and his jurisprudential writings became increasingly eccentric over the years, but his critique of CCL 10 resonated with German jurists. In March 1947, roughly as the Justice trial was getting underway, the *Süddeutsche Juristen-Zeitung* dedicated a special number to a discussion of "crimes against humanity and their punishment." It featured a vociferous attack on CCL 10 by Dr. Hodo Freiherr von Hodenberg, president of the high district court (OLG) in Celle and a prominent professor of law at Heidelberg.[45] Fiercely nationalistic and rigidly positivistic in his jurisprudence, but untainted by any official association with Nazi justice, Hodenberg invoked the likes of Montesquieu, Beccaria, and Feuerbach in defending *nulla poena* as a bulwark against arbitrary power. Noting that the American military government in its occupation zone had promulgated as its most basic law the principle that "No charge shall be preferred . . . or punishment inflicted for an act, unless that act is expressly made punishable by law at the time of its commission," Hodenberg cheekily insisted that CCL 10 violated America's own laws of occupation. Anticipating the arguments of Müllereisert, he went on to note the similarities between CCL 10 and Nazi law, particularly in their shared disregard of the bar against retroactivity:

> With respect to sentencing, National Socialism claimed to satisfy the true requirements of justice. As a result of the influence of political interests, the sentences of promulgated law were tossed aside by retroactive criminal law. Now arises the fresh danger that draconian punishments are being demanded as the result of the influence of political perspectives, punishments that cannot be justified by an objective grasp of the situation.[46]

CCL 10 was not without its defenders among German jurists. In 1946, Gustave Radbruch, one of the great German jurists of the century and a former minister of justice in the Weimar Republic, articulated his theory of "lawful illegality" (*gesetzliches Unrecht*)—the notion that a properly promulgated piece of legislation ceases to have the properties of law if it is "intolerably unjust" (*unerträglich ungerecht*).[47] Now, in the same number of *Süddeutsche Juristen-Zeitung*, Radbruch pushed Hodenberg's logic to its grotesque conclusion:

> Does one really want to draw the conclusion that under the mantle of euthanasia, acts of institutional murder must go without punishment because they were based on a secret order of Hitler's?[48]

Radbruch powerfully noted the absurdity of barring prosecutions for crimes against humanity on the grounds that such cases would retroactively criminalize conduct authorized by Hitler's secret orders. Yet despite the acuity of Radbruch's argument, Hodenberg's broadside carried the day among German jurists.

The debate was hardly just academic. Within the British zone, where Germans conducted the greatest number of prosecutions under CCL 10, courts demonstrated a reluctance to return convictions for crimes against humanity—and when they did, they imposed notably lenient punishments.[49] Concerned by this mounting resistance, R. H. Graveson, a prominent scholar of international law at King's College London, pointedly addressed his German colleagues, warning that "he who refuses to apply this law [CCL 10] . . . in effect refuses to apply law." He continued:

> There is no legal foundation for such a refusal. . . . Under normal conditions within a legal order . . . the application of NPSL [*nulla poena sine lege*] will contribute to the realization of justice and legal order. This is not the case when applied to a legal system that tossed every ethical foundation overboard.[50]

In 1948, the freshly minted central court of appeals (*oberstes Gerichthof*) for the British zone handed down a decision sharply reiterating Graveson's point—that CCL 10 was binding as a matter of strict positive law.[51] German courts largely fell in line with this ruling, but their compliance was no more than an act of submission to the reality of CCL 10, and certainly not a sign of any agreement with the law itself.[52] If anything, forced compliance only stiffened the resistance to CCL 10 and to the larger Allied war crimes trial program. Many German politicians in the fledgling Federal Republic came to eschew use of the term *Kriegsverbrecher* (war criminal) altogether; Hans Ewers, a member of the Bundestag, demanded that the term be avoided altogether, since "for the most part they are not criminals, after all."[53] In the place of "war criminal,"

Germans now spoke of *Kriegsverurteilter* (war-condemned) and *Kreigsgefangener* (war prisoner).[54] Whether a consequence of strategic manipulation or genuine ignorance, this semantic shift served to turn perpetrators into victims. (Decades later, Demjanjuk's defense lawyer in Munich, Ulrich Busch, would use the identical term—*Kriegsverurteilter*—to describe his client.)

The church also joined the chorus of criticism. Moving comfortably from theology into jurisprudence, Cardinal Josef Frings, Germany's foremost Catholic clergyman, delivered a sermon on New Year's Eve 1946, castigating the IMT Charter as a violation of *nulla poena*. Protestant clergymen attacked the American military's trial program on the same grounds. "As Christians," wrote Protestant Bishop Otto Dibelius, "we refuse to recognize the Nuremberg verdicts as justice."[55] Sounding a theme that countless German politicians, jurists, and social thinkers would echo in the decades to come, Hanns Lilje, bishop of the largest *Landeskirche* (regional church) in Germany, insisted that it was time to draw a *Schlussstrich* with the past—a decisive line that would put an end to trials dealing with now distant crimes. "A deep understanding of the Christian teaching of forgiveness of sins," he wrote, "can be demonstrated by turning our view from the past and decisively directing it to the future."[56] The year was 1949. Forgiveness came early, indeed.

Exacerbating the situation were the unfortunate remarks of some American jurists and politicians. In 1948, Charles Wennerstrum, the presiding judge in the so-called Hostages case (one of the twelve "successor" cases at Nuremberg), wrote of the American zonal trials that "[they] were to have convinced the Germans of the guilt of their leaders. They convinced the Germans merely that they lost the war to tough conquerors."[57] Supreme Court Justice William O. Douglas similarly decried the entire American trial program as an exercise in victor's justice.[58] In the US Senate, Joseph McCarthy of Wisconsin publicized allegations that SS men charged with massacring American soldiers at Malmedy had been physically abused while awaiting trial in a US army court in southern Germany. McCarthy used these allegations to attack the American war crimes program as "Communist inspired," a charge repeated by his colleague William Langer of North Dakota, who likened the American trials to Stalinist purges.[59] Today it seems incredible that an American politician could hope to score political points by defending persons who had *massacred* Americans; imagine, a senator hoping to curry political favor by championing the cause of Khalid Sheikh Mohammed and his lieutenants. But new Cold War realities and the heavily German-American constituencies in the Midwest made such grandstanding not just politically feasible but tactically shrewd.

* * *

Deliverance, at least for reluctant German jurists burdened with applying occupation law, came in 1951 in the form of Allied High Commissioner's Order Nr. 243, which repealed the authorization tasking German courts with trying cases under CCL 10. Many commentators have asserted the repeal effectively barred German courts from trying Nazi-era perpetrators for crimes against humanity, but such a construction is highly misleading.[60] As Martin Broszat has noted, an exercise of parliamentary will could easily have rectified this situation, incorporating crimes against humanity into domestic German law, just as genocide later was.[61] This exercise of will was noticeably absent. Although not all of Germany was unanimous in its rejection of CCL 10—state representatives from Niedersachsen, Nordrhein-Westfalen, and Berlin agreed that something like CCL 10 was necessary to deal with the legacy of the Nazis' mass crimes[62]—these remained minority positions, and nothing was done. As one commentator observed, the idea of passing a German law for the punishment of Nazi crimes "was never really discussed."[63]

Certainly the fact that the political and judicial branches were now stacked with former Nazis did little to encourage a spirit of legislative experimentation.[64] In the early years of the Federal Republic as many as 80 percent of the judges in the BGH, Germany's highest appellate court, had served in the judiciary or as state officials during the Third Reich.[65] Examples abound. Edmund Mezger, a prominent jurist who had supported "racial-hygenic measures for the elimination of criminal tribes," retained his prestigious professorship at Munich, and his commentary on the criminal code of the Federal Republic became the most popular postwar teaching textbook.[66] Werner Best, erstwhile in-house counsel to the SS, condemned to death in absentia in Denmark, emerged as an influential adviser to the Free Democrats, specializing in questions of Nazi-era crimes (about which he presumably had ample firsthand knowledge).[67] Whether this rapid rehabilitation of Nazi jurists aided or frustrated the transition to democracy can be debated; as America learned in its disastrous effort to disband Saddam Hussein's army, ambitious campaigns of lustration can create dangerous power vacuums and toxic resentment in transitional societies. It has become something of a shibboleth of the literature of transitional justice that a reckoning with the past is a necessary condition for overcoming the legacy of authoritarianism. Yet avoidance and suppression may be just as efficacious, at least in the early years of transition. As Swiss-German philosopher Hermann Lübbe observed, "The new [German] state had to be constructed against the ideology and politics of National Socialism. It could not be constructed against the majority of the people"—who, after all, had been "part of the National Socialist reality."[68]

Once reinstalled in positions of judicial power, former Nazi jurists had little incentive to pursue crimes committed by their former colleagues. Indeed, the entire history of the Federal Republic reveals not a single case of the successful prosecution of a former Nazi jurist by a German court.[69] In the wake of the repeal of CCL 10, German domestic prosecutions in the 1950s of Nazi-era crimes came to a virtual halt, ushering in a period marked by what one observer has described as "amnesty, integration, and normative distancing"—and selective, occasional punishment.[70] More bluntly, in 1953 an Allied High Commission report described German attitudes toward the "war criminal question" as indicative of a "national psychosis."[71]

This unhappy inventory, however, only partially explains German jurists' "extreme adherence" to *nullum crimen* in the years from 1946 to 1951. Certainly bad faith—a willful effort to frustrate prosecutions of former Nazis—played a role. Particularly among the jurists who led the attacks on CCL 10, it remains difficult to say where sound legal arguments ended and calculated political machinations began. There is no doubt, for example, that Hodenberg was jurisprudentially conservative and politically nationalistic. He was a member of the Heidelberg Circle (Heidelberger Kreis) that included leading law professors and attorneys who had participated in the IMT defense.[72] The Heidelberg Circle was particularly active in petitioning for the creation of a joint Allied-German clemency board that would review the sentences of all the *Kreigsgefangene*. Yet the Circle did not carry the obvious taint that attached to a group known as the Essen Amnesty Committee, which included in its ranks Ernst Aschenbach, who had helped arrange deportations of French Jews to Auschwitz, and which was characterized by John McCloy as a "right-wing lunatic fringe."[73]

If Hodenberg cannot be simply dismissed as a Nazi apologist, then what are we to make of his opposition? As we've seen, even the notoriously slippery Carl Schmitt accepted Nuremberg's prosecutions based on crimes against humanity. (This, of course, did not stop him from spearheading calls for amnesty, with the exhortation "amnesty is the power of forgetting.")[74] To understand Hodenberg's critique, we need to look more closely still at exactly what crimes against humanity meant to a German jurist writing in 1947. As defined in the IMT Charter and in CCL 10, crimes against humanity named two distinct types of offenses—*atrocity* crimes and *persecution* crimes. Allied jurists clearly understood crimes against humanity as atrocity crimes, acts that included, *pace* CCL 10, "extermination," "enslavement," and "torture" directed against "any civilian population." To this list, we should add genocide, as Raphael Lemkin's neologism found frequent use in the trials conducted by the US military even as it awaited its full elevation to an independent crime in international law.

For Hodenberg, however, "crimes against humanity" meant something altogether different. As we have seen, in giving German courts a conditional grant of jurisdiction to try Nazi-era criminals, Allied occupiers limited the grant to cases involving crimes committed by Germans against other Germans or stateless persons. Certainly atrocity-like crimes were committed against members of both groups; in his vigorous defense of CCL 10, Radbruch had referred specifically to the "institutional murders" (*Anstaltsmorde*) of the disabled perpetrated by the Nazis in the name of eugenics.[75] Nonetheless, as we've noted, the overwhelming majority of the Nazis' worst atrocities were perpetrated against non-Germans, cases over which the jurisdictional grant did not extend. Even the bulk of the atrocities perpetrated against German citizens and stateless persons—such as the deportation and extermination of German Jews—remained beyond the authority of German courts, as the Allies typically treated these crimes as one element in the larger exterminatory process directed against all of European Jewry. Britain's broad jurisdictional grant to German courts in its occupation zone specifically excluded crimes against German Jews, as the British simply did not trust German courts to handle such cases responsibly.[76]

As a result, German courts typically handled cases involving a very different type of crime against humanity—namely, acts of denunciation.[77] These cases involved persons who, during the Nazi era, had denounced neighbors, relatives, and even spouses, for making anti-Nazi or defeatist statements, resulting in the denounced persons' incarceration or, in some cases, execution.[78] Such denunciations hardly constitute the kinds of acts one typically associates with crimes against humanity, but they did satisfy CCL 10's definition of "persecution-type" offenses—that is, acts of persecution "on political, racial or religious grounds." And because these crimes were typically German-on-German, they formed the bulk of the CCL 10 cases brought before German courts. According to one study, denunciation comprised 38 percent of all Nazi-era criminal cases tried in German courts between 1945 and 1949, while only 1.2 percent of cases involved acts of extermination.[79] The punishments doled out to those convicted of denouncing countrymen in the Nazi era were hardly trivial. In 1949, a Düsseldorf court sentenced Hans Wienhausen, a Gestapo informer, to life imprisonment for denouncing his employer.[80]

These cases are critical to our discussion, for, in contrast to acts of extermination and genocide, crimes of denunciation *did* raise bona fide problems under *nullum crimen*. Indeed, when Hodenberg penned his critique of CCL 10, his concern was precisely with such prosecutions of denouncers. Hodenberg worried about the application of the law to cases involving "true believers" (*Überzeugungstäter*), writing that "perhaps the person who filed a complaint felt an internal obligation [*eine innere Verpflichtung*]."[81] Trials of denouncers and informers could, he warned, raise "the danger of political persecution."[82] Whatever else we may think about these arguments, they are not trivial; it is entirely plausible to believe that at least some denouncers believed they were performing a patriotic duty in fulfillment of a legal obligation. This is not to say that such informers were wrongly prosecuted but that such cases did raise genuine concerns about retroactivity—concerns that would have looked grotesque if raised in cases involving atrocity-type crimes against humanity.

And yet Hodenberg's critique had a fatal consequence, as concerns about trying denouncers served to erode whatever willingness Germans might have had to use crimes against humanity as a tool for trying atrocity-type offenses. By the time the Allies repealed CCL 10 in 1951, the concept of crimes against humanity had already been irretrievably tainted by the controversial informer cases. Without the positive law compulsion provided by CCL 10, German jurists emphatically turned against trials for crimes against humanity, and did so at the very moment when German courts, for the first time, inherited jurisdiction over *all* Nazi crimes, including extermination and genocide. Because public sentiment, particularly within the German legal community, continued to associate these charges with the vexed punishment of denouncers, the incrimination lost credibility as a tool with which Germany could forcefully address its worst atrocities. Thus did perpetrators of genocide and extermination become the principal beneficiaries of a jurisprudential argument tailored to shield denouncers.[83]

Obviously, for some, this was less a disastrous result than the intended outcome of a conscious effort to shield all perpetrators from prosecution. But for many others, the story was clearly more complex. It is far from clear, for example, that Hodenberg anticipated that his critique of CCL 10 would deliver an argument that would insulate perpetrators of extermination from prosecution. What is clear is that an argument that was not unreasonable on its own terms ended up frustrating the prosecution of the most heinous Nazi-era crimes. Perhaps even more disappointing is the alacrity with which German jurists today continue to believe that the *Rückwirkungsverbot* properly barred prosecuting Nazis for crimes against humanity or genocide. It remains a discomfiting irony that the rewards of a legitimate debate about retroactivity came to be reaped by the perpetrators of the Nazis' worst acts of atrocity.

* * *

Once German jurists rejected the very incriminations designed to facilitate the prosecution of Nazi exterminators, the question remained: what charges *could* be brought? Given the posture of postwar German jurists, only an incrimination already in place during the Third Reich could survive a challenge based on *nullum crimen*. Theoretically, German jurists might have concluded that even the most heinous Nazi atrocities violated *no law* in place at the time. But a blanket bar on prosecuting Nazi atrocities was simply and obviously untenable. Such a bar would have made a mockery of the postwar judiciary's effort to legitimate itself as an instrument of the rule of law. And so German jurists relied on the old penal code and specifically the crime of "murder."

On one level, that decision seems straightforward and uncontroversial. After all, "murder" obviously was a crime on the books in the Third Reich, and people were still prosecuted and convicted of murder under the operative statute. But the conclusion that the statute in place at the time could now be used to prosecute Nazi exterminators was hardly unproblematic. For the argument to work, one had to conclude that those who ordered, organized, and participated in Nazi extermination were in violation of German law in place at the time. But this, as we've seen, was already a matter of strenuous debate at the time of Professor Jahrreiß's testimony at the Justice trial, and the debate has never really been settled to this day. Henry Friedlander, among other prominent scholars, has insisted that "at no time was it 'legal' to kill Jews or gypsies; no law legalizing such killing was ever promulgated."[84] By contrast, Gerhard Werle, a leading scholar of human rights law, among others, has argued that under the Nazis, "genocide was authorized by law because it was provided legal cover by the will of the political leadership." "In the Third Reich," Werle notes, "the will of the Führer was recognized as a source of law. Regardless of whether it was issued in written or oral form, even a secret order could create and alter law."[85] Werle's argument echoes both Schmitt's 1935 formulation, *Das Gesetz ist Wille und Plan des Führers* ("Law is the will and plan of the Führer"),[86] and Jahrreiß's insistence in court testimony that the Führer's orders constituted law. But where Jahrreiß hoped to insulate Nazi jurists from criminal liability, Werle, by contrast, means to undermine the claim that the "legal standards of *damals* [back then]" can supply a proper ground for present prosecutions—a claim he dismisses as "historically false and juridically a fiction"[87] Reminding us of the radical jurisprudential challenge posed by what Jaspers called the *Verbrecherstaat* (criminal state), Werle insists that only special law—the very incriminations repudiated by German jurists—could have enabled adequate and proper German prosecutions.[88] For Werle, it is absurd to claim that in ordering or approving acts of extermination, Hitler made himself a criminal under then-operative German law, as he was the source of law itself. Such an argument conveniently obscures the power of the *Verbrecherstaat* to overwrite and pervert the content of law.

And yet it was precisely this juridical fiction that supplied the foundation for German prosecutions of Nazi criminals. Using German criminal law as the foundation for the punishment of Nazi crimes by German courts had consequences that were far-reaching, both conceptually and practically.[89] As a conceptual matter, it meant that all Nazi crimes, including acts of extermination and genocide, would be treated as "ordinary crimes," no different, except perhaps in scope, from ordinary murder. The fact that such crimes had been sponsored by the state itself would, so the argument went, create no obstacle to prosecution, as the state, it was assumed, was acting in violation of its own valid legal norms when it authorized, organized, and conducted its exterminatory practices. Effectively, although the state was found in violation of its own legal norms, the underlying laws of the Reich were "normalized and validated" by this approach.[90]

What, then, did the operative law of murder look like? In 1871, the German criminal code defined a murderer as "a person who kills another person with premeditation [*Überlegung*]." This was changed on September 4, 1941, ostensibly to bring German law in conformity with the law of several other European countries.[91] Before we examine the text of the new murder statute, it is worth asking what "law making" meant in Nazi Germany. With no functioning legislature, Nazi Germany essentially placed the legislative process in the hands of the executive. A Reich ministry, of which there were fifteen, typically took the lead in drafting a bill, which was then circulated to other concerned ministries. A revised bill might then be drafted collaboratively by different ministries, with Hitler ultimately responsible for examining the resulting proposal. Concerned ministers and Hitler himself would sign the final draft, after which the new law would be published in the *Reichsgesetzblatt* (Reich Law Report).[92] In the early years of the Reich, bills were actually discussed at cabinet meetings, but Hitler dispensed with this practice after 1937. To speak, then, about Nazi law making, in contrast to Hitler's secret orders or oral commands, is still to reference a highly informal process that falls far short of law making by ordinary legislative assembly.

It also bears noting that the alteration to Germany's murder statute in September 1941 occurred at a legally fraught moment in Reich history. It was around this time that the killing operations in the East first assumed the qualities of systematic extermination. That same September, the *Reichsgesetzblatt* announced a new law prohibiting all German and Austrian Jews over the age of six from appearing in public without displaying the yellow *Judenstern*. Two months later, in November 1941, came the law stripping German Jews who took up residence outside the Reich of both their property and status as German legal subjects; for the purposes of this law, forced deportation to one's death counted as a legal change of residence.[93]

Against this grim backdrop, the 1941 law defined *Mord* (murder) in a provocative new manner. Like its 1871 forerunner, the law still focused on the actor, not the act, but it now defined a murderer as a person who "kills another human being out of bloodlust, for satisfaction of sexual impulses, out of greed or otherwise base motive [*niedrige Beweggründe*]; treacherously or steathily [*heimtückisch*]; cruelly [*Grausam*]; with means dangerous to the public; or in order to commit or to cover up another crime.[94] The new definition did not arise sui generis; evidently it was simply borrowed from the Swiss penal code.[95] Whatever its provenance, its consequences were dramatic. In the name of tightening the definition of what constituted murder, the new law in fact gave judges in the Nazi period a "free hand to decide how [they] wanted in each specific case."[96] In particular, the criterion of "base motives" placed vast discretionary power in the hands of judges, providing them with a pretext either to vent moral outrage or to show uncommon understanding, depending on their feelings toward the accused. All this was consistent with the Nazi goal of bringing German law in harmony with the "healthy sensibility of the Volk."[97] It is telling that Roland Freisler, the notorious chief judge of the *Volksgericht*, had strongly supported the change, arguing that it now permitted the judge to dispense "substantive justice" in the form of a "moral assessment of the perpetrator."[98]

The 1943 case of Max Täubner provides a fine, if ghoulish, example of this discretionary power and also offers a vivid illustration of how the killing of Jews was treated in the SS's own courts.[99] That the SS *did* have their own courts is a fact not to be forgotten; indeed, the punishment of SS men, particularly for corruption, could be severe. Karl-Otto Koch, former commandant of Sachsenhausen, Buchenwald, and Majdanek—and husband of "bitch" Ilse—was famously convicted and executed for his corrupt practices. The insistence that genocide must be perpetrated decently was notoriously a principal article of Himmler's code of ethics.[100] SS judges such as Konrad Morgen, who charged Koch, saw themselves as scrupulous upholders of SS law, seemingly oblivious to the insanity of fastidiously upholding legal standards in an utterly perverted ethical system.[101] In applying the German law of murder, Morgen recognized three forms of acceptable or lawful killing: euthanasia killing; "lawful" executions at concentration camps (basically anything could justify an execution—the point was not to pass judgment on the soundness of the reason but simply to require that a reason existed); and the officially decreed extermination of Jews.[102] None of these acts constituted punishable offenses under SS law.

What *was* punishable, however, was murdering Jews without prior order. So while herding Jews into gas chambers or shooting Jews in mass graves was acceptable and indeed approved conduct, shooting them for sport was not. Max Täubner was convicted on May 24, 1943, for engaging in precisely such sport killing. The SS court condemned Täubner's "Bolshevik methods" as a violation of the "German way" of conducting the "necessary extermination of the worst enemy of our people."[103] The judgment typified how SS courts treated the unauthorized killing of Jews—not as murder or even manslaughter but as acts of disobedience or lack of discipline. Thus Täubner's offense was not murder but "breach of troop discipline," a violation of §92 of the Code of Military Justice. In considering whether Täubner had been motivated by "base motives," one of the factors that statutorily elevated a killing to murder, the court observed that "the driving motivation of the defendant has been genuine hatred of Jews."[104] While we might be tempted to view race hatred as the very definition of a "base motive," the SS court treated it as an *exculpatory* factor. The fact that Täubner was motivated by "genuine hatred" of Jews showed that he did not act out of bloodlust, greed, or the like; to his credit, he shared the view that the "Jews must be exterminated." His methods, not his motives, demanded punishment. Sentenced to ten-years imprisonment, Täubner served little more than one: Himmler amnestied him in 1945, and postwar jurists concluded that the bar against double jeopardy precluded retrial.[105]

The postwar German jurisprudence of Nazi-era murder showed both disturbing continuities and important breaks with SS jurisprudence. In the sharpest repudiation of SS case law, postwar German courts now treated "race hatred" as a base motive. This might seem an obvious correction of an odious doctrinal aberration, but here again the *nulla poena* bugaboo raised its head. In an article in *Juristenzeitung* (Lawyers News) in 1976, a law professor named Ernst-Walter Hanack questioned whether racial hatred, "which from today's perspective looks like an obvious case of base motives," could be applied without violating the bar against retroactivity.[106] Arguing that what "constitutes a base motive is an ideological construct," Hanack insisted that using race hatred as a criterion of culpability was to "judge the behavior of the perpetrator from a viewpoint that was not valid in the legal order under whose force the perpetrator acted."[107] Hanack recognized that "this result may be shocking," but his larger argument could be read less as an attack on the justice of prosecutions than as a reductio ad absurdum of the German postwar obsession with retroactivity. At the very least, Hanack encouraged German prosecutors to place greater emphasis on the objective qualities of the act than on the subjective motives of the actor. How, after all, could one prove that a person killed out of race hatred? In the case of the principal architects of Nazi genocide—Hitler, Himmler, Heydrich, and Göring, a list that was later expanded to include Odilo Globocnik and Christian Wirth, chief functionaries in the planning and implementation of Aktion Reinhard—racial hatred could be directly imputed from their statements and actions. After all, if the decision to implement a continent-wide campaign of murdering every last Jewish man, woman, and child does not indicate race hatred, it is hard to imagine what does. But what of the "ordinary" killers of Jews or the so-called *Schreibtischtäter*, the "desk perpetrators," bureaucrats who helped organize genocide while swiveling in an office chair: how was one to distinguish between those who killed out of race hatred and those who killed because it was their job?

In the case of direct participants in killing, courts could find persons guilty of murder in the absence of "base motives," provided that the killing was committed with "treachery" or "cruelty." These were understood as qualities of the act itself, divorced from the actor's internal mental states. Yet when it came to parsing these objective qualities, German courts often adopted tortured formulations, holding, for instance, that cruelty "cannot be imputed if the victim was not caused to suffer pain, misery or suffering in excess of the goal of killing [*Tötungszweck*]." Courts did manage to agree that death by gassing was indeed characterized by cruelty, and that the method of herding the victims to their death—by having SS men in white coats assuring them the "showers" were for hygienic purposes—constituted treachery. Given that the statute required a showing that a killer had acted with base motives *or* with cruelty *or* with treachery, it seemed that postwar German courts had the doctrinal tools to convict vast numbers of persons who had participated in Nazi genocide.

Were it only that simple. Complicating everything was the bewildering subjectivity of the doctrine that distinguished a perpetrator (*Täter*) of murder from a mere accessory (*Gehilfe*). This doctrine found early expression in the so-called Bathtub Case of 1940.[108] A pair of sisters from a farm in Mosel had both become pregnant by the same man, an abusive tyrant. Fearing the social opprobrium that would come from having a child out of wedlock, Maria Anna R. secretly gave birth, and soon thereafter asked her sister to drown the newborn in a bathtub. The sister complied. Convicted of murder, which at the time carried a mandatory death penalty, the sister appealed to the Reichsgericht (the high court of the Third Reich), which set aside the lower court's verdict. According to the Reich court, showing that the accused "killed with intention and forethought" did not suffice to convict for murder. Decisive was whether the accused "wanted the act as her own" and did not simply "want to support a foreign act." The question of whether the act is "one's own" in turn depended on "the degree of personal interest one has in its success." In this case, Maria Anna R. clearly was far more invested in the success of the killing than was her sister, who did the actual drowning. The high court thus concluded that the trial court should have convicted the sister of manslaughter, or as an accessory, but not as a perpetrator.[109]

This Nazi-era case received an influential doctrinal elaboration by the BGH in the famous Staschinsky case of 1962.[110] We recall that back at his first deportation hearing in 1984, John Demjanjuk claimed that the KGB would assassinate him if he were sent to another country. Asked by the OSI's lawyer to identify even one Ukrainian assassinated abroad, Demjanjuk named Stepan Bandera, the Ukrainian nationalist assassinated by a KGB agent in Munich in the summer of 1959. In a scene straight out of a John le Carré novel, Bandera had just opened the door to his apartment building (coincidentally located just around the block from the Munich courthouse where Demjanjuk would be tried) when he was shot in the face with cyanide fired from a spray gun that a KGB assassin had concealed in a newspaper. Bandera's killer was a Soviet agent named Bohdan Staschinsky, who two years earlier had assassinated Lev Rebet, another prominent Ukrainian nationalist, also by cyanide spray gun.

In 1961, on the eve of the construction of the Berlin Wall, Staschinsky defected to West Berlin, and was arrested. His trial and subsequent appeal provide a fascinating example of how legal doctrine emerged from the collision of Cold War politics and National Socialist history. Tried for murder, Staschinsky was instead convicted as a mere accessory and sentenced to eight-years imprisonment, a verdict upheld by the German high court. Although it might seem remarkable to find German courts extending such leniency to a KGB assassin at the height of the Cold War, the fact that Staschinsky was, by the time of his trial, a valued defector no doubt inclined the court to leniency. Yet if the courts were inclined to leniency, they had to get around the fact that German law requires a mandatory life sentence for perpetrators of murder. (The death penalty, at stake in the Bathtub Case, had been abolished by the Basic Law [*Grundgesetz*] of the Federal Republic in 1949.) Given the rigidity of the German statute, the only way for the court to show leniency toward Staschinsky—barring outright acquittal—was to convict him as an accessory.

It seems bizarre to conclude that an assassin who carefully tracked his victim, shot him in the face with poison, and left him dying in a street acted as a mere accessory to murder. But that is precisely what the trial court concluded and the high court affirmed. Building on the Bathtub holding, the court concluded that in the case of state-sponsored crimes, a perpetrator is someone who "willingly gives in to murderous incitement, who silences the voice of conscience, who makes foreign criminal goals the foundation of his convictions and actions."[111] Such a perpetrator was contrasted with persons "who disapprove and buck against the criminal orders but who nevertheless follow them out of human weakness, because they are overwhelmed by the excessive power of state authority, or because they lack the courage of resistance or the intelligence for effective evasion."[112] In a characteristically tortured construction, the high court concluded that "there is no sufficient legal reason to treat such persons without exception and necessarily in the same way as . . . those perpetrators who unhesitatingly act out of conviction." And who, in the court's judgment, was that "unhesitating perpetrator"? Not the lowly KGB assassin, plagued by crises of conscience (the defendant had testified to such crises). According to the court, the perpetrator was none other than Alexandr Shelepin, the director of Soviet state security.[113]

The audacity of the ruling was matched only by its strategic brilliance. For at the same time that the high court essentially cast Soviet leaders as murderers, it also by implication transformed virtually all participants in Nazi genocide into mere accessories—the feckless unfortunates who found themselves "overwhelmed by the excessive power of state authority" or who "lack[ed] the courage of resistance or the intelligence for effective evasion." To claim that this lengthy opinion about a KGB assassin was at its core about Nazis involved in the Holocaust is not to hazard a clever interpretation of artfully concealed subtexts. Nazi mass crimes were clearly very much on the court's mind. Acknowledging that history has long been plagued by politically motivated murder, the court observed:

> Recently, however, certain modern states, under the influence of radical political views—in Germany, under the influence of National Socialism—have come to plan political murder and mass murder, and to order the implementation of such bloody deeds. Those who carry out the orders of these administratively directed crimes do not exhibit the impulses explored by standard criminology. . . . More often, these people find themselves trapped in an ethically confusing situation by their own state, whose unquestioned authority is maintained by artful propaganda. . . . These people follow the directions [to commit the most despicable crimes] under the influence of political propaganda or because of the power of the ordering authority or as the

> result of similar influences from their own state, which reasonably could have been expected to act as the protector of law and order. . . . The special circumstances of state-ordered crimes in no way relieve participants from criminal guilt. . . . Nonetheless, under special circumstances state-sponsored criminal orders may provide a reason for mitigation.[114]

In reading this astonishing paragraph, one might easily forget that it addressed a case involving a trained KGB assassin, and not a lowly SS guard. To its credit, the court was attempting to do what the larger German legal system steadfastly refused to: adapt its ordinary jurisprudence to the reality of state-sponsored crimes of atrocity. But whether it successfully addressed the jurisprudential problems posed by the *Verbrecherstaat* is another matter entirely. At the very least, we should pause over the implied equivalence that the court draws between the Soviet and the Nazi states—and the alacrity with which the court conflates politically motivated murder with acts of mass extermination. And while the court rightly notes that the motives and psychology of participants in state-sponsored crimes confound standard criminology, its exertions to explain such crimes as the product of state propaganda should also leave us troubled—not least because they are offered simply as dicta, without a scintilla of supporting evidence.

The Staschinsky case created a doctrine that powerfully influenced the prosecution of Nazi genocide. As Werle has put it, the case established a lapidary rule: "He who executed an order is an accessory."[115] The rule informed a generation of cases. Of the former members of *Einsatzgruppen* convicted in German courts, 90 percent were found to have acted as accessories,[116] including Otto Bradfisch, commander of an *Einsatzgruppe* responsible for murdering some fifteen thousand Jewish men, women, and children, many of whom he shot personally. Equally dreary examples abound in cases involving death camp functionaries. Gustav Münzberger was an SS guard at Treblinka responsible for herding Jews into the gas chamber. In one documented instance, the chamber was packed full and so Münzberger shot and killed a mother and her two children who could not fit inside; a trial court reasoned that, although fanatically dedicated to Hitler, Münzberger had not internalized the "will of the perpetrator" and thus acted as an accessory. Alois

Häfele was an *SS-Untersturmführer* (second lieutenant) at Chelmno, where he helped organize the camp and personally shoved victims into the gas vans. Because he lacked the "intentions of the perpetrator," he was convicted as an accessory. Robert Mulka was the camp adjutant at Auschwitz, a senior position indeed; along with twenty-one other camp functionaries, Mulka was tried at the famous Frankfurt-Auschwitz trial, which lasted from 1963 to 1965. Supplied with evidence that Mulka had ordered the immediate execution of a prisoner who had conversed with a Jew who had just alighted at the train ramp at Birkenau, the trial court concluded that "by means of the punishment of the prisoner, Mulka wanted to deter similar deeds and so assure the frictionless accomplishment of the ordered extermination action, for which he was responsible."[117] In a different normative universe, this sentence might serve as a prelude to a murder conviction. Instead, it parsed Mulka's conviction as an accessory. Startling as these results sound, they were made possible—even inevitable—by the holding that the person who fires the weapon is a murderer only if he does so out of "inner conviction" with the regime's genocidal politics.

Who, then, was a perpetrator? As we've noted, when it came to the main perpetrators, German law treated the Holocaust as if entirely the work of six or seven men: Hitler, Himmler, Heydrich (at times Kaltenbrunner), Göring, Odilo Globocnik, and Christian Wirth, all of whom were conveniently dead. Because German law treated the follower of an order as an accessory, it was well-nigh impossible to convict a *Schreibtischtäter* (desk killer) as a perpetrator; had Eichmann been tried in Germany, as numerous commentators urged at the time, he might well have been convicted as an accessory.[118] (In fact, in the 1950s Eichmann wrote to Adenauer, volunteering to return to Germany to stand trial, evidently in the expectation that, if convicted, he would be given a light sentence.)[119] Indeed, it was difficult to charge bureaucrats with any crime. Since they had not killed with their own hand, jurists reasoned that they could not have acted cruelly or treacherously; and barricaded behind a desk, they had had few opportunities to evince base motives. All this became moot after 1968, as in that year Germany passed a law that *inadvertently* amnestied all so-called desk killers.[120] At the time, German prosecutors were preparing a massive case against former functionaries associated with the Reichssicherheitshauptamt (Reich Security

Main Office), a sprawling bureaucracy that oversaw the *Einsatzgruppen*, the Aktion Reinhard apparatus, and the extermination program at Auschwitz-Birkenau. What would have been the largest atrocity proceeding in German history, involving potentially three hundred defendants and eighteen separate trials, was brought to a screeching halt by a seemingly innocuous change to the criminal code (paragraph 50, section 2) that had the effect of treating bureaucratic participation in the killing process as a lesser criminal offense whose statute of limitations had already expired.[121]

To qualify as a perpetrator, then, one typically had to have killed or authorized killing without orders: only then could a court conclude that one had the "inner conviction" of the perpetrator. Put somewhat differently, to be found guilty of committing murder, one had to act as an *Exzeßtäter* (excess killer); like Täubner, one had to kill in excess—that is, in violation of SS law.[122] Of course, by the lights of SS justice, the wrong of these "excess acts" was not the killing of Jews, but disobedience or more typically lack of discipline.[123] Nonetheless, in judging the actions of those who operated the machinery of death, postwar German courts essentially employed SS standards of legality, limiting the universe of perpetrators to individuals who, like Täubner, could have been condemned by the SS' own tribunals. Those who met this standard were a select group of monsters, fanatics, and bloodthirsty sadists—sociopaths such as Treblinka's Kurt Franz, the SS officer known as "Lalka" (doll) for his boyish good looks, who would sic his German shepherd on prisoners with the command "Man [that is, the dog], bite the dog [the Jewish inmate]!"[124]

Treblinka's Ivan Grozny fit this model perfectly. Recall the testimony of Eliahu Rosenberg at Demjanjuk's Jerusalem trial:

> I would see him holding a sword in his hand . . . and sometimes he would cut off a piece of nose, a piece of ear . . . you just cannot comprehend why, why. . . . After all, there was no very good reason why he should go up to a person and cut off a part of his ear. He was not a human being. . . . But this sort of torture—this brutalizing—this torturing people by cutting off parts of their ears? Nobody had ordered him to do so. He did it all on his own accord. I never heard a

6.1. Kurt "Lalka" Franz, the baby-faced SS sociopath. Courtesy of Yad Vashem.

German tell him to do so. . . . A little later, a German, in fact, told him to keep off doing such things."[125]

Ivan was the ultimate *Exzesstäter*, a beast whose cruelty and zeal for murder far exceeded what was required by the policy of extermination. In reserving the category of perpetrator to such excess killers, German jurisprudence contributed to a distorted image of the SS man as a brutal psychopath, prompted by an unnatural joy in killing—an image that popular culture was more than happy to run with.

Whether all this followed perforce from the court's fateful ruling in the Staschinsky case can be debated. Kerstin Freudiger, a German scholar, has argued that the Staschinsky decision never explicitly limited the category of perpetrators to those who had engaged in excess killing.[126] Rather, she argues, the ruling left it to lower courts to fill in what objective acts revealed the requisite internal attitude of the perpetrator, and it was the lower courts that subsequently framed the standard of "excess killings." Whatever we make of this argument, two things remain clear. First, German courts carved out a special jurisprudence for Nazi crimes that differed quite dramatically from its ordinary treatment of murder. As far back as 1956, the BGH appeared to repudiate the Bathtub precedent, holding that "he who kills a person with his own hand is a perpetrator even when he acts . . . in the interest of another."[127] By this token, the Staschinsky decision did less to restore the subjective Bathtub standard than it carved out its special application in cases involving state-sponsored criminality. In cases involving "normal criminality," the court continued to apply the more objective standard from 1956.[128] Keeping in mind Jaspers' concept of the *Verbrecherstaat*, we can say that German courts recognized the unusual juridical problems posed by state-sponsored crimes, but did so by treating participants in genocide with a leniency that was conspicuously denied to those who participated in "ordinary" acts of murder.

Second, and more crucially, this jurisprudence effected something of a double shift. Because the category of perpetrator came to be reserved for a select group of sadistic excess killers like Ivan Grozny, courts treated persons nonetheless deeply implicated in hands-on killing—those who shot Jews in mass graves or pushed them into gas chambers—as mere accessories. The category of accessory was thus filled with persons who had played an active and demonstrable role in acts of killing—persons, that is, who otherwise might have been treated as perpetrators. As a consequence, those whom we might have expected to be treated as accessories—such as ordinary members of killing units or guards at death camps—were treated as guilty of nothing at all. In cases involving these persons, evidence of an *Einzeltat*—an individual act of killing (assumed to be required for a successful prosecution after the 1969 appellate holding in the Auschwitz proceeding)—was difficult to come by. In these cases, the very efficiency of the murderous operations guaranteed few survivors, and fellow travelers were rarely willing to testify against their former colleagues in extermination. And so while the vast majority of deeply implicated killers could only be convicted as accessories, thousands of lowly foot soldiers of genocide were never even prosecuted in the first place.

We recall, then, Christiaan Rüter's pessimistic prognostication expressed on the eve of the Demjanjuk trial. The professor's concern turned out to be fully justified; indeed, anyone familiar with Germany's jurisprudence of Nazi extermination should have been surprised that the case was even going to trial. Yet in addition to skepticism about the trial's outcome, Rüter expressed something else as well: indignation.

Introducing a trope that would be used time and again by the defense in the trial, he characterized Demjanjuk as a "small fish." Rüter was outraged that the German legal system—a system that for decades had variously amnestied, failed to indict, acquitted, and released far bigger fish—would now choose to go after a superannuated Ukrainian minnow.

7

Memory into History

In his opening statement at Demjanjuk's Jerusalem trial, prosecutor Shaked had foretold the day when it will no longer be "possible to bring to the stand witnesses who can say, 'We were there.' The subject sooner or later will have to step down from the witness stand and become a part of history."[1]

Demjanjuk's Munich trial heralded the arrival of that day. In preparing their case against him, German prosecutors had to decide whether to call to the stand two Sobibor survivors who claimed to remember their past captor. We recall that back in the summer of 1993, just after the Israeli Supreme Court overturned its conviction, Esther Raab had suddenly stepped forward, claiming to be able to identify Demjanjuk. Now, in the run-up to the Munich trial, Raab revived her claim and volunteered to testify in Germany.[2] On May 19, 2009, David Rich, an OSI historian, emailed German prosecutor Hans-Joachim Lutz, advising against calling her as a witness. "OSI does *not* believe," Rich wrote, "that Raab can identify Subject Demjanjuk."[3] A second Sobibor survivor named Aleksej Waizen, who lived in a retirement home in Russia, also surfaced during the trial, claiming he could positively identify Demjanjuk.[4] Following the OSI's advice, the court's response was a polite "*nein, danke*." The court in Munich was not about to risk a repeat of the disaster in Jerusalem.

Without witnesses who could point a finger and say, "I saw him do it," the Munich trial became a trial by history. The evidence against the accused came from dusty archives rather than the lived memory of survivors. This change emerged poignantly during the testimony of the

Nebenkläger, or "lay accusers"—victims and members of their families who, under German law, are permitted to attach themselves to prosecutions. In the Demjanjuk trial, the *Nebenkläger* consisted of three Sobibor survivors and three dozen relatives of persons murdered at the camp.[5] Almost all were Dutch. As we have noted, Sobibor, Belzec, and Treblinka were built to exterminate Jews in occupied Poland, but as the Final Solution turned into a continent-wide killing program, the camps were also used to murder Jews from other countries. During the five-plus months of Demjanjuk's service, virtually all the Jews killed at Sobibor—at least those whose deaths could be documented—came from the Netherlands.[6]

German law confers numerous rights on *Nebenkläger*. They may have legal representation in court, and no fewer than ten lawyers, led by Cornelius Nestler, a professor of criminal law in Cologne, represented them. These lawyers made for a formidable team; organized and knowledgeable, they were far more aggressive in inserting themselves into the proceeding than the two prosecutors. The *Nebenkläger* may appear before the court, not as witnesses, but as persons whose lives have been irrevocably harmed by the accused. Typically they figure at the conclusion of the trial, their statements resembling the "victim impact statements" permitted in the sentencing phase of American capital cases. In an ill-considered step, however, the defense challenged the certification of the *Nebenkläger*, attempting to cast doubt on their ability to prove that their relatives had in fact been murdered at Sobibor during the period in question. Nestler cleverly petitioned to have the *Nebenkläger* appear as witnesses, testifying, in effect, to their own authenticity. And so the very first witnesses to appear before the Munich court were relatives of the murdered.

Although their testimony supplied the trial with some of its most emotional moments, the *Nebenkläger* told the court no stories of horror, resistance, and survival. Nor did they share stories of the ordeal of the ghetto or the malignancy of the camp. These were victims of an entirely different sort from those who had testified in Jerusalem at the Eichmann trial or the first Demjanjuk trial. The *Nebenkläger* were second-generation victims, many of them orphaned by the Holocaust—men and women, now in their early seventies, who quietly told the court about early loss that in some cases preceded the formation of

7.1. Professor Cornelius Nestler, lead lawyer for the *Nebenkläger*. Photo by Thomas Hauzenberger.

memory itself. Rudi Cortissos, born in 1939 and a small boy during the war, produced a letter that his mother had hastily written in the hours before her deportation from Westerbork, the Dutch transit camp. She had tossed the letter into the street without a stamp, yet somehow it had made its way to the Cortissos house. When Presiding Judge Alt asked for the letter, Cortissos broke down, as if fearful that the court would keep it, his only connection to a mother he never knew. David van

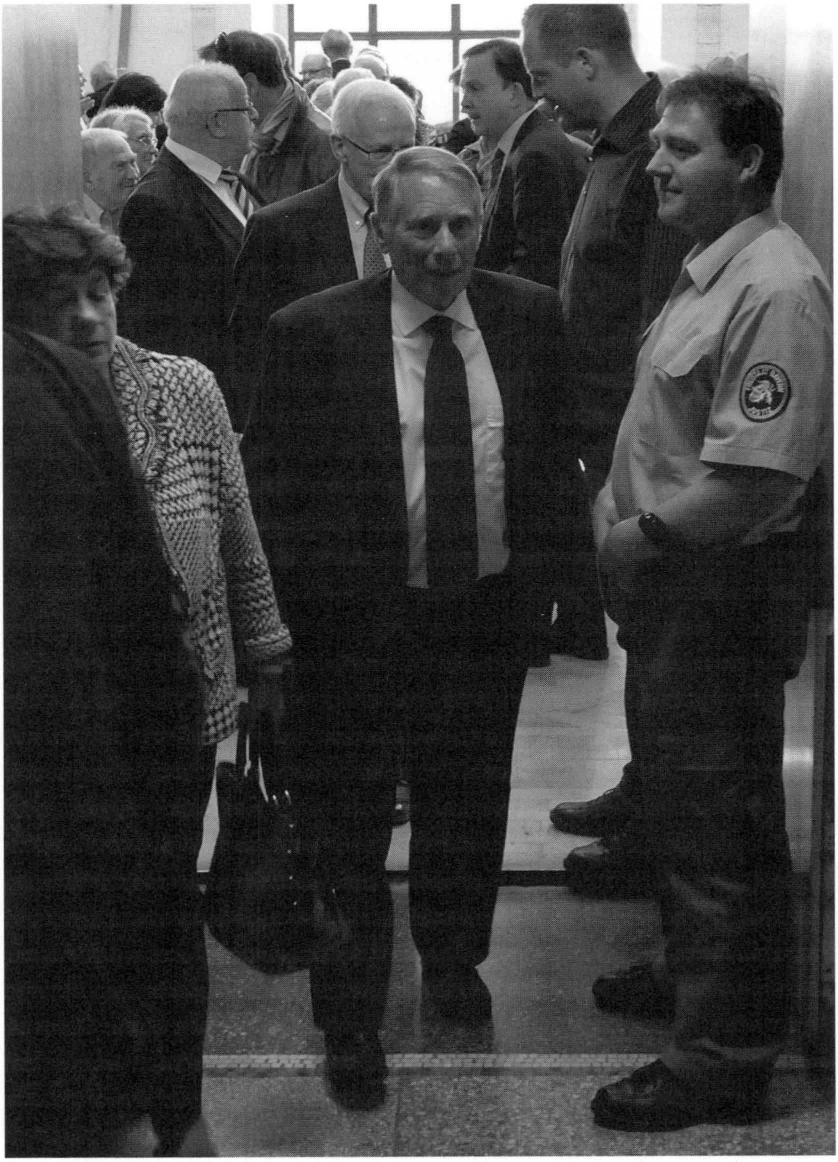

7.2. *Nebenkläger* Rudi Cortissos. Photo by Thomas Hauzenberger.

Huiden testified that his mother, stepfather, and sister were murdered at Sobibor. The day his family was seized, he had been sent out to walk the family dog, a German shepherd. "Nobody figured a Jewish boy would be walking a German shepherd, so I wasn't stopped. Neighbors took me in." Speaking excellent German, he politely thanked the court "for giving me the opportunity to say something."

The *Nebenklägers*' stories were brief. Later, they would have an opportunity to speak more generally, but for now their remarks simply described the losses that "entitled" them to join the prosecution. The contrast between the brevity of their stories and the vast passage of time that they had had to wait to tell them made their testimony exceptionally moving. A seventy-year-old man struggles to describe the long-ago day of his boyhood when his parents vanished from his life forever: the story lacks detail, and that very paucity signals the inestimable loss. The memory of absence and the absence of memory have become one.

Like van Huiden, many of the *Nebenkläger* concluded with words of gratitude to the court. But none addressed his or her words to Demjanjuk or even so much as cast him a glance, which was just as well, as the defendant appeared to sleep through the entire session. As Martin Haas, a seventy-three-year-old professor of medicine at the University of California, San Diego, began to tell the court about the murder of his mother, father, sister, and brother, Demjanjuk's lawyer rose to remind the court that the afternoon session was up. Haas was told he could resume his narrative the next morning—except that the next morning the defendant was a no-show. Demjanjuk had woken up complaining of a headache and joint pain and, according to Dr. Albrecht Stein, the flamboyant court-appointed physician responsible for monitoring the accused's health, had a slightly elevated temperature of 99.5: "Trivial in a younger person, but in light of Herr Demjanjuk's advanced age . . ." So court for the day was canceled.

This began a pattern that would plague the trial, as even the abbreviated schedule recommended by physicians proved too much for the defendant. When he did appear, Demjanjuk remained propped on his gurney, blue baseball cap pulled low over his brow, sunglasses shielding his eyes. There he would lie, inert and silent. At his side was his interpreter, Oksana Gerlach, a Ukrainian-born, German-educated lawyer, whose dutiful whisper supplied a soothing undertone to the court's proceedings.[7] But she might as well have been addressing the concrete wall, for Demjanjuk never gave a sign of attending to the happenings in the courtroom, ignoring the words of the judges, lawyers, and witnesses alike. (He did, however, perk up during the breaks, chatting with Busch.) Not only did the trial unfold without survivors who could identify the defendant; the defendant himself was essentially absent: an old man on a gurney, oblivious and mute.

And then there were the days that the defendant truly was absent. Roughly a quarter of the trial's dates would fall victim to Demjanjuk's complaints of headache, joint aches, chest pains, vertigo, dehydration, and general feelings of unwellness. As these cancelations grew in number so too did the suspicion that they were part of a conscious defense strategy to stall the proceeding in the hope that at some point the defendant would be declared unfit and the trial called off. It was a ploy Demjanjuk had been using without success since the days of his second denaturalization trial. (That his infirmities were exaggerated was confirmed when Dr. Stein disclosed to me that the accused was far more alert back at the Stadelheim jail, where he liked to flirt with his nurses.) Demjanjuk no doubt hoped that Judge Alt would prove as receptive to "defendants' disease" as some German courts had in earlier cases. Karl Frenzel was a former *SS-Oberscharführer* (staff sergeant) at Sobibor, where he served as the head of camp 1, which housed the small Jewish workforce. Convicted of murder in 1966, Frenzel saw his life term set aside on a legal technicality; retried in 1985, he was again convicted but served no additional time, released on grounds of his "deteriorating health." He lived another eleven years, finally dying in 1996. Helmut Bischoff was a former *SS-Obersturmbannführer* (lieutenant colonel) who headed the Gestapo in Madgeburg, where he oversaw the deportation of the city's Jews. In May 1970, toward the conclusion of a lengthy trial, Bischoff was deemed too ill to continue to participate in his defense and freed. Efforts to retry him failed. He died nearly a quarter century later, in 1993. German judges were generous indeed when it came to dispensing what came to be known as "biological amnesty."[8]

Demjanjuk was, of course, an old man, and old men suffer health problems. Alt had to be mindful of his legitimate complaints without letting them completely derail the trial. Ultimately, the mild-mannered judge would lose patience with the defendant, responding to the news that "Herr Demjanjuk doesn't feel well today" with the dry observation, "Many people on trial do not feel well." Still, nine months would pass before Alt actually ordered Demjanjuk to appear on a day he claimed to be under the weather. More often he would yield to the defendant and Dr. Stein. For those associated with the case, these cancelations would prove an aggravation. The lawyers representing the *Nebenkläger* lived in Frankfurt, Berlin, and Amsterdam, and when court was canceled they would glumly duck into taxis and head back to their rooms in the Sofitel in the hope that the defendant would recover by the next day.

For Martin Haas, Demjanjuk's 99.5 was more than aggravating. Haas had flown in from California to tell the story of his family's murder, and the trial was not scheduled to resume until after Christmas and New Year's—not for another three weeks. Either he would now have to spend these weeks in Munich or again fly in from San Diego if he wanted to finish his story. In the end he chose neither. Haas would return to Munich at the end of the trial to make a statement, but his testimony would remain incomplete, his story of life disrupted having suffered its own dismaying rupture.

* * *

When the trial did proceed, in fits and starts, it drew on the testimony of several witnesses qualified to detail how genocide operated. The three death camps of Aktion Reinhard were all constructed according to the same blueprint, differing only in size. Sobibor was larger than Belzec but smaller than Treblinka. But even Treblinka was not large; all three camps packed a great deal of lethality into a small operation. As we've noted, at Sobibor, no more than 15 to 20 SS men and an additional 100 to 120 Trawniki-trained guards oversaw a killing machine that in the eighteen months of its operation consumed the lives of at least 167,000 Jews. A camp like Majdanek-Lublin was purposely placed near a large urban area as a means of intimidating the local population; the death camps of Aktion Reinhard, by contrast, were sited in obscure locales chosen for secrecy and proximity to rail lines. Surrounded by dense pine forests on the eastern frontier of the Generalgouvernement, an easy walk to the Ukrainian border, the tiny cuff of Sobibor had never tallied many more than the 350 inhabitants it has today. The death camp was erected a kilometer from the village.

Following the template of the three Aktion Reinhard camps, Sobibor was divided into several parts.[9] The *Vorlager*, or "fore-camp," housed the SS living quarters and the barracks of the Trawniki guard force. A small post office was retrofitted to serve as the commandant's office, and a former forestry house became home to the camp's administration.[10] A number of other tidy structures with quaint names such as *Schwalbennest* (Swallows' Nest) and *Gottes Heimat* (God's Home) filled out the fore-camp.[11] Gravel paths lined with flowers ran between the cottages. There was a vegetable garden and stalls for horses, pigs, and chickens. Such amenities served both to make life comfortable for the SS men and to conceal the nature of the camp from arriving Jews.[12] Sub-Camp 1 contained the barracks of the Jewish workforce, their kitchen, and their work areas. Sub-Camp 2 contained the storehouses of goods seized from the murdered; this was also the undressing zone for those who would then be herded down a narrow lane called the *Schlauch* (tube) or *Himmelfahrtstrasse* (road to heaven) into Sub-Camp 3, which contained the gas chambers, capable of killing its occupants in about twenty minutes. In July 1942 and again in September of the same year, the extermination process had to be briefly suspended when marshy terrain made the rail tracks to Sobibor unusable. The ever-enterprising organizers of Aktion Reinhard put the interruptions to good use: the existing gas chambers were enlarged and three additional chambers constructed, increasing the camps' killing capacity to twelve hundred at any given moment.[13]

The life span for a Jewish arrivee at Sobibor was around three hours. The only Jews spared immediate extermination were those selected to serve at the camp. The number of these *Arbeitsjuden*, or "work Jews," fluctuated between six hundred and seven hundred, and probably never exceeded one thousand. In the camp's early days, the SS would periodically liquidate this population and replace it with a fresh group, but the resulting loss of know-how proved tiresome, and so the camp came to have a somewhat stable population, with fresh arrivals chosen only to replace those work Jews who had been killed for any of the long list of reasons that got work Jews killed, including no reason at all. The work Jews were pressed into performing many of the tasks essential to the running of the camp. The *Bahnhofkommando* (train station commandos) comprised forty to fifty Jews, who were responsible for unloading

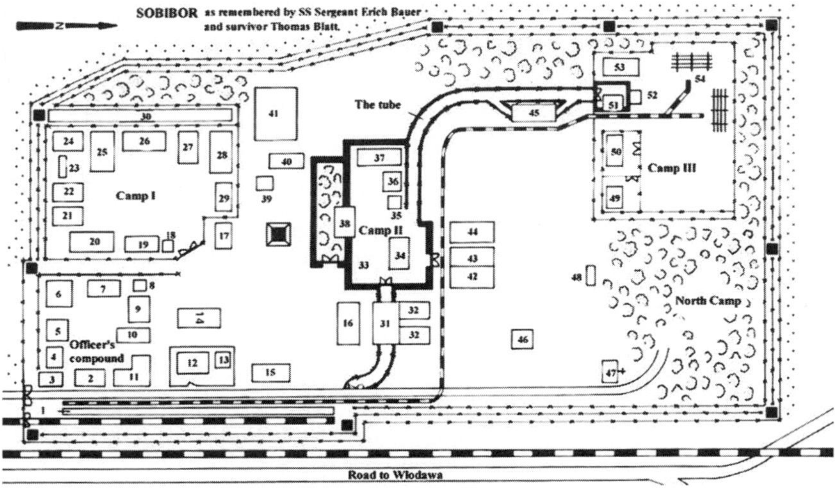

7.3. Sobibor layout. This map was originally prepared for the Sobibor Hagen trial 1965–66, and later modified. Courtesy Aktion Reinhard Camps website, www.deathcamps.org.

7.4. One of the few extant photos of the Sobibor camp. Michael Tregenza collection. Courtesy Aktion Reinhard Camps website, www.deathcamps.org.

freshly arrived trains, as well as removing the luggage and the infirm or dead. The hundred or so members of the *Lumpenkommando* (the rags commando) were responsible for sorting through the vast amount of clothing left behind by the exterminated and bundling it for future use. The *Goldjuden*, the "gold Jews," consisted of a score of jewelers and watchmakers responsible for sorting valuables. The *Hofjuden*, or "court Jews," included in their ranks tailors, shoemakers, and carpenters—persons responsible for maintaining the upkeep of the barracks and attending to the needs of the SS men. The *Waldkommanndo*, the "forest commandos," were responsible for chopping wood used to heat the camp and burn the dead. A variety of other chores, such as cleaning, cooking, washing, sewing, and tending the flower and vegetable garden were handled by 150 Jewish women. Then there were the Jews segregated in Camp 3, who performed the camp's unimaginable tasks. They removed the corpses from the gas chambers and hosed down the interiors to remove the blood and human waste that marked the last struggles of the murdered. This group was also tasked with carrying or dragging the corpses to the mass graves and later, beginning in the summer of 1942, digging up the decomposed bodies and burning them on giant outdoor spits.[14]

On October 14, 1943, the Jews of Sobibor staged an uprising. Three hundred managed to escape the camp, of whom less than fifty survived the war. Thereafter Sobibor closed as a killing center, and five months later, in March 1944, it was dismantled by order of Himmler and its records destroyed.[15] The grounds were plowed up, pine saplings planted, and a farmhouse hastily constructed. By the time the Soviets overran the area in July 1944, virtually no traces of the killing center remained.[16]

Of the three dozen *Nebenkläger* attached to the case, three were survivors of Sobibor—Jules Schelvis, Philip Bialowitz, and Thomas Blatt. All three are tiny men, barely five feet tall, and were dwarfed in court by a bevy of outsized German jurists. Judge Alt and Associate Judge Lenz, *Nebenkläger* lawyer Nestler, and chief defense counsel Busch are all gigantic men, standing well over six feet. I was pleased that one of the lawyers for the *Nebenkläger*, a Dutch Jew named Manuel Bloch, was also outsized, and so helped to correct an unwelcome image of giant Teutons towering over little old Jews. Schelvis, a Dutchman, testified,

7.5. Present-day archaeological excavation at Sobibor. Excavations have been conducted since 2007, under the oversight and with the support of Yad Vashem and Ben-Gurion University. Wojciech Mazurek and Yoram Haimi / Yad Vashem.

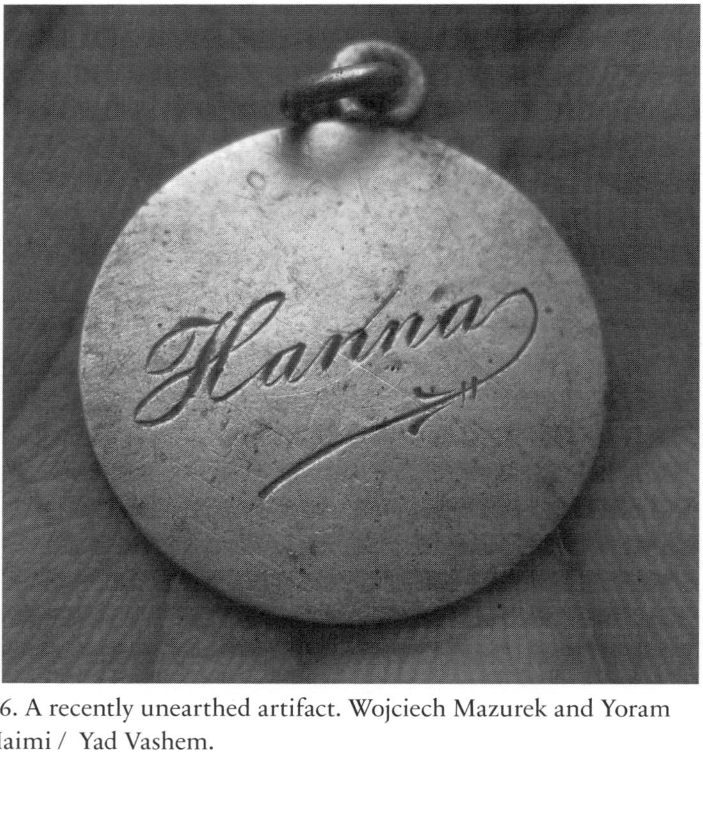

7.6. A recently unearthed artifact. Wojciech Mazurek and Yoram Haimi / Yad Vashem.

7.7. From left to right: survivor Jules Schelvis, survivor Philip Bialowitz, and the defendant. Courtesy ddp images / Sebastian Widmann / Sipa USA.

albeit briefly. Deported from Westerbork with his wife and wife's parents, who were sent directly to the gas chambers, Schelvis never actually entered the camp, as he had the relatively good luck of being chosen to join a group of men sent to dig peat at the nearby Dorohucza labor camp. After the war he wrote a history of Sobibor, a work that has became a standard reference,[17] but because he never actually entered the camp proper, Schelvis' testimony was largely confined to describing the trip from Westerbork to Sobibor.

Blatt and Bialowitz, by contrast, knew the camp all too intimately, and represented a quarter of the living Jewish links to Sobibor left on the planet. Coincidentally both men grew up in the same small town in Poland, Izbica, and arrived at Sobibor on the same transport, a pair of trucks that trundled six dozen Jews the seventy kilometers from their hometown to the death camp. A conceit of treating survivors as a unified group is the assumption that its members share fraternal bonds. But survivors are no more likely to share such ties than any other group tossed together by fate. Despite—or maybe as a consequence of—being acquainted since childhood, Blatt and Bialowitz do not exactly get along. It was only thanks to the cajoling of Bialowitz's son Jeffrey, a public school physical education teacher who accompanied his father to Munich (and whom I chanced upon demonstrably doing push-ups in the middle of the Feldherrnhalle, the commemorative loggia where police confronted Nazis during the Beer Hall Putsch of 1923), that the two agreed to sit beside each other in the Munich courtroom.

Like Schelvis, both Blatt and Bialowitz have written about Sobibor (though Bialowitz's memoir was published in 2010, some ten months after he appeared on the stand). The books by the three survivors make clear how dramatically life at Sobibor deviated from the picture of camp life delivered in standard histories and in popular culture. None of the work Jews received tattoos; the camp was so small that it needed no registry, and the plan was to ultimately exterminate the Jewish workers once their labors were complete anyway. Nor were the *Arbeitsjuden* issued inmate clothing; they worked in civilian garb, which could be readily exchanged for newer garments, given the vast amount of clothing entering the camp. The only uniformed Jews were the members of the *Bahnhofkommando*, the Jews who worked the train ramp, who wore blue overalls and matching blue caps with the letter *B* embroidered inside a yellow triangle.[18] The jaunty uniforms served two functions: they made the train station Jews readily identifiable to the guard force, and so helped prevent their accidental extermination, and they projected order and professionalism to those freshly arrived, who, at least in the case of the Dutch Jews, had no inkling of what awaited them. (Bialowitz, who was not a member of the *Bahnhofkommando* but at times was ordered to assist at the ramp, describes in his book a family of Dutch Jews who offered him a tip for helping to carry their bags.)[19] Food at the camp, at least during the months in question, was ample, as the transports from Westerbork arrived laden with provisions, which could often be obtained through barter with the Ukrainian guards. For the Jewish workers, the rule forbidding men from entering the women's barracks was laxly enforced, permitting romantic trysts and sexual encounters.[20] Every few weeks, there would be an evening of music; the SS men would clap and sing while the Jewish prisoners danced. To conclude,

7.8. Survivor Thomas Blatt: "the Leute waren dead." Photo by Thomas Hauzenberger.

however, that life for the *Arbeitsjuden* was somehow comfortable would be a grave mistake: both the SS and Trawniki guards exercised absolute power over the Jewish inmates, resulting in countless acts of brutality, viciousness, and terror. None of the Jews expected to survive.

Blatt was the first to testify (see figure 7.8). On the eve of his testimony, I bumped into him in the lobby of my hotel; it turned out that he too was staying there. I recognized him from photos; in fact, I had spent the better part of the day reading *From the Ashes of Sobibor*, one of two books he has written about the camp. We fell into conversation, and he gaily told me, "I am thirty-eight—only reverse the numbers please." He wore a pair of red suspenders over a white shirt, and observed me with bright skeptical blue eyes. Accompanying him in Munich were two friends from southern California, where Blatt has lived for over fifty years. Grant, a retired electronics and software engineer, told me that Blatt had given him his first job, installing car stereos, forty years ago. Anita, Grant's partner, had worked as a commercial pilot with US Airways, flying 737s and she, too, was now retired. Having come to support Blatt in court, Grant and Anita were then planning to trek the way of St. James across France and Spain to the Shrine of the saint in the great cathedral in Santiago de Compostela.

The four of us dined together in the hotel's restaurant. Blatt spoke with the same heavy, now nearly extinct Yiddish accent that brought back memories of my long-dead grandfather. About him hovered the mysterious aura of history. He described Izbica, the town where he grew up: "It was the only town in all Poland without a church," he said. "Thirty-six hundred Jews and only two hundred Poles. On Friday nights before the Sabbath the whole town smelled of kerosene because the Jews were too poor to afford soap and used kerosene to wash their hair and kill the lice." His father was a free thinker who ate ham and smoked on the Sabbath.[21] After the German invasion, the SS essentially treated Izbica as a ghetto unto itself, later transforming it into a *Judenstadt*, a "Jew town," to serve as a collecting point for over twenty thousand Jews from the Reich, Czechoslovakia, and Posen destined for the death camps.[22] During a roundup Blatt saw a woman cry out, "Oh, God, I'm innocent. I'm not a Jew. I'm an honest Catholic, please help me." Some Poles confirmed her "innocence," and she escaped her brush with death.[23] A number of years ago Blatt returned to Izbica; a Pole roughly his age was now living in the Blatt family house. *I know why you've returned*, the Pole told him. *To reclaim the treasure that your family buried. Please, we can split it.* When Blatt next returned to Izbica, he found the house abandoned and in disrepair. A neighbor told him that the previous occupant had trashed the house looking for the hidden treasure.

Having written two books about Sobibor, Blatt now hoped to write one about his postwar years. It would be a collection of fragments, he told me, about his survival after the war until he left Poland in 1959. "Some of the stories are not so nice," he confessed. "I'm not such a nice man. I'm tired. I don't think I'll live more than two years. I take two pills, one for depression, one for high blood pressure. But maybe I don't have time to die."

About Demjanjuk, he had little to say: "He's an old man. If he's convicted is not so important. Whatever happens, he cannot go back to his home in Cleveland. That is punishment enough. What's important is for the victims to tell their story, to tell about Sobibor, which even today is not so well known."

The morning of his testimony, Blatt was withdrawn and visibly exhausted. The night before, he had given a talk at the Jewish Center in Munich, where he was introduced as a living "vehicle of memory." During the talk, which was well attended and enthusiastically received, Blatt told some of the same stories he had told me the night before, and also showed clips from *Escape from Sobibor*, a TV movie starring Alan Arkin that earned Blatt a screenplay credit. But the event kept him up late, and he slept poorly. Despite being on antidepressants, Blatt is often gravely depressed in the morning, bothered by thoughts of suicide. "Then he takes a shower," Grant said, "so hot you could cook an egg. That seems to help him."

The entrance to the hotel was cluttered with camera crews and journalists eager to interview Blatt. Later Blatt would clip these articles; he meticulously maintains an album of all his interviews: "Though for who? I don't know. My children don't want this. They've had enough. I made a mistake of taking my son to all my talks when he was a boy. It made him antigovernment. He doesn't have a driver's license so the government can't follow him. I wanted to buy him a car, but he won't get the license. He's almost fifty."

For Blatt's testimony, the courtroom, less than full in recent days, was once again packed, and security extremely tight. But before Blatt could take the stand, Demjanjuk's towering lawyer, Ulrich Busch, rose to lodge an objection. One of two lawyers representing Blatt was Martin Mendelsohn, the hard-boiled, politically connected lawyer who had ruffled feathers during his brief tenure as head of the Special Litigation Unit of the INS. For Busch, the presence of a former senior OSI official was nothing short of a scandal. Mendelsohn, he roared, was a central figure in the OSI's crusade against Demjanjuk. He accused Mendelsohn and the OSI of having practiced *Justizmord* against his client—judicial murder, a term commonly applied to the death sentences handed out willy-nilly by Nazi special courts.

Summarily dismissing Busch's overheated objections, the court invited Blatt to describe life in Sobibor. Blatt is hard of hearing, and his German lawyer had to bellow into his ear, repeating every question posed by the court. Worse, Blatt's answers emerged in a mishmash of English, German, and Yiddish, a linguistic goulash that left the court bewildered. "How *war ist möglich so viele* millions in *so kurzer Zeit* to murder?" "*Wir* arrived in Sobibor on trucks and *wir sehen, es war shayn*!" "Straight to the gas chambers, the *Leute waren* dead." During the first break, exiting my role as scholarly observer, I pulled Blatt's German lawyer aside and advised him to *order* his client to testify in English. Either the directive was never communicated or Blatt was too stubborn, exhausted, or confused to accept it; in any case, after the break, the survivor continued to baffle the court with his polyglot narrative. Judge Alt eyed Blatt with sympathy and respect, but took conspicuously few notes. The court reporter demonstratively looked at his watch. Thomas Lenz, the associate judge with the thickly gelled hair, gazed disdainfully down at Blatt, as if barely able to control his irritation at the waste of time.

Lenz was also not about to make any concessions to the age or experiences of the witness. His questions were sharp, pointed: "In your book, Mr. Blatt, you include diary entries. Was this a diary that you kept contemporaneously, or was this a diary that you later imagined?"

"*Meisten* my own memory *gehabt*"—mostly I had my own memories, an answer that clarified nothing.

"You quote from a diary," the associate judge pressed forward. "Is this a contemporaneous statement or a memory that you later wrote down?"

Blatt's lawyer re-shouted the question. Blatt shook his head. Either he could not remember or had not fully understood the question.

His only clear answer came in response to Judge Alt's question: Could he identify the defendant?

"I can't remember the face of my own mother and father," he said.

It was a poignant response, and also a revealing one. For Blatt had made the identical remark on numerous previous occasions, most recently in a interview in *Der Spiegel* that ran in the days before the start of the trial.[24] Despite his own attestation, "*Mein* memory *ist nicht* so good," there was nothing exactly wrong with Blatt's memory; the problem on display was not memory dulled by the passage of time, but memory volatized by repetition. At the time of his appearance in Munich, Blatt was already well known in Holocaust circles, a kind of professional survivor. He had been interviewed countless times; had given hundreds of lectures to schools and synagogues and civic centers; had been a witness at the trial of Sobibor guards in Hagen in 1965 and again at the retrial of Sobibor staff sergeant Karl Frenzel in 1985; had written two books about the camp; and had served as a consultant to documentaries and feature films. Over time, these stories and images had become enfolded back into the original content of Blatt's memory.

The historian Dick de Mildt has described an episode from the trial of Karl Streibel, the ex-commandant of Trawniki, who, together with five other Trawniki functionaries, was tried in Hamburg in the mid-1970s.[25] Testifying for the state, a Jewish survivor of the camp who had since settled in America, identified one of the SS functionaries as "*Obersturmbannführer* Klink." No other survivor could identify this particular SS lieutenant-colonel by name, so the witness' identification was crucial. But prosecutors had no record of an SS man named Klink at Trawniki, and were perplexed by the odd name. It came out that the survivor had apparently confused her Trawniki tormentor with another man—namely, the bungling monocled colonel who presided over the fictitious Stalag 13 in the American sitcom *Hogan's Heroes*.[26] So it was with Thomas Blatt, except that in his case, he had helped write the show that sowed the confusion. Memory had become unstable through its repetition, recitation, and collision with other representations of death-camp life. Blatt could no longer distinguish between memory and the memory of memory.

His struggles on the stand made for painful watching, yet Demjanjuk's lawyer did not know how to leave well enough alone. Instead, Busch pressed Blatt in an effort to discredit his testimony—testimony that had really done the accused nothing in the way of damage. Blatt never claimed to be able to identify Demjanjuk; his testimony meant only to provide a firsthand account of Sobibor. Even before his struggles became clear, it was evident that the court had called him less to accumulate evidence than to discharge an obligation. The court, with the exception of Lenz, treated Blatt like a fragile showpiece in a museum of memory, a precious artifact one is obligated to behold before moving on. Busch, however, insisted on lingering. He quoted from the decision of the court in the retrial of Frenzel in 1985, which questioned the value and accuracy of Blatt's memories. The gesture served no purpose other than to humiliate the witness. But Busch still wasn't finished. "In 1960," he asked, referring to Blatt's first interview with the Central Office for the investigation of Nazi crimes in Ludwigsburg, "you said there were 200 Trawniki *Wachmänner*, [and] now you say between 120 and 150."

The question, meant to show that Blatt had changed his statements to accommodate what he later learned in researching the camp's history, provided the eighty-three-year-old survivor a welcome opportunity to show his quickness.

"I wasn't a statistician at Sobibor," Blatt answered. "I was a prisoner."

"Did you voluntarily register to work with the Germans?" Busch asked.

Blatt had been a half year shy of sixteen when he arrived by truck at Sobibor. While the rest of his family—his parents and ten-year-old brother—immediately perished, he had survived by claiming to be a locksmith. Busch now wanted to know how a boy of fifteen managed to be chosen for work in the camp. How did this underage boy happen to get chosen? Did he "volunteer"? If so, how was this different from the Ukrainians who "volunteered" as guards?

The questions revealed a great deal about the tactics of the defense. During the course of the trial Busch would argue, seriatim, that the trial was a political show, that his client was fully innocent, that Demjanjuk never trained at Trawniki and had never served as a guard at Sobibor or at any other camp; and that even if he had, he had had no more choice than the Jews who worked the camp. The overdetermined quality of the defense called to mind Freud's story of a man who, charged with breaking a borrowed teakettle, insisted, "In the first place, he returned the kettle undamaged; in the second place, it already had holes in it when he borrowed it; and in the third place, he never borrowed it at all." Busch's grab-bag defense managed to be both internally contradictory and often outrageous, and his insistence that Demjanjuk—assuming, for the sake of argument, that he had served as a guard—had been every bit as much a victim as Thomas Blatt left many in the courtroom visibly appalled. Even then, most observers had missed the ugly cynicism in the question Busch put to Blatt. For the word Busch used for "chosen"—*auserwählt*—is typically reserved for the expression *das auserwählte Volk*: the chosen people. The gesture was utterly gratuitous, designed only to provoke.[27] But if Blatt missed the gratuitous phrasing, he clearly grasped the thrust of Busch's question. "*Ich bin das selber wie* the *mann* over there?" he answered. "*Nur ein Idiot konnte das sagen*"—"I'm the same as the man over there? Only an idiot could say that."

Philip Bialowitz had an easier time on the stand. Reading in English from a prepared statement, Bialowitz, who has lived most of his adult life in Queens, appeared clear and focused. He described a day at Sobibor when he was enlisted to cut the hair of women to be gassed; a Dutch woman, oblivious of her fate, beseeched him not to trim her hair too short. In contrast, the Polish Jews, who often arrived half-dead and deranged with thirst from the intolerable conditions of their journey, knew exactly what awaited them. "Even my seven-year-old niece knew she was going to die," Bialowitz said. He described further how during the camp revolt, the Jews had called out to the Ukrainian guards, "Come join us, the Red Army is near," but the guards continued shooting at them. Remarkably, both Bialowitz and his older brother, now living in Israel but too infirm to travel, managed to survive.

The judges listened attentively. Politely posing a few questions, they largely abstained from examining the witness. In attending to Bialowitz's words, it was as if the court were not confronting an actual living witness but laying a judicial wreath.

* * *

One final witness from *damals*—back then—appeared before the court: Alex Nagorny, the ex-Flossenbürg guard discovered during Thomas Walther's obsessive explorations of Demjanjuk's "microcosmos" of friends in his years as a displaced person. Nagorny was Walther's most remarkable discovery, a Trawniki-trained former guard who could testify not only to having served with Demjanjuk in Flossenbürg but to having lived with him in the same apartment in Landshut.[28]

But Nagorny also proved to be a difficult witness in ways altogether different from Thomas Blatt. If Blatt suffered from having remembered too much too often, Nagorny seemed determined to remember nothing at all. In part, the caginess of this small, wiry Ukrainian was understandable. Alt informed him of his right to remain silent, as any mention of his prior service at a death camp could prove incriminating. (After the trial, prosecutors would in fact investigate allegations that Nagorny had participated in killings at Treblinka.) As a consequence,

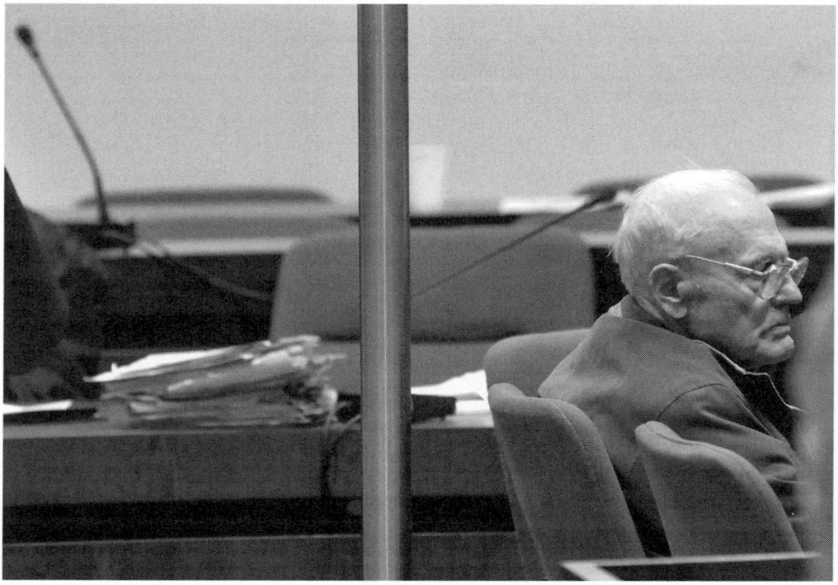

7.9. Former guard Alex Nagorny, a member of the "microcosmos." Photo by Thomas Hauzenberger.

Nagorny spoke exclusively about his service at Flossenbürg, where he claimed to have met Demjanjuk. Like Demjanjuk, Nagorny had been a Red Army soldier captured by the Germans and interned in a POW camp, before being selected for training at Trawniki. Testifying in Ukrainian (Nagorny had lived in Landshut ever since his days as a DP, but still spoke broken German and claimed to be illiterate),[29] he insisted that he had never heard of Sobibor—and also claimed to have no memory of the stone quarry at Flossenbürg, a frankly incredible assertion, given that the camp was created to service the quarry.[30] Nagorny further insisted that he never actually oversaw prisoners on their work details, but had worked exclusively in the guard tower, looking out. Pressed by Alt, Nagorny suffered a coughing fit that required a five-minute break. He was, however, able to recall serving with Demjanjuk at Flossenbürg, and casually noted that "Ivan lived in my apartment" in Landshut. (Indeed, the two managed to get in trouble in the DP camp. An illegal firearm was discovered in a truck they shared; Demjanjuk insisted that the gun belonged to Nagorny, and the infraction effectively prevented Nagorny from emigrating to the United States.) Asked for further details, Nagorny stonewalled, declaring, "I can't even remember what I had for breakfast today,"[31] a remark that oddly echoed Blatt's moving statement about not being able to remember the faces of his parents.

Nagorny's testimony offered a second, more remarkable moment of courtroom déjà vu. Asked if he could currently identify Demjanjuk, Nagorny steadied himself with his cane and approached the defendant, who did not stir on his gurney. At the judge's request, Demjanjuk removed his sunglasses. It was as if the Munich court were restaging the moment in Demjanjuk's Jerusalem trial when Eliahu Rosenberg claimed to recognize the murderous eyes of Ivan the Terrible. Only this time the witness shook his head. "He doesn't resemble him at all," Nagorny declared. (*"Er ist [ihm] überhaupt nicht ähnlich."*)[32] Had this been an American jury trial, Nagorny's emphatic statement would have represented a disastrous setback for the prosecution, supplying one of those sensational "if the glove don't fit, you must acquit" moments endlessly rehearsed and replayed in media coverage of a trial. In Munich, however, the court received Nagorny's declaration with aplomb and the media barely gave it a mention. After all, Nagorny had previously identified Demjanjuk from both his Trawniki service ID and his visa photo from 1951, and no one disputed that the visa photo pictured a younger version of the old man in the courtroom. Nagorny's failure to connect the two had, then, no bearing on his statement about serving with Demjanjuk.

And yet his insistence that the defendant "doesn't resemble" Ivan could be heard in a different way—as suggesting that the gap between *damals* and now had grown so vast that the inert old man no longer bore any resemblance to the strapping youth whom Nagorny had known. This, of course, was very much the story line of the defense. In his steadfast silence and pantomimes of decrepitude, Demjanjuk sought to sever whatever vestigial connections might have linked him to his lived past. He was, or so he wanted the court to believe, a relic dislodged from memory, an invalid disconnected from his own history.

8

The Trial by History

With oversized glasses, dishwater blonde hair combed boyishly across his brow, and a rapid-fire delivery, Dieter Pohl looks and speaks like an eager graduate student. In fact, Pohl is a well-known historian at the University of Klagenfurt. At the time of the trial, he was on the faculty of the Center for Contemporary History in Munich, the prestigious research institute that has prepared hundreds of expert reports for courts trying cases involving Nazi crimes. Called by the judges as an expert witness, Pohl read his testimony from a prepared text. German academics are notorious for reading their lectures in a flat and uninflected voice, their eyes glued to their text, and for the next two-plus hours Pohl rigorously subscribed to this dreary protocol—at times reading so quickly that Ms. Gerlach, Demjanjuk's interpreter, had to plead with the court to remind the professor to slow down. This he managed for just a few minutes before his delivery again accelerated, leaving the interpreter in despair.

Pohl began with a general overview of the Reich's *Judenpolitik*—its "Jewish policies"—and moved on to a discussion of Sobibor and the Trawniki *Wachmänner*.[1] The general lines of the story he told are by now familiar: Göring gives Heydrich the authorization for a *Gesamtlösung*, a "complete solution," to the *Judenproblem* . . . . The total number of victims at Sobibor is hard to estimate (his best guess, around 170,000). . . . Seven mass graves have been identified by archaeologists. . . . Trawniki lies forty kilometers from Lublin, at the site of a former sugar factory. . . . The guards were like auxiliary police. . . . As Pohl droned on, the judges dutifully took notes while the two *Schöffen*—

the lay deliberators—gazed at the professor with their familiar expression of feigned attention.

Pohl was not necessarily the ideal historian to summon as an expert. Originally, the court had considered calling Peter Black, who, since leaving the OSI in 1997, has worked as a public historian at the United States Holocaust Memorial Museum. Black is perhaps the world's foremost expert on the Trawniki camp and its guard force, whereas Pohl is more an expert on the history of the Ukraine during the war. But Germans close to the case, and Black himself, worried that his previous association with the OSI might create a needless distraction; Black then suggested that Pohl testify in his stead.[2] It was not an altogether happy substitution. Not only did Pohl prove to be a dull witness, but he also revealed certain stubborn scholarly prejudices and idiosyncrasies. Perhaps foremost among them was his instinctual distrust of Soviet testimony. Where fellow historians might have treated material with wariness, Pohl moved straight to open doubt; for example, he questioned the reliability of Danilchenko's seemingly precise statements, offered decades apart, describing his service with Demjanjuk at Sobibor and Flossenbürg. And in an effort to appear rigorously objective, Pohl couched every answer to questions posed by the court in needless qualifications.[3]

Yet for all his dullness and hedging, Pohl proved to be the trial's most important witness. To understand why, we must distinguish his testimony from earlier notable appearances of historians in Holocaust trials. At the Eichmann trial, the very first witness had been Salo Baron, a prominent scholar of Jewish history at Columbia, who delivered a lengthy lecture on two millennia of anti-Semitism culminating in the Holocaust. At Demjanjuk's Jerusalem trial, the first witness had been Yitzhak Arad, a prominent Israeli historian and the then director of Yad Vashem, who lectured the court on the Holocaust and Aktion Reinhard. And in the trial of Maurice Papon, the former French budget minister convicted in 1998 for his actions as a police official during the Nazi occupation of France, Robert Paxton, a noted authority on Vichy, offered a nuanced account of the Nazi occupation of France.

In appearing as historical experts, Baron, Arad, and Paxton provided context and background. Pohl also offered background on Aktion Reinhard, but the ultimate purpose of his testimony was altogether different. As we've noted, the prosecution's case would turn less on specific evidence of what John Demjanjuk did than on historical evidence about what people in Demjanjuk's position *must have done*. This was the critical function of Pohl's testimony: it told the court what Demjanjuk must have done at Sobibor. As such, it represented a significant evolution in the role of the historical expert, and a necessary one. In 1997, the famous French historian of Vichy, Henry Rousso, declined to testify in the trial of Maurice Papon, expressing concern about what he called a "judicialization of the past"—trials in which "beyond the judgment of particular individuals, the declared goal is to illuminate an entire era and its politics."[74] Such a critique made no sense in Demjanjuk's Munich trial—or rather, if accepted, it would have simply rendered the trial impossible. For in a trial essentially without witnesses, basic legal questions were *unanswerable* without the insights of professional historians. Whether Demjanjuk was being used, as Rousso worried, to "illuminate an entire era" can be debated; the defense, of course, insisted that he was, but the complaint missed the larger point. The Munich trial witnessed a far more interesting use of history. The defendant was less used to shine light on Nazi atrocity, than a detailed historical understanding of an exterminatory process was deployed in order to illuminate the actions of a single individual. To put it somewhat differently, at Munich the juridical determination of personal guilt turned on basic answers to aggregate historical questions.

We have noted that the prosecution, lacking evidence that the accused had killed with his own hand, developed a rather brilliant theory specifically tailored to the realities of service at a death camp. The argument was as simple and irresistible as a syllogism:

All Sobibor guards participated in the killing process.
Demjanjuk was a Sobibor guard.
Therefore Demjanjuk participated in the killing process.

The reasoning was deductive, and so the conclusion had to be true if both premises were true. The minor premise—that Demjanjuk had served as a Sobibor guard—was solidly established by the same documents used by the OSI in the second denaturalization trial. (Here Nagorny's testimony, which helped prove Demjanjuk's assignment to Sobibor by triangulating it with evidence of his service at Majdanek and Flossenbürg, represented the only substantive advance over the OSI's case.)

It was the major premise, then, that commanded the attention of the court: *all Sobibor guards participated in the killing process*. Proving this was an altogether different undertaking from proving Demjanjuk's service at Sobibor. True, it also entailed a careful examination of the documentary record; but more to the point, it required a full narrative history of how the camp and its guards functioned. In essence, the major premise was an aggregate historical claim, and as such could *only* be proved by a comprehensive historical study of Sobibor and its Trawniki-trained guards. Here documents were not marshaled to reconstruct a chronology, but rather were used to create a nuanced and complete *history*. The Munich proceeding was, at its heart, a trial by history.

To this end, Pohl's testimony established two critical facts. The first was that Sobibor was a death camp. This, of course, was hardly a novel insight; we've seen that, as early as 1950, a Frankfurt trial court described Sobibor as a pure killing center. All the same, the distinction between Majdanek and Auschwitz, on the one hand, and Treblinka, Belzec, and Sobibor, on the other, often blurred in the minds of jurists. The holding in the Frankfurt-Auschwitz trial, which introduced the *Einzeltat* requirement, appeared to recognize the difference between hybrid camps (e.g., Auschwitz) and killing centers, pure and simple. (Recall that around one hundred thousand people survived Auschwitz, while 120 Jews survived the Aktion Reinhard camps.) And yet the holding worked instead in the opposite fashion, eliding the difference between hybrid camps and death camps, and leaving investigators scrambling to find evidence of specific acts of hands-on killing in all cases. Pohl's testimony helped to restore conceptual clarity about the nature and function of the Aktion Reinhard camps.

As a second matter, Pohl attested that *all* guards at Sobibor were generalists. We've noted that the entire supervisory force at Sobibor consisted of twenty or so SS men and 100 to 120 Trawniki-trained guards. The Trawnikis were divided into three companies: the first was responsible for guarding the camp perimeter; the second guarded the work Jews; and the third were on standby. The companies rotated through these tasks in eight-hour cycles. When transports of Jews arrived, however, the entire bare-bones operation was mobilized.[5] Some guards would have continued to man the guard towers while the rest were dispatched to the train ramp to manage the well-rehearsed process of extermination.[6] In manning the towers—that is, in guarding against escape or disorder—or working the train ramp, *all* the Trawniki men facilitated the camp's function: the mass killing of Jews. This point was crucial; if the defense had been able to demonstrate that some Trawniki men worked, say, exclusively as cooks, the prosecution's major premise would have been considerably weakened, as the indictment turned not on what Demjanjuk personally did, but on the function he must have performed.[7] By establishing that Sobibor was a killing machine and that *all* guards participated in the machine's killing operation, the prosecution could claim that Demjanjuk's complicity followed in lockstep. Pohl's testimony left no doubt, then, that at Sobibor all Trawniki men served as accessories to murder because *that was their job*.

This point, however, did not end the inquiry. For even if the court accepted the prosecution's theory of criminal liability, it still had to answer perhaps the most vexing question raised by the case. Had Demjanjuk served at Sobibor voluntarily? As Manuel Bloch, the Jewish lawyer from Amsterdam who represented the Sobibor Foundation, remarked in private what was on the mind of presumably everyone associated with the trial: "There's only really one interesting question here, *nicht*?" Remarkably, in all the years that the Demjanjuk case had consumed the attention of lawyers and judges, this question had never been addressed, much less answered. Indeed, it had never even been considered. In its landmark *Fedorenko* ruling, the US Supreme Court held that the voluntariness of service was not germane in denaturalization cases; in Israel, the question also never arose—Ivan the Terrible was the ultimate *Exzesstäter*, a sadistic sociopath, and the defense had argued mistaken identity.

The voluntariness question thus represented terra novum for the Demjanjuk case. It was, of course, a legal question that only the court could answer. A historian can no more tell a court that an action was voluntary than a ballistics expert can tell a court that a shooting was premeditated. Complicating the inquiry was the fact that for decades, German courts in Nazi cases had been exceptionally receptive to the defense of "putative necessity." In contrast to a pure necessity defense, which must show that the defendant had no choice but to engage in the criminal act, putative necessity must show only that the defendant *believed* that he lacked choice, and that this belief, even if erroneous, was reasonable under the circumstances. This defense must also be distinguished from the "superior orders" defense that, to the indignation of German jurists, had been barred at Nuremberg. In a superior orders defense, the accused argues that he assumed his actions were legal because they were ordered by a properly recognized superior. The putative necessity defense, by contrast, works from the assumption that the defendant knew of the criminality of his received orders but reasonably believed that the failure to comply would have put him in danger of life or limb.

As we've seen, the acquittal in 1950 of the head of Sobibor's *Schuhkommando*, Johann Klier, represented a pioneering success of the necessity defense.[8] It was the first of many. In 1963, eight SS functionaries of the Belzec death camp were set to stand trial in Munich, including such notorious figures as Erich Fuchs and Werner Dubois, both of whom had serviced the Belzec gas chamber (and both later served at Sobibor). A pretrial motion by the defendants resulted in the dismissal of all charges against seven of the eight defendants on grounds of putative necessity. (Josef Oberhauser, who had overseen the expansion of Belzec's gas chambers and had been personally promoted by Himmler, was the sole defendant whose case went to trial. Oberhauser was convicted, but only as an accessory, with the court concluding that he had not acted with the "will of a perpetrator" but only "with the will to fulfill duty.")[9] We've noted that a major trial of Sobibor functionaries ended in 1966 with the outright acquittal of five of eleven former SS men, again on grounds of putative necessity. (Among the acquitted was Erich Lachmann, who, as head of the camp's Trawniki-trained guard force, had been Demjanjuk's senior commanding officer.)[10] A decade later, in 1976, a Hamburg court acquitted former Trawniki commandant Karl Streibel and five other SS functionaries at the camp of all criminal charges, rul-

8.1. Trawniki Commandant Karl Streibel, center, with recruits. Tried in Hamburg, Streibel was acquitted on all charges in 1976. Staatsarchiv Hamburg.

ing that the evidence failed to prove that the commandant and his support staff had known the nature of the work the trainees were being prepared to perform.[11]

Such rulings fuelled the outrage of defense counsel Ulrich Busch, who never tired of reciting the litany of Nazi perpetrators let free by German courts or never even tried in the first place. How, he railed, could a system that acquitted the likes of Streibel and Lachmann possibly convict someone as inconsequential as Demjanjuk?

Busch meant his question rhetorically, but it could be answered. As a matter of German case law, SS men acquitted on grounds of putative necessity essentially profited from the ignorance of earlier trial courts. The result in the scandalous Belzec case, for example, was the predictable consequence of two crucial problems with the prosecution's case. To impeach a claim of putative necessity, the prosecution could pursue two possible avenues. First, it could present evidence that the accused had acted as an *Exzesstäter*, committing acts in excess of what his orders required; such zeal would presumably prove that the accused had not acted out of fear for life or limb. Alternatively, the prosecution could attack the claim that the accused had any reason to fear for his life. The first approach required survivor witnesses, as few SS men or Trawnikis were willing to testify against one another. In the case of Belzec, the very success of the camp as an exterminatory machine made this impossible—indeed, only a single survivor remained alive at the time of the start of the Munich proceeding in 1963, and this survivor, Rudolf Reder, proved unable to say much about the conduct of the specific defendants. Without witnesses who could impeach the claims of the defendants, the court had had little choice but to accept the former SS men's own insistence that they had not engaged in acts of excess.

The second alternative called for directly challenging the claim that SS men had reasonably believed they faced death or great bodily harm if they opted out of the killing process. This, however, required detailed historical knowledge about the larger culture of the SS and how refusals to exterminate were treated. At the time of the Belzec and Sobibor trials, this knowledge was largely lacking. Courts had little choice, then, but to accept the statements of men such as Hans Globke, whose role in drafting the Nuremberg Race Laws of 1935 had not interfered with his postwar rise to Adenauer's state secretary and who testified at the Belzec case that the consequences of opting out were draconian. As a prominent German prosecutor grudgingly noted, "Because putative necessity could not be excluded in these cases, the principle of in *dubio pro reo* (doubt favors the accused) required the suspension of legal proceedings."[12]

Over the years, however, as historians came to better understand SS culture and practices, German courts became far less receptive to the putative necessity defense. An extraordinary research effort was dedicated to exploring the question of duress, and the results were astonishing: historians failed to uncover so much as a single instance in which a German officer or NCO faced "dire punishment" for opting out of genocide.[13] Experts of all ilks examined the question, including those who obviously hoped to find material supportive of the defense of former SS men. But no cases turned up. *Not a single one.*

And it was not because cases of opting out could not be found. People did opt out—not as many as one might have hoped, but enough to draw conclusions. It seems fair to say that opting out was not a brilliant career move. One faced being ostracized from the group, branded a coward or a Jew lover, transferred to a position on the front, or even tried before an SS court. (In cases that went to trial, the punishments were invariably minor.) None of this would have been pleasant, to be sure. Yet as one commentator has observed, "An absence of promotion, humiliation, damage to one's reputation, or unpleasant treatment by superiors" does not constitute putative necessity.[14] "Without doubt, he [the refuser] would have suffered disadvantages," notes Kurt Schrimm, head of the Central Office in Ludwigsburg; yet, "no supervisor or underling [*Befehlsempfänger*] ever lost his life because he refused to shoot a prisoner or escort him to the gas chamber."[15] Perhaps the most frequent disadvantage, according to Schrimm, would have been losing a "relatively cushy position in a camp." And often enough the refusers suffered no consequences at all.

Over time, this accumulation of historical evidence made it increasingly difficult for former SS members to argue putative necessity. Nevertheless, it did not necessarily address the special case of the Trawniki-trained *Wachmänner*. German courts had long avoided trying non-Germans; the Demjanjuk prosecution in fact represented a dramatic break with established (non)practice. Part of the problem was jurisdictional—German courts used weak, if not specious, jurisdictional arguments to refuse cases involving non-Germans. But the deeper problem again involved putative necessity. In a longstanding practice, the Central Office had simply neglected investigating Trawnikis out of the assumption that all such cases were vulnerable to a putative necessity defense.[16] Emblematic were the comments of Helga Grabitz, prosecutor in the failed trial of Trawniki commandant Streibel (and spouse of Professor Wolfgang Scheffler, the OSI's expert witness in Demjanjuk's first denaturalization trial).[17] In a book published in 1988, Grabitz concluded that the Trawnikis had volunteered in order to "escape certain death from starvation, exposure or disease."[18] "In the Fall, 1941," the prosecutor wrote, "Soviet POWs had faced two choices: die in camps or accept the offer to register with SS Trawniki training."[19] In light of these circumstances and the hierarchy within the training camp, Trawnikis "confronted incomparably different psychological pressures . . . than regular Germans [*unvergleichbar anderen psychologischer Drucksituation*]." In Grabitz's account, the slightest violations of discipline by the Trawnikis occasioned extreme punishment: "Refusal of orders . . . was out of the question; given their special situation, they could have reckoned with their own shooting in case they resisted orders."[20]

In Munich, the prosecution essentially insisted that Grabitz had gotten it all wrong.[21] Nearly a quarter century had passed since she had published her conclusions, and in that time historians had radically revised our understandings of the Trawnikis. Here again Professor Pohl served as the court's conduit for these fresh insights, though they came less from his own work than from Peter Black's. Black had carefully examined the claim that Soviet soldiers in German captivity faced a draconian choice: either train with the SS or die in a POW camp. It is true that of the 5.7 million Red Army soldiers taken as POWs by the Wehrmacht, an astonishing 3.3 million died in captivity. The camps for Red Army POWs were often little more than open-air enclosures, lacking sanitation, reliable food supply, medical facilities, and even the barest protection from the elements. As temperatures plummeted in the fall of 1941, conditions in these camps became untenable; disease, particularly dysentery and typhus, raged uncontrolled; and the combination of exposure, starvation, and disease resulted in a mass die-off of Soviet POWs between December 1941 and January 1942. Nonetheless, not all Red Army POWs faced the identical treatment. Jewish POWs, for example, were sorted out for immediate killing. Ukrainian POWs meanwhile tended to fair far better than their Russian brethren. By the end of January 1942, the Germans had for various reasons released some 280,108 Red Army POWs; of these 270,095 were Ukrainians. Not one was Russian.[22] By the time of Demjanjuk's capture in the Kerch campaign in May 1942, the prospects for POWs had improved inasmuch as the Nazis had decided that, instead of letting captured Red Army soldiers starve to death, they would henceforth be used as forced laborers.[23] (The decision was designed in part to compensate for Jewish labor lost to genocide; in this sense, Soviet POWs were the first beneficiaries of the decision to exterminate the Jews.) And so the choice facing a captured Ukrainian in the spring of 1942 was not between collaboration and death, as Grabitz had formulated it, but between collaboration and forced labor.

This is not to say with certainty that Demjanjuk knew of these improved prospects. It is possible that Ukrainian POWs still believed that collaboration offered the only meaningful alternative to death.[24] Moreover, those who agreed to collaborate had no idea what that would entail, at least not at the outset. Once Demjanjuk began his training at Trawniki, the general nature of his assignment would have been clear. The Trawniki facility maintained a small Jewish slave-labor camp that permitted recruits to practice "pacifying" Jews and other techniques of "racial security."[25] And once a *Wachmann* was detailed to Sobibor, the purpose of the camp would have been immediately obvious. Still, none of these facts proves voluntary service. Nor do they challenge Grabitz's belief that the Trawnikis were cowed and fearful lackeys of the SS, a claim that found its echo in Busch's insistence that the Trawnikis were closer in status to their Jewish captives than to their SS overseers—that Demjanjuk was in much the same boat as Blatt.

But here is where Black's scholarship as presented by Pohl showed its greatest force. Black demonstrated that Trawnikis categorically ceased to be POWs once they entered Trawniki. In a textured, granular analysis, Black showed that trainees received uniforms, at first captured Polish army uniforms dyed black, later earth-brown Belgian uniforms; they received firearms, typically rifles captured from Russians, but also German carbines, automatic rifles, and pistols; and they were paid, receiving, during Demjanjuk's tenure at Sobibor, an across-the-board wage increase to forty-five Reichsmarks per month, paid in Polish zlotys, the currency of the Generalgouvernement.[26] The *Wachmänner* received regular days off, when they could enjoy ready access to tobacco, vodka, and women; they drew paid home leave, which the Germans continued to award even in the face of evidence that many Trawnikis failed to return to service after their leave; they received free medical care in German military hospitals; and if killed in the line of duty, they were eligible for burial with honors.[27] They were eligible for promotion, with some advancing to the rank of *Oberzugwachmann*, or Senior NCO, and the SS encouraged fraternization between SS enlisted men and the Trawniki NCOs. Black even located cases of Trawnikis opting out of service. A guard named Victor Bogomolow successfully requested discharge on grounds that "I'm not suited to guard service [*Da ich mich zu dem Wachdienst nicht eigne*]."[28] In short, Black's research demonstrated that the difference between the death-camp inmates and the Trawnikis who guarded them was "stark and unequivocal."[29] In the case of Sobibor, no one could in good faith continue to argue that the Trawniki *Wachmänner*, armed and outnumbering members of the SS by at least five to one, were no more than glorified prisoners. To the contrary, they were entrusted with maintaining the smooth operation of the death camp; without their efforts, the small group of two hundred SS men detailed to Aktion Reinhard could never have murdered as many as 1.7 million human beings.[30] The contribution of the Trawnikis was not merely vital; it was valued and rewarded.

Which is not to say that the Trawnikis always rewarded the trust placed in them. Cases of drunkenness, corruption, sleeping on duty, theft, plundering, curfew violations, and unauthorized leave abounded. We've already seen that Demjanjuk received punishment for indulging his appetite for "salt and onions" during a Majdanek lockdown. According to one German policeman, the Trawnikis "stole like magpies," and a German commander complained that they "stood first in line when it came to robbery and deadly assault."[31] In addition to serving as death-camp guards, Trawnikis often participated in regional mass shootings and in ghetto clearings, a task that involved the emptying of old-age homes, orphanages, and hospitals. In performing these tasks, they often distinguished themselves with their brutality, often behaving more wantonly than members of the SS.[32]

But most of all, they deserted. They deserted early and often. Peter Black has estimated that of the five thousand Trawnikis, *at least* one-fifth—fully a thousand men—deserted. According to Pohl, around 30 percent of the Trawniki men assigned to Belzec deserted.[33] These astonishingly high desertion rates may have had little to do with any moral qualms about genocide. As the winds of war shifted, many Trawniki guards clearly came to reconsider the wisdom of collaborating with the SS—witness the spike in desertions after the Germans' defeat at Stalingrad. The very success of Aktion Reinhard may also have contributed to an uptick in desertions; with no more Jews to exterminate, opportunities for plunder and self-enrichment dwindled.[34] It is difficult to say how many Trawnikis deserted specifically from Sobibor, since the camp's records were destroyed by the SS. Still, Sobibor was a mere hour's walk from the Ukrainian border, just over the River Bug, and the temptation must have been great—a point the court could appreciate in light of the historical documentation showing that consequences of attempting to desert were significantly less severe than had been commonly believed. While surviving records from Belzec suggest that Trawnikis who fled with their weapons were assumed to have shifted alliances and faced possible execution if caught, those who left their weapons behind and later were captured typically suffered far less draconian punishment. Indeed, most were soon back at their guard duties.

All in all, this wealth of historical detail directly challenged the conclusions of Grabitz that formed a bulwark of Demjanjuk's defense in Munich. Far from being glorified prisoners, the Trawnikis were vital and valued assistants in genocide. The fact that so many chose to desert—and that the consequences of a failed attempt were often far from severe—powerfully suggests that those who remained did so for reasons other than simply fear for life or limb. Indeed, the prosecution's case turned on this point. For the prosecution, Demjanjuk had a moral and a *legal* obligation to desert. The argument was not without its difficulties, as it raised a vexing question: when did the obligation to desert attach? On the very day that a *Wachmann* first became aware of his duties in the killing operation? What of the guards who deserted after months of service? Had they not acted voluntarily until the moment they fled?

Perhaps fortunately, the prosecution did not have to face these questions. Instead, it sufficed to argue that Demjanjuk's failure to desert represented a *choice* to continue to assist in mass murder. This was not to claim Demjanjuk would have elected to serve in a death camp from the get-go. But once he found himself serving, he chose to stay put, and that choice, even if constrained by circumstance, was voluntary. Constrained choice, after all, is crucially different than no choice whatsoever. Perhaps Demjanjuk remained because he shared the SS' ideological ambitions. Perhaps he did so because he soberly calculated that his chances of surviving the war were higher if he assisted in genocide than if he struck off on his own. Perhaps he enjoyed the material comforts of being a camp guard despite the distasteful tasks he had to perform. Any or all of these considerations might have played a role. Yet however one reconstructed his motives, the same conclusion emerged: given the range of available options, Demjanjuk voluntarily chose to continue working as a guard in a death camp.

* * *

The trial would turn on whether the court agreed. Alas, Demjanjuk's defense, instead of placing the question of voluntariness front and center, pursued a scattershot strategy that distracted the court from "the only interesting question." Demjanjuk's defense team consisted of two lawyers. The court-appointed counsel was Günther Maul. Already seventy-three at the trial's outset, Maul was an experienced attorney at the end of his professional career, and he remained a passive figure during the trial, a silent observer methodically chewing gum. He did file a handful of motions concerning the terms of his client's detention, but these were mostly modest requests to extend Demjanjuk's bimonthly calls home from thirty to forty-five minutes, or to request a multiband radio so Demjanjuk could listen to Ukrainian news and music.[35]

While Maul worked at the edges, Ulrich Busch orchestrated the central elements of the defense. Like Maul, Busch was paid by the court—Demjanjuk's family, with decades of legal costs behind them, could not afford to hire private counsel—but unlike Maul, he had been directly retained by the Demjanjuks. (Busch's wife, Vera Kostiuk-Busch, a cheerful stout American with rosy cheeks and a friendly face, hails from a Ukrainian family that settled in Detroit; an acquaintance in Cleveland asked her husband to serve on the defense. In recognition for helping to arrange representation for Demjanjuk, Vera was honored in 2009 as "Ukrainian of the Year" by the Ukrainian Graduates of Detroit and Windsor, Ontario, a local professional organization.)[36] Bearded, gigantic, and frequently disheveled, Busch is an excitable man with a choleric temper. At critical junctures during the trial, his face would redden in a frightening, infarction-heralding manner, as if he, and not his client, was about to succumb to the stresses of the trial. Early in the proceeding, he publicly lost his temper with his elder co-counsel, bellowing in easy earshot of journalists, "I can't work with people who stab me in the back. Quit the defense if you think the court is right!"[37]

Busch has enjoyed at least one notable success in his career. In 2006 the European Court of Human Rights offered a landmark ruling in a case he had appealed to Strasbourg, involving two drug dealers who had died after German police had forcibly used emetics in order to "obtain" the swallowed evidence. The European Court, citing the Supreme

8.2. Lead defense lawyer Ulrich Busch. Photo by Thomas Hauzenberger.

Court's famous *Rochin* decision, which held that similar conduct violated substantive due process, ruled that the forced use of emetics constituted a violation of basic rights.

That success notwithstanding, the Demjanjuk case represented the biggest of Busch's career. Whether he was up to the challenge was, however, far from clear. Compared to the lawyers of the *Nebenkläger*, who had digitized their entire case and could call up documents in an instant, Busch often seemed disorganized, fumbling to locate papers. His endless motions included those written by hand in obvious haste, and on one occasion, Professor Nestler, lead lawyer for the *Nebenkläger*, calmly proffered Busch a copy of his own mislaid motion. On another occasion Busch portentously asked a witness, "Would you be surprised to learn . . . ?" The witness seemed genuinely caught off guard. "Yes," he answered, "I would be surprised . . ." But there was no follow-up. Busch shuffled papers, cleared his throat, and pursued a fresh line of questioning.

This lack of organization exposed him to embarrassing mistakes. Two days before Thomas Blatt was to testify, I mentioned to Busch during an interview that I had bumped into Blatt in my hotel lobby. As a separate matter, I told him that I had just returned from a visit to the Central Office in Ludwigsburg. Somehow these two incidents became confused in Busch's mind, and in court he began his questioning of Blatt by asking the survivor if he had ever visited the Central Office. Yes, Blatt answered, forty years ago. "Were you in Ludwigsburg on Monday?" Busch demanded. Blatt shook his head. The line of questioning confused everyone in the courtroom—it was not clear what Busch hoped to prove anyway, except, perhaps, that Blatt had been coached by German investigators—and I alone knew its origin. In person, Busch was affable, quick to laugh, and generous with his time. At times, he spoke movingly of fighting the good fight, of engaging in a David versus Goliath struggle against the formidable legal forces arrayed against his client. He also often spoke of his defense of Israeli drug dealers in Germany and of his friendship with a Swiss rabbi named Michael Goldberger, presumably in the hopes of demonstrating that his zealous advocacy on Demjanjuk's behalf was not motivated by anti-Semitism.[38] All the same, he seemed incapable of quieting a mouth that naturally produced howlers, as when he shared with me the speculation that Thomas Blatt had testified to boost the sales of his books.[39]

On any given day, Busch would begin by reading from a litany of motions to dismiss or delay. By the trial's end, the defense would inundate the court with 515 such motions. With the rare exception, the court rejected them all. According to Busch, the German legal system was trying to make up for its pathetic record of dealing with Nazis by trying a man who was neither a German nor a Nazi. The trial was nothing more than an unconstitutional exercise in displacement, in which German guilt for the Holocaust was being shifted from the actual perpetrators onto a handful of foreigners, who themselves had been victims of the Reich. New standards were being invented out of whole cloth for use against his client. The rules of the game were being changed, and changed outrageously. Again and again Busch raised the names of Nazi perpetrators who had eluded justice. Lachmann! Streibel! How could a system that acquitted the SS *leader* of the Trawnikis at Sobibor and the *commandant* of Trawniki now convict Demjanjuk? For decades German jurists failed to try perpetrators right under their nose, yet whom do they now go after?—a man who was as much a victim as Thomas Blatt. Demjanjuk, he railed, was nothing more than a fall guy, a martyr of *Justizmord*, "judicial murder." And let us not forget that his client already spent seven years in an Israeli prison, five awaiting execution!

In his attempt to turn the proceeding into a political trial, Busch plucked a page from the defense of Klaus Barbie, the notorious Butcher of Lyon, whose trial in France began roughly at the same time as Demjanjuk's trial in Jerusalem. In Lyon, Barbie's defense lawyer Jacques Vergès—a highly polished, sinisterly calm advocate who had cultivated close personal ties to Pol Pot and Palestinian terrorists—had launched what he called a "defense of rupture."[40] The aim had been to turn the prosecution of Barbie, a German, into a political trial that laid bare France's shameful record of collaboration and colonial exploitation. Busch's effort, by contrast, focused on the failure of the German legal system to pursue Nazi criminals. His strategy also borrowed from Yoram Sheftel's show trial defense, and, indeed, Busch periodically would call Sheftel in Tel Aviv to discuss the case. But while Sheftel's argument—that the Jerusalem court had permitted the trial's memorializing and didactic ends to overwhelm the legal proceeding—had merit, Busch's insistence that Demjanjuk's trial was the work of an "unconstitutional special court" (*verfassungswidriges Sondergericht*) was little more than a crass rhetorical attempt to taint the Munich court by casting it as a latter-day instrument of Nazi justice. To this end, Busch routinely misappropriated terms used to describe Nazi victims. Thus Demjanjuk had been forcibly deported (*zwangsdeportiert*), a term used to designate the forced removal of Jews, and had been hunted (*gejagt*) and persecuted (*verfolgt*), words again used to describe the Nazis' treatment of Jews. Demjanjuk was a prisoner of war (*Kriegsgefangener*), the very term deployed by Germans in the postwar years to discredit the Allies' war crimes trials, while the OSI was a "criminal organization," the legal designation applied to the SS and Gestapo at Nuremberg.

None of this made any real sense. The Munich court was not a special court; if anything, Judge Alt could have been faulted for bending over backward in his attempt to treat the trial as an ordinary proceeding. Nor was the court applying special law. Indeed, many of the failures of the German legal system decried by Busch followed, as we have seen, from its stubborn refusal to use the special incriminations—crimes against humanity and genocide—designed to facilitate the prosecution of mass crimes. And the notion that the trial amounted to an exercise in displacement, an attempt to lessen or relativize German guilt by "claiming that the Ukrainians and the European neighbors of Germany were the true perpetrators of Nazi crimes,"[41] also did not parse. No one associated with the trial betrayed any confusion about who bore the ultimate and clear responsibility for the Holocaust. Indeed, if there was any relativizing of the Holocaust, it came from the defense. Holocausts proliferated in Busch's tirades. The Holodomor—the great Ukrainian famine of 1932–33—was a Holocaust, as was the mass die-off of Soviet POWs during the winter of 1941–42. Thomas Blatt in fact had survived but one Holocaust, while Demjanjuk had survived two!

Not all of Busch's outrage was entirely misplaced. It is true that Germany managed to successfully try only a tiny fraction of those responsible for the Holocaust. As we have noted, of the 6600 convictions secured in German courts dealing with Nazi-era crimes, around 4600 were handed down during the occupation period, and few dealt with the gravest of crimes. Since the creation of the Central Office in 1958 until Demjanjuk's conviction in 2011, courts in the Federal Republic managed to convict little more than 560 persons for crimes associated with Nazi-era killings.[42] Whole classes of persons were rendered exempt from criminal prosecution thanks to various amnesties, including most notoriously the bureaucrats in the Reich Security Main Office, beneficiaries, as we've seen, of the "cold," or inadvertent, amnesty law of 1968, a fiasco that enabled many of the genuinely big Nazi fish, the true predators, to escape prosecution altogether.

Yet even granting all this, Busch's critique missed the mark by a wide margin. First, we must note that for all its shortcomings, the German criminal justice system nevertheless managed to launch thousands of investigations that in turn gave rise to hundreds of prosecutions and convictions. Certainly it is disappointing that a Hagen court acquitted Erich Lachmann in 1966; still, that same court convicted six Sobibor functionaries, and its written decision showed an understanding of the death camp's operation that powerfully anticipated the approach of the Demjanjuk prosecution. Lachmann's acquittal was less the result of the court's bad faith, and more the predictable outcome of a jurisprudence of murder, which, despite a willingness to embrace a theory of functional participation, lacked an adequate understanding of the realities of death-camp service. Indeed, in the absence of historical evidence to the contrary, the court had little choice but to accept the defendant's defense of putative necessity. German courts were not laggard or tardy in trying the Lachmanns of the world; if anything, the trials came too *early*, before historians had delivered a detailed, precise, and legally compelling understanding of SS culture.

Busch's critique suffered from another defect. In railing against the German legal system, Busch radically compressed time, treating the acquittals of Lachmann and Streibel as contemporaneous events running in parallel to the Demjanjuk trial. Had this been the case, the defense's barks might have had some bite. But decades separated these verdicts. It is impossible to imagine Lachmann being acquitted today. Courts learn over time. Demjanjuk might bemoan the fact that the German legal system embarked on this belated act of self-correction with him in the dock, but he could hardly claim to have suffered an injustice as a consequence. The fact that others had been wrongly acquitted did not grant him immunity from prosecution. No criminal has a right to be the beneficiary of a legacy of legal mistakes.

* * *

When not lambasting the entire proceeding as a political show, Busch did hazard some specifically legal arguments, most of which could be easily dismissed. He argued, for example, that the trial violated the principle of double jeopardy, since Demjanjuk had already been acquitted of the same charges in Israel. This argument both misread the Israeli record and misapplied the doctrine of double jeopardy. In deciding not to retry Demjanjuk, the Israeli Ministry of Justice never held that double jeopardy barred a second prosecution; it simply noted that a double-jeopardy argument *could* be raised, and thus counseled against a second prosecution. The deeper point remained that the Israelis were sick of Demjanjuk and wanted to be done with the entire botched affair. As a second matter, double jeopardy typically does not apply across sovereign legal systems.[43]

Of course, Busch also continued to insist that his client was fully innocent, that he never trained at Trawniki and never served at Sobibor or at any other camp, and that even if he had, he had had no more choice in the matter than the Jewish inmates. The claim of actual innocence had always been Demjanjuk's main line of defense, going back to his first denaturalization trial some three decades earlier. In Israel, the defense of actual innocence fortuitously worked not because the allegations of a KGB conspiracy proved true but because it turned out that the Israelis had the wrong guy. In Munich, there was no wrong guy to be had and so the defense had to double down on the theory that Demjanjuk was the victim of a frameup. Only now, with the Soviet Union long gone, blame could no longer be placed exclusively at the feet of the KGB, which still remained responsible for the original forgeries—some of which had miraculously been smuggled into German archives—framing this otherwise unknown Ukrainian. More recently, other dark forces had assumed the lead in the plot against Demjanjuk. In a series of three declarations written in the first person, as if by the defendant himself but actually penned by Busch, Demjanjuk described himself as a "hounded juridical victim [*Justizopfer*] of the OSI and its behind-the-scenes supporters, the World Jewish Congress and the Simon Wiesenthal centers," organizations that "live from the Holocaust."[44] Put the two conspiratorial forces together, and we were back to Hitler's Judeo-Bolshevik world conspiracy. So inured had the trial's observers grown to Busch's oratorical overkill that few appeared to note the irony of appropriating rhetorical tropes once used to justify exterminating Jews to attack the trial of an accessory to that genocide.[45]

Demjanjuk's second manifesto, delivered to the court on November 23, 2010, as the trial completed its first year, repeated many of these charges, once again branding the OSI as a criminal organization.[46] The key rhetorical feature of this declaration was the repeated use of the formulation *J'accuse, Ich beschuldige die Richter* . . . (I accuse the judges . . .). This gesture—the defendant accusing the judges—is a familiar maneuver of political trials, which seek to unmask the proceeding as a partisan act of political reckoning. What was notable here was the use of Emile Zola's rhetorical figure *J'accuse*, which the French writer famously used to turn the tables on Dreyfus' anti-Semitic accusers. Without mentioning Dreyfus by name, Busch in Munich echoed the charge that had so outraged the judges in Demjanjuk's Jerusalem trial.

Most remarkable in its cheek was Demjanjuk's third declaration, delivered to the court on February 22, 2011. The statement was accompanied by a bit of political theater. On that winter morning, Demjanjuk arrived in court in his wheelchair wearing his usual outfit of green coat, baseball cap, and sunglasses. On his lap, however, he carried a small cardboard placard that bore the handwritten number *1627* (see figure 8.3). According to the accompanying declaration, this was the number of an ultra-secret KGB file that contained a trove of exculpatory material. Not only did the "mother of all files" contain long-suppressed proof that Demjanjuk's service ID from Trawniki was a forgery, but it also proved that Danilchenko's statements had been falsified under torture. Again composed in the first person, Demjanjuk's third declaration put the court on notice:

> Unless [it] accepts the historical facts, uses it's [*sic*] authority to obtain the critical defense evidence not yet before the court and shows the world that it fully accepts its duty to seek justice rather [than] just conduct a political show trial, I will within two weeks begin a hunger strike.[47]

This would not have been Demjanjuk's first hunger strike. Back in July 1982, he publicly declared his refusal to eat in protest of his ordered deportation from the United States—though he somehow managed to gain weight during the alleged strike.[48] In addition to now demanding access to File No. 1627, Demjanjuk also requested that the court summon the Israeli witnesses who had identified him as Treblinka's Ivan the Terrible.[49] If evidence of his service at Sobibor helped overturn his Ivan Grozny conviction, maybe the fact that some survivors continued to place him at Treblinka could save him from the Sobibor charges. Busch's

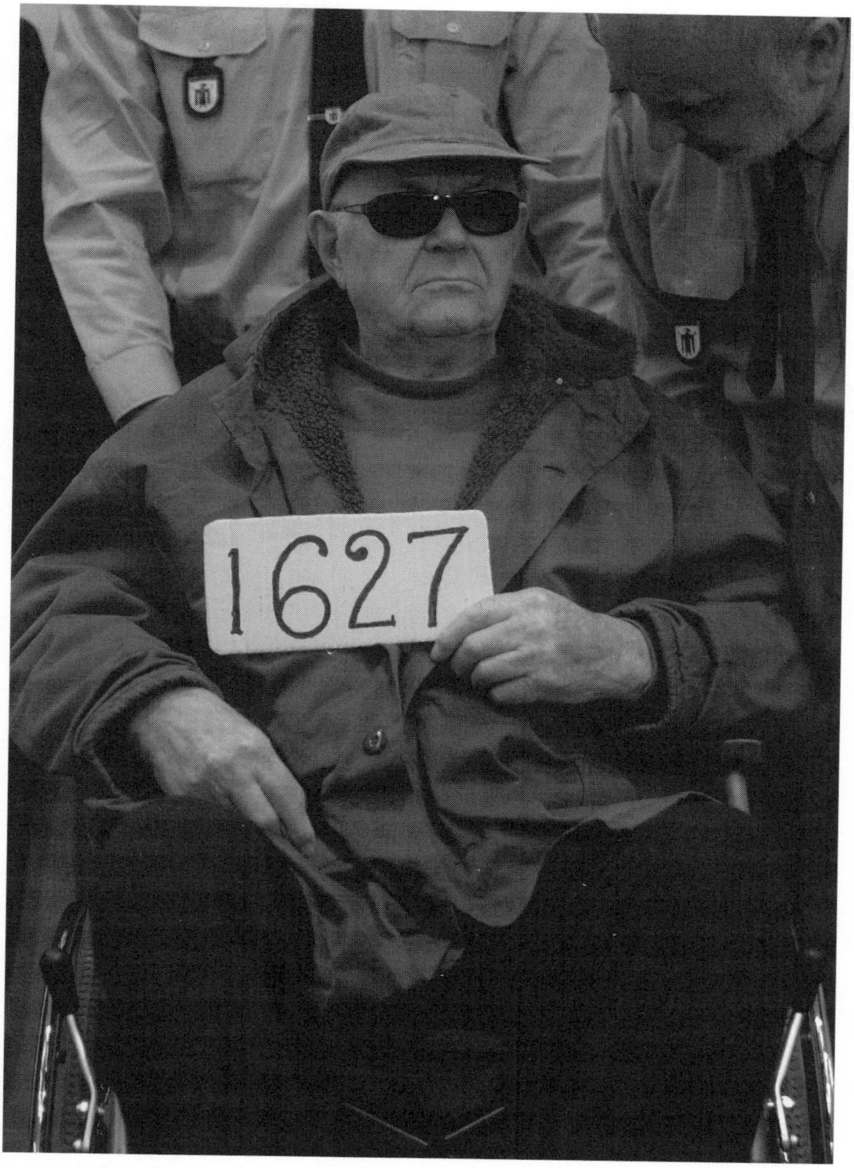

8.3. A defiant Demjanjuk demands the release of the "mother of all files." Miguel Villagran / Getty Images.

brazen attempt to use Treblinka as an alibi brought smiles to the faces of journalists covering the case; the lawyers for the *Nebenkläger* were less amused. ("The man has no shame," Nestler observed.)

The 1627 gambit did, however, manage to create a stir. No one actually credited the claim that the file contained exculpatory material, and most observers doubted its very existence; still, photos of Demjanjuk in his wheelchair holding his handwritten placard ran prominently in all of Germany's leading news outlets. In point of fact, there *was* a File No. 1627, and its existence had been known at the time of Demjanjuk's second denaturalization trial a decade earlier. At the time, Demjanjuk's American lawyer, Michael Tigar, had also reacted excitedly to the possibility that this undisclosed file in Russian hands was chock full of exculpatory material. Although comprising some six volumes, File No. 1627 evidently was no more than a compendium of noninvestigative materials, including Israeli government requests from the time of Demjanjuk's Jerusalem trial, Soviet field reports, twenty years' worth of US Justice Department requests, and internal Soviet/Russian inquiries and responses. It would have been standard practice for the KGB to compile such a file—and to refuse researchers access to its contents. But far from frustrating the defense, the inability of researchers to gain access to File No. 1627 in fact served its interests nicely, as it allowed Busch to indulge his Judeo-Bolshevik conspiracy theories. As for the threatened hunger strike, this never materialized.

However unsustainable, the defense of actual innocence nevertheless forced the court to revisit issues that had been considered ad nauseam over the decades, such as the authenticity of Demjanjuk's Trawniki service card. As we saw in chapter 3, Armand Hammer had secured the ID for the Israeli prosecution of Demjanjuk. With the unraveling of the Soviet Union, the ID had remained in the possession of the Israelis, who had no use for it and eventually gave it to the OSI's Eli Rosenbaum during a personal trip he had taken to the country in July 2000. (During the return flight from Israel, the constitutionally cautious Rosenbaum refused to be separated from the ID even to use the airplane lavatory.) In the run-up to the Munich trial, Rosenbaum expressed his incredulity to German prosecutors that "any objective person could genuinely doubt that the Dienstausweis is authentic."[50] Indeed, the ID had become one of the most exhaustively examined documents in legal history, and

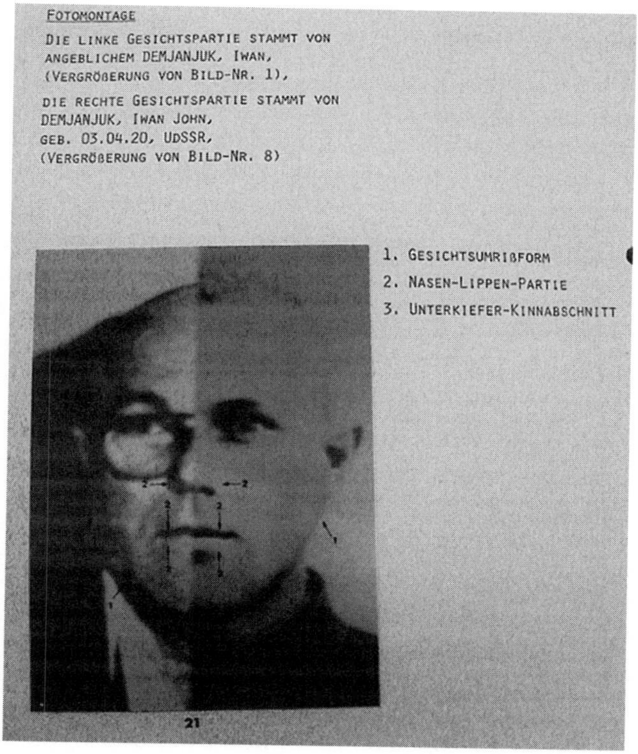
FOTOMONTAGE
DIE LINKE GESICHTSPARTIE STAMMT VON
ANGEBLICHEM DEMJANJUK, IWAN,
(VERGRÖßERUNG VON BILD-NR. 1),
DIE RECHTE GESICHTSPARTIE STAMMT VON
DEMJANJUK, IWAN JOHN,
GEB. 03.04.20, UDSSR,
(VERGRÖßERUNG VON BILD-NR. 8)
1. GESICHTSUMRIßFORM
2. NASEN-LIPPEN-PARTIE
3. UNTERKIEFER-KINNABSCHNITT
21

8.4. Photomontage comparing photo of Demjanjuk from the Trawniki service ID No. 1393 with a later photo of the accused. Courtesy Office of Special Investigations, DoJ.

as Rosenbaum noted, even Demjanjuk had not challenged its authenticity at his second denaturalization trial. Yet in part because Busch insisted on challenging the Trawniki card, and in part because the court had to satisfy itself, the trial brought an influx of documents experts to Munich to consider the matter. A Hebrew-speaking expert arrived to testify about a tiny mark, no more than one millimeter in length, above Demjanjuk's photograph on the ID. Theories abounded about this tiny mark—was it an aleph, a Hebrew letter left by an earlier Israeli investigator as a way of classifying evidence? It could be an aleph, said the expert. The court thanked her for her time. An American documents expert named Larry Stewart flew in from Florida to testify about the rust stains on the card left by staples.[51] Anton Dallmayer, a German documents expert in the Bavarian State Criminal Administration, testified on the make of the typewriter used to fill out the card, an Olympia 12 manufactured in Erfurt by AEG in 1930. Dallmayer also testified that his painstaking comparison of Demjanjuk's card with three other original Trawniki service IDs left no doubts about its authenticity. Busch triumphantly offered his own teakettle explanation for these similarities. "Here are three counterfeit dollars," he declared, "and they are compared with a fourth. And then all four are declared authentic!"[52] Perhaps *all four* cards were KGB forgeries. (At the very end of the trial, the AP also ran a story that the FBI had long ago concluded that 1393 was a forgery; although the 1985 FBI report had been prepared by agents who had not directly investigated the case and had never examined the ID firsthand, the AP piece nevertheless led to a couple of days of frantic headlines.)[53]

The defense of actual innocence wasn't merely contradicted by all the available evidence—it was contradicted by Busch himself, at every turn. Why, for example, insist that the mass die-off of Soviet POWs constituted the "first Holocaust" except to show that any rational person in Demjanjuk's position would have collaborated? Why emphasize the impossible conditions that Red Army POWs experienced if the upshot of the story was that Demjanjuk nevertheless decided to tough it out as a POW? Why provocatively and tendentiously compare his client to Thomas Blatt, except to explain his service as a guard? If anything, the logic of the defense supported rather than challenged the charge of collaboration.

The overdetermined arguments of the defense—the scattershot insistence that Demjanjuk never worked as a guard, but if he did, he exercised no more choice than the Jews who worked at the camp—did the defendant a more troubling disservice still. In the parlance of American law, putative necessity is a *defense*—it concedes that the accused engaged in the wrongful conduct, but argues that he had a legally compelling justification or excuse for doing so. Such an argument, however, has to be *made*; it cannot simply be waved at. In the words of Hardy Langer, a lawyer for the *Nebenkläger*, the defense of putative necessity "is a matter of what a concrete defendant thought and not what he abstractly might have felt in the situation."[54] It makes no sense to say, "I never engaged in the act, but if I had, I would have done so only because I would have felt my life was threatened."

In view of this fact, it is possible that the case might have had a different outcome had Demjanjuk dropped his obdurate refusal to acknowledge his service. Imagine the following confessional story. *Before arriving at Sobibor, Demjanjuk had naively imagined it to be a camp like any other. Upon his arrival he was horrified to discover a diabolical factory of death, and immediately began planning his desertion, but on the day before he was to attempt his escape, two colleagues, who had deserted the week before, were captured, brought back to the camp, and executed on the spot, overwhelming him with the fearful certainty that his only choice was to continue as a guard or die—and with the dreaded knowledge that he was not heroic enough to risk the latter.* Such a declaration from the defendant would have created grave difficulties for the prosecution—"not," as Professor Nestler put it, "because we'd necessarily have to believe him, but because there's absolutely no certain evidence to the contrary." Because Demjanjuk's first line of defense had always been denial, he foreclosed reliance on his own strongest argument. His obstinate and implacable silence did the prosecution an immense favor.

* * *

Notwithstanding its weaknesses and incoherences, Busch's scattershot approach served one overriding purpose: delay. The blizzard of mutually contradictory arguments and the avalanche of frivolous motions slowed the trial to a crawl. Busch presumably hoped the delay would provide Demjanjuk's rude health an opportunity to genuinely deteriorate, forcing the court to discontinue the trial. All the same, it would be wrong to say that delay was Busch's exclusive end. For Busch behaved like a crusader and brought moral fervor to the cause. His defense of the poor, scapegoated Ukrainian moved few observers, but it evidently moved Busch himself—how else to explain the tears that often welled in his eyes? And for all his provocations, Busch also yearned to be liked. As Professor Nestler once quietly observed, Busch was "not the kind of defense lawyer who can tolerate or even enjoy being hated by everyone." He was no Jacques Vergès or Yoram Sheftel. He took the court's rebukes personally. For all his raging, he seemed genuinely surprised to find himself castigated by the court instead of praised. Alas, this only made him rage more.

So a proceeding expected to run four months limped on for eighteen. The long gaps between court dates, the frequent cancelations due to the defendant's alleged infirmities, and most of all Busch's endless barrage of motions and filibusters spread disappointment and frustration among the *Nebenkläger*. "It's a tormenting process for everybody here," commented Rolf Kleidermann, one of their lawyers.[55] The Dutch *Nebenkläger* had clear memories of Slobodan Milošević, who succeeded at dragging out his trial in The Hague to literally terminal lengths. Delay and deteriorate, stall and die—the *Nebenkläger* came to fear the strategy would work for Demjanjuk, too. They needn't have worried; according to the doctors associated with the case, Demjanjuk's health actually *improved* in the course of the trial. (In a dig at the American medical system, a blood specialist assured the court that Demjanjuk received better medical care as a prisoner in Germany than as a civilian in the United States, where he lacked health insurance altogether. This prompted Demjanjuk's son, John Jr., to defend the care his father had received in the United States and to pointedly note that as a Ford retiree, his father received excellent benefits.)[56]

In the early weeks of the proceeding, Judge Alt indulged the defense and its antics, perhaps because he believed that a display of tolerance would give the lie to the charge that the court was conducting a political show trial. Soon, however, the concerns began to circulate, particularly among the lawyers for the *Nebenkläger*, that the mild-mannered chess aficionado was not in control of his courtroom. Perhaps the criticism got back to Alt, or perhaps Busch simply exhausted the judge's reserves of patience; whatever the cause, Alt eventually tired of the defense lawyer's antics and began to show a different side, prickly and sarcastic. When Busch pushed a witness to name whom exactly the Trawnikis assisted at Sobibor, Alt sardonically quipped, "Presumably not the Red Cross," as laughter rippled through the gallery. Such an interjection, unthinkable in an American trial, is not uncommon in German proceedings, where judges—with no jury to worry about influencing—feel more free to show their lack of regard for questions they deem frivolous, tendentious, or simply stupid. Alt's sarcasm provoked

Busch to angry retorts; Alt, in turn, would interrupt Busch's tirade with a terse directive to cease; and if this failed, he would simply turn off Busch's microphone, an act that would only further excite the splenetic defense attorney. All the same, Alt had to take care not to let himself be provoked into actions that could open the door to an appeal. In this, he was not always successful. During Busch's summary argument—a rambling, mind-numbingly repetitious filibuster that lasted an incredible *fifteen* hours—*Nebenkläger* lawyer Nestler briefly left the courtroom in disgust, leading Alt to quip, "Alas, the court cannot leave out of protest." The remark, audible to all, was incautious.

Relations between Busch and Judge Alt, however, were nothing short of cordial compared to those between Busch and Associate Judge Lenz. With his slicked-back hair and imperious gaze, Lenz treated everyone in the courtroom with chilly arrogance. But for Busch he reserved a special contempt. On several occasions, the two engaged in unseemly shouting matches. Lenz's antipathy for the lead defense counsel was so transparent that Busch himself seemed taken aback, once asking plaintively, "Why are you always having temper tantrums with me, Herr Associate Judge? I don't understand, I'm entirely relaxed."[57] The situation became so delicate that Professor Nestler took the extraordinary step of privately telling the judge to tone it down. Observers worried that with all his frivolous motions alleging the court's *Befangenheit*—prejudice—Busch had prodded Lenz into precisely the kind of behavior that could make such a charge troublesome on appeal.

The court's sarcasm and contempt notwithstanding, many observers also continued to feel that Alt had permitted Busch to take the trial hostage. Assessing Alt's performance, Martin Mendelsohn borrowed a well-known criticism of Jimmy Carter. "He was weak when he should have been strong, and strong when he should have been weak."[58] In retrospect, the criticism seems unfair; Alt did, in fact, gradually place limits on Busch and succeeded in shepherding the trial to conclusion. At the time, however, appreciation for Alt's efforts was in short supply. Journalists covering the case turned to black humor. They dubbed the silent defendant *Ivan the Corpse*, *Ivan the Inert*, and *Ivan the Recumbent*. Why, they wondered, should court be canceled just because a defendant who never spoke and seemed wholly oblivious to the proceedings was

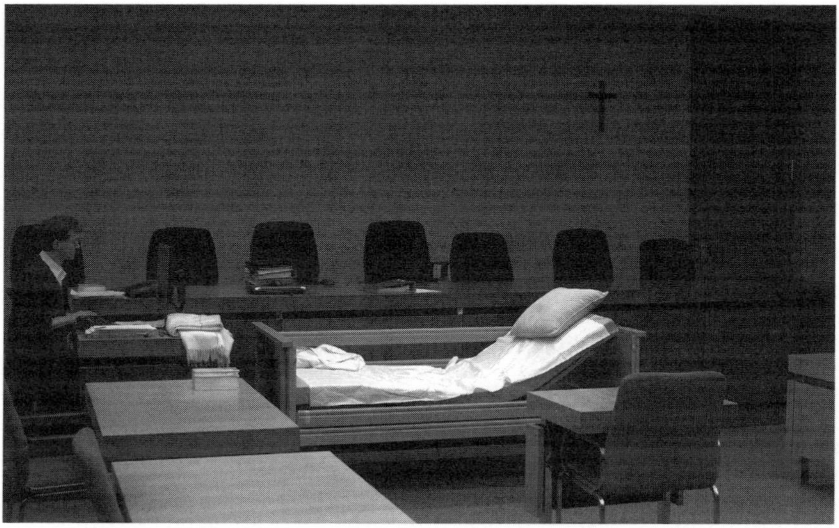

8.5. The absent defendant. Photo by Thomas Hauzenberger.

feeling ill? A mannequin could take his place. Or a fellow journalist, for that matter. How hard could it be to lie there on a gurney, occasionally yawning for good measure?

On one of my trips to Munich to attend the trial, the entire week of proceedings fell victim to the defendant's medical complaints, and so I found myself free to explore the city. I visited the splendid Alte Pinakothek, saw an exhibition of Neo Rauch paintings, attended a reading by Hertha Müller, and admired a city that, once the hub of Nazism, now projects the kind of decency that comes with a willingness to generously invest in civic institutions designed to benefit all its inhabitants. I read *Holocaust Cabaret*, a play based on Demjanjuk's trials written by a Canadian named Jonathan Garfinkel, which was playing to packed houses at a theater in Heidelberg. One evening I dined with a group of *Nebenkläger* lawyers. Pessimistic over the delays, tired of endlessly discussing the case, they sought distraction. Nestler talked about golf. Manuel Bloch, the Dutch Jewish lawyer who represented the Sobibor Foundation, argued about Wagner with Michael Koch, a Munich lawyer and a skilled musician. Koch, the German, groaned at the mention of the bombastic, nationalistic anti-Semite. Bloch, the Dutch Jew, shook his head, dismissing Koch's criticism as tired cliché. Nothing, he said, is more beautiful and moving than the beginning of *Parsifal*.

The next day, court was again canceled; in the afternoon, I bumped into Busch, who, like me, was browsing in the Hugendhubel bookshop on the Marienplatz. "Killing time?" he asked.

I shrugged. "And you?"

"We went to the BMW museum near the Olympic park."

"How was it?"

"For me, not too interesting," he laughed. "I drive Mercedes!"

On it dragged. A milestone was reached on July 22, 2010, roughly nine months into the trial: Alt ordered Demjanjuk to appear in court despite the defendant's insistence that he did not feel well.[59] Another milestone of sorts came in early March 2011, when the court decided that forthwith Busch would not be permitted to use up court time reading his motions; instead, the court would rule on all written submissions in due time.[60] No more delays would be tolerated. By this time, however, frustration and pessimism had taken hold, and the atmosphere in the courtroom remained gloomy.

Trials tell stories, but the story that emerged during the Demjanjuk trial turned into a parody of a David Foster Wallace novel: hopelessly digressive, difficult to follow, largely unplotted, needlessly long, and tediously repetitive. Whatever else one may think about American criminal trials, the fact that lawyers must play to a jury requires them to craft a coherent narrative of the case—even to the point of sacrificing fidelity to reality. German trials—arguably more focused on the truth—have no such requirement. The judges largely speak to themselves. They control the presentation of evidence, choosing to hear what they deem necessary to their judgment. In Munich, countless days were devoted to reading into the record documents from earlier Trawniki depositions and earlier court decisions. Handwritten documents in Cyrillic would appear on an overhead projector, while the German translation was read aloud.[61] To an observer, the trial skipped around in a seemingly arbitrary manner, following its own opaque logic. Key concepts in the case, such as putative necessity, remained completely unexplained. There was no need to explain them. The judges understood them well enough already.

Rebecca West described the Nuremberg trial as a "citadel of boredom," and perhaps boredom is inevitable when the expectation of spectacle collides with the reality of law's sobriety. The beginning of any highly publicized trial is a heady time: packed courtroom, drama in the air, an audience bristling with nerves. As weeks and months pass, the trial settles into a routine, and with routine comes tedium. And yet the Demjanjuk trial seemed to achieve a dullness all its own. Security, extraordinarily tight and thorough in the opening days, grew lax. Only a handful of journalists continued to follow the case closely—an Italian stringer for the AP, a few writers from the Netherlands, and a couple of radio journalists from Germany. For long stretches, the trial largely disappeared from newspaper accounts and remained alive only in the blogosphere, where a desultory group of Ukrainian nationalists, anti-Semites, and neo-Nazis posted their misspelled and syntactically challenged support for Demjanjuk.

If not for a steady stream of teachers bringing their classes into *Gerichtssaal* 101 for a field trip, the spectators' banks would have often been empty. Still, it wasn't always clear who or what was being taught. One day, a group of sixteen-year-olds studying to be hairdressers at a nearby vocational school spent thirty minutes in befuddled attendance, before being replaced by a class of tenth graders from a local *Gymnasium*. I asked a boy in lime-green surfer shorts what he thought the trial was about.

"Nazis," he said, with a shrug.

9

The Right Wrong Man

And then, suddenly, we were there. On the morning of May 12, 2011, Judge Alt addressed the defendant, who as usual sat reclined on his gurney, hands clasped behind his head.

"You have the last word," Alt said.

After ninety-three open sessions over eighteen months, there remained the hope that Demjanjuk might choose to speak—not to confess, not even to apologize to the *Nebenkläger*, but simply to acknowledge the enormity of the dreadful events in which he had participated. "My dream," said Thomas Walther, whose chance Google search had set the historic trial in motion, "would be for Demjanjuk to stand up and say, 'It was so.' "[1] The same wish was voiced by Hardy Langer, a lawyer for the *Nebenkläger*, who in his closing argument acknowledged Demjanjuk's right to remain silent, but then implored him to say *something*: "Find the strength to give us a detailed account of what you experienced," he beseeched. "Demjanjuk, use this last chance to break your silence!"[2] Thomas Blatt's German lawyer, Stefan Schünemann, echoed this sentiment: "Legally his silence cannot be held against him," Schünemann acknowledged, "But even if he tried to downplay his own contribution, as many guards have done over the years, he could have at least confirmed the reality of the death camps and the suffering of the murdered. . . . This we may expect from him even today."[3] *Nebenkläger* David van Huiden wondered aloud why Demjanjuk had never once expressed remorse. The sharpest words came from Martin Haas, the oncology professor from San Diego, who a year and a half earlier had had his opening testimony interrupted by the first of Demjanjuk's many sick days. Showing an anger that few *Nebenkläger* shared, Haas likewise acknowledged the defendant's right to remain silent, but accused him of cowardice in exercising it:

> We, the *Nebenkläger* victims in this trial, expected that for the sake of historical truth and to free yourself from the burden you have carried your entire life, you would testify in this trial and tell the Court, the *Nebenkläger*, and the world of your involvement in Extermination Camp Sobibor. . . . Mr. Demjanjuk! We expected you to apologize to the many dead victims and their next of kin present in this courtroom, and [to] say that you are truly sorry for having . . . willingly participated in this murderous operation.[4]

But to the end, Demjanjuk stubbornly demurred. Now asked by Judge Alt if he would like to make a final statement, Demjanjuk muttered a single word to his lonesome Ukrainian interpreter: *Ne*. No translation was needed. I recalled Iago's utterance: *What you know, you know. From this time forth I never will speak word.* As Shakespeare understood, silence is the captured villain's last retort, his dying blow against those seeking a moral account.

Not that anyone should have expected anything different from Demjanjuk. Indeed, the problem of the silence of the perpetrator had long emerged as something of a trope in Holocaust trials. At the end of *The Music Box*, the Hollywood film partially inspired by the Demjanjuk case, the daughter, played by Jessica Lange, upon learning of her father's complicity in atrocities, screams, *Why can't you try to say the truth?* In 1964, during the famous Frankfurt-Auschwitz trial, Fritz Bauer, the German-Jewish attorney general of Hessen, said in an interview that he had often dreamed that "sooner or later, one of the accused would step forward and say, '. . . what took place, it was horrific, I'm sorry.' . . . Then the entire world would exhale, as would all the survivors of those killed at Auschwitz, and the air would be cleared—if only at last one humane word were uttered." And yet Bauer ruefully noted, "it has not been uttered, nor will it be."[5]

Still, it is not altogether correct to say that Demjanjuk never broke his silence. He did speak at the trial, indeed, at great lengths—through

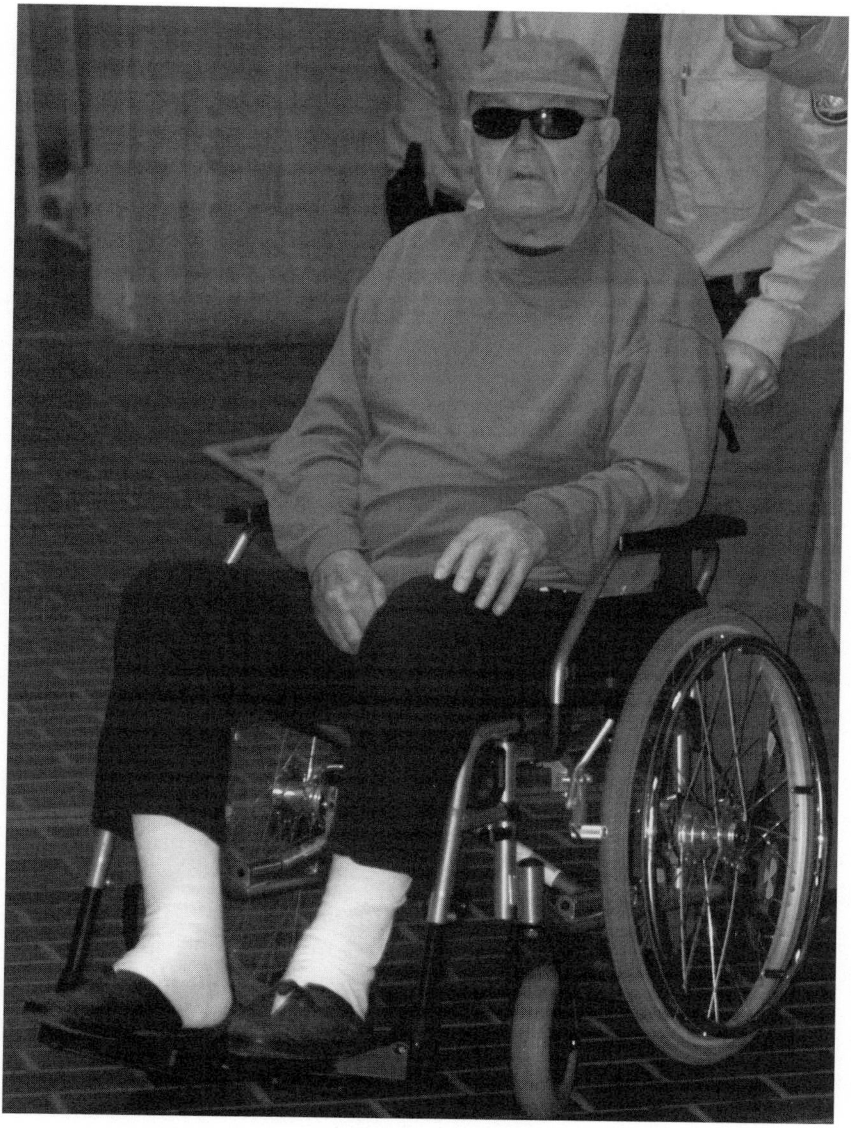

9.1. Ivan the Silent. Photo by Thomas Hauzenberger.

his lawyer, Busch. He spoke through Busch's examination of Thomas Blatt. He spoke through his three declarations. He spoke through Busch's fifteen-hour closing argument later self-published by the lawyer as *Demjanjuk—der Sündenbock* (Demjanjuk: The Scapegoat).[6] And what he said over and over was quite clear: *I am the victim*. The problem with Haas' plea that Demjanjuk free himself "from the burden you have carried your entire life," is that it assumed Demjanjuk had been carrying such a burden. Clearly that was not the case. Even if he had done what the *Nebenkläger* and their lawyers asked of him, even if he had cleared his throat and spoken, what would he have said?

To hazard an answer requires no imaginative leaps, for Demjanjuk was not always such a stony presence. Years before, on the stand in Israel, he had been downright voluble. And while he never admitted to training at Trawniki or serving as a guard, in a remarkable exchange with Judge Levin, who asked him to clarify certain statements he had made to Arye Kaplan, an undercover policeman at Ayalon prison, Demjanjuk came close to explaining how he rationalized his service as a death-camp guard.

> Levin: You sa[id] to Kaplan, why should people who had collaborated with the Germans . . . why should such people be brought to trial?
>
> Demjanjuk: Well, it depends. . . . If somebody did something bad, . . . had killed somebody, well then he is responsible for his deeds, but if he was acting under coercion, or because he was forced to do it, that is another matter.
>
> . . .
>
> Levin: . . . If the Germans sa[id] to someone who collaborated with them, you have to kill 15 people, and he kills them on the basis of orders from his German superior, then in such a case, according to your opinion, he should not be punished, because he fulfilled an order.
>
> Demjanjuk: It depends on how. I don't know. I didn't see that, but I know that if I were told to do that, I would have run away. I would never in my life have done that. I could have not carried that out. I would have run away.
>
> Levin: Well, we are not talking about you. As far as I gather . . .

you couldn't kill a chicken. . . . We are asking what would your attitude to an order—

DEMJANJUK: I can't even kill a chicken.

LEVIN: Yes, we know that. . . . The question is as follows. . . . If the Germans . . . told him to kill five, and [he] killed fifty, because of his [own] initiative, he went further, then that person should be punished?

DEMJANJUK: Of course.

LEVIN: . . . If he only does what the Germans tell him to do . . . he shouldn't be punished, but if he does more than the Germans tell him to do, then he should be punished, that is your thesis.

DEMJANJUK: . . . If he could refuse, or if he could have refused, then he should be punished, but if he was not able to refuse . . . then what should he be punished for?

. . .

SHAKED: In other words in this conversation with [Kaplan] you were speaking about yourself. . . .

DEMJANJUK: That is how it would seem, yes.[7]

In this revealing exchange, Demjanjuk appeared to acknowledge that in his candid conversation with Kaplan, he was really speaking about himself. It is also worth noting that Demjanjuk's position essentially tracked how the German legal system handled such cases at the time. Demjanjuk clearly believed that *Exzesstäter*—those who on their own initiative killed fifty when ordered to kill five—should be punished. He also held out the possibility of punishing persons who killed by their own hand even when following orders—if the killing was done cruelly and there had been a chance to opt out. But if a person found himself ordered to kill and unable to refuse, then what was he to be punished for? In Jerusalem, these telling words were overlooked as the court focused on the actions of Ivan Grozny, the ultimate excess killer.

By the time of the Munich trial, the views Demjanjuk voiced in Jerusalem had hardened into an inflexible structure of excuse, self-pity, and resentment. Its central tenet was: *I, too, am a victim*. During an interrogation in Jerusalem, Demjanjuk had said, "Why are you making such a fuss of my matter, like with Eichmann? Eichmann was big, while Ivan is little, and what is more . . . there is a mistake in identification."[8] True, there had been a mistake in identification, but his first response—*Eichmann was big, while Ivan is little*—stated his abiding credo. A quarter century later in Munich, Demjanjuk basically repeated the line when he irritably snapped at a film crew outside the court, "What's up? I'm not Hitler."

So it is not hard to imagine what Demjanjuk might have said, had he answered the calls to speak. *I was twenty-two. I survived the Holodomor holocaust. I never asked for any of this. Of course, I was a guard, so what? I wasn't a hero but I also wasn't a beast. I watched which way the wind was blowing. I kept my head down and my nose clean. For thirty years I've been hounded. What exactly am* I *supposed to be apologizing for? Let the Germans apologize, they are the ones who made this whole mess.* Rationalization, self-pity, weariness, resentment. But one humane word from Demjanjuk?—it was not going to happen.

* * *

Having duly received the defendant's *Ne*, the court recessed to deliberate. This lasted little more than two hours—not altogether unusual for a German court, which discusses the case while the trial is ongoing. To an American observer, however, the brevity was shocking, and even some German journalists found such speed unseemly. At 1:30 in the afternoon, the defendant was wheeled before the judges, still wearing the dark glasses that had obscured his eyes for the last year and a half.

In German trials, in an inversion of American trial practice, it is the judges who rise to pronounce judgment. Staring down at the defendant, Judge Alt announced that the court found John Demjanjuk guilty of serving as an accessory to the murder of at least 28,060 Jews at the Sobibor death camp. Alt noted that while a small number of these victims arrived from the Polish town of Izbica by truck, the overwhelming majority had arrived at Sobibor on fifteen Dutch trains. "The transport from April 6, 1943, arrived on April 9, 1943, with 1992 persons," he intoned, reading from a draft of the judgment. "At least 1900 were killed in the gas chambers on the day of their arrival; included in this group were the brother of *Nebenklägerin* Aleida Kessing, the parents of *Nebenkläger* Robert Fransmann, as well as the parents and brother of *Nebenkläger* Max Degen."[9] During Alt's steady recitation, which assumed something of the tone and rhythm of a requiem, many of the *Nebenkläger* quietly wept. The judge placed special emphasis on the transport of June 8, 1943, the so-called *Kindertransport*, in which one-third of the three thousand passengers had been children under the age of fourteen.[10] He noted that the youngest victim during Demjanjuk's service had been only a few weeks old, while the oldest had been born in 1848. "This ninety-five-year-old," Alt read, "had the right to die with dignity."

Its recitation complete, the court condemned Demjanjuk to five years of prison. Then, as if in an afterthought, it lifted the order of arrest that had kept the defendant in jail and released him pending appeal. No gavel sounded the end of the trial. The judges collected their binders and quietly exited *Gerichtsaal* 101. The trial was over.[11]

Afterward, a crowd filled with journalists milled outside the courtroom, trying to absorb what the court had done. Busch excitedly told his client, "You're a free man!" "Am I dreaming?" Demjanjuk mused aloud. He then removed his glasses and cap, letting himself be seen for the first time since the trial began. His features were calm, settled, and vaguely defiant; and one had to acknowledge that for all his legal travails and alleged infirmities, Demjanjuk looked remarkably young for his age. (During the latter stages of the trial, having abandoned his theatrics of suffering, Demjanjuk would often lie half reclined on his gurney, with his hands casually clasped behind his head and his legs crossed, as if sunning himself.) Perhaps he did not grasp that his release was a technicality and that he had just been convicted as an accessory to the murder of tens of thousands. Busch seemed surprised and pleased by the lifting of the arrest warrant, even as he announced to reporters his intention to lodge an appeal.

The *Nebenkläger*, for their part, seemed accepting of Demjanjuk's release. They expressed a mix of feelings: relief that the ordeal had concluded in a conviction; appreciation of the respect they had received from the German court; and melancholy that the trial failed to live up to the impossible expectations that such proceedings inevitably raise. While journalists hurried off to file their stories, other observers lingered outside the court building, as if reluctant to bring to an end the most convoluted and lengthy case to arise from the crimes of the Holocaust.

In the hours and days that followed, pundits in Europe and America weighed in on the ruling. Some were harshly critical: Rabbi Marvin Hier, head of the Simon Wiesenthal Center in Los Angeles, called Demjanjuk's release "an insult to his victims and the survivors," a view that among the three dozen *Nebenkläger* was perhaps shared only by Martin Haas. Others chose to focus on the verdict of guilt. Jules Schelvis, the Dutch Jew whose young wife had been gassed at Sobibor and who later became a historian of the camp, had actually urged the court to release the convict. "Out of respect for my humanistic parents," Schelvis said in his closing statement, referring to his father who died at Sachsenhausen and his mother who survived, "I urge the court to convict but not to punish this very old man who has already spent nine years in prison."[12] In the *New York Times*, Holocaust historian Deborah Lipstadt opined that justice had been served, however belatedly. A rather different note was struck in the Ukraine and its diaspora community; Askold Lozynskyj, a former president of the Ukrainian World Congress, ruefully noted, "We've been scapegoats for a lot."[13]

Largely lost in the coverage and commentary, at least in the United States, was the recognition that in convicting this elderly Trawniki, Alt's modest, Solomonic verdict had managed something that no German court had done since the founding of the Federal Republic. However vexatious the trial had been, with its delays, detours, and distractions, the court had reached an important and perhaps a lasting outcome. The German press better grasped the significance of the conviction. *Der Spiegel*, the newsweekly, might have erred in awarding credit for the approach that "brought clarity into a befogged juristic brain" to Thomas Walther instead of to Kirsten Goetze, but it was clearly correct in praising the verdict as a crucial, if belated, rupture with existing German case law.[14]

True, the breakthrough, as we have seen, was not without antecedents. In his closing statement in Munich, Professor Nestler provided a detailed "excursus into legal history" in which he faulted German jurists for having long clung "to a comfortable but incorrect legal analysis."[15] In Nestler's telling, the BGH's Auschwitz-Frankfurt decision had led German jurists astray from the more promising paths paved by earlier German courts. He quoted at length the judgment of the Hagen court from 1966, which had accepted the idea that SS men could be convicted based on their "functional participation" (*funktionelle Mitwirkung*) in the process of mass murder. For Nestler, the task facing the Munich court had been to acknowledge the false turn taken by German legal doctrine and to resuscitate the promising doctrinal antecedents that had failed to take hold.

The writings of Fritz Bauer supplied yet another antecedent. At the time of the Treblinka-Düsseldorf trial in 1965, Bauer had insisted that "whoever works on this machine of murder is guilty of contributing to murder, regardless of what he did."[16] Bemoaning the fact that "trials of NS crimes [had] deviate[d] from [a] widely accepted praxis," Bauer argued, "Anyone who belongs to a band of robbers . . . or to a group of gangsters like a Murder Inc. is certainly guilty of murder . . . regardless of whether as 'boss' he gave the order to murder, whether he delivered the pistol, whether he cased the joint, or whether he did the shooting with his own hand."[17]

Perhaps the clearest antecedent to the Demjanjuk verdict was to be found in the words of Hannah Arendt. In a short but probing critique of the Frankfurt-Auschwitz trial, Arendt had noted, "What the old penal code [namely, the statutory definition of murder] failed to take into account was nothing less than the everyday reality of Nazi Germany in general and of Auschwitz in particular."[18] As a result of this insufficiency, "a man who had caused the death of thousands because he was one of the few whose job it was to throw the gas pellets into the chambers could be criminally less guilty than another man who had killed 'only' hundreds, but upon his own initiative and according to his perverted fantasies."[19] To correct this mangling of legal categories, Arendt insisted, "'mass murder and complicity in mass murder' was a charge that could and should be leveled against every single SS man who had ever done duty in any of the extermination camps."[20]

To acknowledge precursors of the Munich verdict in Arendt's critique, Fritz Bauer's agitations, and the Hagen court's decision is in no way to undercut the distinctiveness or importance of Alt's holding. First, there was the simple fact of the conviction itself, which represented the first time a German court had ever tried, let alone convicted, one of the thousands of auxiliaries who served as the foot soldiers of Nazi genocide. Second, we must credit and applaud the years of historical research that made the jurisprudential breakthrough possible. Without the painstaking archival work and interpretive labors of the OSI's historians, the court could never have confidently reached its two crucial findings: that in working as a Trawniki at Sobibor, Demjanjuk had necessarily served as an accessory to murder; and that in choosing to remain in service when others chose not to, he acted voluntarily. This "trial by history" enabled the court to master the prosecutorial problem posed by the auxiliary to genocide who operates invisibly in an exterminatory apparatus.

Then there was the larger legal breakthrough. Those who argue that, because earlier courts had anticipated the theory of functional liability, the Demjanjuk ruling represented less a paradigm shift than a correction of doctrine that had wandered off in the wrong direction may be technically correct.[21] Yet there is no denying that for decades, German jurists tortured history by pigeonholing Nazi atrocities into the conventional murder statute. In reviving a theory that had never properly taken hold in German case law, the Munich court found a way to grasp the essential logic of genocide while still working within available statutory strictures. The result was a crucial reorientation. In Arendt's terms, the Demjanjuk trial succeeded at correcting the "pernicious" and "common illusion" that the "crime of murder and the crime of genocide are essentially the same."[22]

Certainly this reorientation was late in coming, a fact that can fuel skepticism. Cynics may note that the generation of perpetrators essentially had passed before this self-correction was waged. But the claim that change came only when it was safe for it to do so ignores the power of law to shape a contested social reality. Such a dismissive view may serve as a corrective to the naive belief that law operates exclusively by its own empyrean logic, but it is too crudely deterministic to capture the complex workings of legal doctrine and the determined labors of jurists. However late in coming, the Demjanjuk verdict was not inevitable or easy or safe. It never would have happened without the stubborn exertions of the OSI and the Central Office. Despite the troubled histories of these organizations, it was their historians and lawyers who worked tirelessly and creatively to bring the case to a worthy and just conclusion.

* * *

Several days after the verdict, *Bild Zeitung*—Germany's *New York Post*—ran the headline "The Miraculous Recovery of the Evil Guy." The accompanying story showed pictures of the ninety-one-year-old Demjanjuk strolling the grounds of Pflegerheim St. Lukas, a nursing home in Upper Bavaria, with no wheelchair in sight.[23] It was in this nursing home—with its wellness area, sun terrace, senior swimming facilities, and monthly cost of between eighteen hundred and three thousand euros, paid by German taxpayers—that Demjanjuk spent his last months. He died on March 17, 2012, some ten months after his conviction. His body was returned to his family in America; the location of his grave has not been released.

Demjanjuk's death provided his indefatigable lawyer, Ulrich Busch, with the chance to accuse the nursing home of manslaughter; having long insisted that Demjanjuk was at death's door, Busch now claimed that only criminal negligence or malfeasance could have brought down his sturdy client. The death also gave Busch occasion to assert that because his client's appeal had never been heard, he died an innocent man. Technically speaking, it is true that Demjanjuk's conviction never took legal effect, but this of course did not change the fact that he died having been convicted of participating in mass extermination.

Demjanjuk's death brings us one step closer to the day when the Holocaust will pass from the memory of those who lived it—victims and perpetrators alike—and become an artifact of history. By then, we will have arrived at the end of the era of galvanic Nazi atrocity trials that began at Nuremberg. That this era should close not with a Göring or an Eichmann in the dock, or even an Ivan the Terrible, but rather with Ivan the Minnow, may strike some as disappointing. But in a deep sense it is fitting. For Demjanjuk truly was what Eichmann claimed to be: a faceless facilitator of genocide. A man whom prosecutors first mistakenly pursued for his alleged singular viciousness ultimately was convicted in Munich as a replaceable cog in an exterminatory machine. His conviction reminds us that the Holocaust was not accomplished through the acts of Nazi statesmen, SS henchmen, or vicious sociopaths alone. It was made possible by the thousands of lowly foot soldiers of genocide. Through John Demjanjuk, they were at last brought to account.

Postscript

Fritz Bauer can now exhale. On April 21, 2015, on the opening day of his trial in Lüneburg, a town near Hamburg, Oskar Gröning, a former SS guard at Auschwitz, faced the court. "It is beyond question that I am morally complicit," he said. "This moral guilt I acknowledge here, before the victims, with regret and humility."[1]

The Gröning trial would never have been possible without Demjanjuk's conviction. Armed with the Munich precedent, the Central Office in Ludwigsburg promptly began investigating dozens of guards and low-level killers whom the old model had essentially shielded from legal scrutiny. Prosecutors announced that they were weighing charges against as many as thirty former guards.[2] (Included in this group was Alex Nagorny, Demjanjuk's former bunkmate at Flossenbürg who suddenly faced the possibility of charges stemming from his earlier service at Treblinka.) To aid their work, investigators employed state-of-the-art computer imaging technology to establish sight lines of former Auschwitz guards who continued to dispute having known of gas chambers and crematoria.[3] Whether any of these fresh investigations would actually culminate in a trial remained, however, unclear. In December 2013, German prosecutors dropped charges against a former SS guard at Auschwitz-Birkenau named Hans Lipshis after Lipshis was diagnosed with dementia. In July 2014, Germany sought the extradition of Johann Breyer, an American by birth who was raised in Europe and later served in the SS, allegedly guarding the rail ramp at Auschwitz. On the very day that a federal judge in Philadelphia upheld Germany's extradition request came word that Breyer had died.[4]

Along with a healthy defendant, prosecutors also needed a case that would fit the Demjanjuk precedent. As we have seen, Goetze's theory of culpability did not ask the Munich court to repudiate the *Einzeltat* requirement, the fateful doctrinal legacy of the Frankfurt-Auschwitz proceeding; rather, her theory found a way around this doctrine by attending to the distinctive realities of the pure death camp. To use the Demjanjuk precedent against a former guard at a hybrid facility such as Auschwitz, it would be necessary to show that he had performed a task necessarily connected to the exterminatory process.

The case against Oskar Gröning satisfied these conditions. Gröning, a former SS *Unterscharführer* (junior squad commander), had served at Auschwitz for two years, during which time he had been responsible for sorting currency obtained from arriving Jews—thus his sobriquet, "the book-keeper of Auschwitz." The indictment—which charged Gröning as an accessory to the death of three hundred thousand Jews—did not, however, concern itself with the entirety of his tenure at Auschwitz. Rather, it focused narrowly on his service during a two-month period, from May 16, 1942, until July 11, 1942—the most concentrated period of killing in Auschwitz's murderous history.[5] During these weeks, some 137 trains carrying 425,000 Jews from Hungary arrived at Birkenau, the massive extension to Auschwitz where the camp's main killing center was located. At least 300,000 of these Jews from Hungary were murdered, most gassed within hours of their arrival. During this time of hectic mass murder, Gröning was stationed at Birkenau, where he was responsible for overseeing the removal of suitcases of the freshly arrived Jews, and then searching the suitcases for cash that would be counted and forwarded to Berlin. Because his tasks—which included *Rampendienst* (working the train platforms)—had directly and necessarily served the exterminatory process, Gröning, so the indictment reasoned, was an accessory to murder.

In importantly acknowledging his moral complicity, Gröning fell short, however, of confessing legal guilt. Gröning had never denied his service at Auschwitz; to the contrary, for years he had made statements and given interviews to give the lie to arguments of Holocaust deniers. All the same, he did not consider himself a criminal. In an interview with *Der Spiegel* in 2005, he emphasized that he had been no more than a "cog in the gears."[6] In 2005, such a statement remained tantamount to a denial of participation in a crime; a decade later the legal landscape had importantly changed. Thanks to the Demjanjuk verdict, Gröning's insistence that he had been no more than a "cog" now constituted an admission of guilt.

His conviction on July 15, 2015 by the Lüneburg court hardly came, then, as a surprise. But it was welcome—again, not because it is important to imprison nonagenarians. (Gröning received a four-year sentence though it remains unclear at this writing whether he will do any time, as the 94-year-old is in frail health and remains free while his conviction is appealed.) Rather, the case enabled a German court to use the Demjanjuk precedent to condemn not a foreign auxilliary impressed into service, but a German SS volunteer, who, by his own lights, had been *adolftreu* (loyal to Hitler). No longer can it be said that the last Nazi trial involved a man who was neither a German nor a Nazi.

Whether more convictions will follow remains to be seen. But even if the Gröning conviction was, in a sense, the first and last application of the Demjanjuk decision, the importance of the breakthrough in Munich remains undiminished. For its significance, I have argued, should not be measured simply in terms of the prosecutions it sponsors or the convictions it secures; its importance lies in the renewal of judgment as a meaning-positing act. In convicting Demjanjuk and Gröning, German courts demonstrated the power of legal systems to learn from past missteps and to self-correct. They offered powerful proof of how criminal trials can deploy history in a responsible way to shift and recenter doctrine. And while nominally working within the troubled German framework that treated the Holocaust as an "ordinary" crime, these courts managed to comprehend the Holocaust as a crime of atrocity. Demjanjuk and Gröning were rightly convicted not because they committed wanton murders, but because they worked in factories of death.

To convict only on proof of personal viciousness is to treat the crimes of the Holocaust as acts of garden-variety villainy. The courts in Munich and Lüneburg, by contrast, recognized the death camp as a site of organized destruction. Their verdicts understood that in judging state-sponsored atrocities, guilt is not to be measured by acts of cruelty or savagery alone; guilt follows *function*. Such was the simple, terrible, and great insight of these courts.

ACKNOWLEDGMENTS

Many helped, some a great deal.

This book could not have been written without the support of fellowships from the National Endowment of the Humanities, the American Council of Learned Societies, and the Mandel Center for Advanced Holocaust Studies at the United States Holocaust Memorial Museum (the latter came in the form of the Ina Levine Invitational Scholar Award). Support also came from Amherst College, in particular from President Biddy Martin and Dean of Faculty Greg Call.

The book started as an essay I wrote for *Harper's* about Demjanjuk's Munich trial ("Ivan the Recumbent, or Demjanjuk in Munich"); at *Harper's* I'd like to thank the expert editing of Chris Beha and Ellen Rosenbush. I'd also like to thank Bill Wasik and Cullen Murphy for helpful guidance. Peter Carstens of the *Frankfurter Allgemeine Zeitung* helped arrange publication of an earlier essay of mine on Demjanjuk in the pages of the FAZ.

I had the good fortune of receiving a digitized version of the entire sixteen volume Munich case file as well as a complete digitized version of the OSI's investigatory files. I thank those who made this material available to me; you know who you are.

Many people generously answered my questions and plied me with other material. At the Justice Department's Human Rights and Special Prosecutions Section (formerly the OSI), I'd like to particularly thank the generous assistance of Eli Rosenbaum, David Rich, and Elizabeth ("Barry") White. I also greatly benefited from conversations with the following persons formerly with the OSI: Peter Black, Todd Huebner, Jonathan Drimmer, Judy Feigin, Norman Moscowitz, and Martin Mendelsohn. (And thanks to Sherman Katz for facilitating.) In Israel, I benefited from the help offered by former Supreme Court Justices Aahron Barak and Gabriel Bach, Tom Segev, Leora Bilsky, and Yehudit Dori Deston. In Germany, at the *Zentrale Stelle* Ludwigsburg, help came from Kurt Schrimm, Thomas Walther, and, most of all, Kirsten Goetze. Among the lawyers for the *Nebenkläger*, I'd like to thank Manuel Bloch,

Hardy Langer, and especially Cornelius Nestler, who offered extraordinary assistance in all sorts of ways. Defense lawyer Ulrich Busch was generous with his time. Journalists also helped out, especially Rainer Volk of *Bayerischer Rundfunk* and Andrea Beer of *Südwestrundfunk*. I greatly benefited from the time I was able to spend with Thomas Blatt. And a special thanks to Thomas Hauzenberger, my talented assistant, who took notes for me during the long stretches when I could not be in Munich.

When it came time to turning a pile of research into a book, I again received lots of help that came from many people in many different places. Particular thanks go to Gerhard Werle, Kim Priemel, Annette Weinke, Joachim Perels, Dick de Mildt, Christiaan Rüter, and Charles Sydnor. At the Mandel Center at the USHMM, I'd like to thank Jürgen Mattäus, Martin Dean, Suzanne Brown-Fleming, Paul Shapiro, and Robert Ehrenreich. Also, in no particular order, thanks go to Devin Pendas, Michael Marrus, Jonathan Bush, Larry May, Rebecca Wittmann, and Jens Meierhenrich.

At Amherst, thanks go to my colleagues in the Department of Law, Jurisprudence, and Social Thought: David Delaney, Nasser Hussain, Austin Sarat, Adam Sitze, Martha Umphrey, and our invaluable assistant, Megan Estes. Thanks, too, to the assistance that came from several students: Natascha Schiel, Marc Daalder, Chlöe MacKenzie, Krya Ellis-Moore, and (my son!) Jacob Douglas.

The manuscript was read in whole or part by several friends who helped improve things: John Kleiner, Elizabeth Kolbert, Laura Moser, Viveca Greene, Teresa Shawcross, Alex George, and my wife, Nancy Pick. A very large and special thanks to Rand Cooper, the dude who read the entire manuscript with a deft editorial hand.

Owen Fiss, *again*, helped arrange the early contract. Thanks also goes to Daniel Greenberg, my agent. Ian Malcolm first took the book on. Eric Crahan at Princeton extended great support and expertly shepherded the book to publication. Also at Princeton I greatly benefited from the excellent work of Kathleen Cioffi, Ben Pokross, and Julia Haav.

I'm grateful to you all.

NOTES

Unless otherwise indicated, translations from the German are my own.

Introduction

1. Heinrich Wefing, "Das letzte große NS-Verfahren geht zu Ende. Was sagt der Demjanjuk-Prozess über die Schuld des Angeklagten? Und was sagt er über uns, die Nachgeborenen?," *Zeit Online*, May 2, 2011, www.zeit.de/2011/18/Demjanjuk-Prozess.

2. "Für Völkermord gibt es keine Verjährung," *Der Spiegel*, October 3, 1965, www.spiegel.de/spiegel/print/d-25803766.html.

3. Jaspers, *Wohin treibt die Bundesrepublik?*

4. International Military Tribunal, *Trial of the Major War Criminals before the International Military Tribunal, Nuremberg, 14 November 1945–1 October 1946*, vol. 2, 155.

5. Lemkin, *Axis Rule in Occupied Europe*, 79.

6. See Schabas, *Genocide in International Law.*

7. Arendt, *Hannah Arendt/Karl Jaspers Correspondence, 1926–1969*, 39.

8. See Douglas, *The Memory of Judgment.*

9. Hausner quoted in ibid., 106.

10. Arendt, *Eichmann in Jerusalem*, 233.

11. Rückerl, Adalbert. *NS-Verbrechen vor Gericht*, 111.

12. Trials conducted by East German courts in the Soviet occupation zone, at least until 1948, mostly were not defective show trials (some of these proceedings in fact anticipated the idea of functional participation recognized in Demjanjuk's Munich trial); later trials, such as the Waldheim trials of 1950, often amounted to judicial shams.

13. See generally Weinke, *Eine Gesellschaft ermittelt.*

14. For a careful quantitative breakdown, see Eichmüller, "Die Strafverfolgung von NS-Verbrechen."

Chapter 1. The Beginning of the End of Something

1. Heribert Prantl, "Die ganze Welt auf 147 Plätzen," *Süddeutsche Zeitung*, May 17, 2010. www.sueddeutsche.de/politik/prozess-gegen-john-demjanjuk-die-welt-auf-plaetzen-1.126704.

2. Alexander Krug et al., "Du glaubst nicht, was hier los ist," *Süddeutsche Zeitung*, January 21, 2009, 3.

3. See Wiesenthal Center Annual Report on the Prosecution of Nazi War Criminals, 2009. Summary at www.wiesenthal.com/site/apps/nlnet/content2.aspx?c=lsKWLbPJLnF&b=5711841&ct=6929435#.VBhRVmTF_DE "most wanted."

4. Susi Wimmer, "Entschuldigung für Pannen," *Süddeutsche Zeitung*, February 12, 2009, 37.

5. Alexander Krug, "Profil: Ralph Alt," *Süddeutsche Zeitung*, March 12, 2009, 4.

6. See introduction to Meierhenrich and Pendas, *Political Trials*.

7. See "Is Demjanjuk Too Sick to Be Deported?," www.youtube.com/watch?v=84QpF1nL900.

8. Roger Boyes, "Sobibor Families Vent Anger . . . ," *Times* (London), March 12, 2012, www.thetimes.co.uk/tto/news/world/europe/article2601446.ece.

Chapter 2. John in America

1. *State of Israel vs. Ivan (John) Demjanjuk, Criminal Case No. 373/86: Verbatim, Unedited Minutes*, 6832.

2. See Snyder, *Bloodlands*, 42–46.

3. Transcript of Proceedings, *United States v. Demjanjuk*, US Immigration Court, Case No. A8237417 (Deportation Proceedings), January 16, 1984, 48.

4. *State of Israel vs. Ivan (John) Demjanjuk, Criminal Case No. 373/86: Verbatim, Unedited Minutes*, 7407.

5. Ibid., 6846, 6847.

6. Transcript of Proceedings, United States v. Demjanjuk, US Immigration Court, Case No. A8237417 (Deportation Proceedings), January 16, 1984, 55–56.

7. *State of Israel vs. Ivan (John) Demjanjuk, Criminal Case No. 373/86: Verbatim, Unedited Minutes*, 6843.

8. Ibid., 6836.

9. Ibid., 6840.

10. Ibid., 6841.

11. Ibid., 6850.

12. See, for example, AEFDP Registration Record, Demjanjuk, Iwan, 27.8.1947 (Desired Destination: Canada). On file with author. See Actin Sheet Annex C to Administrative Order 29, 22.3.1948 (Country of first preference: Argentina). On file with author.

13. Friedlander and McCarrick, "Nazi Criminals in the US: The Fedorenko Case," in Marrus, *The Nazi Holocaust*, 9:683.

14. Fletcher, Friedlander, and Weinschenck, "United States Responses," 19.

15. Anthony Leviero, "Reaction Is Angry," *New York Times*, July 16, 1948 1.

16. Displaced Persons Act of 1948, Pub L. No 80-774, 62 Stat. 1009, http://library.uwb.edu/guides/usimmigration/62%20stat%201009.pdf.

17. Wyman, *DPs*; Dinnerstein, *America and the Survivors of the Holocaust*. Raphael Lemkin, the Polish-Jewish refugee who in 1944 coined the term genocide, recalled in his autobiography that only a steady diet of bribes kept his family's farm running. Lemkin, *Totally Unofficial*, 12.

18. Teicholz, *The Trial of Ivan the Terrible*, 46.

19. *State of Israel vs Ivan (John) Demjanjuk, Criminal Case No. 373/86: Verbatim, Unedited Minutes*, 6915.

20. Ibid., 7227.

21. Ibid., 6917, 7227.

22. *US v. Demjanjuk*, Case No. A8237417 Deportation Proceedings, transcript of proceedings, Tuesday, February 7, 1984, 176.

23. Yet when asked in a deposition an innocuous background question about his union membership, Demjanjuk responded defensively, emphasizing that everyone had been a member; he appeared reluctant to acknowledge that he had ever voluntarily joined *any* organization.

24. *US v. Demjanjuk*, Case No. A8237417, Deportation Proceedings, transcript of proceedings, Monday, January 16, 1984, 25.

25. *State of Israel vs Ivan (John) Demjanjuk, Criminal Case No. 373/86: Verbatim, Unedited Minutes, 7421*.

26. Ibid., 69, 70.

27. Teicholz, *The Trial of Ivan the Terrible*, 49.

28. "Michael Hausiak, activist and journalist, 93," *People's World*, September 21, 2007, http://peoplesworld.org/michael-hanusiak-activist-and-journalist-93/.

29. Steinlauf, *Bondage of the Dead*, 148.

30. Ibid.

31. Hanusiak, *Lest We Forget*, 11.

32. Immigration and Nationality Act of 1952, Pub. L. No. 414 §241(a)(19), 66 Stat. 163, 260 (1952) (codified as amended at 8 USC §1451(a) (1982).

33. This process required each applicant to be interviewed first by a representative of the International Refugee Organization of the United Nations (IRO) and then by an official of the Displaced Persons Commission. For a fuller description of the process, see the Supreme Court's ruling in *US v. Fedorenko* 449 US 490 (1981).

34. Irving Engel et al., "Screening of DPs," Letters to the Editor, *New York Times*, January 12, 1949, http://query.nytimes.com/mem/archive/pdf?res=9A02E1DF1F38E23BBC4A52DFB7668382659EDE.

35. Reverend Luigi Ligutti et al., "Admitting Displaced Persons," Letters to

the Editor, *New York Times*, February 3, 1949, http://query.nytimes.com/mem/archive/pdf?res=9803EFDD173FE03ABC4B53DFB4668382659EDE.

36. See Friedlander and McCarrick, "Nazi Criminals in the United States: Denaturalization after Fedorenko."

37. Lichtblau, *The Nazis Next Door.* Lichtblau appears to have gotten his figure from former OSI director Allan Ryan, who offered the guesstimate decades earlier.

38. Charles R. Allen Jr., "Nazi War Criminals Living among Us," *Jewish Currents*, 1963.

39. Douglas Martin, "A Nazi Past, a Queens Home Life, an Overlooked Death," *New York Times*, December 2, 2005, www.nytimes.com/2005/12/02/international/europe/02ryan.html?pagewanted=all.

40. Taylor, *Nuremberg and Vietnam.*

41. Ralph Blumenthal, "Ex-Chief Immigration Trial Attorney Quits Abrupthy; Feared Retaliation Social Favors," *New York Times*, December 8, 1973.

42. Application for Immigration Visa and Alien Registration No. 1272219, Iwan Demjanjuk, December 27, 1951 (listing Sobibor, Poland as residence, 1934–43). On file with author.

43. Nor was it an isolated reference: investigators would later discover Demjanjuk's Application for Assistance filed with the International Refugee Organization in Regensburg on March 3, 1948—that is, over two and a half years earlier—in which Demjanjuk listed having worked as a farmer and driver in the village of Sobibor, though for a shorter period of time, from 1937 to 1943. Other documents from the same period also list Sobibor as his wartime domicile. See Application for Assistance, PCIRO, 3.3.1948 (listing Sobibor-Chelm as residence, 1937–43); Final DP camp record, Demjanuk (*sic*), Iwan, (listing Sobobor [*sic*] under *allgem. Vormerkungen* [general notes]), 2.1.1952. On file with author.

44. Feigin, *Striving for Accountability*, 31.

45. "In the Matter of the Extradition of John Demjanjuk aka John Ivan Demjanjuk, aka John Ivan Demyanyuk [*sic*]," Misc. No. 83–349, April 15, 1985, 612 F. Supp 544, 557.

46. *Demjanjuk v. Petrovsky* 776 F.2d 571 (Sixth Circuit, 1985), 582.

47. Immigration and Nationality Act of 1952, Pub. L. No. 414 §340(a), 66 Stat. 163, 260 (1952) (codified as amended at 8 USC §1451(a) (1982).

48. Transcript of Radiwker interview with Eugen Turowski, Headquarters, 12:00 10.5.76. On file with author.

49. Transcript of Radiwker interview with Abraham Goldfarb, Headquarters, 13:00 9.5.76. On file with author. The records of the interviews suggest that Goldfarb was interviewed before Turowski, but the trial court reports that

Turowski was interviewed first. See *The Demjanjuk Trial: In the District Court of Jerusalem 373/86*, 121.

50. Transcript of Radiwker interview with Josef Czarny, Headquarters, 14:15, 21.9.76. On file with author.

51. Transcript of Radiwker interview with Gustav Boraks, Haifa, 10:10, 30.9.76. On file with author.

52. Boraks interview with Radiwker.

53. Czarny interview with Radiwker.

54. Report to House Subcommittee on Immigration, Citizenship, and International Law, 30.

55. Nearly a year was needed to assemble a team of four trial attorneys, two INS investigators, an archivist, and four graduate students fluent in German (though none had any particular expertise in Nazi genocide). Mendelsohn interview with the author.

56. Ryan, *Quiet Neighbors*, 60.

57. Saidel, *The Outraged Conscience*, 124–26.

58. Inteview with the author.

59. Wiseman, "Report of the Special Master," 29.

60. Ibid., 33.

61. See Friedlander and McCarrick, "Nazi Criminals in the United States: Denaturalization after Fedorenko."

62. Pnina Lahav, "The Chicago Conspiracy Trial as a Jewish Morality Tale," in Sarat, Douglas, and Umphrey, *Lives in the Law*, 38.

63. *United States v. Walus*, 453 F.Supp. 699 (N.D.Ill.1978).

64. Feigin, *Striving for Accountability*, 77.

65. *United States v. Walus*, 616 F2d 283 (Court of Appeals, 7th Circuit 1980), parag. 5.

66. Feigin, *Striving for Accountability*, 82.

67. Quoted in ibid., 64.

68. Report to House Subcommittee on Immigration, Citizenship, and International Law, iii.

69. Martin Mendelsohn undertook several trips to the Soviet Union in an effort to establish better working relations, a necessary condition for prosecutorial success, though it wasn't until 1980, after the creation of the OSI, that an unofficial understanding ushered in a period of greater cooperation. Mendelsohn interview; see also Ryan, *Quiet Neighbors*.

70. Lichtblau, *The Nazis Next Door*, 144–45.

71. Report to House Subcommittee on Immigration, Citizenship, and International Law, 28.

72. Feigin, *Striving for Accountability*, 85.

73. It has been well established that Demjanjuk spent some weeks at the

Rovno POW camp; doubts remain, however, about whether he was ever interned at the POW camp in Chelm.

74. *United States v. Fedorenko*, 455 F. Supp. 893 (Dist. Court, SD Florida 1978).

75. Ibid., 899.

76. Ibid., 903, 907.

77. Ibid., 918, 921.

78. Memo, Martin Mendelsohn, Chief, Special Litigation Unit, INS, to the Solicitor General, September 15, 1978. On file with author.

79. *United States v. Fedorenko*, 597 F. 2d 946 (Court of Appeals, 5th Circuit 1979).

80. *Fedorenko v. United States*, 449 US 490 (1981).

81. Ibid., 505, 510, 512, 514.

82. *United States v. Fedorenko*, 455 F. Supp. 893, 902 (Dist. Court, SD Florida 1978).

83. *Fedorenko v. United States*, 449 U.S. 490 (1981), 494.

84. *United States v. Fedorenko*, 455 F. Supp. 893, 913.

85. *Fedorenko v. United States*, 449 US 490, 538, 534.

86. In his famous discussion of the Gray Zone, Primo Levi acknowledged, "It is naïve, absurd, and historically false to believe that a system such as National Socialism sanctifies its victims." All the same, Levi insisted that to confuse the murderers with their victims amounts to "precious service rendered . . . to the negators of truth." Levi, *The Drowned and the Saved*, 40.

87. See *Fedorenko v. United States*, 449 US 490, 512, note 34.

88. Mendelsohn's removal turned into a substantial headache for Rockler; Holtzman raised objections with the attorney general, while Harvard's Jewish Law Students Association wrote to President Carter to express "outrage" at Mendlesohn's ouster. Saidel, *The Outraged Conscience*, 131.

89. In the solicitor general's office, Ryan had initially recommended that the government drop its appeal in *Fedorenko*, which he described as a "dead end"; he later changed his mind and drafted the government's sturdy appellate brief submitted to the Supreme Court.

90. Peter Black interview with the author.

91. "Treblinka-Prozess." Urteil von LG Düsseldorf vom 3.9.1965, 8 I Ks 2/64.

92. Feigin, *Striving for Accountability*, 112.

93. See US v. Demjanjuk Case No. C77-923, Deposition of defendant, April 20, 1978, 36–37, 45–46.

94. *US v. Demjanjuk*, Civil Action No. C 77-923. Trial Proceedings, March 4, 1981, 1105.

95. Demjanjuk was not alone in the effort to remove traces of the SS blood-

type tattoo. KGB interrogations show that this was a process followed by numerous other auxiliaries. Soviet investigation files include photographs of the results of these efforts.

96. By the fall of 1942, the recruitment of POWs tailed off; thereafter, most of the Trawniki recruits were Ukrainian civilians. See Black, "Police Auxiliaries for Operation Reinhard."

97. Matyiychuk, "Punishment Will Come," *News from Ukraine*, September 1977, 3.

98. *US v. Demjanjuk*, Civil Action No. C 77-923. Trial Proceedings, March 4, 1981, 1107.

99. Application for Immigration Visa and Alien Registration No. 1272219, Iwan Demjanjuk, December 27, 1951 (listing hair: brown; eyes: grey). On file with author.

100. Historians in the OSI have also speculated that perhaps Demjanjuk *was* 175 cm (5'8") at the time of his arrival at Trawniki, but then experienced a rapid growth spurt. In support of this seemingly outlandish claim (Demjanjuk was, after all, about to turn twenty-two when he arrived at Trawniki), OSI historians point to scientific studies that demonstrate the dramatic effects of proper caloric intake on young adults who have suffered severe malnutrition early in life; these effects include remarkable late growth spurts.

101. Author interview with David Rich.

102. Wyman, *DPs*. 69.

103. www.columbia.edu/cu/lweb/digital/collections/rbml/lehman/pdfs/0737/ldpd_leh_0737_0131.pdf.

104. *United States v. Demjanjuk*, 518 F. Supp. 1362 (Dist. Court, ND Ohio 1981).

105. During the Eichmann trial, Scheffler had served as an observer for the Auswärtiges Amt (the German Foreign Office) and would later testify at Demjanjuk's trial in Jerusalem. See Pohl, "Prosecutors and Historians," 117–29.

106. Ibid., 8.

107. *United States v. Demjanjuk*, 518 F. Supp. 1362 (Dist. Court, ND Ohio 1981).

108. "Ohio Man Accused of Nazi Crimes," *New York Times*, February 11, 1981, www.nytimes.com/1981/02/11/us/ohio-man-accused-of-nazi-crimes.html.

109. Philip Shenon, "The Demjanjuk Aggravation," *New York Times*, February 17, 1987, www.nytimes.com/1987/02/19/us/washington-talk-the-buchanan-aggravation.html?module=Search&mabReward=relbias%3As%2C%7B%221%22%3A%22RI%3A5%22%7D.

110. Buchanan, "The True Haters," April 14, 2009, http://buchanan.org/blog/pjb-the-true-haters-1495.

111. "Pat Buchanan's Unrelenting Defense of John Demjanjuk," Anti-Defamation League Background Report, 2, http://archive.adl.org/special_reports/pb_archive/pb_demjanjuk_1993.pdf.

112. 101 Federal Rules Decision 1.

113. Congress later changed this and now the same standard controls both proceedings.

114. The attorney general long enjoyed the discretionary power to intervene at the last moment to bar deportation if he or she believed it might subject the deportee to, among other things, "personal or family hardship"—a rather permissive equitable standard to apply in cases involving a person about to be forced from home and country. Elizabeth Holtzman properly put an end to that. In 1978, Congress passed the so-called Holtzman Amendment to the Immigration and Nationality Act, which, among other things, barred the attorney general from stepping in at the last second to upend years of legal work. See text at www.justice.gov/criminal/hrsp/statutes/stats/holtzman-amend.pdf.

115. Transcript of Proceedings, *United States v. Demjanjuk*, US Immigration Court, Case No. A8237417 (Deportation Proceedings), February 7, 1984, 84.

116. Transcript of Proceedings, *United States v. Demjanjuk*, US Immigration Court, Case No. A8237417 (Deportation Proceedings), January 16, 1984, 84.

117. Wiseman, "Report of the Special Master," 8–9.

118. Germany's Basic Law prohibited the extradition of its own nationals. This blanket prohibition was changed with the adoption of the Framework Decision on the European Arrest Warrant and Surrender Procedures between Member States of the European Union. See Martin Rademacher, "Extradition Proceedings in Germany: The Legal Procedure for Dealing with Incoming Requests for Extradition," www.auslieferungsverfahren.de/pdf/Auslieferungsverfahren_englisch.pdf.

119. *Demjanjuk v. Petrovsky*, 776 F.2d 571 (Court of Appeals, 6th Circuit 1985), 576.

120. *Matter of the Extradition of John Demjanjuk*, aka John Ivan Demjanjuk, aka John Ivan Demyanyuk [*sic*]. Misc. No. 83-349.603 F. Supp. 1468 (N.D. Ohio 1985).

121. *Matter of Extradition of John Demjanjuk*, 612 F. Supp. 544, 553 (N.D. Ohio 1985).

122. Also manslaughter, and grievous bodily harm. *Demjanjuk v. Petrovsky*, 776 F.2d 571 (Court of Appeals, 6th Circuit 1985).

123. Convention on the Prevention and Punishment of the Crime of Genocide, December 9, 1948, Art. 2, file:///Users/lrdouglas/Downloads/IHL-51-EN.pdf.

124. Nazis and Nazi Collaborators (Punishment) Law, 5710-1950, Article

1(b), www.icrc.org/applic/ihl/ihl-nat.nsf/0/aacf823ae32ab469c12575ae0034c1fe/$FILE/Law%20no.%2064.pdf.

125. Arendt, *Eichmann in Jerusalem*, 269.

126. Taylor, "Large Questions in Eichmann Case," *New York Times*, January 22, 1961.

127. Porat, in Finder and Jokusch, *Jewish Honor Courts*, 7.

128. Novick, *The Holocaust in American Life*.

129. Porat, in Finder and Jokusch, *Jewish Honor Courts*.

130. Ibid., 16.

131. Ibid., 25. The last collaboration trial technically took place in 1972; the *Barenblat* opinion was written by Moshe Landau, who presided over the Eichmann trial.

132. Criminal Appeal 377/88, *Demjanjuk v. Israel*, Judgment of Israeli Supreme Court, 44.

133. *Matter of Extradition of John Demjanjuk*, 612 F. Supp. 544, 567–568 (N.D. Ohio 1985).

Chapter 3. Ivan in Israel

1. Pyle, *Extradition, Politics, and Human Rights*, 264, 276.

2. "Valerian Trifa, an Archbishop with a Fascist Past, Dies at 72," *New York Times*, January 29, 1987.

3. Hausner, *Justice in Jerusalem*, 291.

4. *Trial of Adolf Eichmann* 5:2146.

5. "Absolute Gerechtigkeit," *Der Spiegel* November 1986, 190, www.spiegel.de/spiegel/print/d-13517583.html.

6. Quoted in Teicholz, *The Trial of Ivan the Terrible*, 269.

7. (UPI) "Israel Copies Eichmann Trial for Demjanjuk," *Bryan Times*, March 18, 1986, http://news.google.com/newspapers?nid=799&dat=19860318&id=eMIdAAAAIBAJ&sjid=IVgEAAAAIBAJ&pg=6228,7246728.

8. Qutoed in Teicholz, *The Trial of Ivan the Terrible*, 81.

9. Quoted in ibid., 169.

10. *State of Israel vs Ivan (John) Demjanjuk*, Criminal Case No. 373/86: Verbatim, Unedited Minutes, 6871.

11. Teicholz, *The Trial of Ivan the Terrible*, 73.

12. Simpson, *Blowback*, 270.

13. Teicholz, *The Trial of Ivan the Terrible*, 76.

14. *Matter of the Extradition of John Demjanjuk* 603 F.Supp 1468, 1473 (N.D. Ohio 1985).

15. *Demjanjuk v. Petrovsky*, 776 F2d 571, 576. (6th Cir., 1985).

16. On January 14, 2011, five month's before Demjanjuk's conviction in Munich, Spain issued an international extradition order, seeking to gain custody of Demjanjuk in the case of his acquittal in Germany. Although Spain sought Demjanjuk in connection with crimes against humanity and genocide, the Spanish National Court's order was not, technically speaking, based on universal jurisdiction, as Demjanjuk was charged with participating in the murder of Spanish citizens, sixty of whom were alleged to have perished at Flossenbürg during Demjanjuk's tenure as a guard at the camp.

17. *State of Israel vs Ivan (John) Demjanjuk*, Criminal Case No. 373/86: Verbatim, Unedited Minutes, 8.

18. Ibid., 9.

19. Most commentators agree that the international application of double jeopardy (*non bis in idem*) cannot be considered an article of customary international law or a general principle of international law. See R. N. Daniels, "*Non bis In Idem* and the Rome Statute of the International Criminal Court," http://law.bepress.com/cgi/viewcontent.cgi?article=6282&context=expreso

20. See Reydams, *Universal Jurisdiction*.

21. Finkielkraut, *Remembering in Vain*, 3.

22. Roth, *Operation Shylock*, 61.

23. Wefing, *Der Fall Demjanjuk*, 65.

24. Roth, *Operation Shylock*, 61.

25. Francis X. Clines, "Survivor of Death Camp Indentifies Accused Guard at Trial in Israel," *New York Times*, February 24, 1987, www.nytimes.com/1987/02/24/world/survivor-of-death-camp-indentifies-accused-guard-at-trial-in-israel.html.

26. *State of Israel vs Ivan (John) Demjanjuk*, Criminal Case No. 373/86: Verbatim, Unedited Minutes, 160–61.

27. Thomas L. Friedman, "Treblinka Trial Becomes an Israeli Obsession," *New York Times*, March 13, 1987, www.nytimes.com/1987/03/13/world/treblinka-trial-becomes-an-israeli-obsession.html?module=Search&mabReward=relbias%3Ar%2C%7B%221%22%3A%22RI%3A11%22%7D.

28. Ibid.

29. Arendt, *Eichmann in Jerusalem*, 15.

30. See Douglas, *The Memory of Judgment*, 123–49.

31. *State of Israel vs Ivan (John) Demjanjuk*, Criminal Case No. 373/86: Verbatim, Unedited Minutes, 1076.

32. Ibid., 1079.

33. Ibid., 1018.

34. Mary Sedor, "Demjanjuk's Attorney Challenges Description of Ivan," *AP News Archive*, March 11,1987, www.apnewsarchive.com/1987/Demjanjuk-s-

Attorney-Challenges-Description-Of-Ivan/id-3d27324ab119e3ec67015284c69 71290.

35. Roma Hadzewycz, "Interview: Yoram Sheftel, Israeli Defender of John Demjanjuk," *Ukrainian Weekly* 64, no. 28 (July 14, 1996): 7.

36. Ibid., 2.

37. *State of Israel vs Ivan (John) Demjanjuk,* Criminal Case No. 373/86: Verbatim, Unedited Minutes, 6828.

38. Ibid., 6831, 6871, 6974.

39. *US v. Demjanjuk* (US District Court, Northern District of Ohio) Deposition of John Demjanjuk, April 20, 1978., 27. On file with author.

40. *State of Israel vs Ivan (John) Demjanjuk,* Criminal Case No. 373/86: Verbatim, Unedited Minutes, 7128.

41. Ibid., 7164, 7135.

42. Ibid., 6861, 7159, 7158.

43. Ibid., 7176, 7171.

44. Ibid., 7178.

45. PCIRO, Application for Assistance, March 3, 1948. On file with author.

46. *State of Israel vs Ivan (John) Demjanjuk,* Criminal Case No. 373/86: Verbatim, Unedited Minutes, 6917.

47. Ibid., 7375.

48. Ibid., 7441–42.

49. Ibid., 7377, 7379.

50. Ibid., 6924, 7522, 7517, 6924.

51. Ibid., 7263.

52. Ibid., 6988.

53. Ibid., 7562.

54. Author interview with Gabriel Bach.

55. Protocol of witness interrogation, Ignat Danilchekno, November 21, 1979; no. 1429-2038, p. 5.

56. In yet another demonstration of the vulnerability of eyewitness memory, Danilchenko said the transfer to Flossenbürg occurred in March or April 1944, when in fact it took place in October 1943.

57. Wefing, *Der Fall Demjanjuk*, 79.

58. Feigin, *Striving for Accountability*, 48.

59. Author Interview with OSI historian David Rich. That said, other historians have noted that without the full name and date of birth of the defendant, it was "almost impossible to trace . . . files in the relevant KGB archives." Dean, "Displaced War Crimes Trials."

60. This was the so-called "Amnesty to Soviet citizens who collaborated with the enemy during the Great Patriotic War, 1941–1945." See Feldbrugge, *Encyclopedia of Soviet Law*, 46.

61. Minutes of Interrogation, Ignat Danilchenko, Dniepropetrowsk, March 2, 1949, 10–12. On file with author.

62. Meldung von der Hundestaffel. January 20, 1943. On file with author.

63. Application for Immigration Visa and Alien Registration, No. 1272219. December 27, 1951.

64. Claims that Marchenko survived the war, returned to Soviet soil, and died in peace, have never been substantiated.

65. *The Demjanjuk Trial: In the District Court of Jerusalem 373/86*, 263–64.

66. http://mfa.gov.il/MFA/AboutIsrael/State/Law/Pages/STATEMENT%20BY%20JUSTICE%20MINISTER%20LIBAI%20ON%20DEMJANJUK%20D.aspx.

67. Decision of Israel Supreme Court on Petition Concerning John (Ivan) Demjanjuk.

68. Teicholz, *The Trial of Ivan the Terrible*, 301.

69. Roth, *Operation Shylock*, 13.

70. Ibid., 63.

71. Duncan Campbell, "I Felt I Had Befouled Myself," *Guardian*, January 30, 2004, www.theguardian.com/film/2004/jan/30/4.

72. Pat Buchanan, "Acquit Demjanjuk: The Case is Weak," *New York Times*, March 31, 1987, www.nytimes.com/1987/03/31/opinion/acquit-demjanjuk-the-case-is-weak.html?module=Search&mabReward=relbias%3As%2C%7B%221%22%3A%22RI%3A5%22%7D.

73. *The Demjanjuk Trial: In the District Court of Jerusalem 373/86*, 211–15.

74. Sereny, "John Demjanjuk and the Failure of Justice," 34.

75. See also Sereny, *The German Trauma*, 309–57.

76. For text of law, see http://nolegalfrontiers.org/israeli-domestic-legislation/criminal-procedure/criminal01?lang=en.

77. Associated Press, "Nazi Expelled by U.S. Executed: Fyodor Fedorenko Dies by Soviet Firing Squad," July 27, 1987, http://articles.latimes.com/1987-07-27/news/mn-4129_1_soviet-union.

78. *Manson v. Brathwaite*, 432 US 98 (1977).

79. The quoted example comes from the State of Wisconsin, "Model Policy and Procedure for Eyewitness Identification," www.doj.state.wi.us/sites/default/files/2009-news/eyewitness-public-20091105.pdf.

80. *The Demjanjuk Trial: In the District Court of Jerusalem 373/86*, 121.

81. Loftus and Ketcham, *Witness for the Defense*, 219.

82. The arrangement was born in part as an effort to keep Benjamin Halevi from presiding over the Eichmann trial. Halevi's conduct during the Kastner trial had raised concerns about his objectivity toward Eichmann. See Douglas, *The Memory of Judgment*, 155–56.

83. *The Trial of Adolf Eichmann*, 5:2082.

84. *The Demjanjuk Trial: In the District Court of Jerusalem 373/86*, 39.
85. Ibid., 11.
86. Ibid., 10.
87. Ibid., 93.
88. Wagenaar, *Identifying Ivan*.
89. *The Demjanjuk Trial: In the District Court of Jerusalem 373/86*, 199.
90. *The Trial of Adolf Eichmann*, 5:2083.

Chapter 4. Demjanjuk Redux

1. Decision of Israel Supreme Court on Petition Concerning John (Ivan) Demjanjuk, 36.
2. Ibid., 34.
3. Ibid., 34, 36.
4. See Lichtblau, *The Nazis Next Door*, 154–69.
5. Author interview with Kirsten Goetze.
6. "Ukraine Willing to Admit Demjanjuk, Leader Says," *New York Times*, July 31, 1993, www.nytimes.com/1993/07/31/world/ukraine-willing-to-admit-demjanjuk-leader-says.html.
7. The Clinton administration considered appealing the ruling to the Supreme Court but, in a sudden volte-face, decided not to, a reversal that signaled widening rifts in the Justice Department. Clyde Haberman, "Israel Again Puts Off Demjanjuk Deportation," *New York Times*, September 3, 1993, http://www.nytimes.com/1993/09/03/world/israel-again-puts-off-demjanjuk-deportation.html.
8. Joel Greenberg, "Israeli Court Bars Demjanjuk's Leaving," *New York Times*, August 2, 1993.
9. Ibid., www.nytimes.com/1993/08/02/world/israeli-court-bars-demjanjuk-s-leaving.html.
10. Clyde Haberman, "Israeli Court Clears Way to Deporting Demjanjuk," *New York Times*, August 18, 1993., www.nytimes.com/1993/08/18/world/israeli-court-clears-way-to-deporting-demjanjuk.html.
11. Clyde Haberman, "Woman Says Demjanjuk Was at Nazi Camp," *New York Times*, August 25, 1993, www.nytimes.com/1993/08/25/world/us-woman-says-demjanjuk-was-at-nazi-camp.html.
12. Clyde Haberman, "Aboard Flight, Demjanjuk Hears Different Verdict," *New York Times*, September 23, 1993, www.nytimes.com/1993/09/23/world/aboard-flight-demjanjuk-hears-different-verdict.html.
13. Renee Redman, "The Trials of John Demjanjuk," in Finkelman and Alexander, *Justice and Legal Change*, 15, 18.

14. *City of Seven Hills v. Aryan Nations*, 76 Ohio St. 3d 304, 667 N.E.2d 942 (1996).

15. Jean Marbella, "Demjanjuk's Community on Defensive," *Baltimore Sun*, September 23, 1993, http://articles.baltimoresun.com/1993-09-23/news/1993266002_1_john-demjanjuk-ss-cleveland.

16. Stephen Labaton, "At the Bar; A successful prosecutor of war criminals may be remembered for the case that fell apart," *New York Times*, August 27, 1993, www.nytimes.com/1993/08/27/news/bar-successful-prosecutor-war-criminals-may-be-remembered-for-case-that-fell.html.

17. Bill Sloat, "Court Reopens Case of 'Ivan the Terrible,'" *Cleveland Plain Dealer*, June 6, 1992, http://blog.cleveland.com/pdextra/2011/05/corut_reopens_case_of_ivan_the.html. For the *Vanity Fair* article, see Dannen, "How Terrible Is Ivan?"

18. Finkelman and Alexander, *Justice and Legal Change*, 14; Feigin, *Striving for Accountability*, 158.

19. Wiseman, "Report of the Special Master," 2.

20. *Demjanjuk v. Petrovsky*, 10 F. 3d 338, 36 (Court of Appeals, 6th Circuit 1993), 10:36.

21. Ibid., 10, quoting Parker at 38.

22. Ibid., 10:17–18, 18.

23. Ibid., 10:16, 17.

24. Ibid., 10:19, 18.

25. Yossi Melman, "Who Lied about Demjanjuk?," *Ha'aretz*, November 14, 1997; Finkelman and Alexander, *Justice and Legal Change*, 14; www.willzuzak.ca/lp/merrit01.htm.

26. Indeed, historians now believe four persons operated the gas chambers at Treblinka. Peter Black interview.

27. Wiseman, "Report of the Special Master," 96. At least one source I spoke to speculated, however, that Moscowitz's request may never have been forwarded by the State Department, the department through which all such requests had to pass. Aiding OSI investigations was never a top priority with the State Department.

28. Author interview with Peter Black.

29. Some continue to question the timing of the memo; at least one former OSI lawyer I spoke to, suspicious that it had been backdated, wished it could have been subjected to metadata analysis. Author interview with Jonathan Drimmer. Moscowitz insists he never saw the memo until years later.

30. Gladwell, "Connecting the Dots."

31. Wiseman, "Report of the Special Master," 204–5.

32. Even before the Demjanjuk debacle, the OSI had put into place in its

other cases a model that relied on documentary evidence prepared in close collaboration between lawyers and historians.

33. Redman, "Trials," in Finkelman and Alexander, *Justice and Legal Change*, 20.

34. In particular the cases researched by OSI historian Peter Black relied heavily on the documentary approach. These included the Maikovskis, Kairys, Trifa, and Schellong cases.

35. Author interview with Peter Black. Black notes that this collaborative model was not embraced by other war crimes units in Canada, Great Britain, and Australia, where prosecutors also failed to match the OSI's successes.

36. Sydnor, "Expert Report of Charles W. Sydnor Jr.," 23.

37. The *Dienstausweis* was typically issued when the recruit was about to be detailed outside the camp proper. The Trawniki man would turn in the service ID on his return to the camp, next receiving it at the time of his next deployment.

38. Sydnor, "Expert Report of Charles W. Sydnor Jr.," 24.

39. Huebner notes that record keeping at Trawniki was such a mess that ID numbers did not reliably ascend by order of arrival: men assigned higher numbers often had arrived before those with lower numbers. That said, numbers in roughly the same sequence were typically assigned on the same day, and evidence indicated that the recruit assigned ID No. 1392 arrived on June 13.

40. Ibid., 29.

41. Coming some three months after his arrival at Trawniki, this was presumably his first assignment upon "graduation." Whether this was in fact his first assignment is, as the report notes, impossible to say with absolute certainty; it's possible that an earlier summer assignment went unrecorded on his ID, as unrecorded assignments early in one's training were not unheard of.

42. Sydnor, "Expert Report of Charles W. Sydnor Jr.," 36–37.

43. Ibid., 48.

44. Author interview with Todd Huebner and Jonathan Drimmer.

45. The roster of Trawniki guards detailed to Sobibor includes both Demjanjuk's name as well as Danilchenko's.

46. At Flossenbürg, Demjanjuk was technically no longer part of the Trawniki system.

47. See Benz, Distel, and Königseder, *Flossenbürg*.

48. The blood-type tattoo was also given by the SS to Trawniki-trained guards at camps such as Buchenwald and Mauthausen.

49. Sydnor, "Expert Report of Charles W. Sydnor Jr." 99.

50. And yet, as we have seen, the *Fedorenko* holding, by making the volun-

tariness of service irrelevant in denaturalization matters, encouraged those who had unlawfully acquired citizenship to lie.

51. Drimmer took over the case after the lead lawyer, Edward Stutman, who had worked the case for four years, fell ill with lymphoma, and had to withdraw. Huebner drafted the questions for Drimmer's direct examination of Sydnor—that is, the historian drafted the questions about the report that he himself had written. Odd as this may sound, it was in fact not uncommon in OSI proceedings (and in other government litigation, for that matter) for expert reports to be independent in name only, as the greatest expertise resided in house. But it would be misleading to suggest that Sydnor's task was only to become an expert on the contents of Huebner's document. By the time of the trial, Sydnor had undertaken his own research trips to Russia and Germany, and, working in collaboration with Huebner, had introduced certain revisions and additions to the expert report.

52. "Findings of Fact," *US v. Demjanjuk*, Case No. 1:99CV1193 (N.D. Ohio Feb. 21, 2002), 4–5.

53. Around this time, Demjanjuk's camp turned suddenly internally litigious. In January 2006, Jerome Brentar, the Cleveland travel agent cum Holocaust denier who had bankrolled much of the defense, turned around and sued the family for the $2 million that he had spent on Demjanjuk's behalf. Demjanjuk, who four years earlier had allegedly been too cognitively infirm to participate in the second denaturalization trial, took the stand and cogently argued that Brentar had always presented his support as a charitable gift, not as a loan with the expectation of repayment. The jury in the case returned something of a mixed message, ordering the family to repay $90,000 in expenses.

54. Author interview with Eli Rosenbaum.

55. Bartosz Wielinski "Die Ukraine will keinen Antrag auf Auslieferung Demjanjuks stellen," translation of article from *Gazeta Wyborcza*, May 24, 2008. Staatsanwaltschaft München I, Verfahrensakten 1578. On file with author.

56. "Beschluss über die Einstellung des Verfahrens" Institut für nationales Gedenken IPN, Lodz, December 19, 2007. Staatsanwaltschaft München I, Verfahrensakten 1862-1874. On file with author.

57. Letter to Kurt Schrimm regarding Johan Leprich case, Auswärtiges Amt, 22. Juni 2004. On file with author.

58. Aktenvermerk, Überprüfungsverfahren gegen John Demjanjuk, Ludwigsburg, 28.05.2008 Staatsanwaltschaft München I, Verfahrensakten 58–62, 59.

59. "Vermerk über die Dientreise zur Auswertung der Akten des US DOJ,

OSI" Ludwigsburg, 20.08.03. Staatsanwaltschaft München I, Verfahrensakten 3238-3240, 58.

Chapter 5. Demjanjuk in Munich

1. Volk, *Das letzte Urteil*, 51.

2. See Langbein, *Comparative Criminal Procedure*.

3. For example, an audio recording of the famous Frankfurt-Auschwitz trial (1963–65) was permitted as an aide-mémoire for the court.

4. Hrycyk to Christian Schmidt-Sommerfeld, 12.5.09; Alt to Hrycyk, 16.6.09; Staatsanswaltschaft München I, Verfahrensakten HA 2432, 2433, 2434. On file with author.

5. Behind the scenes, Lutz did coordinate on behalf of the court inquires from the court to the OSI for documents or information. Such collaboration between court and prosecution is, again, not unusual in the German system.

6. Anklageschrift in der Strafsache gegen Demjanjuk, John, 115 Js 12496/08; Staatsanswaltschaft München I, Vefahrensakte; pp. 3002ff. On file with author.

7. See, for example, Beschluss des Landgerichts Dresden vom 20. Dezember 1993. Lfd. Nr. 1411e, BSRH 0434/93, allowing indemification in the case of former guard who had been sentenced to prison by a Soviet occupation court and had had his assets seized. Also, Beschluss des Landgerichts Dresden vom 12. April 1996, Lfd. Nr. 1411g, BSRH 0434/93, indemnifying a former guard for costs of trial that resulted in his conviction based on a theory of "collective guilt."

8. See Lemkin, *Axis Rule in Occupied Europe*.

9. Vogel, *Ein Weg aus der Vergangenheit*.

10. Miquel, *Ahnden oder Amnestieren?*, 27–35.

11. Vogel, *Ein Weg aus der Vergangenheit*, 33–34.

12. Ibid., 33–34.

13. Ibid., 36.

14. "The Nazi Criminals," *New York Times*, February 24, 1965, http://query.nytimes.com/mem/archive/pdf?res=9E01EED7143CE733A25757C2A9649C946491D6CF.

15. Vogel, *Ein Weg aus der Vergangenheit*, 32.

16. See "'Holocaust': Die Vergangenheit kommt zurück," *Der Spiegel*, May 1979, 17–28, http://magazin.spiegel.de/EpubDelivery/spiegel/pdf/40350860.

17. Osterloh and Vollnhals, *NS-Prozesse und deutsche Öffentlichkeit*, 375.

18. LG Frankfurt/M., Urteil v. 19./20.8.1965, Az: 4 Ks2/63, reprinted in *Justiz*

und NS-Verbrechen, Bd. XXI, Lfd. Nr. 595a, p. 882. The court's holding was upheld by the BGH in Urteil v. 20.2.1969, Az: 2StR 280/67, reprinted in *Justiz und NS-Verbrechen*, Bd. XXI, Lfd. Nr. 595b, pp 881ff.

19. "Findings of Fact" *US v. Demjanjuk*, Case No. 1:99CV1193 (N.D. Ohio Feb. 21, 2002), 84–85.

20. Author interview with Thomas Walther.

21. Rückerl, *NS-Verbrechen vor Gericht*, 329.

22. See generally Weinke, *Eine Gesellschaft ermittelt gegen sich selbst.*

23. Ibid., 161.

24. Ibid., 11–28.

25. Jurists and lawmakers argued that investing the Office with this power would violate the federated structure of the German judicial system. Bryant, *Eyewitness to Genocide*, 26.

26. Weinke, *Die Verfolgung von NS-Tätern im Geteilten Deutschland*, 339. See also Perels, *Das Juristische Erbe des "Dritten Reiches,"* 19.

27. Eichmüller, *Keine Generalamnestie, Die Strafverfolgung von NS-Verbrechen in der frühen Bundesrepublik.*

28. Quoted in Müller, *Hitler's Justice*, 257.

29. Dietrich Strothmann, "Ein Toter gleich 10 Minuten Gefängnis?" *Die Zeit* May 25, 1962. www.zeit.de/1962/21/ein-toter-gleich-10-minuten-gefaengnis/komplettansicht.

30. Eichmüller, *Keine Generalamnestie, Die Strafverfolgung von NS-Verbrechen in der frühen Bundesrepublik*, 626.

31. Like Eichmann, Schwammberger had fled to Argentina. German authorities petitioned for his extradition as early as 1973 but it was not until 1990 that he was returned to Germany to stand trial.

32. Interview with Kurt Schrimm.

33. Ibid.

34. Interview with Thomas Walther.

35. On file with author.

36. See Jardim, *The Mauthausen Trial*; U.S. v. Altfuldisch, et al., Case No. 000-50-5.

37. *Kairys v. Immigration and Naturalization Service*, 981 F2d 937 (7th Circuit, 1992), paragraph 14.

38. *Justiz und NS-Verbrechen*, Lfd. Nr. 594, 2 StR 71/64, 594c, p. 352.

39. LG Frankfurt/M., Urteil, v. 25.8.1950, Az.:52 Ks 3/50, reprinted in *Justiz und NS-Verbrechen*, Bd. VII, Lfd. Nr. 233, p. 286.

40. LG Frankfurt/M. *Justiz und NS-Verbrechen*, Bd. VII, p. 286. See also Gerhard Werle and Boris Burghardt, "Zur Gehilfenstrafbarkeit bei Massentötun-

gen in nationalalsozialistischen Vernichtungslagern—Der Fall Demjanjuk im Kontext der bundesdeutschen Rechtsprechung."

41. *Justiz und NS-Verbrechen*, LG Hagen vom 20.121966, 11 Ks 1/64, Lfd. Nr.642a, p. 217. One of the twelve defendants, Kurt Bolender, committed suicide on October 10, 1966, before the verdict was announced.

42. Hannah Arendt, "Auschwitz on Trial," in Arendt, *Responsibility and Judgment*, 243.

43. At the Munich trial, however, Professor Cornelius Nestler, chief lawyer of the *Nebenkläger*, attacked the 1969 ruling as a "doctrinal aberration." Nestler, "Ein Mythos."

44. Klier's acquittal was based both on necessity and on evidence that he did not share the SS' exterminatory aims and had worked to alleviate the suffering of the camp's Jews (this despite evidence that he had beaten some Jews with a whip).

45. Snyder, *Bloodlands*, 253–54. *Three* Jews survived Belzec, and one of them, Chaim Hirszman, was murdered by right-wing anti-Semites on March 19, 1946, hours after testifying about the camp before the Jewish Historical District Commission in Lublin. Only thanks to the Jewish uprisings did Treblinka and Sobibor have as many survivors as they did.

46. Anklageschrift in der Strafsache gegen Demjanjuk, John, 115 Js 12496/08; Staatsanswaltschaft München I, p. 6 . On file with author.

47. Zentrale Stelle, Demjanjuk Abschlussbericht, 115 J 12496/08, p.125 On file with author.

48. Reichsbürgergesetz vom 25. November 1941. RGBL 1 1941, p. 722. www.verfassungen.de/de/de33-45/reichsbuerger35-v11.htm.

49. Beschluss des zweiten Senats vom 14. Februar 1968. BverfGE 23, 98 (2 BvR 557/62).

50. Rosenbaum interview with the author.

51. See Frei, *Vergangenheitspolitik*.

Chapter 6. Was damals Recht war . . .

1. See, for example, the judgment in the case of *Public Prosecutor v. Jorgic*, Oberlandesgericht Düsseldorf, and the discussion in Luc Reydams, *Universal Jurisdiction*, 150–57. Jorgic was convicted of genocide and sentenced to four life terms. For Judgment, see www.trial-ch.org/en/ressources/trial-watch/trial-watch/profils/profile/283/action/show/controller/Profile.html.

2. Sobibor-Prozess (Berlin)—Urteil, LG Berlin vom 8.5.1950, PKs 3/50, www.holocaust-history.org/german-trials/sobibor-urteil-berlin.shtml.

3. See Weinke, *Die Verfolgung von NS-Tätern im geteilten Deutschland.*

4. See LeBlanc, *The United States and the Genocide Convention.*

5. Grundgesetz für die Bundesrepublik Deutschland, vom 23.5.1949, veröffentlichte und bereinigte Fassung. Zuletzt geändert durch Gesetz vom 11.7.2012 (BGBl I S. 1478).

6. See Gallant, *The Principle of Legality in International and Comparative Criminal Law.* Technically speaking, *nulla poena* includes, in addition to the bar against retroactivity, a bar against "anaological" jurisprudence, and a stipulation of statutory precision in the specification of a crime. Although the last of these played a role in some arguments detailed in this chapter, the weightiest debates involved the question of retroactivity.

7. Kurt Schrimm, "Die strafliche Aufarbeitung der NS-Vergangenheit in der Bundesrepublik Deutschland vor 1989," 28.

8. Ibid., 29.

9. Interview with Stefan Schünemann conducted by the author, January 13, 2010.

10. *Jackson Report*, 335.

11. Opening Statement by Robert Jackson, in International Military Tribunal, *Trial of the Major War Criminals before the International Military Tribunal, Nuremberg, 14 November 1945–1 October 1946*, 2:146.

12. Christoph Burchard, "The Nuremberg Trial and its Impact on Germany," *Journal of International Criminal Justice* 4 (2006): 800–829, at 807.

13. See Trials of War Criminals before the Nuernberg Military Tribunals under Control Council Law No. 10, Nuernberg October 1946–April 1949, vol. 3. (Hereafter cited as TWC.)

14. Ibid., 3:31.

15. See *Judgment at Nuremberg*, director Stanley Kramer, writer Abby Mann, 1961.

16. CCL 10 also authorized the punishment of persons proven to have been members in an organization deemed criminal by the IMT. Telford Taylor, Final Report to the Secretary of the Army on the Nuernberg War Crimes Trials Under Control Council Law No. 10 (Washington, DC, 1949), appendix D.

17. CCL 10 expanded the range of crimes against humanity to include "atrocities and offenses" such as "imprisonment," "torture," and "rape"—acts not mentioned in 6(c) of the IMT Charter. For a full text of CCL 10. See Taylor, Final Report, appendix D.

18. Admittedly, many of the NMT judges failed to appreciate the significance of CCL 10's severing of the nexus requirement, and historians have labored to offer a satisfactory account of the change. As Robert Wolfe has ob-

served, the tribunals in the Medical, Flick, and Ministries cases all "reaffirmed the IMT opinion that crimes against German nationals antedating September 1939 and not directly connected to aggressive war, . . . however deplorable, were not . . . punishable under international law." Wolfe, "Flaws in the Nuremberg Legacy," 444. In his opening statement in the *Einsatzgruppen* case, by contrast, Benjamin Ferencz specifically called attention to the change effected by CCL 10: "The London Charter restricted the jurisdiction of the International Military Tribunal to crimes against humanity connected with crimes against peace or war crimes. This restriction does not appear in the Control Council enactment, which recognizes that crimes against humanity are, in international law, completely independent of either crimes against peace or war crimes. To deny this independence would make the change devoid of meaning." TWC, 4:49.

19. It remains unclear why Allied lawmakers made this important change. We can hazard the guess that Allied jurists saw CCL 10 as essentially the "legislative product" of a sovereign body acting as a proxy for the German state. Because Nuremberg had jurisdiction exclusively over international crimes, only those crimes against humanity that were connected to international war were deemed justiciable. But because CCL 10 functioned like a domestic German statute, Allied jurists apparently saw no similar need to connect the crimes named within it to the Nazis' war of aggression.

20. Robert Wolfe, "Flaws in the Nuremberg Legacy: An Impediment to the International War Crimes Tribunals' Prosecution of Crimes against Humanity," *Holocaust and Genocide Studies* 12 (1998): 434–53, at 444.

21. It should be noted that Article 6(c) of the IMT Charter appeared to allow the Tribunal to condemn acts permitted under German law, but this construction was rejected by the Tribunal in its judgment. Also, the practical consequence of the judges' stance in the Justice case should not be exaggerated: the Justice case ultimately dealt with crimes against humanity committed during and not before the war, thus reducing the court's comments on prewar crimes to *orbiter dicta*.

22. TWC, 3:977.

23. Ibid.

24. TWC, 3:256.

25. TWC, 3:282, 284.

26. Schmitt and Nunan, *Writings on War*, 135.

27. In part, this unfortunate development may have resulted from the Allies' failure to get the word out. Original plans to publish a German-language edition of the judgment in the Justice case were scuttled amid congressional

budget cuts and escalating Cold War tensions. Taylor was painfully aware of this failure, and his summary report betrays his frustration with the absence of coordinated support for the NMT program: "A failure to disseminate the Nuernberg records and judgments in Germany, accordingly, is not only a failure to make use of their contents to promote the positive aims of the occupation. It is a failure to put the necessary "ammunition" in the hands of those Germans who can make use of the documents presented and testimony given during the trials in reconstituting a democratic German society." Taylor, *Final Report*, 111. Had the United States aggressively disseminated the NMT judgments, Germans might still have rejected domestic trials for crimes against humanity. History by counterfactual is always a tricky enterprise, and there is no clear recipe for orchestrating the successful reception of an extraordinarily ambitious exercise of transitional justice in the defeated land of the perpetrators. But certainly the unwillingness or inability to use political tools to support the juridical lessons of the Justice Case sapped it of its relevance and didactic power. A German-language version of the judgment first appeared in 1969 but only in East Germany; a redacted version was first published in the Federal Republic in 1985, and it wasn't until 1996 that a complete version of the judgment appeared in German translation. By then, the question of the retroactivity of crimes against humanity had long been settled in the law of the Federal Republic. Peschel-Gutzeit, *Das Nürnberger Juristen-Urteil von 1947.*

28. Loewenstein, "Reconstruction of the Administration," 422.

29. TWC, 3:xx.

30. The Frankfurt trial of Sobibor SS men Gomerski and Klier, staged roughly at the same time as the Bauer prosecution, was also anomalous, if for different reasons. Gomerski and Klier were charged not with crimes against humanity but with murder under normal German law, but this hardly made the proceeding any more proper; in prosecuting extraterritorial crimes the Frankfurt trial court also was guilty of exceeding its remit under occupation law.

31. Mildt, *In the Name of the People*, 22.

32. Loewenstein, "Reconstruction of the Administration," 433.

33. Ibid., 447. This was applied only in the case of judges who had joined before 1937.

34. Ibid., 431, 433.

35. See Nobert Frei, *1945 und wir*, 89.

36. Meyer-Seitz, *Die Verfolgung von NS-Straftaten*, 85.

37. SMAD-Befehl (Order of the Soviet Military Administration in Germany) Nr. 201 of 16 August 1947. Wentker, Die juristische Ahndung," 61.

38. Friedlander, *Nazi Crimes and the Law*, 24.

39. Meyer-Seitz, *Die Verfolgung von NS-Straftaten*, 102.

40. Ibid.

41. Ibid. For the use of CCL 10 in the Soviet zone and for the following, see also Ahrens, *Dresdner Bank*, 73–80.

42. See *Der Konstanzer Juristentag.*

43. Ibid., 7. This and the following quotations appear in the discussions.

44. Ibid., 75.

45. Hodenberg, "Anwendung," cols. 113–124. On Hodenberg, see Broszat, "Siegerjustiz," 520–21; and Weinke, *Die Verfolgung von NS-Tätern im geteilten Deutschland*, 41–42.

46. Hodenberg, "Anwendung," col. 120.

47. Gustav Radbruch, "Gesetzliches Unrecht und übergesetzliches Recht," 105–8. The German Constitutional Court made use of the Radbruch formula in its decision retroactively reconferring citizenship on German Jews, noted in the last chapter. In that decision, from 1968, the court held that the Nazi denaturalization law "contradicted principles of justice to such an intolerable extent so as to be void." BVerfGE 23, 98 (Urteil vom 14.21968, Az: 2 BvR 557/62), Paragraph 31.

48. Gustav Radbruch, "Zur Diskussion über die Verbrechen gegen die Menschlichkeit," col. 134.

49. Friedlander, *Nazi Crimes and the Law*, 27.

50. R. H. Graveson, "Der Grundsatz 'nulla poena sine lege,' 280.

51. See Peschel-Gutzeit, *Das Nürnberger Juristen-Urteil von 1947*, 25.

52. Other efforts to encourage acceptance, such as permitting decisions based on *Idealkonkurrenz*—the notion that the wrongdoing represented a violation of both CCL 10 and German domestic law—did little to enamor German jurists of CCL 10. Among German judges, *Idealkonkurrenz* did less to rehabilitate CCL 10 than to demonstrate its irrelevance: if ordinary German law sufficed to condemn the conduct before a court, why also apply this mooncalf of occupation law? And so the very efforts to make CCL 10 more palatable to German jurists only strengthened their opposition. See Broszat, "Siegerjustiz," 529. See also Meyer-Seitz, *Die Verfolgung von NS-Straftaten*, 130–32.

53. Quoted in Müller, *Hitler's Justice*, 242.

54. One might have expected members of the Socialist Party (SPD) to resist this drift, as they had numbered among Hitler's victims. To the contrary, the Socialists helped lead the charge against the unpopular Allied war crimes program as a way of shoring up their credentials as nationalists (during the Weimar Republic they had been discredited as "internationalists") and of scoring points against Adenauer, who became Germany's first postwar chancellor at a

time when the country still remained under Allied occupation. Buscher, *The U.S. War Crimes Trial Program*, 118.

55. Ibid., 93, 98, 100.

56. Perels, *Das juristische Erbe des "Dritten Reiches,"* 67.

57. Quoted in "Charles F. Wennerstrum, 96. Served on Iowa's High Court," *New York Times*, June 6, 1986, www.nytimes.com/1986/06/06/obituaries/charles-f-wennerstrum-96-served-on-iowa-s-high-court.html.

58. Buscher, *The U.S. War Crimes Trial Program*, 43.

59. Ibid., 43, 47.

60. See, for example, Rückerl, *NS-Verbrechen vor Gericht*, 124.

61. Broszat, "Siegerjustiz," 540.

62. Weinke, *Die Verfolgung von NS-Tätern im geteilten Deutschland*, 60.

63. Ratz, *Die Justiz und die Nazis*, 75. When it came to ratifying the European Convention for the Protection of Human Rights and Fundamental Freedoms of 1950, the Federal Republic famously lodged a reservation to the convention's so-called Nuremberg exception (Article 7[2]) to the principle of *nulla poena*: "This [prohibition] shall not prejudice the trial and punishment of any person for any act or omission which, at the time it was committed, was criminal according to the general principles of law recognized by civilized nations." Burchard, "The Nuremberg Trial and Its Impact on Germany," 813. http://conventions.coe.int/Treaty/ger/Treaties/Html/005.htm (21.10.10). The Federal Republic was notably alone in lodging this reservation. Meyer-Seitz, *Verfolgung*, p. 130. In 1973 Germany lodged no similar reservation to the identical Nuremberg exception to Article 15(2) of the International Convention on Civil and Political Rights (ICCPR), but this gesture of forbearance must be understood as political and tactical and not as indicative of a fundamental change of position. Indeed, another thirty years would have to pass before Germany would conceptually, if not formally, abandon its position. See Werle, "Menschenrechtsschutz, " 826–27.

64. Allied efforts in the western zones to keep former Nazis out of the reconstituted German judiciary had quickly fallen by the wayside. The dearth of untainted German judges led Britain, for example, to adopt its controversial 50–50 rule (in Germany known as the *Huckepackverfahren*, or "piggy-back rule"), in which one former Nazi judge could be reinstated for every "clean" judge. See Broszat, "Siegerjustiz, " 508–16; Reinhold, *Der Wiederaufbau der Justiz in Nordwestdeutschland 1945 bis 1949*, 103–4, 130ff; see also Miquel, *Ahnden oder Amnestieren*. The end of the controversial practice arguably only made matters worse, as the British came to realize the impossibility of "reorganizing the judiciary while excluding the mass of former party members." Weinke, *Die Verfolgung von NS-Tätern im geteilten Deutschland*, 35.

65. Perels, *Das juristische Erbe des "Dritten Reiches,"* 215. The figure of 80 percent comes from an examination of BGH judges in 1956.

66. Wolf, "Befreiung des Strafrechts vom nationalsozialistischen Denken?," 2.

67. Perels, *Das juristische Erbe des "Dritten Reiches,"* 20.

68. Hermann Lübbe, "Der Nationalsozialismus im deutschen Nachkriegsbewußtsein," 586.

69. Hubert Rottleuthner, "Krähenjustiz," in Mildt, *Staatsverbrechen vor Gericht*, 158. Evidently there were six convictions of judges of drumhead courts.

70. Weinke, *Nazi Crimes and the Law*, 171.

71. Weinke, *Nazi Crimes and the Law*, 158.

72. Susanne Jung, *Die Rechstprobleme der Nürnberger Prozesse*, 156.

73. Buscher, *The U.S. War Crimes Trial Program*, 105.

74. Perels, *Das juristische Erbe des "Dritten Reiches,"* 69.

75. Radbruch, "Zur Diskussion," col. 134.

76. Meyer-Seitz, *Die Verfolgung von NS-Straftaten*, 87. The British finally granted German courts jurisdiction over crimes against humanity committed against Jews in July 1947, that is, well after the special issue of the *SJZ* and the *Juristentag*, see Pendas, "Retroactive Law and Proactive Justice," 438.

77. See Claudia Bade, "Das Verfahren wird eingestellt."

78. Szanajda, *Indirect Perpetrators*.

79. Eichmüller, "Die Strafverfolgung von NS-Verbrechen," 628. The study, it should be noted, was not restricted to CCL 10 cases, which presumably included an even higher percentage of denunciation cases.

80. See Müller, *Hitler's Justice*, 274–75.

81. Hodenberg, "Anwendung," col. 122.

82. Ibid., col. 122.

83. For an insightful and somewhat more sanguine assessment of the consequences of the rejection of crimes against humanity by German jurists, see Pendas, Retroactive Law.

84. Friedlander, *Nazi Crimes and the Law*, 22.

85. Werle, *Auschwitz vor Gericht*, 35.

86. Wolf, "Befreiung des Strafrechts vom nationalsozialistischen Denken?," 11. Also Schmitt, "Kodifikation oder Novelle?," 924.

87. Werle, *Auschwitz vor Gericht*, 37.

88. Friedlander's claims can in part be reconciled with Werle's more radical critique of Nazi law. For while Friedlander insists that "killing Jews and gypsies" was never "legal," he never says it constituted a punishable crime under then-operative law; and while Werle argues that genocide was authorized by the will of the Führer, he never says it was fully "legal."

89. Werle, *Auschwitz vor Gericht*, 31.

90. Reichel, *Vergangenheitsbewältigung in Deutschland*, 25.

91. Friedlander, *Nazi Crimes and the Law*, 28.

92. Ibid., 17.

93. Ibid., 21, 23. As we have noted, the German constitutional court later retroactively voided this perverse law; obviously, then, not all "duly constituted" law promulgated by the Nazis would continue to be treated as binding for the period in question by postwar German courts.

94. See Strafgesetzbuch (StGB): § 211 Mord, www.gesetze-im-internet.de/stgb/__211.html.

95. Lange, "Mord, Totschlag und Kindestötung."

96. Wolf, "Befreiung des Strafrechts vom nationalsozialistischen Denken?," 8.

97. Ibid.

98. Bryant, *Eyewitness to Genocide*, 211.

99. I am indebted to Mildt's splendid discussion of the case in *Nazi Crimes and the Law*.

100. See Himmler's notorious speech praising the SS's genocidal work, "Most of you will know what it means when 100 bodies lie together, when 500 are there or when there are 1000. . . . To have seen this through and—with the exception of human weakness—to have remained decent, has made us hard and is a page of glory never mentioned and never to be mentioned." www.nizkor.org/hweb/people/h/himmler-heinrich/posen/oct-04-43/ausrottung-transl-nizkor.html.

101. Pauer-Studer and Velleman, *Konrad Morgen: The Conscience of a Nazi Judge*.

102. O'Neil, *Belzec*, 98.

103. Mildt, *Nazi Crimes and the Law*, 105.

104. Ibid., 104.

105. The SS judge in the case, Günther Reinecke, settled in Bavaria and set up a legal practice. Briefly disbarred after his decision in the Täubner case came to light in the early 1970s, Reinecke successfully appealed his disbarment.

106. Hanack, "Zur Problematik," 299.

107. Ibid., 300.

108. RG: Urteil vom 19. Februar 1940. Az. 3 D 69/40 (Badewannen-Fall).

109. RG: Urteil vom 19. Februar 1940. Az. 3 D 69/40 (Badewannen-Fall).

110. BGH: Urteil vom 19. Oktober 1962, Az. 9 StE 4/62 (Staschynskiifall).

111. BGH: Urteil vom 19. Oktober 1962, Az. 9 StE 4/62 (Staschynskiifall), 137.

112. BGH: Urteil vom 19. Oktober 1962, Az. 9 StE 4/62 (Staschynskiifall), 138.

113. In fact, the BGH might have gotten its Cold War history wrong. Shelepin did not become head of the KGB until December 25, 1958. Staschinsky had been tasked with and sent on his mission in 1956, when Ivan Serov was still head of the KGB.

114. BGH: Urteil vom 19. Oktober 1962, Az. 9 StE 4/62 (Staschynskiifall), 136. 137.

115. Werle, *Auschwitz vor Gericht*, 32.

116. Perels, "Perceptions and Suppression of Nazi Crimes by the Postwar German Judiciary," in Friedlander, *Nazi Crimes and the Law*, 95.

117. Freudiger, *Die juristische Aufarbeitung*, 169.

118. Cf. the murder conviction of Hermann Krumey, who worked as Eichmann's assistant in the deportation of the Hungarian Jews. See Freudiger, *Die juristische Aufarbeitung*.

119. Stangneth, *Eichmann before Jerusalem*, 322, 324.

120. See generally Friedrich, *Die kalte Amnestie*.

121. On the question of the inadvertent effects of the change, see also Hubert Rottleuthner, "Hat Dreher gedreht?" http://edoc.bbaw.de/volltexte/2011/1875/pdf/307_Rottleuthner_Hat_Dreher_gedreht.pdf.

122. See Wittmann, *Beyond Justice*.

123. Werle, *Auschwitz vor Gericht*, 38; see also Benz, *Der Henkersknecht*, 165.

124. www.deathcamps.org/treblinka/barry_de.html.

125. Teicholz, *The Trial of Ivan the Terrible*, 125, transcript changed.

126. Freudiger, *Die juristische Aufarbeitung*, 65.

127. BGH Urteil vom 10.01.1956, Az.: 5 StR 529/55. See also Ratz, *Die Justiz und die Nazis*.

128. Müller, *Hitler's Justice*, 252. Matters changed with the adoption of § 25tGB on 1.1.1975, statutorily incorporating the objective standard.

Chapter 7. Memory into History

1. *State of Israel vs. Ivan (John) Demjanjuk*, Criminal Case No. 373/86: Verbatim, Unedited Minutes, 160–161.

2. Indeed, Raab insisted that after the Sobibor uprising, she had seen Demjanjuk at a cinemat in Lublin. See website "The Long Shadow of Sobibor," interview with Esther Raab, www.longshadowofsobibor.com/interview/esther-raab.

3. David Rich to Hans-Joachim Lutz, Re: Survivor from Sobibor Death Camp, sent 19 May 2009, 17:07, HA 1597. On file with author.

4. "Russian Sobibor Survivor Remembers Demjanjuk," *Reuters*, February 3, 2010, www.willzuzak.ca/fc/2009/reuters20100203KyivPost.html.

5. See the website Nebenklage Sobibor: Mitteilungen und Fakten zum Verfahren gegen John Demjanjuk vor dem LG München: "Die Nebenkläger," www.nebenklage-sobibor.de/index.php/das-verfahren/die-nebenklager/.

6. In total, 19 transports with 34,131 Jews were sent from Westerbork transit camp in the Netherlands to Sobibor; these include four transports that arrived before Demjanjuk arrived at the camp. Of these 34,131, eighteen survived. Of the 100,000 Jews deported from Westerbork, an additional 55,000 were sent to Auschwitz; almost 5,000 to Theresienstadt; and, nearly 4,000 to Bergen-Belsen. Eichmann was responsible for arranging the timetable, size, and destination of the transports. The commandant of Westerbork was responsible for preparing the lists of the deportees, a task in which he was assisted by Jewish collaborators within the transit camp. For a list of those deported see, Staatsanswaltschaft München I, Vefahrensakte HA Bd. 15, 6992ff.

7. Defense lawyer Busch had petitioned the court to have his wife Vera serve as the interpreter, a proposal that the prosecution objected to. Staatsanswaltschaft München I, Vefahrensakte HA Bd. 1–3, 1249, 1333.

8. Müller, *Hitler's Justice*, 259.

9. See generally Musial, *Aktion Reinhardt*.

10. Benz, *Der Henkersknecht*, 105.

11. Bialowitz, *A Promise at Sobibór*, 77.

12. Ibid.; Benz, *Der Henkersknecht*, 106.

13. Benz, *Der Henkersknecht*, 109, 59.

14. None of the three Aktion Reinhard camps had anything as fancy as an enclosed crematorium. Arad, *Belzec, Sobibor, Treblinka*; Benz, *Der Henkersknecht*, 108, 109.

15. Himmler had considered turning the camp into a depot for captured munitions; others thought it should be turned into a transit camp, but nothing came of these plans. Sobibor remained in nominal existence until the end of March 1944, still guarded by a contingent of Trawniki *Wachmänner*. Black, "Foot Soldiers of the Final Solution," 41.

16. Arad, *Belzec, Sobibor, Treblinka*. For the past several years, Israeli and Polish archaeologists have been working to identify the exact footprint of the camp. The team's recent discoveries include escape tunnels made by Jewish inmates in preparation of breakout, and the foundation and remnants of four gas chambers. See Ofer Aderet, "Archaeologists Uncover Remnants of Sobibor

Gas Chambers," *Haaretz*, September 17, 2014, www.haaretz.com/jewish-world/jewish-world-news/.premium-1.616331.

17. Schelvis, *Sobibor*.

18. Blatt, *From the Ashes of Sobibor*, 94.

19. Bialowitz and Bialowitz, *A Promise at Sobibór*, 76.

20. Ibid., 91, 90.

21. Blatt, *From the Ashes of Sobibor*, 8.

22. Bryant, *Eyewitness to Genocide*, 134.

23. Blatt, *From the Ashes of Sobibor*, 89.

24. Volk, *Das letzte Urteil*, 44.

25. Mildt, *Staatsverbrechen vor Gericht*, 146.

26. *Justiz und NS-Verbrechen* Lfd.Nr.833LG Hamburg vom 03.06.1976, p. 103.

27. I am grateful to Thomas Hauzenberger for bringing this to my attention.

28. Jan Friedmann, a journalist with *Der Spiegel*, discovered a second Trawniki man who claimed to have served with Demjanjuk at Flossenbürg. Samuel Kunz was a *Volksdeutscher* who after being taken as a POW by the Wehrmacht became an active collaborator. But because Kunz himself was the subject of an active investigation for his service at Treblinka and facing possible indictment, he was not called as a witness by the court.

29. Wefing, *Der Fall Demjanjuk*, 153.

30. Benz, *Der Henkersknecht*, 103.

31. Wefing, *Der Fall Demjanjuk*, 154.

32. Ralf Müller, "Zeuge im Demjanjuk-Prozess: Erinnerung, aber keine Identifizierung," *Nürnberger Zeitung*, February 25, 2010, www.nordbayern.de/nuernberger-zeitung/nz-regionews/zeuge-im-demjanjuk-prozess-erinnerung-aber-keine-identifizierung-1.646955/kommentare-7.478173.

Chapter 8. The Trial by History

1. See generally Pohl, "Die Ermordung."

2. The court also weighed calling Charles Sydnor, the expert from Demjanjuk's second denaturalization trial—though not to serve as a historical expert, but to testify about the American trials. But it came out that in 1989 Professor Sydnor had remarked that "the cause of justice would never be better served" than by Demjanjuk's hanging. Sydnor had made these comments back when Demjanjuk was still believed to be Ivan Grozny; they were thoroughly—even exhaustively vetted—during the second denaturalization trial, where Sydnor openly acknowledged the error; still, Alt feared that Sydnor's appearance

would fuel the defense's hysteria and so decided against summoning him, which probably was just as well. In his summary argument, Demjanjuk's chief lawyer, Ulrich Busch, pushed the limits of hyperbole in railing against Sydnor and his report (which, as we recall, was not even written by Sydnor): "His hatred for the accused oozes like pus from every page!" Final Argument, June 10, 2011, see full text at Busch, *Demjanjuk Der Sündenbock*.

3. Volk, *Das letzte Urteil*, 79.

4. Rousso, *The Haunting Past*, 56.

5. Our understanding of how the guardforce was used at the Aktion Reinhard camps comes largely from interrogations of former Trawniki men conducted by the KGB, the very material that Pohl otherwise treated with exagerated skepticism.

6. LG München II, Urteil von 12.5.2011, Az.: 1 Ks 115 Js 12496/08, p. 28ff.

7. Among lawyers for the *Nebenkläger* there was some disagreement about the importance of this evidence. Nestler, for example, insisted that even if some guards had served exclusively as cooks, they still would have been guilty of supporting the overall killing process. Hardy Langer, a lawyer from Berlin, by contrast, considered the evidence crucial. Kirsten Goetze, who pioneered the approach, agreed with Langer.

8. It should be noted that the court also based its acquittal on the testimony of Jewish survivors who claimed that Klier had behaved with decency.

9. In imposing a sentence of four years and six months imprisonment, the court noted that the defendant had led an upstanding life (*straffreies Leben*) both before and after the war. Freudiger, *Die juristische Aufarbeitung*, 166, 167.

10. *Justiz und NS-Verbrechen* Lfd.Nr.641 und 642, LG Hagen vom 20.12.1966, 11 Ks 1/64; BGH vom 25.03.1971, 4 StR 47-48/69. Lfd. Nr. 642(a); for discussion of the reasons for acquittal based on putative necessity, see 227–30.

11. *Justiz und NS-Verbrechen* Lfd.Nr.833LG Hamburg vom 03.06.1976, (50) 8/72 BGH vom 09.10.1979, 5 StR 319/79, 652–53. ("In dispatching a guardforce to Warsaw, the accused probably did not reckon or know that persons would be killed; more likely, he assumed the action would in all probability entail the peaceful escorting of a small number of Jews to a work camp.")

12. Grabitz, *NS-Prozesse, Psychogramme der Beteiligten*, 109.

13. Browning, *Ordinary Men*, 170.

14. Jäger, *Verbrechen unter totalitärer Herrschaft*, 81ff.

15. Kurt Schrimm quoted in Monika Dittrich, "Ehemalige KZ-Aufseher müssen mit Anklagen rechnen" *Deutschlandfunk* 21.12.2013, www.deutschlandfunk.de/ns-prozesse-ehemalige-kz-aufseher-muessen-mit-anklagen.724.de.html?dram:article_id=272756.

16. Freudiger, *Die juristische Aufarbeitung*, 170; Wefing, *Der Fall Demjanjuk*, 200.

17. Both Scheffler and Grabitz also testified at Demjanjuk's Jerusalem trial.

18. Georg Bönisch, Jan Friedmann, Cordula Meyer, "Ein ganz gewöhnlicher Handlanger," *Der Spiegel*, June 22, 2009, www.spiegel.de/spiegel/print/d-65794351.html.

19. Grabitz, *NS-Prozesse, Psychogramme Der Beteiligten*, 106.

20. Ibid., 107, 108.

21. Grabitz was not alone in reaching this conclusion. At trial, the court heard the testimony of Hans-Robert Richthof, the judge who presided over Karl Frenzel's retrial in 1985. Richthof likewise expressed the belief that Trawnikis were in a "powerless" position. See DDP, "Ehemaliger Richter sagt im Verfahren gegen Demjanjuk aus," April, 4, 2010, www.t-online.de/regionales/id_41366780/ehemaliger-richter-sagt-im-verfahren-gegen-demjanjuk-aus.html.

22. O'Neil, *Belzec*, 69.

23. Black, "Foot Soldiers of the Final Solution," 8.

24. Ibid., 7, 8.

25. Ibid., 5.

26. Ibid., 13, 12.

27. Ibid., 36, 37; Benz, *Der Henkersknecht*, 68. According to Benz, only Trawnikis who were ethnic Germans were eligible for burial with honors; Black has showed that several such honors were extended to Trawnikis who were not ethnic Germans. Black, "Foot Soldiers of the Final Solution," 37.

28. Black, "Foot Soldiers of the Final Solution," 14, 15.

29. Ibid., 15. It should be noted that the historian Anglelika Benz has offered a somewhat different view of the Trawnikis, presenting them as "tragic figures" occupying a position between the "Jewish victims" and the "German occupiers." Benz, *Handlanger*, 277, 278.

30. This figure includes the 1.5 million killed in the death camps, and another 200,000 Jews killed in shooting actions.

31. Ibid., 33, 34.

32. Ibid., 76; Benz, *Der Henkersknecht*, 72.

33. Pohl, "Die Trawniki-Männer."

34. Black, "Foot Soldiers of the Final Solution," 35.

35. Staatsanswaltschaft München I, Verfahrensakten p. 6942. On file with author.

36. Wefing, *Der Fall Demjanjuk*, 176. Busch's wife's father was an acquaintance of Stepan Bandera, whose Munich assassination gave rise to the famous Staschinsky decision, and she and her husband cultivated ties with the ultrana-

tionalist Swoboda group; in the summer of 2011, a couple of months after the end of the trial, they arranged a meeting between Demjanjuk and Oleg Tyahnybok, the right-wing Ukrainian politician known for his anti-Semitic outbursts. See Volk, *Das letzte Urteil*, 48; Bourcier, *Le dernier procès*.

37. "Kommen Sie auf unsere Seite," *Süddeustche Zeitung*, December 21, 2009, http://www.sueddeutsche.de/politik/demjanjuk-verteidiger-streiten-kommen-sie-auf-unsere-seite-1.58369.

38. Rabbi Goldberger, for his part, did not describe Busch as a friend, but did note that in his defense of the Israeli drug dealers, Busch defended Israel's good name. See Tom Segev, "The Makings of History: A Warning to Every Soldier," *Haaretz*, January 28, 2010, www.haaretz.com/weekend/week-s-end/the-makings-of-history-a-warning-to-every-soldier-1.262303.

39. Author interview with Busch.

40. Douglas, *The Memory of Judgment*, 208–9.

41. Benz, *Der Henkersknecht*, 143.

42. Andreas Eichmüller, "Die Strafverfolgung von NS-Verbrechen," 628.

43. There were, however, precedents that Busch, had he been more resourceful, might have cited in support of his double jeopardy argument. In the *Einsatzgruppen* trial, one of the twelve successor trials conducted by the US military at Nuremberg, nine defendants sentenced to death later escaped the gallows thanks to American commutations. Further capitulating to German pressure, American officials released the last of these convicted mass murderers in 1958. Included in this group was Martin Sandberger, a former SS colonel who had organized killings of Jews in Estonia. Presented with the chance of retrying Sandberger, German jurists concluded that a new proceeding would violate the terms of the *Überleitungsvertrag*, the treaty from 1955 between the Federal Republic and the Western Allies that transferred full sovereignty back to Germany. By the terms of the treaty, German courts were to give full legal effect to decisions of Allied courts, an arrangement meant to prevent German courts from watering down or overturning Allied convictions. With characteristic perversity, German jurists instead interpreted the treaty as raising a bar of double jeopardy that prohibited German courts from retrying mass murderers set free by Allied administrators to appease German public opinion. Sandberger died in a nursing home in March 2010 shortly before his ninety-ninth birthday, just as the Demjanjuk trial entered its fifth month. If Busch knew of this case, he failed to cite it. On the Sandberger case, see Osterloh and Vollnhals, *NS-Prozesse und deutsche Öffentlichkeit*.

44. Demjanjuk, First Statement of John Demjanjuk in Germany, April 21, 2010, www.kyivpost.com/opinion/op-ed/statement-of-ukrainian-native-john-demjanjuk-64500.html.

45. The claim that Jewish organizations "live from the Holocaust" flirted with the canard of Holocaust deniers that Jews invented the story of their own extermination to extract political and financial gains from the rest of the world. As a consequence, four lawyers for the *Nebenkläger* explored the possibility that Busch's statements constituted a violation of Germany's law proscribing Holocaust denial. "Erneuter Eklat vor dem Schwurgericht," March 23, 2010, www.nebenklage-sobibor.de/index.php/2010/03/23/erneuter-eklat-vor-dem-schwurgericht/.

46. Demjanjuk, Second Statement of John Demjanjuk in Germany, November 11, 2010. On file with author.

47. Demjanjuk, Third Statement of John Demjanjuk in Germany, February 22, 2011. On file with author.

48. "Legal Maneuvers Delaying Deportation Proceedings Against Demjanjuk," Jewish Telegraphic Agency, July 29, 1982, www.jta.org/1982/07/29/archive/legal-maneuvers-delaying-deportation-proceedings-against-demjanjuk.

49. The third declaration also declared that Fedorenko, his fellow Ukrainian, prevailed in his deportation trial, a statement that failed to mention that Fedorenko lost on appeal to the Supreme Court, was deported and ultimately executed.

50. Letter from Eli Rosenbaum to Kurt Schrimm, Authenticity of Iwan Demjanjuk Dienstausweis No. 1393, 1.13.09 Verfahrensakten, pp. 42–44. On file with author.

51. Curiously Stewart had his own legal problems, having been prosecuted for having perjured himself during his testimony as a government documents expert in the trial of Martha Stewart (no relation).

52. Wefing, *Der Fall Demjanjuk*, 148.

53. "Demjanjuk Nazi Trial Evidence Reportedly Faked," *Huffington Post*, April 12, 2011, www.huffingtonpost.com/2011/04/12/demjanjuk-nazi-trial-evidence_n_848287.html.

54. Langer, *Schlußvortag, Sobibor Verfahren*, 8.

55. Karin Matussek, "Demjanjuk Nazi Case Punctuated by Delays . . . ," *Bloomberg*, November 11, 2010, www.bloomberg.com/news/2010-11-30/demjanjuk-nazi-case-punctuated-by-delays-fights-with-judge-after-one-year.html.

56. AP, Andrea Jarach and David Rising, "Doctor: No Significant Change in Demjanjuk Health," November 25, 2010, www.boston.com/news/world/europe/articles/2010/11/25/doctor_no_significant_change_in_demjanjuk_health/.

57. Benz, *Der Henkersknecht*, 90.

58. Author interview with Martin Mendelsohn.

59. Reuters, "German Judge Forces Demjanjuk to Appear in Court," July

22, 2010, www.reuters.com/article/2010/07/22/us-germany-demjanjuk-trial-idUSTRE66L3LC20100722.

60. Benz, *Der Henkersknecht*, 196.

61. Wefing, *Der Fall Demjanjuk*, 163.

Chapter 9. The Right Wrong Man

1. Author interview with Thomas Walther.

2. Langer, *Schlußvortag, Sobibor Verfahren*, 14.

3. Schünemann, *Schlussantrag*, 4.

4. Haas, *Plädoyer von Martin Haas*, 1–2.

5. Perels, *Auschwitz in der deutschen Geschichte*, 167. See also Heute Abend Keller Club, TV-Dokumentation, 1964 BRD/Redaktion: Dietrich Wagner/ Hessischer Rundfunk Frankfurt am Main.

6. Busch, *Demjanjuk Der Sündenbock*.

7. *State of Israel vs Ivan (John) Demjanjuk*, Criminal Case No. 373/86: Verbatim, Unedited Minutes, 7449, 7470, 7471, 7453.

8. *The Demjanjuk Trial: In the District Court of Jerusalem 373/86*, 381.

9. Urteil der 1. Strafkammer des Landgerichts München II als Schwurgericht in der Strafsache gegen Demjanjuk, John, 34–35. On file with author.

10. Urteil der 1. Strafkammer des Landgerichts München II als Schwurgericht in der Strafsache gegen Demjanjuk, John, 36. On file with author.

11. The decision announced in court preceded the issuance of the full written opinion. The court's full judgment came out some six months later. A copy of the published opinion can be found in *Justiz und NS-Verbrechen*, LG München II Urteil vom 12.05.2011 Lfd.Nr.924.

12. Schelvis, *Plädoyer von Jules Schelvis*, 9.

13. AP, "Ukrainians Back Demjanjuk, Convicted and Stateless," May 27, 2011, www.foxnews.com/us/2011/05/27/ukrainians-demjanjuk-convicted-stateless/.

14. Gisela Friedrichsen, "'It Was Clear What Happened': The Deeper Meaning of the Demjanjuk Verdict," *Der Spiegel*, May 16, 2011. English version at www.spiegel.de/international/germany/it-was-clear-what-happened-the-deeper-meaning-of-the-demjanjuk-verdict-a-762766.html.

15. Statement of Professor Dr. Cornelius Nestler, lawyer of twelve of the victims and coplaintiffs in the trial against Demjanjuk, 17.

16. Bauer quoted in Freudiger, *Die juristische Aufarbeitung*, 61.

17. Bauer quoted in Frei, *1945 und wir*, 94.

18. Hannah Arendt, "Auschwitz on Trial," in Arendt, *Responsibility and Judgment*, 243.

19. Ibid.

20. Ibid., 243–44.

21. Kurz, "Paradigmenwechsel"; Nestler, "Ein Mythos."

22. Arendt, *Eichmann in Jerusalem*, 272.

23. "Die Wunderheilung des Bösen," *Bild am Sonntag*, May 22, 2011, 20. See also Volk, *Das letzte Urteil*, 119.

Postscript

1. Claudia von Salzen, "Der 'Buchhalter von Auschwitz' sagt aus," *Der Tagesspiegel*, April 24, 2015, www.tagesspiegel.de/themen/reportage/prozess-gegen-oskar-groening-der-buchhalter-von-auschwitz-sagt-aus/11667316.html.

2. "Last Justice: Germany to Prosecute 30 Auschwitz Guards," *Der Spiegel*, September 3, 2013; English at www.spiegel.de/international/germany/nazi-murder-germany-may-prosecute-30-former-auschwitz-guards-a-920200.html.

3. Melissa Eddy, "Chasing Death Camp Guards with New Tools," *New York Times*, May 5, 2014, www.nytimes.com/2014/05/06/world/europe/chasing-death-camp-guards-with-virtual-tools.html.

4. Eric Lichtblau, "Philadephia Man Accused in Nazi Case Dies," *New York Times*, July 23, 2014, www.nytimes.com/2014/07/24/us/philadelphia-man-accused-in-nazi-case-dies.html?module=Search&mabReward=relbias%3As%2C%7B%221%22%3A%22RI%3A5%22%7D.

5. Anklageschrift in der Strafsache gegen Oskar Gröning, LG Lüneburg. 27 Ks 9/14, 1191 Js 98402/13. On file with author.

6. Matthias Geyer, "An SS Officer Remembers: The Bookkeeper from Auschwitz," *Der Spiegel*, May 9, 2005, www.spiegel.de/international/spiegel/an-ss-officer-remembers-the-bookkeeper-from-auschwitz-a-355188.html.

SOURCES

Material from the Demjanjuk Trial in Germany

Documents

Urteil der 1. Strafkammer des Landgerichts München II als Schwurgericht in der Strafsache gegen Demjanjuk, John.

Anklageschrift in der Strafsache gegen Demjanjuk, John, 115 Js 12496/08; Staatsanswaltschaft München I.

Zentrale Stelle, Demjanjuk Abschlussbericht, 115 J 12496/08.

Staatsanswaltschaft München I, Verfahrensakten, 16 vols.

Proceedings

BGH, 09.12.2008–2 ARs 536/08.

LG München II, 02.02.2010–1 Ks 115 Js 12496/08.

LG München II, 12.05.2011–1 Ks 115 Js 12496/08.

Oral Pleadings

Bloch, Manuel. "Plädoyer Manuel Bloch in dem Verfahren gegen John Demjanjuk." LG München II. April 14, 2011. www.nebenklage-sobibor.de/wp-content/uploads/2011/04/SKMBT_C20311041510451.pdf.

Cortissos, Rudolf. "Plädoyer von Rudolf Cortissos." LG München II. www.stichtingsobibor.nl/press/rudie-cortissos-de/.

Degen, Marcus. "Plädoyer des Nebenklägers von Marcus Degen." LG München II. www.nebenklage-sobibor.de/wp-content/uploads/2011/04/SKMBT_C20311041214501.pdf.

Haas, Martin. "Plädoyer von Martin Haas." LG München II. February 6, 2011. www.stichtingsobibor.nl/martin-haas-en.

Langer, Hardy. "Schlußvortag."

Leijden, Marianna. "Plädoyer von Marianna Leijden van Amstel."

Mendelsohn, Martin, and Stefan Schünemann. "Schlussvortrag im Namen von Phillip Bialowitz und Thomas Blatt, Überlebende von Sobibor." LG München II. 2011.

Nestler, Cornelius. "Schlussvortrag von Professor Dr. Cornelius Nestler im

Strafverfahren gegen John Demjanjuk." LG München II. www.nestler.uni-koeln.de/fileadmin/sites/strafrecht_nestler/Demjanjuk/PlaedN-D-End.pdf.

Schelvis, Jules. "Plädoyer von Jules Schelvis." *May 12, 2011.* www.tagesspiegel.de/politik/plaedoyer-des-nebenklaegers-die-wahrheit-ueber-sobibor-muss-ans-licht-/4162474.html.

Schünemann, Stefan. "Schlussantrag im *Ve*rfahren gegen John Demjanjuk, im Namen der Nebenkläger Thomas Blatt und Philip Bialowitz, Überlebende des Vernichtungslagers Sobibor." n.d.

Van Huiden, David. "Plädoyer von David van Huiden im Verfahren gegen John Demjanjuk." LG München II. www.nebenklage-sobibor.de/wp-content/uploads/2011/04/SKMBT_C20311041214511.pdf.

Court Decisions

Germany

Anklageschrift in der Strafsache gegen Oskar Groening 1191Js 98402/13

BGHSt 8, 393. January 10, 1956.

BGHSt 18, 87. October 19, 1962. ("Staschyinskij Case.")

LG Berlin. PKs 3/50. May 8, 1950. ("Sobibor-Prozess.")

LG Düsseldorf. 8 I Ks 2/64. September 3, 1965. ("Treblinka-Prozess.")

LG Frankfurt am Main. *Ks 2/63. August 19/20, 1965. ("Auschwitz-Prozess")*

Nuernberg Military Tribunals. *Trials of War Criminals Before the Nuernberg Military Tribunals under Control Council Law No. 10: Nuernberg October 1946–April 1949.* Vols. 1–15. Washington, DC: US Government Printing Office, 1951.

RGSt 74, 84. February 19, 1940. ("Bathtub Case.")

Rüter, C. F., and D. W. de Mildt, eds. *Justiz und NS-Verbrechen: Sammlung deutscher Strafurteile wegen nationalsozialistischer Tötungsverbrechen, 1945–2012.* 49 vols. Amsterdam: University Press Amsterdam.

Israel

Decision of Israel Supreme Court on Petition Concerning John (Ivan) Demjanjuk, 2004.

The Demjanjuk Trial: In the District Court of Jerusalem 373/86. Tel Aviv: Israel Bar Publishing House, 1991.

State of Israel vs. Ivan (John) Demjanjuk, Criminal Case No. 373/86: Verbatim, Unedited Minutes. (Translators' Pool) Jerusalem, 1988

The Trial of Adolf Eichmann: Record of Proceedings in the District Court of Jerusa-

lem. Jerusalem: Trust for the Publication of the Proceedings of the Eichmann Trial, in co-operation with the Israel State Archives and Yad Vashem, the Holocaust Martyrs' and Heroes' Remembrance Authority, 1992, 9 vols.

United States of America

City of Seven Hills v. Aryan Nations, 76 Ohio St. 3d 304, 667 N.E.2d 942 (Supreme Court of Ohio, 1996).

Demjanjuk v. Petrovsky, 776 F.2d 571 (Court of Appeals, 6th Circuit, 1985).

Demjanjuk v. Petrovsky, 10 F. 3d 338 (Court of Appeals, 6th Circuit 1993).

Fedorenko v. United States, 449 US 490 (Supreme Court 1981).

Kairys v. Immigration and Naturalization Service, 981 F. 2d 937 (Court of Appeals, 7th Circuit 1992).

Manson v. Brathwaite, 432 US 98 (Supreme Court 1977).

Sydnor, Charles W. "Expert Report of Charles W. Sydnor Jr."

United States v. Demjanjuk, Case No. 1:99 CV 1193 (N.D. Ohio Jul 17, 2001).

United States v. Demjanjuk, No. 1:1999 CV 1193 (N.D. Ohio 2011).

United States v. Demjanjuk, 518 F. Supp. 1362 (Dist. Court, ND Ohio 1981).

United States v. Demjanjuk, 367 F.3d 623 (Court of Appeals, 6th Circuit, 2004).

United States v. Demjanjuk, US Immigration Court, Case No. A8237417 (Deportation Proceedings), January 16, 1984.

United States v. Demjanjuk, US Immigration Court, Case No. A8237417 (Deportation Proceedings), February 7, 1984.

United States v. Fedorenko, 455 F. Supp. 893 (Dist. Court, SD Florida 1978).

United States v. Fedorenko, 597 F. 2d 946 (Court of Appeals, 5th Circuit 1979).

United States v. Walus, 453 F. Supp. 699 (Dist. Court, ND Illinois 1978).

United States v. Walus, 616 F. 2d 283 (Court of Appeals, 7th Circuit 1980).

Wiseman, Steven. "Report of the Special Master; Demjanjuk v. Petrovksky No. 85-3435." 1992.

International Conventions and Treaties

United Nations. Convention on the Non-Applicability of Statutory Limitations to War Crimes and Crimes against Humanity, New York, 26 November 1968, General Assembly Resolution 2391 (XX III), www.un.org/ga/search/view_doc.asp?symbol=A/RES/2391%28XXIII%29.

United Nations. Convention on the Prevention and Punishment of the Crime of Genocide, 9 December 1948, *United Nations Treaties Series*, vol. 278, no. 1021. https://treaties.un.org/doc/Publication/UNTS/Volume%2078/volume-78-I-1021-English.pdf.

Other Sources

Aktion Reinhard Camps. "Sobibor Camp History." September 15, 2006. www.deathcamps.org/sobibor/sobibor.html.

Allen, Charles R. *Nazi War Criminals in America: Facts, Action—The Basic Handbook*. New York: Highgate House, 1985.

Allo, Awol K. "The 'Show' in the 'Show Trial': Contextualizing the Politicization of the Courtroom." *Barry Law Review* 15, no. 1 (2010): 41–72.

Aly, Götz. *Endlösung: Völkerverschiebung und der Mord an den europäischen Juden*. Frankfurt am Main: S. Fischer, 1995.

Anti-Defamation League. "Sorting Out the Demjanjuk Case: An Anti-Defamation League White Paper." New York: Anti-Defamation League, 1993.

Arad, Yitzhak. *Belzec, Sobibor, Treblinka: The Operation Reinhard Death Camps*. Bloomington: Indiana University Press, 1987.

Arendt, Hannah. *Eichmann in Jerusalem: A Report on the Banality of Evil*. New York: Viking, 1963.

———. *Responsibility and Judgment*. New York: Schocken, 2003.

———. *Hannah Arendt/Karl Jaspers Correspondence, 1926–1969*. New York: Harcourt Brace Jovanovich, 1992.

Arendt, Hannah, and Joachim Fest. *Eichmann war von empörender Dummheit: Gespräche und Briefe*. München: Piper, 2011.

Association for Jewish Studies. *Journal of the Association for Jewish Studies*. Vol. 36, no. 2. Edited by Christine Hayes and Magda Teter. New York: Cambridge University Press, 2012.

Bade, Claudia. "'Das Verfahren wird eingestellt': Die strafrechtliche Verfolgung von Denunziation aus dem Nationalsozialismus nach 1945 in den Westzonen und in der frühen BRD." *Historical Social Research* 26, no. 2/3 (2001): 70–85.

Beck, Susanne. "Does Age Prevent Punishment? The Struggles of the German Juridical System with Alleged Nazi Criminals: Commentary on the Criminal Proceedings against John Demjanjuk and Heinrich Boere." *German Law Journal* 11, no. 3 (2010): 347–66.

Benz, Angelika. *Handlanger der SS: Die Trawniki-Männer und ihre Rolle im Holocaust*. Berlin: Metropol-Verlag, 2014.

———. *Der Henkersknecht: Der Prozess gegen John (Iwan) Demjanuk in München*. Berlin: Metropol-Verlag, 2011.

Benz, Wolfgang, Barbara Distel, and Angelika Königseder, eds. *Flossenbürg: Das Konzentrationslager Flossenbürg und seine Außenlager*. München: C. H. Beck, 2007.

Berger, Sara. *Experten der Vernichtung: Das T4-Reinhardt-Netzwerk in den Lagern Belzec, Sobibor und Treblinka.* Hamburg: Hamburger Edition, 2013.

Berman, Harold J., and James W. Spindler, trans. *Soviet Criminal Law and Procedure: The RSFSR Codes.* Cambridge, MA: Harvard University Press, 1966.

Bertram, Günter. "Die Fragwürdigkeit eines letzten Strafverfahrens." *Mitteilungen des Hamburgischen Richtervereins (MHR)* no.2 (2009).

Bialowitz, Philip, and Joseph Bialowitz. *A Promise at Sobibór: A Jewish Boy's Story of Revolt and Survival in Nazi-Occupied Poland.* Madison: University of Wisconsin Press, 2010.

Bilsky, Leora. "Transnational Holocaust Litigation." *European Journal of International Law* 23, no. 2 (2012): 349–75.

Black, Peter. "Askaris in the 'Wild East': The Deployments of Auxiliaries and the Implementation of Nazi Racial Policy in Lublin District." In *The Germans and the East*, edited by Charles Ingrao and Franz A. J. Szabo, 277–309. West Lafayette: Purdue University Press, 2008.

———. "Foot Soldiers of the Final Solution: The Trawniki Training Camp and Operation Reinhard." *Holocaust and Genocide Studies* 25, no. 1 (2011): 1–99.

———. "Police Auxiliaries for Operation Reinhard: Shedding Light on the Trawniki Training Camp through Documents from behind the Iron Curtain." In *Secret Intelligence and the Holocaust*, edited by David Bankier, 327–67. New York: Enigma Books, 2006.

———. "Rehearsal for 'Reinhard'?: Odilo Globocnik and the Lublin Selbstschutz." *Central European History* 25, no. 2 (1992): 204–26.

Blatt, Thomas Toivi. *From the Ashes of Sobibor: A Story of Survival.* Evanston, IL: Northwestern University Press, 1997.

———. *Sobibór—der vergessene Aufstand.* Münster: Unrast-Verlag, 2004.

Bloxham, Donald. "British War Crimes Trial Policy in Germany, 1945–1957: Implementation and Collapse." *Journal of British Studies* 42, no.1 (2003): 91–118.

———. *Genocide on Trial: War Crimes Trials and the Formation of Holocaust History and Memory.* Oxford: Oxford University Press, 2001.

Blumenthal, David A., and Timothy L. H. McCormack, eds. *The Legacy of Nuremberg: Civilising Influence or Institutionalised Vengeance?* Leiden: Martinus Nijhoff Publishers, 2008.

Boas, Gideon. *The Milošević Trial: Lessons for the Conduct of Complex International Criminal Proceedings.* Cambridge: Cambridge University Press, 2007.

Bohlander, Michael, trans. *The German Criminal Code: A Modern English Translation.* Oxford: Hart, 2008.

Bourcier, Nicolas. *Le dernier procès.* Paris: Don Quichotte, 2011.

Bower, Tom. *Blind Eye to Murder: Britain, America and the Purging of Nazi Germany—A Pledge Betrayed*. London: Andre Deutsch, 1981.

Brochhagen, Ulrich. *Nach Nürnberg: Vergangenheitsbewältigung und Westintegration in der Ära Adenauer*. Berlin: Ullstein Verlag, 1999.

Broszat, Martin. "Siegerjustiz oder strafrechtliche "Selbstreinigung": Aspekte der Vergangenheitsbewältigung der deutschen Justiz während der Besatzungszeit 1945–1949." *Vierteljahrshefte für Zeitgeschichte Heft* 28, no. 4 (1981): 477–544.

Browning, Christoper. *Ordinary Men: Reserve Police Battalion 101 and the Final Solution in Poland*. New York: Harper Perrenial, 1998.

Bryant, Michael. *Eyewitness to Genocide: The Operation Reinhard Death Camp Trials, 1955–1966*. Knoxville: University of Tennessee Press, 2014.

Burchard, Christoph. "The Nuremberg Trial and its Impact on Germany." *Journal of International Criminal Justice* 4, no. 4 (2006): 800–29.

Busch, Ulrich. *Demjanjuk Der Sündenbock*. Münster: Monsenstein und Vannerdat, 2011.

———. "Demjanjuk rettet Ludwigsburg." Ulrich Busch Blog 'John Demjanjuk.' April 11, 2013. http://jdemjanjuk.blogspot.com/2013/04/demjanju-rettet-ludwigsburg.html.

Buscher, Frank M. *The U.S. War Crimes Trial Program in Germany, 1946–1955*. New York: Praeger, 1989.

Cohen, David. "Transitional Justice in Divided Germany after 1945." In *Retribution and Reparation in the Transition to Democracy*, edited by Jon Elster, 59–88. Cambridge: Cambridge University Press, 2009.

Cohen, Gerard Daniel. *In War's Wake: Europe's Displaced Persons in the Postwar Order*. Oxford: Oxford University Press, 2011.

Conference of Teachers of International Law and Related Subjects. *Proceedings of the Sixth Conference of Teachers of International Law and Related Subjects: Held at Washington, D.C., April 27–30, 1938*. Washington, DC: Carnegie Endowment for International Peace, 1938.

Dagerman, Stig. *German Autumn*. Translated by Robin Fulton Macpherson. Minneapolis: University of Minnesota Press, 2011.

Dean, Martin. "Displaced War Crimes Trials: The Investigation and Prosecution of Nazi War Criminals from the Soviet Union in Australia, Great Britain, and Germany, 1987–1999," Presentation presented at European Science Foundation Workshop on East/West European Prosecution on Nazi War Crimes in the Soviet Union: From a Local to a Transnational Perspective, Berlin, Germany, March 27–29, 2014.

Del Pizzo, Lisa J. "Not Guilty—but Not Innocent: An Analysis of the Acquittal of John Demjanjuk and Its Impact on the Future of Nazi War Crimes Trials."

Boston College International & Comparative Law Review 18, no. 1 (1995): 137–78.

"The Demjanjuk Case Factual and Legal Details," 2004.

Diestelkamp, Bernhard. "Die Justiz nach 1945 und ihr Umgang mit der eigenen Vergangenheit." *Rechtshistorisches Journal* 5 (1986): 153–74.

Dinnerstein, Leonard. *America and the Survivors of the Holocaust*. New York: Columbia University Press, 1982.

Douglas, Lawrence. "From IMT to NMT: The Emergence of a Jurisprudence of Atrocity." In *Reassessing the Nuremberg Military Tribunals: Transitional Justice, Trial Narratives, and Historiography*, edited by Kim Christian Priemel and Alexa Stiller, 276–95. New York: Berghahn Books, 2012.

———. *The Memory of Judgment: Making Law and History in the Trials of the Holocaust*. New Haven: Yale University Press, 2001.

———. "Was damals Recht war: Nulla Poena and the Prosecution of Crimes against Humanity in Post-War Germany." In *Jus Post Bellum and Transitional Justice*, edited by Larry May and Elizabeth Edenberg, 44–73. Cambridge: Cambridge University Press, 2013.

Dreier, Ralf, and Wolfgang Sellert, eds. *Recht und Justiz im "Dritten Reich."* Frankfurt am Main: Suhrkamp, 1989.

Ehrlich, Paul R., Loy Bilderback, and Anne H. Ehrlich. *The Golden Door: International Migration, Mexico, and the United States*. New York: Ballantine, 1979.

Eichmüller, Andreas. *Keine Generalamnestie: Die Strafverfolgung von NS-Verbrechen in der frühen Bundesrepublik*. Berlin: De Gruyter Oldenbourg, 2012.

———. "Die Strafverfolgung von NS-Verbrechen durch west-deutsche Justizbehörden seit 1945." *Vierteljahrshefte für Zeitgeschichte* 56, no. 4 (2008): 621–40.

Eisfeld, Rainer, and Ingo Müller, eds. *Gegen Barbarei: Essays Robert M. W. Kempner zu Ehren*. Frankfurt am Main: Athenäum, 1989.

Feldbrugge, Ferdinand, ed. *Encyclopedia of Soviet Law*. Berlin: Springer, 1985.

Finder, Gabriel, and Laura Jokusch, eds. *Jewish Honor Courts: Revenge, Retribution, and Reconciliation in Europe and Israel after the Holocaust*. Detroit: Wayne State University Press, 2015.

Finkelman, Paul, and Roberta Sue Alexander, eds. *Justice and Legal Change on the Shores of Lake Erie: A History of the United States District Court for the Northern District of Ohio*. Athens: Ohio University Press, 2012.

Finkielkraut, Alain. *Remembering in Vain: The Klaus Barbie Trial & Crimes against Humanity*. New York: Columbia University Press, 1992.

Fletcher, George, Henry Friedlander, and Fritz Weinschenck. "United States Responses to World War Two War Criminals and Human Rights Violators:

National and Comparative Perspectives." *Boston College Third World Law Journal* 3, no. 8 (1988): 17–33.

Forster, Karl, ed. *Möglichkeiten und Grenzen für die Bewältigung historischer und politischer Schuld in Strafprozessen*. Würzburg: Echter-Verlag, 1962.

Frei, Norbert. *1945 und wir: Das Dritte Reich im Bewußtsein der Deutschen*. München: Deutscher Taschenbuch Verlag, 2009.

———. *Adenauer's Germany and the Nazi Past: The Politics of Amnesty and Integration*. Translated by Joel Golb. New York: Columbia University Press, 2002.

———. *Vergangenheitspolitik: Die Anfänge der Bundesrepublik und die NS-Vergangenheit*. München: C. H. Beck, 1996.

Freudiger, Kerstin. *Die juristische Aufarbeitung von NS-Verbrechen*. Tübingen: Mohr Siebeck, 2002.

Friedlander, Henry. "The Deportation of the German Jews: Post-War German Trials of Nazi Criminals." *Leo Baeck Institute Yearbook 29, no. 1 (1984)*: 201–28.

———. "The Judiciary and Nazi Crimes in Postwar Germany." *Museum of Tolerance Online—Multimedia Learning Center of the Simon Wiesenthal Center. 1997.* http://motlc.wiesenthal.com/site/pp.asp?c=gvKVLcMVIuG&b=394973.

Friedlander, Henry, and Earlean M. McCarrick. "The Extradition of Nazi Criminals: Ryan, Artukovic, and Demjanjuk." *Museum of Tolerance Online—Multimedia Learning Center of the Simon Wiesenthal Center.* 1997. http://motlc.wiesenthal.com/site/pp.asp?c=gvKVLcMVIuG&b=395075.

———. "Nazi Criminals in the United States: Denaturalization after Fedorenko." *Museum of Tolerance Online—Multimedia Learning Center of the Simon Wiesenthal Center.* http://motlc.wiesenthal.com/site/pp.asp?c=gvKVLcMVIuG&b=395005.

Friedlander, Henry, and Nathan Stoltzfus, eds. *Nazi Crimes and the Law*. Cambridge: Cambridge University Press, 2008.

Friedman, Tuviah, ed. "Ernennungsvorschlag: SS Sturmbahnführer Streibel, Kommandant der SS-Ausbildungs-Schule in Trawinki, vor Gericht in Hamburg." Haifa: Institute for the Documentation of Nazi War Crimes, 2002.

Friedrich, Jörg. *Freispruch für die Nazi-Justiz: Die Urteile gegen NS-Richter seit 1948—Eine Dokumentation*. Berlin: Ullstein, 1998.

———. *Die kalte Amnestie: NS-Täter in der Bundesrepublik*. Berlin: List, 2007.

Funk, T. Markus. *Victims' Rights and Advocacy at the International Criminal Court*. Oxford: Oxford University Press, 2010.

Futamura, Madoka. *War Crimes Tribunals and Transitional Justice: The Tokyo Trial and the Nuremburg Legacy*. London: Routledge, 2007.

Gallant, Kenneth S. *The Principle of Legality in International and Comparative Criminal Law*. Cambridge: Cambridge University Press, 2010.

Gilbert, Martin. *Holocaust Journey*. New York: Columbia University Press, 1999.

Giordano, Ralph. *Die zweite Schuld, oder von der Last Deutscher zu sein*. Hamburg: Rasch und Röhring, 1993.

Goldoni, Marco, and Christopher McCorkindale, eds. *Hannah Arendt and the Law*. Portland: Hart, 2013.

Grabitz, Helge. "Iwan Demjanjuk zum Tode verurteilt: Anmerkungen zur strafrechtlichen Verantwortung der 'Trawnikis.'" *Tribüne—Zeitschrift zum Verständnis des Judentums* 108 (1988): 176–82.

———. *NS-Prozesse: Psychogramme der Beteiligten*. Heidelberg: C. F. Müller, 1985.

Graveson, R. H. "Der Grundsatz 'nulla poena sine lege' und Kontrollratgesetz Nr. 10." *Monatschrift des Deutschen Rechts* (1947): 278–81.

Gutermuth, Frank, Sebastian Kuhn, and Wolfgang Schoen. *Rückschau: Der Fall Ivan Demjanjuk (SWR)—NS-Verbrechen vor Gericht*. TV documentary. Das Erste.

Haberer, Erich. "History and Justice: Paradigms of the Prosecution of Nazi Crimes." *Holocaust and Genocide Studies* 19, no. 3 (2005): 487–519.

Haldemann, Frank. "Gustav Radbruch vs. Hans Kelsen: A Debate on Nazi Law." *Ratio Jurisprudence* 18, no. 2 (June 2005): 162–78.

Hanack, Ernst-Walter. "Zur Problematik der gerechten Bestrafung nationalsozialistischer Gewaltverbrecher." *Juristen Zeitung* 22, no. 10 (May 1967): 297–303.

Hanusiak, Michael. *Lest We Forget*. Toronto: Progress Books, 1976.

Hartmann, Christian. *Operation Barbarossa: Nazi Germany's War in the East, 1941–1945*. Oxford: Oxford University Press, 2013.

Hartmann, Ralph. "Der Alibiprozeß." *Ossietzky—Zweiwochenschrift für Politik /Kultur/ Wirtschaft*, September 2010. www.sopos.org/aufsaetze/4bdfd55e42f57/1.phtml.

Hasian, Marouf Arif. *Rhetorical Vectors of Memory in National and International Holocaust Trials*. East Lansing: Michigan State University Press, 2006.

Hastings, Max. *Inferno: The World at War, 1939–1945*. New York: Alfred A. Knopf, 2011.

Hausner, Gideon. *Justice in Jerusalem*. New York: Schocken, 1978.

Heller, Kevin Jon. *The Nuremberg Military Tribunals and the Origins of International Criminal Law*. Oxford: Oxford University Press, 2012.

Herdy, Amy, and Miles Moffeit. "Betrayal in the Ranks." *Denver Post*, 2004. http://extras.denverpost.com/justice/tdp_betrayal.pdf.

Hodenberg, Hodo von. "Zur Anwendung des Kontrollratsgesetzes Nr. 10 durch deutsche Gerichte." *Suddeutsche Juristen-Zeitung*, special edition (March 1947): 113–24.

Holborn, Louise W. *The International Refugee Organization, a Specialized Agency of the United Nations: Its History and Work, 1946–1952*. New York : Oxford University Press, 1956.

Horowitz, Irving Louis. *Genocide: State Power and Mass Murder*. New Brunswick, NJ: Transaction, 1977.

Houwink ten Cate, Johannes. "The Activities of Wachmann Iwan Demjanjuk, 1940–2," November 11, 2008. www.chgs.nl, 26; Urteil, 173.

———. "The Demjanjuk Trial: An Interim Assessment." *Jerusalem Center for Public Affairs* 99, no. 1 (July 2010): 1–8.

———. "Looking Back on the Demjanjuk Trial in Munich." Jerusalem Center for Public Affairs. March 1, 2012. http://jcpa.org/article/looking-back-on-the-demjanjuk-trial-in-munich/.

Jackson, Robert H. *Report of Robert H. Jackson, United States Representative to the International Conference on Military Trials, London, 1945*. US State Department. Washington, DC: Department of State, Division of Publications, Office of Public Affairs, 1949.

———. "The Significance of the Nuremberg Trials to the Armed Forces: Previously Unpublished Personal Observations by the Chief Counsel for the United States." *Military Affairs* 10, no. 4 (Winter 1946): 2–15.

Jäger, Herbert. *Verbrechen unter totalitärer Herrschaft: Studien zur nationalsozialistischen Gewaltkriminalität*. Frankfurt am Main: Suhrkamp, 1982.

Janson, Matthias. *Hitlers Hiwis: Iwan Demjanjuk und die Trawniki-Männer*. KVV Konkret, 2010.

Jardim, Tomaz. *The Mauthausen Trial: American Military Justice in Germany*. Cambridge, MA: Harvard University Press, 2012.

Jaspers, Karl. *The Question of German Guilt*. Translated by E. B. Ashton. New York: Fordham University Press, 2001.

———. *Die Schuldfrage*. Heidelberg: Lambert Schneider, 1946.

———. *Wohin treibt die Bundesrepublik?* Munich: Piper, 1988.

Kastner, Klaus. "'Der Dolch des Mörders war unter der Robe des Juristen verborgen': Der Nürnberger Juristen-Prozess 1947." *Juristische Arbeitsblätter* (1997): 699–706.

Kaufman, Mark Ira. "Untangling John Demjanjuk." *Midstream* 56, no. 2 (October 2010).

Kelman, Herbert C., and V. Lee Hamilton. *Crimes of Obedience: Toward a Social Psychology of Authority and Responsibility*. New Haven: Yale University Press, 1989.

Kempner, Robert M. W. "The Nuremberg Trials as Sources of Recent German Political and Historical Materials." *American Political Science Review* 44, no. 2 (June 1950): 447–59.

Kenntner, Markus. "Der deutsche Sonderweg zum Rückwirkungsverbot." *Neue Juristische Wochenschrift* 50, no. 35 (1997): 2265–300.

Klinge, Katharina. *Die Verjährungsdebatte des Deutschen Bundestags im Lichte der deutsch-israelischen Beziehungen*. München: GRIN, 2008.

Klinghoffer, Arthur Jay, and Judith Apter. *International Citizens' Tribunals: Mobilizing Public Opinion to Advance Human Rights*. New York: Palgrave, 2002.

Der Konstanzer Juristentag, 2–5 Juni 1947. Ansprachen, Vorträge, Diskussionsreden. Tübingen: J.C.B. Mohr, 1947.

Kurz, Thilo. "Paradigmenwechsel bei der Strafverfolgugn des Personals in den deutschen Vernichtungslagern?" *Zeitschrift für Internationale Strafrechtsdomatik* 3 (2013): 122–29.

Kuwalek, Robert. *Das Vernichtungslager Belzec*. Translated by Steffen Hänschen. Berlin: Metropol-Verlag, 2014.

Lahav, Pnina. "Theater in the Courtroom: The Chicago Conspiracy Trial." *Law and Literature* 16, no. 3 (2004): 381–474.

Landau, Asher Felix. "The Demjanjuk Appeal." Israel Ministry of Foreign Affairs. July 29, 1993. www.mfa.gov.il/mfa/aboutisrael/history/holocaust/pages/the%20demjanjuk%20appeal-%20summary%20by%20asher%20felix%20landa.aspx.

Langbein, John H. *Comparative Criminal Procedure: Germany*. St. Paul: West Group, 1977.

Lange, Harald. "Mord, Totschlag und Kindestötung im deutschen und schweizerischen Strafrecht." PhD diss., Tübingen, 1946.

LeBlanc, Lawrence J. *The United States and the Genocide Convention*. Durham: Duke University Press, 1991.

Lemkin, Raphael. *Axis Rule in Occupied Europe; Laws of Occupation, Analysis of Government, Proposals for Redress*. Washington, DC: Carnegie Endowment for International Peace, Division of International Law, 1944.

———. *Totally Unofficial: The Autobiography of Raphael Lemkin*. New Haven: Yale University Press, 2013.

Lerner, Natan. "The Convention on the Non-Applicability of Statutory Limitations to War Crimes." *Israel Law Review* 4, no. 512 (1969): 512–33.

Leslie, Michelle, and Bill Sloat. "The Devil Knows Where." *Cleveland Plain Dealer*, November 13, 1994, special supplement.

Levi, Primo. *The Drowned and the Saved*. New York: Vintage, 1989.

Levine, Michael G., and Bella Brodzki, eds. "Trials of Trauma: Comparative and Global Perspectives." Special issue, *Comparative Literature Studies* 48, no. 3. University Park: Pennsylvania State University Press, 2011.

Lichtblau, Eric. *The Nazis Next Door: How America Became a Safe Haven for Hitler's Men*. Boston: Houghton Mifflin Harcourt, 2014.

Lipstadt, Deborah E. *The Eichmann Trial*. New York: Schocken, 2011.

Locke, John. *Two Treatises of Government and A Letter Concerning Toleration*. New Haven: Yale University Press, 2003.

Loewenstein, Karl. "Reconstruction of the Administration of Justice in American-Occupied Germany." *Harvard Law Review* 61, no. 3 (February 1948): 419–67.

Loftus, Elizabeth F. *Eyewitness Testimony*. Cambridge, MA: Harvard University Press, 1980.

Loftus, Elizabeth F., and Katherine Ketcham. *Witness for the Defense: The Accused, the Eyewitness and the Expert Who Puts Memory on Trial*. New York: St. Martin's Griffin, 1992.

Luban, David. "A Theory of Crimes against Humanity." *Yale Journal of International Law* 29, no. 1 (2004): 85–167.

Lübbe, Hermann. "Der Nationalsozialismus im deutschen Nachkriegsbewußtsein." *Historische Zeitschrift* 236 (1983): 579–99.

Machura, Stefan. "Geschorenen- und Schöffengericht." Working paper presented at the Institut für Rechts- und Kriminalsoziologie, Vienna, Austria, March 6, 2009. www.irks.at/assets/irks/Publikationen/Working%20Paper/IRKS_WP10_Machura.pdf.

Maguire, Peter. *Law and War: An American Story*. New York: Columbia University Press, 2001.

Maier, Regina. *NS-Kriminalität vor Gericht: Strafverfahren vor den Landgerichten Marburg und Kassel, 1945–1955*. Darmstadt/Marburg: Hessische Historische Kommission Darmstadt, 2009.

Maihofer, Werner, and Peter Schneider. *NS-Verbrechen und Verjährung*. Bonn: Bundeszentrale für Politische Bildung, 1965.

Mankowitz, Zeev W. *Life between Memory and Hope: The Survivors of the Holocaust in Occupied Germany*. New York: Cambridge University Press, 2002.

Marrus, Michael Robert, ed. *The End of the Holocaust. Berlin: Walter de Gruyter, 1989.*

———, ed. *The Nazi Holocaust: Historical Articles on the Destruction of European Jews*. Westport: Meckler, 1989.

———. *The Nuremberg War Crimes Trial, 1945–46: A Documentary History*. Boston: Bedford/St. Martin's, 1997.

———. *The Unwanted: European Refugees in the Twentieth Century*. New York: Oxford University Press, 1985.

McAdams, A. James. *Judging the Past in Unified Germany*. Cambridge: Cambridge University Press, 2001.

Meierhenrich, Jens, and Devin Owen Pendas, eds. *Political Trials*. Cambridge: Cambridge University Press, 2016.

Meyer-Seitz, Christian. *Die Verfolgung von NS-Straftaten in der sowjetischen Besatzungszone*. Berlin: Berlin Verlag Arno Spitz, 1998.

Mildt, Dick de. *In the Name of the People: Perpetrators of Genocide in the Reflection of Their Post-War Prosecution in West Germany: The "Euthanasia" and "Aktion Reinhard" Trial Cases*. Leiden: Brill, 1996.

———, ed. *Staatsverbrechen vor Gericht: Festschrift für Christiaan Frederik Rüter zum 65. Geburtstag*. Amsterdam: Amsterdam University Press, 2003.

Miquel, Marc von. *Ahnden oder amnestieren?: Westdeutsche Justiz und Vergangenheitspolitik in den sechziger Jahren* Göttingen: Wallstein, 2004.

Müller, Ingo. *Hitler's Justice: The Courts of the Third Reich*. Translated by Deborah Lucas Schneider. Cambridge, MA: Harvard University Press, 1991.

Musial, Bogdan, ed. "Aktion Reinhardt": Der Völkermord an den Juden im Generalgouvernement, 1941–1944. Osnabrück: Fibre, 2004.

Nardin, Terry. *Law, Morality and the Relations of States*. Princeton: Princeton University Press, 1983.

Nestler, Cornelius. "Ein Mythos: Das Erfordernis der 'konkreten Einzeltat' bei der Verfolgung von NS-Verbrechen." In *Kriminologie-Jugendkriminalrecht-Strafvollzug Kölner Kriminalwissenschaftliche Schriften* 59. Berlin: Duncker & Humblot, 2014.

Novick, Peter. *The Holocaust in American Life*. Boston: Houghton Mifflin, 1999.

Ogorek, Regina. "Vom 'Stillstand der Rechtspflege' zum Rechtspflegestaat: Hessens Justiz auf dem Weg zur demokratischen Identität." *Rechtshistorisches Journal* 15 (1996): 237–52.

O'Neil, Robin. *Belzec: Stepping Stone to Genocide*. New York: JewishGen, 2008.

Osterloh, Jörg, and Clemens Vollnhals, eds. *NS-Prozesse und deutsche Öffentlichkeit: Besatzungszeit, frühe Bundesrepublik und DDR*. Göttingen: Vandenhoeck & Ruprecht, 2011.

Pappe, H. O. "On the Validity of Judicial Decisions in the Nazi Era." *Modern Law Review* 23, no. 3 (May 1960): 260–74.

Pauer-Studer, Herlinde, and J. David Velleman. *Konrad Morgen: The Conscience of a Nazi Judge*. New York: Palgrave Macmillan, 2015.

Pendas, Devin Owen. *The Frankfurt Auschwitz Trial, 1963–1965: Genocide, History and the Limits of the Law*. Cambridge: Cambridge University Press, 2006.

———. "Retroactive Law and Proactive Justice: Debating Crimes against Humanity in Germany, 1945–1950." *Central European History* 43, no. 3 (2010): 428–63.

Perels, Joachim, ed. *Auschwitz in der deutschen Geschichte*. Hannover: Offizin, 2010.

———. *Das juristische Erbe des "Dritten Reiches": Beschädigungen der demokratischen Rechtsordnung*. Frankfurt: Campus Verlag, 1999.

Peschel-Gutzeit, Lore Maria, ed. *Das Nürnberger Juristen-Urteil von 1947: Historischer Zusammenhang und aktuelle Bezüge*. Baden-Baden: Nomos, 1996.

Petrovic, Vladimir. "Historians as Expert Witnesses in the Age of Extremes." PhD diss., Central European University, 2009.

———. "Historians as Experts in the First Holocaust-Related Trials." *Institute for Contemporary History* 20, no. 1 (2007): 129–44.

Pohl, Dieter. "Die Ermordung Der Juden Im Generalgouvernment," In *Nationalsozialistische Vernichtungspolitik, 1939–1945: Neue Forschungen und Kontroversen*, edited by Ulrich Herbert, 108–10. Frankfurt am Main: Fischer, 1998.

———. "Prosecutors and Historians: Holocaust Investigations and Historiography in the Federal Republic, 1955–75." In *Holocaust and Justice: Representation and Historiography of the Holocaust in Post-War Trials*, edited by David Bankier and Dan Michman, 177–29. Jerusalem: Yad Vashem, 2010.

———. "Die Trawniki-Männer Im Vernichtungslager Belzec, 1941–1943," In *NS-Gewaltherrschaft: Beiträge zur historischen und juristischen Aufarbeitung*, edited by Alfred Gottwaldt, Nobert Kampe, and Peter Klein. Berlin: Edition Hentrich, 2005.

———. "Ukranische Hilfskräfte beim Mord an den Juden." In *Die Täter der Shoah: Fanatische Nationalsozialisten oder ganz normale Deutsche?*, edited by Gerhard Paul. Göttingen: Wallenstein, 2002.

Priemel, Kim C., and Alexa Stiller, eds. *NMT: Die Nürnberger Militärtribunale zwischen Geschichte, Gerechtigkeit und Rechtschöpfung*. Hamburg: Hamburger Edition, 2013.

Prittwitz, Cornelius. "Notwendige Ambivalenzen—Anmerkungen zum schwierigen Strafprozeß gegen John Demjanjuk." *Der Strafverteidiger* 11 (November 2010): 648–54.

Pyle, Christopher H. *Extradition, Politics, and Human Rights*. Philadelphia: Temple University Press, 2001.

Quint, Peter E. "Judging the Past: The Prosecution of East German Border Guards and the GDR Chain of Command." *Review of Politics* 61, no. 2 (1999): 303–29.

Radbruch, Gustav. "Gesetzliches Unrecht und übergesetzliches Recht." *Süddeutsche Juristen Zeitung* 1 (1946): 105–8.

———. "Des Reichsjustizministeriums Ruhm und Ende: Zum Nürnberger Juristen-Prozess." *Süddeutsche Juristenzeitung* 3, no. 2 (1948): 57–64.

———. *Rechtsphilosophie*. Edited by Ralf Dreier and Stanley L. Paulson. Heidelberg: C. F. Müller, 2003.

———. "Zur Diskussion Über Die Verbrechen Gegen Die Menschlichkeit." *Süddeutsche Juristen-Zeitung* 2 (1947): 131–36.

Radin, Max. *The Day of Reckoning*. New York: Alfred A. Knopf, 1943.

Rajchman, Chil. *The Last Jew of Treblinka: A Memoir.* New York: Pegasus, 2012.

Rashke, Richard L. *Useful Enemies: John Demjanjuk and America's Open-Door Policy for Nazi War Criminals.* Harrison, NY: Delphinium, 2013.

Ratz, Michael. *Die Justiz und die Nazis: Zur Strafverfolgung von Nazismus und Neonazismus seit 1945.* Frankfurt am Main: Röderberg-Verlag, 1979.

Reichel, Peter. *Vergangenheitsbewältigung in Deutschland: Die Auseinandersetzung mit der NS-Diktatur von 1945 bis heute.* München: C. H. Beck, 2001.

Reinhold, Joachim. *Der Wiederaufbau der Justiz in Nordwestdeutschland 1945 bis 1949.* Königstein, 1979.

Report to House Subcommittee on Immigration, Citizenship, and International Law. Washington, DC: US General Accounting Office, May 16, 1978.

Reydams, Luc. *Universal Jurisdiction: International and Municipal Legal Perspectives.* Oxford: Oxford University Press, 2004.

Rich, David Alan. "Reinhard's Footsoldiers: Soviet Trophy Documents and Investigative Records As Sources." In *Remembering For the Future: The Holocaust in an Age of Genocide,* edited by John K. Roth and Elizabeth Maxwell. New York: Palgrave Macmillan, 2001.

Ritz, Christian. *Schreibtischtäter vor Gericht: Das Verfahren vor dem Münchner Landgericht wegen der Deportation der niederländischen Juden, 1959–1967.* Paderborn: Schöningh, 2012.

Roesen, Anton. "Rechtsfragen der Einsatzgruppen-Prozesse," *Neue Juristische Wochenschrift* 4 (1964): 133–36.

Rosenthal, Walter. *Die Justiz in der Sowjetzone: Aufgaben, Methoden und Aufbau.* Bonn: Deutscher Bundes-Verlag, 1962.

Roth, Philip. *Operation Shylock: A Confession.* New York: Simon & Schuster, 1993.

Rothenpieler, Friedrich Wilhelm. *Der Gedanke einer Kollektivschuld in juristischer Sicht.* Berlin: Duncker & Humblot, 1982.

Rottleuthner, Hubert. "Das Nürnberger Juristenurteil und seine Rezeption in Deutschland—Ost und West." *Neue Justiz* 51, no. 12 (1997): 617–23.

———. "Wären die Juristen wirklich Positivisten gewesen, hätten sie sich vielem verweigert: Ein Interview mit Professor Hubert Rottleuthner." Interview by Ulrike Müller, 2000. Arbeitskreis kritischer Juristinnen und Juristen an der Humboldt-Universität zu Berlin. http://akj.rewi.hu-berlin.de/zeitung/05-1/interview-rottl.htm.

Rousso, Henry. *The Haunting Past: History, Memory and Justice in Contemporary France.* Philadelphia: University of Pennsylvania Press, 2002.

———. "History, Memory, and the Law: The Historian as Expert Witness." *History and Theory* 41, no. 3 (2002): 326–45.

Rückerl, Adalbert. *The Investigation of Nazi Crimes, 1945–1978: A Documentation*. Hamden, CT: Archon, 1980.

———. *Nationalsozialistische Vernichtungslager im Spiegel deutscher Strafprozesse: Belzec, Sobibor, Treblinka, Chelmno*. München: Deutscher Taschenbuch-Verlag, 1977.

———. *NS-Verbrechen vor Gericht: Versuch einer Vergangenheitsbewältigung*. Heidelberg: C. F. Müller, 1982.

Rundle, Kristen. "The Impossibility of an Exterminatory Legality: Law and the Holocaust." *University of Toronto Law Journal* 59, no. 1 (2009): 65–125.

Rüping, Hinrich. "Denunziation im 20. Jahrhundert als Phänomen der Rechtsgeschichte." *Historical Social Research* 26, no. 2/3 (2001): 30–43.

Rüthers, Bernd. *Entartetes Recht: Rechtslehren und Kronjuristen im Dritten Reich*. München: Deutscher Taschenbuch Verlag, 1994.

Ryan, Allan A., Jr. *Quiet Neighbors: Prosecuting Nazi War Criminals in America*. San Diego: Harcourt Brace Jovanovich, 1984.

Sa'adah, Anne. *Germany's Second Chance: Trust, Justice, and Democratization*. Cambridge, MA: Harvard University Press, 1998.

Sabrow, Martin, ed. *Bewältigte Diktaturvergangenheit?: 20 Jahre DDR-Aufarbeitung*. Leipzig: AVA—Akademische Verlagsanstalt, 2010.

Saidel, Rochelle G. *The Outraged Conscience: Seekers of Justice for Nazi War Criminals in America*. Albany: State University of New York Press, 1984.

Sands, Philippe, ed. *From Nuremberg to The Hague: The Future of International Criminal Justice*. Cambridge: Cambridge University Press, 2003.

Sarat, Austin, Lawrence Douglas, and Martha Merrill Umphrey, eds. *Lives in the Law*. Ann Arbor: University of Michigan Press, 2002.

Schabas, William A. *Genocide in International Law: The Crime of Crimes*. Cambridge: Cambridge University Press, 2009.

———. "Perverse Effects of the Nulla Poena Principle: National Practice and the Ad Hoc Tribunals." *European Journal of International Law* 11, no. 3 (2000): 521–39.

———. *Unimaginable Atrocities: Justice, Politics, and Rights at the War Crimes Tribunals*. Oxford: Oxford University Press, 2014.

Scheffler, Wolfgang. "A Brief for Humanity." Translated by Nina Morris Farber. *Museum of Tolerance Online—Multimedia Learning Center of the Simon Wiesenthal Center*. http://motlc.wiesenthal.com/site/pp.asp?c=gvKVLcMVIuG&b=395101.

Schiessl, Christoph. "The Search for Nazi Collaborators in the United States." PhD diss., Wayne State University, 2009.

Schlink, Bernhard. *Vergangenheitsschuld: Beiträge zu einem deutschen Thema*. Zurich: Diogenes, 2007.

Schmitt, Carl. *Antworten in Nürnberg.* Edited by Helmut Quaritsch. Berlin: Duncker & Humblot, 2000.

———. *Das internationalrechtliche Verbrechen des Angriffskrieges und der Grundsatz "Nullum crimen, nulla poena sine lege."* Edited by Helmut Quaritsch. Berlin: Duncker & Humblot, 1994.

———. "Kodifikation oder Novelle? Über die Aufgabe und Methode der heutigen Gesetzgebung." *Deutsche Juristen-Zeitung* 40, nos. 15/16 (1935): 919–25.

———. *Writings on War.* Edited by Timothy Nunan. Malden, MA: Polity, 2011.

Schreiber, Hans-Ludwig. "Das Schicksal des Nulla-Poena-Prinzips in der nationalsozialistischen Zeit." In *Gesetz und Richter: Zur geschichtlichen Entwicklung des Satzes Nullum Crimen, Nulla Poena Sine Lege.* Frankfurt am Main: Metzner, 1976.

Schrimm, Kurt. "Die strafliche Aufarbeitung der NS-Vergangenheit in der Bundesrepublik Deutschland vor 1989." In *Die juristische Aufarbeitung der NS-Vergangenheit in der DDR und der Bundesrepublik Deutschland, hrsg. durch die Landesbeauftragte für die Unterlagen des Staatssicherheitsdienstes der Ehemaligen DDR in Sachsen-Anhalt.* Magdeburg, 2005.

Schwartz, Thomas Alan. "Die Begnadigung deutscher Kriegsverbrecher: John J. McCloy und die Häftlinge von Landsberg." *Vierteljahrshefte für Zeitgeschichte* 38, no. 3 (July 1990): 375–414.

Segev, Tom. "Der Prozess gegen John Demjanjuk in Jerusalem." *Bulletin des Fritz Bauer Instituts (Fall 2009): 16–23.*

Sereny, Gitta. *The German Trauma: Experiences and Reflections, 1938–1999.* London: Penguin, 2000.

———. *Into That Darkness: An Examination of Conscience.* New York: McGraw-Hill, 1974.

———. "John Demjanjuk and the Failure of Justice." *New York Review of Books,* October 8, 1992. www.nybooks.com/articles/archives/1992/oct/08/john-demjanjuk-and-the-failure-of-justice/.

Sheftel, Yoram. *Show Trial: The Conspiracy to Convict John Demjanjuk as "Ivan the Terrible."* London: Weidenfeld & Nicolson, 1995.

Shephard, Ben. *The Long Road Home: The Aftermath of the Second World War.* New York : Alfred A. Knopf, 2011.

Simpson, Christopher. *Blowback: The First Full Account of America's Recruitment of Nazis and Its Disastrous Effect on The Cold War, Our Domestic and Foreign Policy.* New York: Collier, 1989.

Slye, Ronald C., and Beth Van Schaack. *International Criminal Law: Essentials.* Austin: Aspen Publishers, 2009.

Smith, Adam M. *After Genocide: Bringing the Devil to Justice.* Amherst, NY: Prometheus, 2009.

Snyder, Timothy. *Bloodlands: Europe between Hitler and Stalin*. New York: Basic, 2010.

Sofsky, Wolfgang. *Die Ordnung des Terrors: Das Konzentrationslager.* Frankfurt am Main: Fischer-Taschenbuch-Verlag, 1999.

Staff, Ilse, ed. *Justiz im Dritten Reich: Eine Dokumentation*. Frankfurt am Main: Fischer-Taschenbuch-Verlag, 1978.

Stangneth, Bettina. *Eichmann before Jerusalem: The Unexamined Life of a Mass Murderer.* Translated by Ruth Martin. New York: Knopf, 2014.

Steinlauf, Michael. *Bondage to the Dead: Poland and the Memory of the Holocaust*. Syracuse: Syracuse University Press, 1997.

Steinweis, Alan E., and Robert D. Rachlin. *The Law in Nazi Germany: Ideology, Opportunism, and the Perversion of Justice*. New York: Berghahn Books, 2013.

Stern, Herbert Jay. *Judgment in Berlin*. New York: Universe Books, 1984.

Stolleis, Michael. *The Law under the Swastika: Studies on Legal History in Nazi Germany.* Translated by Thomas Dunlap. Chicago: University of Chicago Press, 1998.

———. *Recht im Unrecht: Studien zur Rechtsgeschichte des Nationalsozialismus*. Frankfurt am Main: Suhrkamp, 1994.

———. "Reluctance to Glance in the Mirror: The Changing Face of German Jurisprudence after 1933 and Post-1945." *Maurice and Muriel Fulton Lecture Series*. Chicago: University of Chicago Law School Publications, 2001.

Szanajda, Andrew. *Indirect Perpetrators: The Prosecution of Informers in Germany, 1945–1965*. Lanham, MD: Lexington Books, 2010.

Taylor, Telford. *Nuremberg and Vietnam: An American Tragedy*. Chicago: Quadrangle Books, 1970.

Teicholz, Tom. *The Trial of Ivan the Terrible: State of Israel vs. John Demjanjuk*. New York: St. Martin's Press, 1990.

Thiam, Doudou. "Fourth Report on the Draft Code of Offences against the Peace and Security of Mankind." *Yearbook of the International Law Commission* 2, no. 1 (1986): 70–86.

Ueberschär, Gerd R., ed. *Der Nationalsozialismus vor Gericht: Die alliierten Prozesse gegen Kriegsverbrecher und Soldaten, 1943–1952*. Frankfurt am Main: Fischer Taschenbuch Verlag, 1999.

United Nations War Crimes Commission. "Case No. 9: The Zyklon B Case—Trial of Bruno Tesch and Two Others." In *Law Reports of Trials of War Criminals*, English ed., Vol. 1, ix–xi, 93–124. London: His Majesty's Stationery Office, 1947.

US Commission on Civil Rights. *Sexual Assault in the Military: U.S. Commission on Civil Rights 2013 Statutory Enforcement Report*. Washington, DC: United

States Commission on Civil Rights, 2013. www.usccr.gov/pubs/09242013_Statutory_Enforcement_Report_Sexual_Assault_in_the_Military.pdf.

US Congress. Committee of Conference. "Conference Report on Displaced Persons Act of 1948." *Authorizing for a Limited Period of Time the Admission into the United States of Certain European Displaced Persons for Permanent Residence*, 1948. 80th Cong., 2d sess., 1948.

US Congress. House. "Conference Report on Bill Amending Displaced Persons Act of 1948." *Amending the Displaced Persons Act of 1948*, 1950. 81st Cong., 1950

US Congress. House. Committee of the Whole House, and Committee on the Judiciary. *Displaced Persons in Europe and Their Resettlement in the United States*, 1950. 81st Cong., 1950.

US Department of Justice. The Office for Special Investigations. *Striving for Accountability in the Aftermath of the Holocaust*, by Judy Feigin. Washington, DC, 2008. www.justice.gov/criminal/foia/docs/12-2008osu-accountability.pdf.

Vogel, Rolf, ed. *Ein Weg aus der Vergangenheit: Eine Dokumentation zur Verjährungsfrage und zu den NS-Prozessen*. Frankfurt am Main: Ullstein, 1969.

Volk, Rainer. "Der letzte Prozess seiner Art? Eine Bilanz des Demjanjuk-Verfahrens in München." *Bayerische Zeitschrift für Politik und Geschichte* 2 (2011). www.blz.bayern.de/blz/eup/02_11/5.asp.

———. *Das letzte Urteil: Die Medien und der Demjanjuk-Prozess*. München: Oldenbourg, 2012.

Vollnhals, Clemens, ed. *Entnazifizierung: Politische Säuberung und Rehabilitierung in den vier Besatzungzonen 1945–1949*. München: Deutscher Taschenbuch-Verlag, 1991.

Wagenaar, Willem Albert. *Identifying Ivan: A Case Study in Legal Psychology*. Cambridge, MA: Harvard University Press, 1989.

Weber, Jürgen, and Peter Steinbach, eds. *Vergangenheitsbewältigung durch Strafverfahren?: NS-Prozesse in der Bundesrepublik Deutschland*. München: OLZOG Verlag, 1987.

Weckel, Ulrike. *Beschämende Bilder: Deutsche Reaktionen auf alliierte Dokumentarfilme über befreite Konzentrationslager*. Stuttgart: Franz Steiner, 2012.

Weckel, Ulrike, and Edgar Wolfrum, eds. *"Bestien" und "Befehlsempfänger": Frauen und Männer in NS-Prozessen nach 1945*. Göttingen: Vandenhoeck & Ruprecht, 2003.

Wefing, Heinrich. *Der Fall Demjanjuk: Der letzte große NS-Prozess*. München: C. H. Beck, 2011.

Weinke, Annette. *Eine Gesellschaft ermittelt gegen sich selbst: Die Geschichte der Zentralen Stelle Ludwigsburg, 1958–2008*. Darmstadt: Wissenschaftliche Buchgesellschaft, 2009.

———. "Hermann Jahrreiß (1894–1992)—Vom Exponenten des völkerrechtlichen 'Kriegseinsatzes' zum Verteidiger der deutschen Eliten in Nürnberg." In *Kölner Juristen im 20. Jahrhundert*, edited Steffen Augsberg and Andreas Funke. Tübingen: Mohr Siebeck, 2013.

———. *Die Nürnberger Prozesse*. München: C. H. Beck, 2006.

———. *Die Verfolgung von NS-Tätern Im geteilten Deutschland: Vergangenheitsbewältigungen 1949–1969 oder: Eine deutsch-deutsche Beziehungsgeschichte im Kalten Krieg*. Paderborn: F. Schöningh, 2002.

———. "War Crimes, Genocide Trials and Vergangenheitspolitik—the German Case." In *The Genocide Convention Sixty Years after Its Adoption*, edited by Christoph Safferling and Eckart Conze. The Hague: Asser, 2010.

Weinschenk, Fritz. " 'The Murderers among Them'—German Justice and the Nazis." *Hofstra Law & Policy Symposium* 3 (1999): 137–54.

Wentker, Hermann. "Die jurisitsche Ahndung von NS-Verbrechen in der Sowjetischen Besatzungszone und in der DDR." *Vierteljahrshefte für Zeitgeschichte Jahrgang* 35, no. 1 (2002): 60–78.

Werle, Gerhard, and Boris Burghardt. "Zur Gehilfenstrafbarkeit bei Massentötungen in nationalalsozialistischen Vernichtungslagern—Der Fall Demjanjuk Im Kontext Der Bundesdeutschen Rechtsprechung." In *Ein menschengerechtes Strafrecht als Lebensaufgabe: Festschrift für Werner Beulke zum 70. Geburtstag*, edited by Christian Fahl, Eckhart Müller, Helmut Satzger, and Sabine Swoboda, 327–41. Heidelberg: C. F. Müller, 2015.

Werle, Gerhard, and Thomas Wandres. *Auschwitz vor Gericht: Völkermord und bundesdeutsche Strafjustiz*. München: C. H. Beck, 1995.

———. "Menschenrechtsschutz durch Völkerstrafrecht." *Zeitschrift für die gesamte Strafrechtswissenschaft* 109, no. 4 (1997): 809–29.

———. "Rückwirkungsverbot und Staatskriminalität." *Neue Juristische Wochenschrift* 41 (2001): 3001–08.

Wiley, Alexander. *Displaced Persons in Europe. Report pursuant to S. Res. 137, a Resolution to Make an Investigation of the Immigration System*. 80th Cong., 2d Sess., 1948. Senate. Report: No. 950. Washington: US Government Printing Office, 1948.

Wilson, Richard Ashby. "Judging History: The Historical Record of the International Criminal Tribunal for the Former Yugoslavia." *Human Rights Quarterly* 27, no. 3 (2005): 908–42.

———. *Writing History in International Criminal Trials*. Cambridge: Cambridge University Press, 2011.

Wimmer, August. "Die Bestrafung von Humanitätsverbrechen und der Grundsatz Nullum Crimen Sine Lege." *Süddeutsche Juristen-Zeitung* (1947): 123–32.

Wittmann, Rebecca. *Beyond Justice: The Auschwitz Trial.* Cambridge, MA: Harvard University Press, 2012.

Wolf, Gerhard. "Befreiung des Strafrechts vom nationalsozialistischen Denken?" *Humboldt Forum Recht* 9 (1996): 1–14. www.humboldt-forum-recht.de/druckansicht/druckansicht.php?artikelid=79.

Wolfberg, Andrew David. "Israel v. Ivan (John) Demjanjuk: Wachmann Demjanjuk Allowed to Go Free." *Loyola of Los Angeles International and Comaparative Law Review* 17, no. 445 (1995): 445–75.

Wolfe, Robert. "Flaws in the Nuremberg Legacy: An Impediment to the International War Crimes Tribunals' Prosecution of Crimes against Humanity." *Holocaust and Genocide Studies* 12 (1998): 434–53

Wright, Quincy. "The Law of the Nuremberg Trial." *American Journal of International Law* 41, no. 1 (1947): 38–72.

Wyman, Mark. *DPs: Europe's Displaced Persons, 1945–51.* Ithaca: Cornell University Press, 1998.

Zertal, Idith. *Israel's Holocaust and the Politics of Nationhood.* Cambridge: Cambridge University Press, 2005.

Zoller, Elisabeth. *Enforcing International Law through U.S. Legislation.* Dobbs Ferry, NY: Transnational, 1985.

Zur Mühlen, Bengt von, and Andreas von Klewitz, eds. *Die Angeklagten des 20. Juli vor dem Volksgerichtshof.* Potsdam: Chronos, 2001.

Zuroff, Efraim. *Worldwide Investigation and Prosecution of Nazi War Criminals.* Annual Status Report. Jerusalem: Simon Wiesenthal Center—Israel Office - Snider Social Action Institute, November 2010.

INDEX

Page numbers in italics refer to illustrations